Years of Yearning

Memoir of Brother Mel Anderson, FSC
President
1969 - 1997

The selection of *Years of Yearning* for a title is reminiscent of the signature theme in Saint Augustine's *Confessions:* "You stir man to take pleasure in praising you, because you have made us for yourself, and *our heart is restless until it rests in you.*" (Confessions, Book I, i, Early Years.)

To Ed Epstein with gratitude

Brother Mel Anderson, FSC

THIS BOOK IS PUBLISHED BY BROTHER MEL ANDERSON, FSC

AUTHOR'S NOTE: This book is drawn from memories that took place during my presidency at Saint Mary's College of California from 1969 to 1997. The contents of this book are my personal recollections and should not be read as a historical or endorsed publication of the College.

Years of Yearning, A Memoir by Brother Mel Anderson, FSC
President of Saint Mary's College 1969-1997
Copyright © 2011 by Brother Mel Anderson, FSC

Library of Congress Cataloging-in-Publication Data available upon request.

ISBN 978-0-578-09835-7

Printed in the United States of America
December 2011

Brother Mel Anderson, FSC, 1928 Saint Mary's Road, P.O. Box 5150, Moraga, CA 94575

Printed and distributed by Vision Press, San Ramon, CA

To the Saint Mary's College community:
    The Christian Brothers
    The faculty and staff
    The Boards of Trustees and Regents
    The Development Office personnel
    Our generous donors
    The Saint Mary's alumni
    The many supportive committees
    And volunteers
    And our thousands of students,
    All of whom made progress possible
    And a delightful experience

Table of Contents

Introduction

I officially arrived as the President of Saint Mary's College on July 1, 1969, having been appointed by Brother Bertram Coleman, FSC, the Provincial of the Christian Brothers of the San Francisco Province. I had been informed by numerous members of the College community, both Christian Brothers and other faculty members, that the College was philosophically moving away from the traditions that had been its hallmark for nearly 30 years, during which time I had been a student. It was a philosophical position that was deeply imbedded in a liberal arts and Catholic intellectual tradition to which I was personally attached and which I saw as an academic, social, religious and personal strength, a worthy investment for one's future. Furthermore, it was apparent to even a casual observer that the facilities, which occupied approximately 400 acres of Moraga Valley real estate, were in serious need of refurbishing and creative landscaping.

Since I had been elected to the fifteen-member Board of Trustees in 1968, I was aware of the precarious financial condition of the College and that fundraising via the development department was hobbled by inconsistent leadership and a limited staff that sorely needed inspiration. It was also apparent that the political tensions within the faculty were not constructive. Identifiable faculty forces, led by the then Academic Vice President, had developed a concept on curriculum, calendar and student choice, for which they then gained approval from the Board following Presidential approval.

The concept was based on progressive theories of higher education designed to free students from academic formalism and requirements, which in the case of Saint Mary's were, in part, the philosophical and some theological traditions characteristic of much of Catholic higher education at the time. Unfortunately, the philosophical supports of the pre-1969 curriculum had begun to atrophy, opening the door to reactionary free-spirited, political and literary trends. The seemingly liberating academic concepts were synchronous with widespread societal activism that opposed the Vietnam War and compulsory military draft, symbolized by the Free Speech Movement initiated by protestors on the nearby University of California, Berkeley, campus. Many of the misguided aberrations of Vatican II likewise contributed to the societal and academic turmoil that surrounded and affected the Moraga campus.

This was the Saint Mary's I found and is the beginning of a jumbled, tangled tapestry that took many years to unravel and then to reweave, a section at a time. When I left the presidency in 1997, the most difficult aspect of the reweaving, namely, its liberal arts, Catholic and Lasallian characteristics had

1

only just begun, but the beginning was, I believe, a significant step forward.

In 1994, a diverse and perceptive group of faculty, alumni, Trustees, Regents and students developed, over a period of a year, a well-conceived mission statement. The committee was named the New Century Committee in view of the new millennium commencing but a few years hence. With the completion of the mission statement, part two of the plan envisioned an incorporation or immersion of the mission statement within every School and department. The success of this immersion was something that could only be a hope or a yearning to be fulfilled in the future, undoubtedly after considerable faculty soul-searching and active implementation.

Because of the success of the advancement office under the able hand and mind of the late Brother Jerome West, I left my successor with expanded and improved facilities, significant financial reserves, increased endowment, an enlarged student body that was self-sustaining and a suggested blue print for engaging in the difficult task of implementing a new curriculum for our time in view of the substantive Catholic intellectual tradition I cherished.

The Years of Change

The history of Saint Mary's College from 1969 to 1997 may be called transitional years, because major changes in both calendar and, more importantly, in curriculum, expressed the diverse yearnings of both mind and spirit within factions among the Christian Brothers, the lay faculty, alumni and students. The changes were religious, cultural, philosophical, pragmatic, political, conservative, liberal and financial -- in total, a potpourri of conflicting agendas. The saga of the College during a tumultuous era in the nation's history would be incomplete and most likely incoherent without a preamble addressing at least the two academic years preceding my presidency.

The accelerating academic and campus political activity preceding 1969 culminated in consequential and radical changes in the curriculum, calendar and requirements that included several reorganizations of the World Classics or Great Books seminars, religious studies programs and the elimination of requirements in language, mathematics, philosophy, science and history for all students. These profound changes commenced in fall of 1969 and affected the subsequent 28 years in one way or another. The elimination of requirements implied the necessity for assigned faculty advisors to meet in congenial face-to-face meetings with each student to discuss the selection of courses for creating a program of studies tailored to the interests of each student. However, after two years it became evident that requirements from selected areas of study had to be reinserted into the academic programs for all students, beginning with a program in better writing. One of the failures of secondary education in general at that time (and one that prevails in general to the present) was ineffective instruction in English grammar and composition.

In the academic years from fall of 1967 through the spring of 1969, Brother Michael Quinn, FSC, PhD, was in the last two of his seven and a half years as president, having been appointed in February 1962, following a fatal automobile accident near Lake Tahoe in which his predecessor, Brother President, Albert Plotz, FSC, was killed, along with two of his confreres: retired artist, author and curator of the Keith Gallery, Brother Cornelius Bragg, FSC, and retired Spanish instructor, Brother Julius Rodriguez-Paneda, FSC. When he was appointed President, Brother Michael was a member of the College Psychology Department, having received his doctorate in clinical psychology from Loyola University of Chicago.

By the fall of 1967, Rafael Alan Pollock, PhD, was beginning his sixth year as Academic Vice President and Dean of the College. Pollock had earned his doctorate in English from Yale University and held an appointment in the English department at the University of Notre Dame in Indiana, at the time of his appointment as Academic Vice President and Dean at Saint Mary's in August 1962. I had been principal at Saint Mary's College High and Residence School and financial administrator of the Saint Mary's Grammar and Residence School in Berkeley since 1964 and was elected to membership on the Board of Trustees for the 1968-1969 scholastic year, on the recommendation of my predecessor, Brother Michael Quinn.

Nationally, the prolonged, and in general unsupported, war in Vietnam spawned free-speech protests over the draft and the real or conjectured machinations of corporate America, especially multinational business enterprises and those supplying materiel for the war. The Civil Rights Movement, increasingly and graphically portrayed through the media, heightened the awareness of most Americans that basic constitutional rights had for far too long been denied African-Americans, Hispanics, Asians and other minority groups. In certain areas of the South and Southwest, widespread discrimination against people of color--particularly in education, employment and housing--curtailed or even precluded opportunities for full participation in the attainment of the American dream. Though women are not a minority, the inequities in employment, education, athletics and leadership opportunities, often cited as the glass ceiling, eventually assumed a greater competitive position on the civil rights agenda.

Within the fabric of the College and the religious life of the Christian Brothers, the effects of major changes in the Catholic Church, either mandated by the Ecumenical Council known as Vatican II (1962-1965) or both liberally and conservatively interpreted by free spirits and cautious conservatives, added another dimension to the upheaval of the times.

Movements the magnitude of those associated with the Vietnam conflict and civil rights efforts generated new forms of political activism that inspired changes in the attitudes of many Americans, especially those of collegiate age. Such activism is bound to exhibit excesses, sometimes unfortunate or tragic ones on both sides of such emotionally charged and widespread issues. Colleges and universities were particularly vulnerable to political activism, especially its excesses, since the majority of those enrolled in undergraduate higher education in the '60s and early '70s were between 18 and 22 years of age, and males were facing the prospect of being drafted and sent to Vietnam to fight a war that many citizens, among them a majority of faculty members in most institutions of higher education, believed was either difficult or impossible to justify. Many faculty members, though cognizant of the limitations of academic freedom (that is, speaking freely within one's area of expertise), were inclined to stretch its meaning to speak their minds about politics and other matters on campus in casual conversations or even in their classrooms. They were less restricted by academic protocols in off-campus locations, such as in public forums, letters to editors and on the lecture circuit.

Many extolled the virtues of progressive socialism, while condemning what President Eisenhower had characterized as the military-industrial complex, the political influence of so-called big business, alleged American political arrogance, and indifference to the plight of the disadvantaged and marginalized at home and abroad. Many also saw as symbolic in the so-called Free Speech Movement the paradox that violated the free speech of others who spoke in opposition to the liberal, politically correct, politics of the time. The destabilization that the Free Speech Movement signaled throughout higher education was perceived by many as an opportunity to promote, in addition to complaints on foreign policy and issues of social injustice, what has been broadly labeled as the liberal or progressive social and political agenda. Society in general, especially among younger adults, had become socially less constrained and culturally less refined, most likely as an expression of disdain for existing mores and personal moral propriety. The moral compass of many wavered in the face of political rhetoric, unrestrained activism and seductive expression. The philosophies of modern existentialism and nihilism and claims of God's demise eroded the very source of moral stability. Yet, through the smoke, anguish and excesses of battle, ground was gained in redressing years of injustice to many segments of American society by at last fulfilling major tenets of the *"Declaration of Independence."*

Misunderstanding of Vatican II and resultant confusion among American Catholics was abundant among both laity and some clergy on matters such as liturgy, music, developing the Christian community, sexuality (birth control, abortion, homosexuality and premarital and extra-marital sex), marriage and whether to encourage young men to enter the priesthood and young men and women to enter religious life. Opposing views on such topics as the role of women in the Church, patronizing clericalism, the exercise of authority and the authentic meaning of ecumenism, as well as societal, business and medical ethics, were also the cause of numerous tensions. Secular notions of relativism, skepticism and overwhelming media liberalism along with a prevailing view that religion, faith and morality are solely private matters, challenged the thoughtful dialogue between faith and reason and compromised moral standards. The Church, many claimed, was outdated, authoritarian and rigid. Students and some faculty alike saw the institutional Church as irrelevant to the real world, in spite of the many changes in the Church that either confronted or adapted to some imperatives of modern societies. In the United States, Catholics had long invested heavily in their own educational institutions from grammar grades to graduate and professional schools, and the Church was now faced with an educated laity who rightfully raised thoughtful concerns about numerous critical issues. For American Catholics, various changes in the liturgy and other aspects of the modern Church, though holding fast to basic Christian doctrine, were added to the combustible ingredients in the mix of moral and political issues of secular society.

Saint Mary's College, located approximately 15 miles from the University of California Berkeley, was still a single-sex institution with most of the student body expected to face the draft and possibly the Vietnam conflict upon commencement. What occurred on the campuses of other institutions of higher education, and especially on the UC, Berkeley campus and its environs, was duly noted by Saint Mary's students and faculty. Thus, the anti-war, anti-draft, free-speech, free-love and other so-called freedom movements, as well as expressions of intense interest in civil rights, conscientious objection, the burning of flags and draft cards and out-of-country relocation, affected attitudes and activism at Saint Mary's.

The New Order in the Making

While many Saint Mary's students were sympathetic with the well-publicized protest activities on the University of California campus and the streets of Berkeley, the main focus of Saint Mary's freewheeling activism for the most part turned inwardly.

As early as January 1961, the faculty Liberal Arts Committee (which also included a few students) stated in a report entitled *The Record* that its purpose was to "explore the problem of dealing with the liberal arts within a four-year college program." *The Record* stated, by way of criticism and recommendation, that: "The Saint Mary's College program is overcrowded and much too specialized. Students pack too many classes into their schedules. Seven courses a semester create an impossible and unrealistic burden. Such crowding makes for all kinds of superficiality. Students fail to concentrate as they should but are content merely to rush through their appointed tasks with the minimum of effort ... Ideally the student should not engage in more than four courses each semester. A two-year program at the lower division level should allow all students to feel that they are learning together and that they are creating a genuine intellectual community." (*The Record*, edited by James Townsend, Jr. of the English department, Jan. 17, 1961, as reported in *The Seminar at Saint Mary's College* by Ed Porcella, page 13, *Distillations*, Oct. 5, 1992, St. Mary's College Archives.)

In December 1967, a spontaneous mimeographed newspaper entitled *The Student*, was slipped under the doors of the residence halls in an effort to alert and hopefully inspire excitement among students regarding the issues facing them -- the Vietnam War, the draft and "those movements and ideals which are commanding an increasing amount of attention in the world."

A new organization that would claim leadership in forwarding an anticipated enlightened academic order was called SPAN (Students for Progressive Action Now). In a prologue to the all-encompassing SPAN proposals on curriculum, coeducation, residence hall regulations, facilities, admissions and recruiting, finances, food services, and capital development, the authors expressed urgency for action, ironically because of the alleged "level of intellectual alienation among the student body ..."

Edgar Z. Friedenberg, a professor of education and sociology at the State University of New York at Buffalo, was invited by parties unidentified to deliver two addresses on what was termed a *Day of Conscience* on the Saint Mary's campus, April 26, 1968, the same day that the new Saint Albert

Library was being dedicated. In a memo to students and faculty dated April 24, 1968, Academic Vice President Pollock stated that Professor Friedenberg: "takes special interest in questions of education and social behavior which are of great concern to contemporary young people. He expressed great delight at being given the opportunity to address you in the morning as well as in the afternoon, and I hope that you will be able to reciprocate by attending." (*Memorandum* by R. A. Pollock, April 28, 1968, Saint Mary's College Archives.) Classes were cancelled by the Academic Council so that students could avail themselves of Professor Friedenberg's progressively astute comments. As Academic Vice President and Dean, Rafael Alan Pollock was the leader of the academic community and chairman of the Academic Council. He played a sometimes discreet, but active, role in supporting both faculty and student liberal politics and a major role in engineering the impending calendar reorganization and startling academic changes.

The campus newspaper, *The Collegian,* carried an article in the April 24, 1968, issue on the *Day of Conscience,* stating that a group of students had circulated a petition to be delivered to Pollock asking that he revoke the decision of the Academic Council to cancel classes, "on the grounds that such a small minority of students and such a small organization (SPAN) should not have the influence and the threat of canceling classes." The article further noted that, "Some students suggested that the cost ... of going to class one day be returned to them or be collected in a fund for Vietnamese missions or for the Red Cross." Following the publication of the letter to Alan Pollock, it became clear that some students were willing to reveal their conservatism at the risk of being identified as neither contemporary nor relevant.

The majority of the members of the Philosophy Department were the object of particular criticism from activist students, the Academic Vice President and some members of the Academic Council, because of the department's conservative, and in the minds of some, stultifying curricular stance. In addition, there were those among both the political and nonpolitical faculty who rejected what they perceived as the ascendant and doctrinaire attitude of some members of the Philosophy Department in insisting on an inordinate share of required courses to the detriment of other academic disciplines or majors. A student petition submitted to the Academic Council on May 9, 1968, requested a reduction in the 17 required units in philosophy, a not uncommon sort of requirement in many Catholic universities and colleges at the time. Student spokesman, Rick Anderson, '70, appeared before the Academic Council on May 22, 1968, to offer his observation that the Philosophy Department maintained "a distinctively Catholic approach in philosophy which aims at certain truths in a philosophical system." He then opined that the department employed a "too strong emphasis on abstraction," and noted that students "want involvement in concrete realities, such as the poverty program, civil rights and the peace movement." In the discussion that ensued following Anderson's presentation, a member of the Academic Council stated that "theology is not doctrinaire as presently taught, but philosophy is, and that there is no toleration for opposing views." Another Academic Council member declared that "future students will want more self-determination and that the College should now give serious consideration to its program in light of this eventuality." (Minutes of the Academic Council, May 22, 1968, Saint Mary's College Archives.)

After extended discussion, a member of the Academic Council moved "that upper division philosophy be reduced to six units of the student's choice, and that discussion between students and faculty on requirements in philosophy and other areas be initiated ..." Following a special meeting of the Academic Council on May 27, 1968, to discuss philosophy requirements, Vice President Pollock suggested that the Academic Council endorse the submission of a ballot for a faculty vote on philosophy requirements, following an open discussion among faculty. An extraordinary faculty meeting was called on June 3, 1968, close to the end of the semester, with the agenda limited to "philosophy courses and philosophy requirements." For many students and faculty members, the Philosophy Department found it difficult to justify requiring 17 units for all liberal arts students, (nine upper-division, that is, those in junior and senior standing, and eight lower-division units, those below junior standing.) The Academic Council proposed to the faculty that a maximum six-unit modification of the upper-division philosophy requirements be enacted, to become effective in the fall 1968. The members of the Academic Council, one member noted, had called for the extraordinary meeting in order to clarify issues and to conduct the vote at least a day following the discussions, thus giving "an opportunity for a wider vote." Following the discussion at the extraordinary meeting, no vote was recorded. One faculty member proposed placing a motion to the Faculty Assembly at its first meeting in the fall "registering strong disapproval of separating discussion from voting." The meeting was apparently adjourned following this intervention.

The minutes of the first Faculty Assembly meeting of the fall semester, 1968, simply indicated that the "philosophy requirement motion which was passed last spring, had been approved by the president and that it is effective immediately." (Minutes, Faculty Meeting, 9/5/68, Saint Mary's College Archives) The announcement did not sit well with a number of faculty members, particularly with philosophy professor Brother Robert Smith, FSC, PhD, an insightful, articulate and influential member of the faculty. During the October 30 meeting he noted that ballots were distributed and some collected before the public discussion that had been held on the previous June 3, that a motion to delay the vote was ruled out of order, that the Academic Council should have "assured wider student and faculty discussion" and that private discussions "should have been brought to public scrutiny." Implicit in Brother Robert's observations was that political chicanery and manipulation had ruled the day. He moved that the Academic Council be censured for "separating vote from discussion in the matter of changing the College philosophy requirements." Alan Pollock spoke against the motion, noting that it would be "regarded as censuring him." Brother Robert protested that such was not his intent. It was finally agreed that "the motion would appear on the next agenda." (Minutes of the Faculty Assembly Meeting, Oct. 30, 1968.)

The motion did appear in lengthy written form on the next agenda for the Faculty Assembly of Nov. 20, 1968. After a short review of the issue it was again postponed to an extraordinary Faculty Assembly meeting scheduled for Dec. 4, 1968. After a discussion at the end of the extraordinary meeting, the motion "for a faculty-wide referendum, by secret ballot on the resolution ..." was soundly defeated by a vote of 9 yea and 36 nay. (Minutes of Faculty Assembly Meeting, Dec. 4, 1968.) As it turned out, the lengthy motion seemed more concerned with procedure than it did with the issues of philosophy requirements, and the majority of the faculty did not seem anxious to become embroiled in governance or in further concern over reinstituting three units of philosophy requirements they felt were unnecessary.

In a lead article appearing in the Dec. 1967 of *The Student* entitled *Some Thoughts on The Possible Life or Death of an Experimental College at Saint Mary's College,* the chair of the moribund Department of Education, Professor Hubert O. Brown, proposed that Saint Mary's become an experimental college, while at the same time cynically expressing doubt that such would occur because of recalcitrant philosophical, sentimental or outdated religious forces within the faculty. "Experimental colleges," Brown noted, "are supposed to cater to the immediate, existential needs of individual students. Traditionally speculative education ends in itself. While it is possible that such speculation is of greater value, such a hierarchy would have to be accepted on faith or sentiment. (I discount the argument about what is *proper* to man as nonsense.)" The experimental college, Brown asserted "would certainly provide some welcome relief from the trivial quasi-Aristotelianisms (Thomisms) we currently substitute for thought."

Brown's characterization as nonsense of what is proper to man or human nature may refer to John Dewey's view that natural inalienable rights are derived from the social-political process rather than inherently existing prior to politics. (See *The Good Society*, page 294, Robert N. Bellah et al, Vantage Books, NY, 1991.)

Brown's apparent modern or postmodern relativist encounter with Aristotle and St. Thomas Aquinas seems to have brought on a fit of existential angst. Since 1942 the College had been devoted to Great Books education, a program that included texts in its seminars from Plato, Aristotle, Augustine, Aquinas, Hume, Kant and many other intellectual giants. In my view it became apparent that Brown's educational background and activist leanings were ill-suited for his engagement with the intellectual traditions that formed the foundation of the deeper elements of both secular and Catholic thought at Saint Mary's, as well as with much of Catholic higher education at the time.

SPAN — Let Us Begin Anew

The criticisms by both faculty and students of the philosophy department and the philosophy requirements along with the faculty vote favoring a reduction in the number of required philosophy units, captured the attention of Students for Progressive Action Now. A SPAN manifesto, *Let Us Begin Anew*, argued that the philosophy department views its role at Saint Mary's as "subservient to the teaching *Magisterium* of the Church," illustrating what State University of New York at Buffalo Professor Friedenberg observed about collegiate institutions not permitting "their students much voice or choice about what kind of person they shall be encouraged to become."

Friedenberg's views apparently had a significant impact on a number of SPAN members, who cited his claims in the SPAN *Manifesto*, "The schools are an integral part of the system by which the dominant social and economic institutions of our society staff themselves and propagate their values." The SPAN document applied the Friedenberg critical principle to the existing College curriculum, noting that its desideratum proposed not only the "assimilation of the student into his 'Western Cultural Heritage' but also holds true for assimilation into the 'magisterial truth' of the Roman Catholic Church." (SPAN document, *Let Us Begin Anew*, Spring 1969, Saint Mary's College Archives.)

On Feb. 18, 1969, the results of a meeting presided over by Student Body President and senior Daniel K. Whitehurst (later to become a two-term mayor of his hometown of Fresno, Calif., and a Democratic candidate for U. S. Senate) listed proposals developed by "the academic community and SPAN." Who or how many in the "academic community" represented the whole were not identified, but regardless, the "academic community" and SPAN had "joined forces to work together in bringing about change." (*Minutes* of the Second Meeting of SPAN, Feb. 18 1969.)

"How can our education," the joint *SPAN-academic community* proposal asked, "'strive to teach every subject in a liberal and liberating spirit as stated in the College Bulletin?" The College Bulletin addressed the purpose of a liberal arts education as liberating or freeing one from ignorance and prejudice and providing means for developing the mind (or what can be cited as the intellectual virtues or developing critical thinking), thus allowing a person to pursue the intellectual life in all of its forms and even to pursue the most exalted of intellectual goals. The question the students posed appeared to be a worthy one. However, from what was being touted as a new gospel, some students were most likely confusing the language of liberal arts education as found in the College Bulletin with the common meanings of liberal politics voiced stridently in the late '60 and early '70. That was not an uncommon error.

The SPAN answer to the curriculum and student-life controversy was offered in 12 proposals or demands affecting the academic and student-life ambience of the College. (SPAN document, *Let Us Begin Anew,* February 1969, Saint Mary's College Archives.)

The first of eight academic proposals was that the College **adopt the 4-1-4 calendar**, requiring that each student take four courses in the first semester of 13 weeks, one course in a four-week January term and four courses in the second semester of 13 weeks. The second proposal was **to eliminate all academic requirements.** (General requirements as listed in the College Bulletin in 1968-1969 for the student in the School of Liberal Arts included 16 units of theology or religious studies, 16 units of World Classics, four units of English composition, 16 units of foreign language, 16 to 17 units of philosophy, eight or more units of laboratory science, six to eight units of mathematics, six units of history and three units of *American Institutions,* which was a state requirement up to 1973.) The third proposal would **expand the faculty-student counseling relationship** (an imperative necessity once requirements were abolished.) The fourth would **abolish final examinations and would establish a pass-fail, plus a prose evaluation** of each student in each course to replace the standard letter-grade evaluation. (A changeover to prose evaluations assumed that a common evaluative language for higher education prevailed, so that prose evaluations could be universally and accurately understood.) The sixth would **abolish mid-term grades and send final grades to the student only.** (Subsequent federal legislation, known as the *Buckley Amendment* banned the sending of grades or disciplinary information to parents of any adult student, that is, any student 18 or older.)

The seventh proposal was to **incorporate fine arts and humanities into the curriculum in a** "creative, aesthetical, historical and intellectual manner, **to establish courses in journalism, and other aspects of communications, as well as courses in social analysis, urban studies, racism, war, the draft and black studies."** The eighth was that the academic list under **curriculum** suggest courses in contemporary issues and creativity and noted that students desire political involvement, "as seen in the Civil Rights Movement, in the Peace Corps, in Vista, in protest against the war in Vietnam, and even more significantly in the campaigns of Robert Kennedy, Eugene McCarthy and George McGovern." The ninth proposal moved beyond the academic and urged that **coeducation be instituted in 1969-1970.** Coeducation, an issue under discussion for several years, was perceived as fundamental for a full education, since the young men of the College would experience the "emotional, physical, intellectual and social presence of women as an integral part of our life in this college community." (The document omits discussing the benefits that would accrue to women in the coeducational environment. One can surmise benevolently that the writers anticipated that women would benefit in a manner similar to men.) Extending themselves beyond curricular and other strictly academic matters, the students proposed greater student involvement in residence hall regulations, College financial management, food services and even campus landscaping.

The 10th proposal sugessted that **Dormitory Regulations** were to be "student centered" with conduct to be, **"decided by a majority of the students residing in each residence hall"** and that the composition of residents in each hall be drawn from all classes, freshmen through seniors. Segregation by class was to be eliminated, speculating that freshmen and sophomores would learn to live and study responsibly through day-to-day contact with upper classmen. (Some faculty observers likened the proposal to the rhetoric of the Marxist classless society, and others opined that placing freshmen with older students, who could legally obtain liquor, would not be conducive to good residence hall order. A major objection to having freshmen distributed throughout the residence halls was that freshmen would find it difficult to form class unity, one of the lifelong values of residential collegiate life.) Under **admissions and recruiting** the 11th proposal suggested that the

College make "a concerted effort to recruit **non whites, non Catholics, non Californians and women.**" Admissions policies should be revised, it stated, to attract students with, "qualities which will contribute to the kind of institution Saint Mary's is trying to become," namely, it seemed, the ambiguous goal of the reformers who stood against many of the traditional academic and social goals outlined in the College Bulletin.

The claim was made that the College "is bound in mediocrity," and that a new effort in recruitment should seek out students interested in an education designed to discover "fundamental principles." While the language "fundamental principles" mirrored that in the catalog describing liberal arts education, its meaning in the SPAN document described principles guiding the activist agenda. One could easily extrapolate from the various proposals being circulated that immersion in politically liberal principles inherent in the political and social issues of the day would be central. The 12th proposal on **finances,** would provide a **guaranteed tuition plan,** so that the tuition would remain the same from the day students entered until they completed their collegiate career. (This proposition could be addressed if tuition charges in the freshman year and each subsequent year represented the average anticipated charges over the four years of college.) In view of the long-standing liberal arts and Catholic traditions of the College, its finances and a competitive marketing perspective, the plan was financially naive.

The last part of the report addressed problems with Hi Continental, (a subsidiary of Del Monte, Inc.), the College food service contractor at the time, as well as the need for refurbishing facilities and landscaping the campus. "Students should be in control of landscaping," the report contended, and be fully informed of "impending changes." At the time the 40 year old physical facilities -- namely, Augustine, De La Salle and Aquinas residence halls, Dante and Galileo classroom buildings, the administration facilities, the dining room, Dryden Hall, the Chapel and the so-called Madigan Gymnasium, subjected to rigorous use by the U. S. Navy Pre-flight School during World War II -- had deteriorated, and maintenance of both buildings and grounds had not kept pace with either the aging process or the need to upgrade facilities and infrastructure for the coming high-tech age. An example of the latter issue was the number of TV antennae hanging from windows and dotting the roofs of residence halls, creating a scene resembling the New York tenements from *West Side Story*. Students did recognize that the potential for attractive landscape architecture in a natural bucolic setting was a yearning and an opportunity yet to be realized.

As SPAN was offering its proposals to the College community, I was the principal at Saint Mary's College High School in Berkeley. In the spring of 1968, Brother President Michael Quinn, FSC, PhD, recommended my election to the Board of Trustees for a three-year term to serve as one of the six to eight Christian Brothers on the Board as required by the bylaws. During the scholastic year 1968-1969, as a member of the Board, I, along with 14 Board colleagues, was required to vote on the most significant academic issues brought before it since 1941. The two major academic proposals were **the adoption of the 4-1-4 calendar** and the **reduction and realignment of collegiate requirements.**

Alan Pollock, PhD, Academic Vice President, 1962-1971

The man who helped construct and then persuaded -- (some say, cajoled) -- and successfully implemented the basic academic plan that, with numerous adjustments and modifications, spanned at least 40 years, was Alan Pollock, the Dean and Academic Vice President from 1962 to 1971.

Alan Pollock was intellectually gifted; could speak extemporaneously with eloquence; wrote with an animated, effective and rhetorical style; was passionately devoted to politically liberal causes; and exercised his commitment tirelessly. He earned his doctorate in English literature from Yale University and was a professor of English at the University of Notre Dame prior to his being offered an appointment by Brother Michael Quinn in 1962 as Dean of the College and Academic Vice President. Pollock possessed an abundance of academic political shrewdness and was blessed with energy, though he exhibited one crucial blind spot, namely, his seeming confidence that no person or group could exercise sufficient political or philosophical influence to frustrate the efficacy of his plans for the future. He hosted faculty members at his home and called the like-minded together when he believed his agenda required solidarity. A convert to Catholicism, Pollock regularly practiced his faith and often attended Sunday student Masses on campus with his spouse, "Meg" or Margaret, and all or several of their seven children. His views on Catholic higher education were in keeping with a number of other modern Catholic educators who believed that Catholic institutions should become more open to the American mainstream in admissions, in developing curriculum, and in commitment to a larger religious purpose than simply protecting the faith of Catholics in a pluralistic society. He endeavored to promote the commendable goal that the College set an example of Christian commitment to underprivileged and minority populations, a proposal at the heart of the Christian Brothers founder, Jean Baptiste De La Salle.

Given that Alan Pollock's appointment as Dean and Vice President was scheduled for renewal at the end of the 1970-1971 academic year, and in view of the mixed but casual reviews I received when I was appointed President, I decided that it would be appropriate to engage in a formal assessment of the Academic Vice President's performance by confidentially consulting with each senior faculty member, that is, those with tenure. After privately interviewing the tenured faculty I compiled the varying appraisals, noting that a slim majority favored a change in academic leadership. Though Pollock's virtues were articulately praised by a strong minority, others alleged that his brinkmanship politics in dealing with the faculty were unacceptable, and that he was leading the College toward secularization through a political activism that placed social and political goals over objective intellectual goals and principles of traditional Catholic higher education. In other words, he had a penchant for juxtaposing liberal social principles alongside the principles of liberal arts education. This is not to say that he dismissed the Catholic nature of the College, rather it was that his view of being Catholic differed in several respects from a number of more traditional, but moderate views, on this essential issue.

Pollock's analysis of members of the faculty was usually perceptive, though he may not have perceived the full mentality or the number of those who found him wanting. He enjoyed command and exercised influence over a diverse constituency and sometimes tended to disregard his adversaries and those he felt were academically ineffective, pushing forward his plans through persuasion and procedures that had the appearance of democracy conducted within a loose governing structure. Most in administration realize that governance looseness will favor maneuvering. The most vocal and persistent critics claimed that Pollock was at heart a politically liberal authoritarian, and that his tactics evoked an aura of suspicion and cynicism. Some were disconcerted over having to consider issues in haste, due, they believed, to a lack of planning. Others attributed the push for hasty decisions as tactical politics.

The divisions among the faculty became more clearly drawn as the interviews came to a close. There were those who fully believed in him as being on the cutting edge of academic insight, an authentic academic innovator and a compassionate champion for the disadvantaged. Others acknowledged the quality of his mind but found him domineering, politically progressive and close-minded, in effect, a man with a cause and the persuasive power to further it.

There were few faculty in the middle, and in assessing those few, I was not sure whether they were cautiously attempting to discern reality, or simply not sure which way the political wind was going to blow. Very few faculty members remained aloof from the politics of the time.

At the beginning of the 1970 fall semester Alan Pollock delivered an address in Dryden Hall to the College community entitled, *The Political Morality of the College.* He proposed several theses, supporting them with sociological statistics taken primarily from a study by Alexander "Sandy" Astin that appeared in *The Educational Record*, summer 1970 edition. His first thesis was that colleges and universities engage in a "sorting out process," which meant that "American higher education exists for its own sake, for the sake of selectivity, that is to say, for the sake of exclusion and perhaps for the sake of social channeling." In the matter of curriculum and requirements Pollock observed, "… what is to be learned is determined usually in no way by the students, by their interests or the needs they feel or even, for that matter, by their parents, but is rather imposed on them … by people, in short, who are very far away from students."

Concerning academic evaluation he said, "I believe that the worst deeply rooted feature of the system, as it exists, is the process of evaluation by grades, degrees and the spirit of competition for these arbitrary, factitious rewards which the system fosters." This latter view may have provided the rationale for the benign neglect and ultimate dissolution of *Alpha Pi Gamma Upsilon*, the former Saint Mary's Honor Society. In his concluding remarks Pollock stated that "colleges generally should move toward a truly open admission policy without compulsion, without the compulsory aspect at all." And, that as "Dr. Astin suggests, again logically, that it might be a good idea if we allowed the whole process of evaluation and the accomplishment of students to be undertaken by those who really profit from it, namely, as he called them 'the consumers' of students. Let graduate schools discover if the students have those abilities they really need to pursue courses of study at those schools. Let businesses, factories and firms devise means for discovering whether students have those abilities that they really need to pursue these employments. The position of the college and the university in such an arrangement would be no longer, again, to use Astin's words 'in the position of a handicapper,' but rather of a trainer preparing students to meet the demands of the real world."

The address expressed serious doubts concerning many common attitudes and practices in institutions of higher education which, he believed, sustained the hegemony of the elite and did little to assist the poor or ameliorate the plight of those who were otherwise disadvantaged or written off by society. While Pollock proposed that colleges and universities be more attentive to social goals, he also proposed that various traditional foundational requirements that were intimately linked to intellectual achievement be made relevant and contemporary, globalized and diversified, or even abandoned. He recommended such practices as open admissions (a long-standing policy of community colleges), the elimination of grades, since grades were, he stated to the Faculty Assembly, "vacuous," and the elimination of most past requirements that would thus allow students to determine their own curriculum, with the assistance of faculty counselors, based on "felt student needs." A diverse array of faculty believed that such concepts would turn the College into an academic smorgasbord rather than an institution guided by philosophical principles intrinsic to intellectual order and the ultimate pursuit of truth. To his credit, however, he strongly supported the long-standing World Classics or Great Books program for all students, renamed, Collegiate Seminars. Pollock's address echoed portions of Friedenberg's philosophy that was voiced in his addresses in 1968 and eagerly embraced by the membership of SPAN.

In a lengthy, more carefully crafted, paper addressed to the *President's Council, Subcommittee on Goals*, dated Nov. 18, 1970, Pollock repeated and embellished his major views as outlined in his September address and supported them with such references as, *The Brother of the Christian Schools in the World Today, A Declaration,* a publication emanating from the Christian Brothers 1967 General Chapter in Rome, the writings of Thomas Jefferson, Ivan Illich (former priest, contemporary educational innovator), Alexander Astin, Horace Mann, *The President's Commission on Campus Unrest,* and studies from the U. S. Office of Education. In his summary he softened the radicalism expressed earlier in *The Political Morality of the College* in recognition of such realities as selective admissions, grading and limited academic requirements inherent in most four-year collegiate institutions. He was intensely interested in what later became known as *affirmative action,* a promotion of more aggressive means for offering higher education to those who did not have the opportunity, resources or background to avail themselves of its benefits, as well as hiring members of minority groups to fulfill various functions in higher education. He saw this as a significant mission of both a Catholic college and the Christian Brothers. In addition, he believed that the College should do all it could to upgrade the methods and quality of teaching, so that it truly improved learning.

The criticism of many so-called prestigious and selective institutions, Pollock said, was that such institutions were not pressed to improve student insight through imaginative teaching, since students were selected at the outset with the requisite aptitudes for intellectual success. He reiterated his view that students must become more actively engaged in the educational process and suggested that cooperative, rather than competitive methods be employed in encouraging them to do so. Yet, he observed that some students may take longer than others to reach certain standards of achievement. The paper provided a comprehensive view of higher education, with sections of it being psychologically and pedagogically current, compelling to some, misguided to others. It proposed a number of controversial issues, such as his insistence that the evaluation or grading of students was a matter of sorting out to the detriment of certain groups of younger people in society, a view complementing the growing awareness and effort by major institutions to include more minority students on their rolls. Pollock also proposed that academic cooperation, rather than competition, should become the model in higher education, so that achievement could "be evaluated for the group rather than for individuals." He also recommended "that students as well as faculty be given a genuine role in governance of the College at the highest internal level," and that "the role of Trustees also ought to be reexamined." What a Board of Trustees would look like in Pollock's overview was not disclosed, but his observation that faculty be given a genuine role in governance "at the highest level" left speculators with a number of probabilities that he may have had in mind. They became clearer later.

His view that educational institutions be seen "as agencies of social and political purpose and, indeed, of social change," heightened the increasing conviction of many that Pollock would place the academy at the service of a social-political agenda, a concept abhorrent to those who placed their faith in reasonable and objective academic principles. His seemingly radical views, and his conclusion that the system of American higher education "may, in fact, be working in some measure against" some of the major purposes of higher education, caused some who once sat at his feet to find more distanced places to position themselves. The politicalization of the academy was considered by many faculty members as a foray against the traditional protocols of higher education that were dedicated to authentically open and objective liberal arts principles, even though they fully granted that he had a right to enunciate his views in an institution dedicated to academic freedom. They also acknowledged that a number of his ideas -- particularly efforts to improve undergraduate instruction and to include more minority representation among the student body -- merited consideration.

Brother Michael Quinn Resigns, 1968-1969

During the 1968 fall semester Brother Michael Quinn indicated his desire to retire from the presidency to Brother Bertram Coleman, provincial of the Christian Brothers. In keeping with the College bylaws, the person responsible for the appointment of the president is the provincial, though as a matter of practice he seeks the advice of the Board of Trustees.

Brother Mel Anderson, FSC

I was born to the late Edwin Albert Anderson (of Swedish descent) and Lillian Frances (Redmond) Anderson (of Irish descent) at Merritt Hospital in Oakland, Calif., on Sept. 28, 1928, and named Harold Fabian. The name Fabian was that of an admired friend of my mother's, and she selected it for two reasons: honor her friend and that it would be "distinctive" among the thousands of Andersons in the telephone book. My brother, Edwin Joseph, who was six years older than I, had expressed his desire to have a brother named Harry, thus the name, Harold. But, as it turned out, Harry was an unused moniker.

From an early age, my brother and I were taught to be frugal in our lifestyle. We were Depression children and both of us found ways to provide for ourselves. I first sold Saturday Evening Post magazines then worked at a factory making mattresses, and sold shoelaces and shoe polish door-to-door through a franchise from a friend who managed a GalenKamps shoe store. After I acquired a manual printing press, I learned to set type and did work for neighbors and businesses. I found the theater fascinating having been first inspired by marionette shows at the Treasure Island World's Fair in 1939, and I began creating them myself, along with my older cousin, a commercial artist who painted faces on the characters. I was also a child tap-dancer in a troupe in Oakland that performed on numerous stages in the Bay Area and Santa Cruz, an experience that gave me a liking for the legitimate stage. With the aid of my father I built a small stage in the basement of my home in the Temescal district of Oakland and along with my neighborhood peers conducted variety shows for the neighbors. Since the nation was engulfed in World War II and television had not yet arrived in the Bay Area, local entertainment, such as it was, gained some appreciation -- or at least was not ignored. My early education was at Saint Augustine Grammar School (two years), Chabot Primary School and then Claremont Junior High in Oakland. In 1943 at age 14, I left Claremont Junior High and enrolled at Saint Mary's High School in Berkeley where two zealous Christian Brothers answered many of my questions on religious issues after classes. Among activities, a multitude of such as studying for school and working at the Oakland Real Estate Board in downtown Oakland, participating on stage in U. S. War Bond rallies at Saint Mary's High School and collecting scrap metal for the war effort, I spent many hours exploring religious questions with Brother George Fraser, my Spanish and geometry instructor. History instructor, Brother Bertram Coleman, and Brother George inspired me to enter the Junior Novitiate at Mont La Salle, Napa, in August 1945, just as the atomic bombs were falling on Nagasaki and Hiroshima.

Following my graduation from Mont La Salle in 1947 -- my diploma was officially from Saint Mary's College High School, since Mont La Salle Junior Novitiate was considered a satellite campus of St. Mary's High School at that time -- I entered the Christian Brothers Novitiate and was robed as a Christian Brother on Aug. 14, 1947, choosing my religious name, as was then the custom in the church for members of religious orders, of Brother Timothy Mel. The practice was reminiscent of the biblical story of Jacob, who wrestled with God through an angel. Jacob asked for a blessing and the angel changed Jacob's name to Israel. The change of name indicated a special favor from God to a person who wrestled with God and survived.

Since my mother was of Irish descent, I thought it fitting to select the name of an Irish saint. St. Mel was St. Patrick's nephew. I chose Timothy along with Mel, because the two names together sounded lyrical. I professed my first vows in 1948 and entered the Scholasticate (the Christian Brothers house of studies at Saint Mary's College.). I graduated from Saint Mary's College in 1952 as a philosophy major and was assigned to teach at the Junior Novitiate at Mont La Salle, because I had some training and experience in woodworking. During the Depression years my father had been a dry goods salesman, but with the advent of World War II he became a shipyard craftsman, and his facility with handcrafts was my inspiration for doing pragmatic hand tasks. Part of my instructional duties at Mont La Salle was in a new program that had been instituted to train some Junior Novices in nonteaching capacities. The program eventually failed for several reasons, one of which was that it was not fully planned from the outset, and its juxtaposition to those destined for collegiate education created a disparity in ends and spirit. The following year I was assigned to be a geometry, English, woodshop and religion teacher at Sacred Heart High School in San Francisco. Four years later I was appointed the founding Vice Principal at La Salle High School in Pasadena, Calif., and in 1962 I was assigned to be Principal and Religious Superior of the boys' division at San Joaquin Memorial High School in Fresno. In 1964 I became Director (Religious Superior) and Principal at Saint Mary's College High and Residence School and Financial Administrator of the residence grammar school, both located at Peralta Park in Berkeley. In all of my high school assignments, I was involved in assisting or directing student plays, musicals and concerts, as well as conducting after-class Great Books seminars for interested students or parents.

In 1968, as principal of Saint Mary's High School, I accepted an invitation to serve on the Board of Trustees at Saint Mary's College, an opportunity that continued my strong interest in the future of my alma mater. It was on the Board of Trustees that I first encountered the plans to reorganize both the academic calendar and curriculum of the College, to the detriment of the philosophy department, the department of my own major. In 1969, Brother Bertram, my former high school mentor and then Provincial, persuaded me to become the 23 President of Saint Mary's College. During my 28 year tenure, the College faculty grew from a little more than 85 members to approximately 300 members and the student body expanded from less than 950 male students to more than 4,000 coed students in traditional undergraduate, undergraduate older-adult programs and graduate programs. As the College grew, I oversaw the construction and/or renovation of 28 facilities. At my recommendation, the College opened its doors to women in 1970. My dedication to the original prize-winning John Donovan architecture of 1928 inspired me to seek the services of a campus architect who would respect and complement the original campus design as the College expanded. I was not particularly impressed with the plans drawn by well-known architect Mario Ciampi, FAIA, and sought a different expert. Though I tended to be philosophical in terms of my devotion to the liberal arts, including both the hard and soft sciences along with the humanities, I realized that the College had to adjust to the aspirations of students and their parents if enrollment was to grow and develop an attitude of self-sufficiency for the College. A certain number of undergraduate majors were added, including accounting and communications, which major I hoped would become a modern rhetoric department. I saw that expanding graduate education and other graduate programs, such as the Executive MBA, was an opportunity craving for development in the growing Contra Costa County area. Likewise, undergraduate baccalaureate or certificate programs, such as the Paralegal Assistant Program for older adults, were seen as a means for providing services to the community and utilizing College facilities more efficiently. A well-crafted undergraduate, high-potential program for minority students was developed in answer to a significant societal need and in keeping with the Lasallian spirit of the Christian Brothers.

Since I began my years at Saint Mary's with the college in debt, I was ever conscious of balancing the budget through an aggressive, but quality, development program and increasing enrollment by creating academic programs of stature, the major means for attracting students.

I received five honorary degrees over the years from other institutions of higher education, was included in the Contra Costa County Hall of Fame in 1988, received the Anti-Defamation League's *Torch of Liberty* award in 1993 and was selected as *Moraga Citizen of the Year* in 1994 I also received the Papal *Pro Ecclesia et Pontifice* medal in 1994, a letter of gratitude in 1996 from the Archbishop of Canterbury for my ecumenical work (at the urging of Brother Patrick Moore, FSC, PhD) with the local Anglican parish that makes use of the Saint Mary's College Chapel for its parish activities, the *Distinguished Lasallian Educator Award* in 1997, and proclamations of commendation from the town of Moraga and both the California State Assembly and the California State Senate.

Appointment of Brother Mel Anderson, July 1, 1969

In March 1969, when I was principal at Saint Mary's College High School in Berkeley and during my first year on the Board of Trustees (1968-1969), I was asked to meet the Provincial, Brother Bertram Coleman, in his office in the former Rheem Estate in Moraga. The Rheem Estate had been purchased by the Christian Brothers for the Provincial residence and offices in July 1961 and was subsequently sold to the town of Moraga by the Christian Brothers in 1975. After the normal pleasantries, Brother Bertram took me completely by surprise by asking me to consider assuming the presidency of Saint Mary's College in four months on July 1, 1969. He stated that the then president, Brother Michael Quinn, desired to step down as soon as possible. He also remarked that Brother Michael thought that I understood and appreciated the philosophy and pedagogy of the College, in particular the World Classics (Great Books) and Integrated Liberal Arts programs. "You have the resiliency to absorb faculty criticisms," he said, "and the personality to befriend both students and faculty alike."

He also noted that many of the Brothers were seeking a change in what they considered the trend toward secularization, exemplified by a diminution of the Catholic intellectual tradition. He hoped that I would be able to stem such a movement so that the College would remain steadfastly Catholic. At that time De La Salle Institute not only owned six high schools and a grammar boarding school (grades four through eight), it was the sole owner of Mont La Salle Vineyards, the commercial producers of Christian Brothers wines, champagnes and brandy. Therefore, the Provincial was in a position, with his Council's advice to provide limited aid to College renovation projects, thus making it more attractive to prospective students. Little by way of renovation had been undertaken to upgrade College residence halls, classrooms or other facilities since 1928. The occupation by the U. S. Navy Pre-Flight School during World War II had clearly taken its toll on common facilities and grounds, while at the same time it preserved the existence of the College for the future.

I held a baccalaureate degree in philosophy (1952) and had a significant number of credits toward a California teaching credential, as well as a number of credits toward master's degrees in both theology and philosophy. However, for the past 18 years my teaching and administrative career had been dedicated to secondary education. I responded to the Provincial by saying that I needed some time to consider the offer. I left his office in shock and returned in a little over a week, to say that I did not think that I should accept his kind offer. I quickly sensed that the Provincial was not willing to accept my refusal easily, however, since he began to recite the reasons why I should accept. I asked for more time. Another week passed and the Provincial phoned to ask what I was thinking. I went to see him again and reiterated that I did not think I had either the background or the experience to enter collegiate education at that time. However, I also said that I did take the vow of obedience seriously and would do what the Provincial assigned me to do to the best of my ability. I also added that if he were to insist, I would consider the appointment short-term, and after due investigation would make what seemed to be necessary changes to ameliorate his concerns. Little did I realize how difficult it was to change some faculty attitudes and direction, even though faculty are often perceived in society as leaders in effecting educational and societal change. The Provincial exuded a sigh of relief and appointed me president as of July 1, 1969. My appointment was officially announced to the Christian Brothers of the Province on May 29, 1969 by Brother Bertram. (Memorandum of Brother Bertram Coleman to the Brothers of the District of San Francisco, San Francisco District Archives, Napa.)

I was then asked to speak to a group of Brothers on the faculty regarding the difficulties the College faced and was asked by them what my response might be. I did not believe that I could respond with any depth at that time, but did say that I thought that the philosophy that directed the curriculum was of paramount importance. I also noted that it was gratifying that several of the Brothers on the faculty had received their doctorates in theology, most likely improving the department and its instructional task in manifesting the *Queen of the Sciences*. I could see that the problems facing the College -- from faculty politics to planned changes in the curriculum, from the renovation of facilities already underway to achieving a critical financial stability -- were formidable. Planning for the major changes in both calendar and requirements, under the direction of the Academic Vice President, were verging on completion and would shortly be presented to the Board of Trustees for approval.

As news of my appointment became known, several concerned and generally conservative faculty sought to make appointments to express their views. As I met with them I realized with increasing trepidation the academic, organizational, political and financial difficulties that lay before me.

Having been brought up in the Depression years, my instinct was to examine the audit report, as well as the College by-laws, with care. The internecine political turmoil seemed to be reaching a boiling point, and I had no time to enjoy a honeymoon period, since strong positions had already surfaced. I was expected to embrace the new order, as well as maintain tradition. What I needed was time to become aware of the new movement by evaluating its principles, and to consider political and public relations implications in decisions regarding the future. It was clear that the Academic Vice President along with his intimate colleagues, had gained the upper hand, in turning the long-standing College curriculum in a new direction. I spent considerable time with Academic Vice President Pollock attempting to uncover his personal academic philosophy and what effect it was having on the majority of the faculty, including the Christian Brothers, as well as on the student body. The Academic Vice President even exerted significant influence over residential life, I discovered to my surprise, as well as over the informal culture of the campus at large. The decision as to the renewal of Alan Pollock's appointment as Academic Vice President soon became one of my major concerns.

I was also concerned with the effectiveness of the Admissions Office and whether it was prudent to continue the outmoded single-sex stance of the institution. Brother Jerome West, former Provincial, had been appointed Vice-President for Development concurrently with my appointment, which gave me hope for significant improvement in what seemed to be a lack-luster fundraising effort. I also needed to assure myself that the costly renovation projects sponsored by De La Salle Institute were being accomplished efficiently and aesthetically, in conformity with the existing elegant Spanish-Mediterranean 1928 architecture of the late John Donovan, AIA.

The most daunting difficulty facing the College was clearly financial. The College was in debt by $121,000 and underfunded endowment stood at a mere $1.5 million, an amount that could aid but a few students. Saint Mary's was headed toward serious financial problems by almost anyone's guess, and fundraising had not yet begun to move forward as was so desperately required. Surprisingly, some Brothers in administrative positions, notably Brother Cassian Frye, Dean of Studies, advised me that funding a Development Office was a losing proposition and saw little reason to support it. Enrollment, and thus tuition income, was unpredictable. The all-male student body, most all of whom faced the draft, had been seriously affected by national protests. Likewise, demands for additional funds for minority student financial aid and necessary advising was a difficult hurdle at a time of serious financial stringency. It was particularly difficult to convince both faculty and staff that the financial recession of 1969 was a reality. The athletic program was experiencing its nadir, which probably was the cause for what proved to be a naïve student enthusiasm for club football. Some fiscal solutions offered by faculty, such as the elimination or downgrading of the athletic program, would, I thought, only worsen the financial situation in terms of support from alumni and many friends and could make the recruitment of students even more difficult than it was. I surmised that an athletic regeneration from its embarrassing doormat state might well excite some donors and potential students.

In spending time with members of the administration, faculty, staff and my own confreres, the Christian Brothers, I began to uncover the complexities that guided the diverse factions in College politics. I had to assess the impact that the drastic calendar and curriculum changes, the design of which was a *fait accompli*, would have on academic life, if approved by the Trustees and implemented commencing in the fall of 1969, but a few months away. The proposed changes had become imbedded in the minds of many and especially those of the more liberal faculty. To all appearances they had the support of my predecessor, Brother Michael Quinn.

Given the financial state of the College, the continuing Vietnam War and realistic possibilities for public protests, as well as my own uncertainty as to the financial future of the College and what my role should be regarding the controversial proposed new curriculum and calendar, I thought it prudent to assume office without such fanfare as mounting a costly and protest-vulnerable official inauguration ceremony. That is how my 28 years as president began.

As of this writing I serve as Resident Director in Ageno West residence hall, living in what is jocularly called the high-rent district of the campus, and conduct seminars on the Great Books of the Western World (Collegiate Seminar). Following my presidency I taught the Critical Perspectives or Great Books Seminars every semester in the Extended Education Program. I also served on various Boards of Directors or Board of Trustees, including Goodwill Industries of the East Bay, the School of Applied Theology at the Graduate Theological Union, Berkeley, and the Dominican School of Philosophy and Theology, also a member of the G.T.U. I continue to serve on the Corporation Board for Saint Mary's College.

Years of Recession, 1969-1977

Academic Governance: Familiar to Socrates

Academic Governance in 1969 had been fashioned under the guidance of the Academic Vice President, also known as Dean of the College, Rafael Alan Pollock, PhD, the Academic Vice President and Dean of the College (both titles were used) saw to both the organization and management of the academic life of the College. He was responsible for faculty searches, appointments (though contracts were signed by the president) and the monitoring of faculty performance along with School and Department Chairs and the Rank and Tenure Committee. Normally, in searching for new faculty, the AVP would appoint a search committee that included members from the department in which a potential faculty member would serve and a few members from other departments who would interview and recommend faculty appointments. Appointments were officially made by the president on the recommendation of the Academic Vice President.

The AVP either appointed or called for the election of academic committee members who would assist him in the conduct of academic life. One of the most significant committees, the Rank and Tenure Committee, was charged with making recommendations to the president on the granting of faculty tenure and promotions. Promotions in rank occurred at various stages during a faculty member's appointment. Under normal circumstances, a full-time faculty member was first appointed as an assistant professor and after a period of six years became eligible for promotion to associate professor. Tenure was usually granted concurrently with promotion to associate professor. Teaching competence, the possession of a terminal or ultimate degree (usually a doctorate), as well as scholarly achievement (publication or significant research) and accommodation with colleagues, were normally prerequisites for tenure and promotion to associate professor. After another six years the member would be eligible for promotion to professor (officially called full professor), assuming that the faculty member regularly acquired positive evaluations for teaching from both students and peers, fostered the academic life of the collegiate community and demonstrated clear evidence of scholarship. The academic quality of the institution was dependent on the insight of the evaluations and recommendations of the Rank and Tenure Committee. The Academic Vice President, who normally sat as chair of the Rank and Tenure Committee, would accompany the committee's recommendation with his own evaluative letter to the President.

The two other committees directly advising the Academic Vice President were the Academic Council and the Curriculum Committee. The Academic Vice President also received advice from the Faculty Assembly (a meeting to which all full- and part-time faculty were invited, usually held once a month and for occasional special sessions during the academic year).

After fall 1969 classes commenced, in order to familiarize myself with governance processes, the political climate and the management style of the Academic Vice President, I attended sessions of the Academic Council, the Faculty Assembly and the Rank and Tenure Committee. I thought it curious that the faculty elected a chairperson to conduct Faculty Assembly business, but that the Academic Vice President sat next to the chairperson in front of the Assembly during deliberations, offering his opinions and the rationale for his views on various issues. Academic governance was clearly centered in the person of the Academic Vice President. The Faculty Assembly process resembled nascent Athenian democracy in action where by procedures were neither fully clear nor developed. The faculty had become familiar with what processes there were and though a number of significant faculty were not pleased with what they perceived as political maneuvering under the guise of democracy, they sensed that not much could be done without intervention by the president. Those who approved the direction Alan Pollock envisioned for the College took full advantage of the Faculty Assembly forum that provided them with an opportunity to rule by rhetoric, even before the impact of so-called *political correctness,* or PC had reached Moraga. A number of members spoke well and often. They elicited sympathetic support from those who agreed with them, tended to overwhelm those who straddled the fence or disagreed, and at times verbally confronted those who expressed contrary views or met them with stony silence.

Faculty interchange, disagreement and compromise, one could rightfully assume, was of the essence of a thoughtful and professionally engaged faculty. However, I wondered whether factions in the Saint Mary's faculty were fully engaging each other. I heard grumbling after meetings from the more conservative members, but I did not see, nor was I aware of, any organized effort among the conservatives to marshal opposition against those who were promoting the new agenda. Amendments to curricular requirements were made from time to time to mend a few shortcomings in the new calendar and curriculum. With the exception of the Collegiate Seminar, civics and religious studies requirements, a clear philosophically guided curriculum based on an in-depth understanding of liberal education coupled with the Catholic intellectual tradition was hard to discern.

The Faculty Assembly was considered the final faculty voice, with the exception of a facultywide, written referendum. As is usually the case, those in political ascendancy dominated the Assembly. Attendance was voluntary and the number attending increased or decreased in direct relation to the interests of faculty on agenda items. There were times when the Assembly could pass a measure with less than 10 attendees present. Even Alan Pollock admitted that from time to time "faculty meetings tended to be sparsely attended." (Minutes of Faculty Meeting of Oct. 30, 1968.)

There were some written policies, but in 1969 the most recent Faculty Handbook was dated Jan. 25, 1961. Governance and procedural changes, a number being *ad hoc*, were accomplished by political coalitions and last-minute proposals within the town-hall governance of the Faculty Assembly. Groups were called together and telephone calls were allegedly made prior to what was deemed a critical vote. The most effective way for a minority voice or minority voices to be heard was for a member or a group of faculty to submit a written proposal to the chair of the Assembly for placement on the agenda. Persuasion by the Academic Vice President, often through small, *ad hoc* meetings, telephone networking and from the seat he assumed during deliberations, was a dominant factor in determining policy. Unfortunately, some who expressed contrary views were too often the less politically astute, or some of the same few were not fully effective in the academic classroom. In general, the exercise of what became increasingly a social-political liberal agenda was, I discovered, a one-way street. Proposals developed through considerable debate and careful thought by fairly objective faculty committees, such as the Academic Council, were often voted down at a single meeting if enough opposing votes could be mustered by the dominant faction. Both subtle and not-so subtle campaigns for positions on faculty committees were frequently waged to assure the election of the correctly progressive faculty members. To its credit, however, the faculty held firm to the Collegiate Seminar and Religious Studies requirements for all students, thus supporting two of the traditionally major Saint Mary's academic and liberal arts traditions.

After the Senate was formed in the latter half of the 1980s, some faculty, in retrospect, bemoaned the absence of the excitement that sometimes characterized the give-and-take of the Faculty Assembly. The faculty realized that the Assembly may not have been as effective and efficient as it could have been, and even assumed positions that eventually proved to be unworkable. There were moments that the ebb and flow of emotionally charged participatory democracy morphed into a kind of congestive dead end. There were meetings, punctuated with wit, chagrin, concern and passion, and filled with a bold manifestation of diverse positions and even some small-time political chicanery that was often more intriguing than reading a recent bestselling novel. As several faculty noted after the Senate had been instituted, "The Faculty Assembly used to be fun!"

Prudential governance would normally provide the faculty an opportunity to express ideas or vent feelings through a town-hall type meeting, for if there are pent-up issues, the tension usually subsides when members are able to state their frustrations or objections and hear contrary or modified points of view from their colleagues. However, the Faculty Assembly, given its amorphous inconsistency and vulnerability to political intervention on issues of the moment, could not be taken as seriously as such a learned group should have been regarded.

A widespread breakdown of civil discourse, appropriate language, professional dress, objective reporting, authentically artistic entertainment and cultivated decorum, characteristic in American culture of the '60s and early '70s had a significant and lingering influence on academe. One of the more egregious violations of academic freedom was protests designed to silence or insult speakers whom certain factions judged to be opposed to their views. Fortunately, the College escaped such effrontery for the most part, but not entirely.

Launching New Ideas

First Committees of the New Regime, Goals and Women

In my first semester as President I formed what I believed to be two noncontroversial committees: one to restate the College goals or what is called its *mission statement* that normally appeared in the *Bulletin,* thus providing the academic compass for curriculum development. The other committee was formed to continue the discussion begun several years prior to 1969 and to draw to closure its recommendations regarding the feasibility of instituting *coeducation,* one of the more reasonable recommendations among the SPAN proposals, and one which I thought was not only reasonable but commendable.

Since I believed that the committee should develop its own vision without my interference, some interpreted my noncommittal stance as either timidity or a cloaked and unenlightened conservatism. My ultimate aim was to restore as much as possible what I considered to be the intellectual mission of the College, guided by philosophical and theological principles, and to extricate the College as much as possible from bending its purposes to be in alignment with particular ideological, social and political trends characteristic of the time, well-outlined in both the SPAN proposals and the Academic Vice President's major addresses and memoranda.

The development of new and clear goals in a mission statement proved to be more difficult than I had anticipated and led to renewed, though more subdued, controversy. I requested Brother Robert Smith, FSC, PhD, a philosopher, Chairman of the Integrated Program in Liberal Arts and a man of quality mind to chair the committee on goals. Brother Robert appeared to take the task to heart by engaging the committee in regular meetings for more than a year. At the outset, he and his subcommittee colleagues had to determine whether the subcommittee would compose a document reflecting the rationale for the existing *new* curriculum or would develop a document that contained a vision for the future with the expressed hope of moving toward that vision. My hope was that the statement would demonstrate its commitment to certain philosophical principles, either expressed or implied.

The subcommittee opted for an existential document, given the recent history of controversy over the changes in calendar and curriculum which had both excited and troubled the campus over the prior two years. The statement that emerged, informally tagged the *Robert Smith Draft*, was titled *Saint Mary's College Its Rationale and Reason for Being.* (April 1970, Saint Mary's College Archives) and described the general purposes of the College, the signs of its Catholic tradition, and the current ambiguity of philosophical and theological systems. In addition to preparing students in some way for assuming responsibilities in society, and in acquiescing the College mission as Catholic, the statement noted that its task was "helping Catholic students articulate the meaning of their faith." An historical overview provided the context for College evolution since 1863. During the last 10 years of existence in the city of Oakland (1918-1928) and the early years in Moraga, the document observed that "the College revolved intellectually around two of its own alumni, Brother Leo Meehan, FSC, and James L. Hagerty." Brother Leo was steeped in English literature and was an able author and rhetorician, widely acclaimed and admired by the public. Hagerty was devoted to philosophy and the Socratic method of instruction, though he often conducted seminars as though they were lectures. Historically, the major academic emphasis of the pre-'40 was "literary and to a degree philosophical." Since 1941 the great works of philosophy and literature became paramount. Brother Robert's observations on the changes which occurred in 1969 were contained in restrained criticisms, "Those who are not content that the institution should represent in a living and creative way at least part of the intellectual spectrum around us are a little more pleased with the memory of the College in the '50 and the '60." He then noted that the changes effected in 1969 were "less the consequence of a clearly enunciated theory than a new framework of courses and requirements that can be used differently by people who have diverse theories of education." These tactfully crafted criticisms were deleted in a subsequent revision, informally tagged as the *Collins Revision*.

Brother Robert completed his analysis by placing his hope in the commitment of the Seminar Governing Board to provide students with "some experience of a philosophical and religious tradition useful in helping them form their own opinions and direct their lives wisely" and, more significantly, to produce a "group of teachers capable of talking with one another about important matters." Brother Robert's document was carefully drawn to say more than what appeared on the surface. However, when he submitted his statement to the full Goals Committee and others for criticism, he received a plethora of negative comments and observations. The comments and observations were placed in the hands of a young professor, James Collins, a member of the subcommittee, who was directed to incorporate as many of the suggested amendments as possible while maintaining the original intent of the *Robert Smith Draft*. The *Collins Revision* of Feb. 15, 1971, attempted to include an endorsement of the rationale for the sweeping changes of 1969 but also directed its attention to eschewing any tendencies within the institution of establishing the types of programs found in universities or vocational and technical programs that were similar to those offered in community colleges. The *Collins Revision* stated that "the primary and essential commitment of Saint Mary's is to provide the best possible environment for the education of undergraduate students in a relatively small community of learners centered in a predominantly residential college." The optimum size of the College was suggested to "lie between 1,000 and 1,500 students."

Issues proposed in the Nov. 18, 1970, paper by Alan Pollock, *Goals of the College*, submitted to the Subcommittee on Goals were also added to the *Collins Revision*, namely, a commitment to increase minority enrollment, devising a College program for the improvement of teaching, conducting an examination of the evaluation (grading) process, and creating opportunities for cooperative education, as opposed to competitive educational methods.

The *Collins Revision* was presented to the Administrative Council and after considerable editing, was approved by the Council on Feb. 23, 1971. It was then submitted to the faculty for a vote. The faculty endorsement was lukewarm at best. Approximately half voted on the document, with 28 yea votes and 22 nays. The Trustees expressed serious reservations about the document, and a group of 11 Christian Brothers holding faculty rank moved to reject the document *in toto*. "This statement," the Brothers observed, "is an account of the history of a process that led to the present state of confusion

rather than an affirmation of any present or future purpose." After reviewing the *Collins Revision*, I expressed serious reservations of my own, one of
which was a lack of middle ground that might bring more agreement to the
document. I consequently formed another, smaller committee to consider
the composition of an alternative statement. Brother Robert, who had invested both considerable time and thought in attempting to be both realistic
and compromising of various viewpoints, seemed disappointed with the
end result, and especially with the reaction of his confreres.

A year later, a new Academic Vice President, alumnus Thomas Slakey, PhD,
'52, working with a committee composed of six faculty members and administrators produced, his first lengthy draft of a goals statement. Discussions with the President's Council, the Board of Trustees, the faculty and
the Christian Brothers Community continued through the fall 1972 semester, with a final shortened draft being approved by the Board of Trustees
on March 1, 1973. I held the view that involving the Brothers, the faculty,
the administration, and ultimately the Board of Trustees in the review and
possible alteration of the mission statement approximately every five years
brought faculty, particularly new members, into dialogue across departmental lines in considering the fundamental academic principles characterizing
the College. The final version cited the liberal arts, Catholic and Lasallian
nature of the institution. The order in which the three characteristics were
placed (liberal arts, Catholic and Lasallian) followed a rational and theological order based on the principle that grace builds on nature in the development of the Christian person. The Lasallian element in the mission statement provided a spirituality that viewed students as deserving of the dignity
accorded persons created in the image and likeness of God, that is students,
who possessed an ability to engage in a thoughtful, creative process that results in acquiring the truth, developing both arts and sciences, perceiving
and fostering the good in themselves and others, and especially acknowledging the reality that God is both truth and love.

Coeducation, the Study and Decision

Since groups of faculty had for several years considered the option of coeducation, the conversation was a familiar one to the Committee I appointed to
investigate its possibility. Considerable evidence had been collected in the
form of both pro and con faculty views, as well as through faculty and student polls. A student poll conducted by the freshmen and sophomore class
presidents dated Feb. 19, 1969, revealed that 86.5 percent of the freshmen
and 79 percent of the sophomores favored a change from a single-sex institution to coeducation. Professor William Tauchar, PhD, Chairman of the

School of Economics and Business Administration, concerned as to how the presence of women would affect his School, conducted a poll of 1,076 males in Catholic high schools in California. Four-hundred and eighty-eight or 45.3 percent stated that they "absolutely preferred a coeducational college" and 272 or 25 percent stated that they "preferred a coeducational college," a total of 70 percent indicating a preference for attending a coeducational institution. Tauchar also cited a Princeton University study in which 76.8 percent of high school seniors surveyed stated that, "coeducation increases collegiate attractiveness."

An on-campus faculty poll resulted in 37 favorable responses (70 percent) and 16 (30 percent) unfavorable responses to the concept of coeducation. Comments by faculty members were mixed yet thoughtful. Visiting Professor Robert Sacks, PhD remarked that: "Aristotle is probably right in supposing changes should not be made unless they are clearly good. Arguments opposed to the proposed issue seem to have their foundation in the camaraderie of the beer party which tends to be exclusive with regard to sex. And in spite of the fact that the 'good old days' would be remembered by some, one should weigh the other side. Quite simply we will get better students" Professor Raleigh Scovel of the history department opined that "Coeducation would make it possible to raise the admittance requirements of the College, and it would thus raise the general level of intelligence in the classroom ..." On the contrary, Brother Brendan Kneale, Professor of mathematics, offered 11, "reasons for caution." Though Brother Brendan urged prudential consideration by his use of the word caution he was quietly, but admittedly, opposed to the introduction of coeducation. In his veiled opposition he made his case. "It is not clear," he said, "that we have done the necessary groundwork needed for undertaking responsibility for the education of women ... It is not clear that increased economic support would ensue ... It is not clear that the amateur psychoanalytical arguments for coeducation are beyond refutation ... It is not clear that women electing to come to Saint Mary's would be superior in both ability to study and appetite for study" It was this latter argument that Brother Brendan found most formidable, given what he considered the prevailing attitude of American culture and of many women themselves regarding the pursuit of the intellectual life, at least at that time. In judiciously private conversations, Brother Brendan expressed his concern that the presence of women on campus may lure the young Christian Brothers in training (called Formation) away from their religious vocations.

In his characteristic eloquence, Dean Alan Pollock supported the concept of coeducation stating that "segregation in any form seems anachronistic to most college students and, in this case, is a divorce between intellectual and social life in a society where we must learn to treat each other as equals ..." An article discussing the merits of coeducation appearing in *The Chronicle of Higher Education* (Feb. 10, 1969), observed that, "Another reason cited by advocates of coeducation is that geographic isolation of many sex-segregated schools ... many argue, leads to 'weekly monasticism' and weekend 'orgies.'" The late Brother Kyran Aviani, Professor of Art, who was prevailed upon with the argument that women would add a beneficial dimension to the art program, disagreed in haut sarcasm, stating, "I think moreover that we should enroll old people, children, married couples, and as many races and religions as possible too, because then we would have even more points of view, and things would be better yet." Brother Kyran concluded his skeptical peroration by saying: "... it would perhaps be better simply to go coed for all of the cogent and logically persuasive reasons we have received. And let us, at the same time, change the name of the school to Moraga University to make clear to the world how much we have changed for the better."

The Chairman of the School of Economics and Business Administration, William Tauchar, PhD, was clearly apprehensive regarding the institution of coeducation, since women, he believed, were not wont to associate themselves with either economics or business administration. "The current imputation of sundry desiderata to coeducation," he eloquently stated, "reflects either wish fulfillment (reaction to the assumed plight of private colleges) or a facet of the continuing drift in cultural apperception in the direction of social integration. Resort must therefore be had to justification by emotion, perhaps the ultimate arbiter of all social judgments." (Memoranda and letters on file under *Coeducation,* Saint Mary's College Archives)

I favored coeducation for two major reasons, the primary one being that I believed that men and women should encounter each other on an intellectual level in the academic classroom and seminar setting as they mature together. Women, I thought, would also enhance the cultural, artistic and social life of the College, as my prior experience in a coeducational institution had demonstrated. Secondly, Saint Mary's was the last of the formerly all-male Catholic institutions of higher education remaining in the state, and as long as it remained such, the chances for student-body growth, subsequent academic enhancement and financial stability were unlikely. Tauchar's canvass of California male high school students was persuasive. Saint Mary's enrollment had never achieved the 1,000 mark in its 113 years of existence, even shortly after World War II when the return of veterans who carried the benefits of the GI Bill entered collegiate life throughout the nation. The recruitment of a suitable and sizeable male student body was a continuing problem. If the College were to flourish, that is, develop an authentic liberal arts curriculum, as well as strengthen both the science, and economics and business administration offerings, expand the library holdings, upgrade deteriorating facilities, maintain what was considered at the time an ambitious and competitive athletic program (to which had been added club football in 1966), remunerate faculty appropriately and expand selected offerings in the arts, its progress would depend upon a larger enrollment and subsequent income. Instituting coeducation would open the College to the other half of the world, offering women as well as men the benefits of a distinctive Saint Mary's education. Ironically, one of the unanticipated costs of a coeducational student body was government intervention requiring long overdue equal opportunity for women in athletics, including athletic financial aid, duplicating to some extent the coaching staff and adjusting schedules for equal use of facilities. However, it is not clear that government intervention has been as fruitful in what are called the spectator sports in terms of women's teams competing with men for spectators. It seems fairly clear that equal opportunity does not mean equal results, at least as far as general public interest in women's athletics goes, which has its financial implications as well.

As a matter of professional cooperation and courtesy, particularly with another Catholic institution of higher education, I requested an appointment with Sister Ambrose Devereux, SNJM, PhD, the President of Holy Names College in Oakland, at that time a long standing single-sex institution for women, with alumnae that included the spouses of many Saint Mary's alumni. When Sister Ambrose was told of the possibility of Saint Mary's becoming coeducational, perhaps anticipating the inevitability of the initiative, she said that Saint Mary's had to do what it believed to be in its best interests. She rightfully thought that the change might well have a troublesome effect upon Holy Names, but even so, she said "that should not deter Saint Mary's from doing what it thought best for its own fulfillment." I thanked Sister Ambrose for her candor and congeniality and later asked her to serve as a member of the Board of Trustees of the College. Sister Ambrose graciously accepted the offer. Her administrative experience and academic background became a valuable asset on the Board, particularly in light of the increasing number of women in the student body. It was not too long before Holy Names announced that it, too, would become coeducational. After completing her term as President at Holy Names Sister Ambrose enjoyed a sabbatical year and intended to return to the Saint Mary's Board, but unfortunately, she suffered a debilitating stroke, forcing her to resign from both the Board and her faculty appointment at Holy Names. She retired to the Sisters of the Holy Names center in Los Gatos, Calif. and died several years later.

On Dec. 12, 1969, the *San Francisco Chronicle* ran the headline: Saint Mary's College to Admit Coeds and the article succinctly reported "The Board voted 9-3 with one abstention for the radical change."

Coeducation, Beginnings, 1970-1971

Since women were to become part of the student body commencing with the 1970-1971 academic year, it seemed only proper that a female Associate Dean be appointed as soon as possible. A group of those associated with the residence halls began screening for an associate dean. Pollock complained that he was not included in the search, claiming that the appointment of an Associate Dean of Students was critical, since what happened in the residence halls affected the academic life of the College. At this time, the Academic Vice President was closely aligned in spirit and friendship to the Dean of Students, alumnus Odell Johnson, '58. I responded that more importantly, what happened in the academic classroom had a much more profound effect upon residence hall living than the other way round. "If the academic life is demanding," I said, "residence hall living will be more self-directive." I quickly conceded, however, that an orderly residence hall life was undoubtedly conducive to developing the intellectual life.

The decision by the Board of Trustees in Dec. 1969 for the College to become coeducational followed most other institutions of higher education in California. Although the fall of 1970 was but nine months away, limiting recruitment time for women by the Admissions Office, 138 women enrolled for the fall 1970 semester.

Both Beckett and More residence halls had been designed to accommodate a possible shift to coeducation. Furthermore, in the summer of 1969 both Dante Hall classroom facility and De La Salle residence hall, often identified as center or senior dorm, were renovated. During the summer of 1970, Aquinas residence hall, previously identified as sophomore dorm, was completely gutted and renovated with quasi-apartment-style suites. They did not contain a central common room or kitchen facilities. These initial renovation projects were made possible primarily through assistance from the Christian Brothers De La Salle Institute. The Provincial of the Christian Brothers, Brother Bertram Coleman, fully supported the renewal of College facilities, with the hope that increased enrollment and an aggressive development program would eventually allow the College to become not only operationally self-sufficient but would increase its future fundraising capacity to allow for the construction of needed facilities and the increase of its endowment. The initial renovation projects clearly facilitated the introduction of coeducation.

With the advent of coeducation I sought assurance from the staff that preparations for having women on campus would be completed before the commencement of the fall 1970 semester. The timing for the commencement of coeducation was almost too late for both student recruitment and the posting of job announcements for the position of Associate Dean. Fortunately however, most physical accommodations for women were adequate. A Dominican sister, Theresa Lackie, OP, from the Dominican Congregation of the Most Holy Cross, Edmonds, Washington, upon hearing of the plan for coeducation and the search for an Associate Dean, applied for the position. I favored the appointment of a religious sister in view of the College entering the first-time uncertainties of coeducation, where the vast majority of students during the first two years would be male. Though she seemed mildly conservative, she was organized, reasonable and congenial. She held her baccalaureate from Seattle University and had taught in both elementary school and high school for 27 years. At that time she was engaged in securing her Master's Degree in counseling from the University of San Francisco. She was hired and was able to assist the first 138 women through the throes of pioneering an uncertain male minefield. A number of male students, who felt that their male bonding, weekend beer parties and distinctive manly enclave would suffer with the presence of women on campus, demonstrated their opposition to the presence of the fair sex in curious ways. It was not uncommon for some groups of men to turn their backs on female students with the phrase, "Here come the skirts." Yet, within a short time, women made their presence appreciated among their male counterparts. Several of the men discovered the women of their dreams, and many of the women likewise found the men of their hearts. The faculty was particularly pleased with the academic commitment of women students and the perspective they brought to the academic interchange.

When former Sister Theresa came back for her fifth year, she had decided to return to lay life and was listed in the Student Guide as Miss Theresa Lackie. She tendered her resignation at the end of the 1974-1975 academic year. A search committee, under the direction of the then Vice President for Student Affairs Bill McLeod, selected Patricia Swatfager, a capable young woman as the second Associate Dean.

Campus Ministry, 1969

As was the custom, the Mass of the Holy Spirit was celebrated within the first week or two of the commencement of the new academic year. When the date for the Fall Holy Spirit Mass was announced in early September 1969, I looked forward to its celebration. I recalled my own introduction to the celebration when I was a freshman Student-Brother and part of the choir in 1948 -- the colorful academic regalia of the faculty in solemn procession, the sonorous power of our 30-plus-voice Student Brothers (Scholastics) choir, the majesty of the organ, the student body members in suit and tie filling the Chapel, the dignity of the liturgical celebrants, and the lofty expectations and inspiration voiced in the first homily delivered by the campus minister assigned by the Archdiocese as College chaplain.

In 1969, I joined approximately 25 faculty and administrators, a surprisingly small group, along with the Campus Ministers who had assembled for the processional in the arcade outside the Chapel. At the appointed time the procession commenced. When I entered the nearly empty 700-seat Chapel, I was mortified to find one student with a guitar standing near the sanctuary singing and strumming *Blowing in the Wind.* Since there were less than a handful of students in attendance, the celebrant invited all present to stand around the altar. The scene was clearly a cause for concern and action, given the contrast with the historical context of the opening liturgy. The currently popular Nietzschean notion that *God was dead* had reached the Moraga Valley, or perhaps the evident indifference to the Holy Spirit was evoked by the *au courant* distrust of both religion and the Church. I was so disgusted with the apparent lack of planning and promotion and the absence of student and faculty interest that I suspended the celebration of inaugural Masses of the Holy Spirit until such time that the celebrations could be conducted with the dignity they deserved, coupled with the active participation of significant numbers of administration, faculty, students and staff. The Holy Spirit hiatus lasted for the next two years until plans were forthcoming for an appropriate celebration.

Surveys of religious adherence indicated that approximately 70 percent of the student body in the early '70s was nominally Roman Catholic and a respectable number of students did attend Sunday Mass fairly regularly. The number of self-identified Catholics declined as the student body grew. By 1997 Catholics numbered a little over 50 percent. But in 1969 I, as well as other members of the administration, members of the Christian Brothers Community and other faculty members, were invited to the Sunday student liturgies usually celebrated after the student dinner hour.

In 1969, in a spirit of supporting the Sunday liturgies by my presence and example, I decided to attend one of them, held not in the Chapel, but in Dryden Hall, a large meeting room not far from the Chapel. A portable altar was positioned on the floor with students and others standing near the walls or seated on the floor around the altar in a semicircle. "Students," I was told, "enjoyed the more casual environment of Dryden Hall than the formality of the Chapel." Guitars provided the musical background for the post-Vatican II hymns. The Mass proceeded in its customary way until it was time for the consecration of the bread and wine in reenactment of the Last Supper, when several loaves of Columbo French bread were consecrated at the altar. When the moment for Holy Communion arrived, the full loaves were handed to students nearest the altar. Each student tore off a portion of a supposedly consecrated loaf and passed it on to the next person. Since the crust on French bread crumbles profusely, the floor was littered with supposedly consecrated crumbs.

It would be accurate to say that the vacuum cleaners on Monday morning became temporary tabernacles, so it seemed, though some theologians would argue that Columbo French bread was an invalid kind of bread for use at Mass, and thus the consecration was not only unlawful by Canon Law but also invalid.

Acquiescence to the aberrant interpretations of Vatican II and the deconstruction of some cultural and religious traditions indulged students rather than urged them to consider with care the principles that infused popular -- some would say vulgar -- notions or cultural changes. While adapting the changes to more communal celebration of the liturgy, Campus Ministry could have seized the moment by advocating a profound faith in the authentic meaning of the Mass and the many insightful concepts enunciated in the documents of Vatican II. Unfortunately the ministry seemed to fall into the post-Vatican II confusion itself, since the contending elements within the Church at the time became a formidable challenge for anyone associated with campus ministry.

When alumnus Tom Slakey, PhD, was appointed Academic Vice President in 1971, he expected to participate in the Mass of the Holy Spirit at the beginning of the academic year. He found that I had temporarily suspended the Holy Spirit Mass. Slakey strongly believed that the Mass of the Holy Spirit marking the beginning of the academic year should be restored and spoke to me about its restoration. I fully agreed in principle on the condition that the Mass be conducted with significant dignity and that means be taken to encourage student attendance. Discussions on the promotion of student attendance resulted in a creative solution by seeking cooperation from student body and class officers, who were invited to participate in the beginning processional, in the offertory procession by offering gifts symbolic of each class, and in the recessional. They were also urged to encourage student participation. Students responded to the urging and the Mass returned to a more inspirational and celebratory quality, even though it would be some time before more traditional or new and more elegant compositions of liturgical music were again heard in the Chapel.

Governance

The Corporation and the Board of Trustees

The bylaws of the College divide the Governing Board or Board of Directors into two tiers or parts, namely, the **Corporation** and the **Board of Trustees**. Membership on the Corporation was composed of 15 Christian Brothers, 10 from the College faculty and five from the Christian Brothers San Francisco Province-at-large. In 1969 the **Board of Trustees** was composed of 15 voting members (increased to 18 in 1996), a minimum of six being Christian Brothers, with two of that number being the Christian Brother President and the Provincial of the San Francisco Province (District) designated as *ex officio* members. The limited, but comprehensive, responsibilities of the **Corporation** were specified as approving the bylaws or composing new bylaws, approving changes in existing bylaws and approving the sale of all or almost all of the College assets.

This two-tiered model was instituted in many Catholic institutions of higher education to protect religious or apostolic interests, usually considered the *mission of the sponsoring religious body*, though many Catholic institutions jettisoned this model in governance, either to eliminate overbearing control or interference by Provincials or Provincial advisors (Provincial Councils) or to place the increasingly complex issues of higher education upon the president and the Board of Trustees regarding the prescripts of academic freedom and the conduct of an institution as a community of scholars capable of self-direction under the guidance of a competent academic administration. American higher education is significantly different from secondary or primary educational institutions or other kinds of educational or apostolic activity, though the Provincial would normally have an obligatory interest in whether the apostolic mission of the institution was being fostered appropriately.

The responsibility of the **Board of Trustees** at Saint Mary's has been to establish operating policy for the management and enhancement of the College as a liberal arts, Catholic and Lasallian institution of higher education.

The two *ex officio* Christian Brothers, namely, the President and Provincial, and the minimum of four remaining Brothers on the Board of Trustees may be from the faculty, administration or other Christian Brothers institutions.

The local Accreditation Commission policy states that faculty from an institution should not be appointed as members of the Board of that institution on the principle that faculty would not be free from the temptation of self-serving interests and the resultant loss of objectivity and thus be vulnerable to the criticism of conflict of interest. The Accreditation Visitors had several times cited the presence of Brothers from the faculty as being in violation of Accreditation policy. However, when I had the opportunity I noted to both the chairman of the Accreditation Visiting Team, the Executive Director and the Accreditation Commission that faculty Brothers had served on the Board since incorporation in the early 20th century and because the Brothers were not affected by salary adjustments, they would not be members with conflicts of interest. Yet, members of the Commission countered with the argument that Brothers who are faculty are subject to the President, whereas as faculty on the Board, the President is subject to them. That seemed to them to be an undesirable anomaly. I responded that the Brothers on the Board acted in consort with the Board and brought a point of view that represented the mind of the Brothers, who saw their representatives on the Board as acting as guardians of an apostolic enterprise or religious mission to which they had committed their lives. "Brothers from the faculty would bring intimate views about the College that may at rare moments differ from those of the President, but," I stated, "Trustees should take such views into account when reflecting on serious decisions." Therefore, I observed, "Brothers from the College faculty must have voice and vote on the Board, albeit as a minority." Faculty Brothers on the Board, I facetiously noted, were an incentive to keep the President and administrators "transparent" at least to the Board. Christian Brothers from other provinces or from other institutions in the province could also be named as voting members, thus enriching the Board with a welcome, but perhaps different, perspective. One difficulty with Brothers from other parts of the country is that they are not familiar with California law, the spirit and peculiar characteristics of Saint Mary's College or the intense academic environment in which Saint Mary's exists when considering both public and independent institutions located in the San Francisco Bay Area.

Other members, from six to nine, could be members of the clergy and laymen or women. The Board of Trustees is a self-perpetuating body, however, no member with the exception of the *ex officio* members could serve more than two five-year terms, later revised to three three-year terms, so enacted to be in conformity with changes in the California Corporations Code. The Provincial Visitor serves *ex officio* during his time as Provincial Visitor, which is now limited to a maximum of two four-year terms, unless for significant reasons beyond the concerns of the College an extension is allowed. The president serves *ex officio* for whatever his time in office might be.

Though the College is officially incorporated under California corporation law, I did not believe that the Board should assume the characteristics of a corporate business board, though business decisions were inevitable. It was, in my opinion, important that every member of the Board acquire a familiarity with both faculty and student attitudes so that faculty and students would be acknowledged as forming a community of scholars with administrators and the Board. Faculty should be considered as partners in the crucial enterprise of education and not be considered simply as employees or the students as impersonal customers or clients. Such protocols as the granting of tenure to faculty solidify that partnership, and the Trustees must take this principle into account in working with the faculty.

I inherited such wide-ranging responsibilities as the granting of tenure to faculty after appropriate review and recommendation by the Rank and Tenure Committee; finalizing faculty and administrative appointments; signing contracts for Vice Presidents, Deans, Athletic Directors, the campus architect, major coaching appointments and other administrative personnel; the appointment of College legal counsel; and signing contracts for construction projects, consultants and other major commitments, after Board review and approval on budget for architectural plans and administrative personnel needs.

Board member, James Harvey, who was at that time President and CEO of Transamerica, Inc., counseled against enlarging the Board beyond its 15 members. Maintaining a membership of approximately 15 members, he believed, was reasonable and workable, especially since all major matters were brought before the entire Board for due consideration. If the Board were expanded, he observed, it would not be too long before an Executive Committee would be formed that would act much like the existing Board. Board members not on the Executive Committee could be reduced to second-class membership, though they would be members of an enlarged number of permanent committees. A committee increase and larger committee structure was deemed unnecessary at the time. There are positive and negative effects to a large committee structure. The positive ones are that Trustee expertise in certain areas may well enlighten the function of committees and thus guide the College prudently. The negative effects could be unnecessary interference in the efficient management of certain areas best left to administrators, including the President, who hopefully have demonstrated their effectiveness.

Major development or fundraising functions became the task of the Board of Regents rather than the Board of Trustees, though the Board of Trustees was intimately involved in the planning of capital campaigns and approving unusual contacts.

Chairmen of the Board of Trustees, 1968-1997
Dan Cullen, 1968-1970; Brother Bertram Coleman, 1970-1971; George Gordon, JD, 1971-1972; Brother Cassian Frye, 1972-1973; William P. Niland, EdD, 1973-1975; Sister Mary Ambrose Devereux, SNJM, PhD; 1975-1976; Ross B. Yerby, 1976-1978; Brother Cassian Frye, 1978-1980; Chancellor of the Contra Costa Community College District Harry Buttimer, PhD, 1980-1982; James McCloud, 1982-1983; Elaine McKeon, 1983-1985; Raymond O'Brien, 1985-1987; Hon. Arthur Latno, 1987-1989; Brother Mark Murphy, 1989-1993; Maryellen Cattani, JD, 1993-1995; B. J. Cassin, 1995-1997.

A complete list of all members of the Board of Trustees from 1969 through 1997 can be found in the Appendix

Maneuvering with the Board of Trustees
The new calendar and curricular proposal that the Academic Vice President, his colleagues and some students had been engaged in designing during the latter years of Brother Michael Quinn's presidency was readied for Board of Trustee approval at the April 24, 1969 meeting of the Board, only one month from the end of the 1968-1969 academic year. The proposal that Alan Pollock had compiled and hoped would be implemented in the fall of 1969 was strategically divided for presentation to the Board into two segments, a division that appeared to avoid what might have generated strong Board opposition had the entire proposal been presented at once and at such a late date. The first segment addressed the institution of a new academic calendar and the second, the changes in requirements.

The 4-1-4 Calendar
The proposal to change the academic calendar substituted what was called the 4-1-4 calendar for the existing two-semester calendar of 15 weeks for each semester or 30 weeks of instruction per year. The proposed calendar divided the traditional academic year of 30 weeks of instruction into two 13-week semesters and a January term of four weeks, or the required 30 weeks per year. It was identified as the 4-1-4 calendar, meaning that students would enroll in four courses each 13-week semester and one course in January, for a

total of nine courses per academic year. In order to fulfill the standard time allotments for traditional courses, 10 minutes were added to each class in the 13-week semester, thus altering the standard "Carnegie" 50-minute class hour to a 60-minute standard hour.

The Board was presented with the proposal for the adoption of the 4-1-4 calendar on April 24, 1969. In response to questions by members of the Board, Alan Pollock assured the Board that the calendar change would not require additional expense. Furthermore, he eloquently described a future curriculum in which, "exciting and innovative courses would be possible" under the proposal. Pollock also elaborated under questioning that the reduction of course loads would "eliminate busy work and fragmentation of the curriculum." Though his academic goals gave the impression that greater coherence and academic intensity were the intention of the calendar change, one had to wonder why busy work would characterize any academic classroom at Saint Mary's, regardless of calendar, or why a calendar change with fewer courses would eliminate an undefined academic fragmentation, that he believed existed. The somewhat mysterious nature of his rhetoric unfolded in May when the second part of the academic proposal, namely the curriculum revisions were presented. The "exciting" variety of "innovative courses" Pollock stated, would come through the January Term, controlled by a governing committee or board, as yet unnamed. Why such a program would not lead to the greater academic fragmentation that he saw as hostile to quality academic endeavors was not clear. The governing board, he stated, "must reflect Catholic values, though its members do not need to be Catholic themselves." This was another of those ambiguous statements that came too quickly for careful Board analysis. He also emphasized that there was *no connection between the 4-1-4 calendar and any reduction in requirements, either in courses or in subject matter.*

After considerable discussion by the Board, the Chairman, Dan Cullen, who was Chairman of the Board of Directors of Walston and Co., at that time a prestigious San Francisco brokerage firm, turned to the President, Brother Michael Quinn, and asked what he preferred. Brother Michael responded that he supported the 4-1-4 calendar. Cullen, sensing that discussion had run its course, called for a motion. Whether several on the Board realized that a reduction in course load implied a necessary change in requirements is not ascertainable since almost all of the Board members from that time are no longer living. Brother Cassian Frye, Dean of Studies, moved that the 4-1-4 calendar be approved. Brother Michael Quinn seconded. Judging from the provisions attached to his motion, Brother Cassian was aware of discussions well under way regarding changes in requirements. In moving for acceptance of the 4-1-4 calendar, Brother Cassian added that the new calendar "not involve any changes in the proposed budget (for the forthcoming year), that it be subject to periodic evaluative review and that the motion in no way "prejudge the question of changed requirements." The Board approved the motion on the 4-1-4 calendar with a vote of 7 yea, 3 nay and 1 abstention. (Minutes of the Board of Trustees, April 24, 1969.) Within 34 days major changes in academic requirements would be placed before the Board for approval.

Alan Pollock reported his *Proposal for Reduction and Reform of Collegiate Requirements* to the Board on May 28, 1969, as outlined in a memorandum to the President, Brother Michael Quinn, dated the same day. The Board minutes record that "considerable discussion of the need for requirements and of the validity of the proposed courses in meeting the intellectual ideals of Saint Mary's College followed." Board member George Gordon moved that the proposal be deferred until the next meeting. I seconded the motion, and it passed unanimously. (Minutes of the Board of Trustees, May 28, 1969, Saint Mary's College Archives.)

A special meeting of the Board was called for July 2, 1969, and in the absence of the Board Chairman, I presided, having assumed office as of July 1, 1969. Following a history and analysis of the changes in curriculum by Professor El Gelinas of the Philosophy Department, the Trustees realized what the changes would mean. Gelinas also outlined the faculty discussion on the proposal. Alan Pollock was introduced to explain the proposal in detail. Discussion by the Board centered on two issues, the first regarding the revision of requirements, including details on the required Collegiate Seminars, their content, methodology and the evaluation process, and the second regarding, the role of a proposed Seminar Governing Board. The Collegiate Seminar program, which was at the core of the liberal arts curriculum, would be governed by a Collegiate Seminar Governing Board comprised of three faculty members and two students appointed by the Academic Vice President. Faculty member appointments were to be approved by the Academic Council and the student appointments were to be approved by the Associated Students Executive Council. In reality, appointments by the Academic Vice President would rarely be challenged by the Academic Council, and nonapproval by the Associated Students Executive Council would likewise be unusual. The entire proposal evoked a discussion among Trustees on the haste and lack of planning which seemed to characterize the process of developing both the calendar and the academic requirements proposals. There was some concern expressed as to the efficacy of students on the seminar board, but given the weightiness of the matter before the Trustees, that concern was muted.

In defense of eliminating all but a few requirements, the exceptions being four courses in Collegiate Seminar, two in religious studies and the state-mandated American Institutions course on federal and state government structure, Pollock enunciated the proposal to the Board that he had submitted in his memorandum to Brother Michael Quinn dated May 28, 1969. "Although many of the present collegiate requirements may contribute significantly to the education of some students," he declared, "the present structure of requirements appears excessive and incoherent. It is not evident how coverage of material in language, mathematics, philosophy, theology, history and so forth will tend to foster such liberal goals as a mature, inquiring mind, intellectual discipline, commitment to wisdom and to truth, enlightened understanding of the Christian heritage." (Pollock memorandum to Brother Michael Quinn, May 28, 1969, Saint Mary's College Archives.) There was little persuasive evidence by way of research or assessment that eliminating almost all requirements would accomplish the intellectual discipline, quest for wisdom and understanding of Christian heritage that Pollock so eloquently envisioned for all students while faulting the existing curricular requirements for their "incoherence and excesses."

The elimination of former requirements was disturbing to many faculty members, especially those in the departments of language, mathematics, history and in particular, philosophy and since philosophy was traditionally understood in Catholic institutions as academically architectonic in developing coherent curricular principles, the traditional curricular infrastructure designed for developing insight, living life coherently and thus affording students the very means for avoiding "fragmentation" in real life. Several members in the School of Science strongly objected to the 4-1-4 calendar with its interim or January Term, since they believed that the long break between semesters would disrupt continuity in science courses from the first semester to the second.

When asked by a Board member what would happen if the Board did not approve of the plan, Pollock replied that disapproval or postponement would have a "very bad effect upon the morale of both faculty and students." Though no attitudinal documentation was produced to support his contention, the statement was most likely an accurate reflection of the possible reaction of those faculty members and students who helped create and then supported the Pollock plan. During the course of discussion, Board member Brother Cassian Frye, FSC, Dean of Studies, referred to his earlier compromise curriculum plan, (dated March 25, 1969, Saint Mary's College Archives) by adjusting existing requirements to fit the 4-1-4 calendar, thus countering the intellectual vacuum created by the minimal requirements in the Pollock proposal. However, Brother Cassian's proposal was not considered. Pollock emphasized the importance of faculty advising in view of the new calendar with its minimal requirements, thus in fact allowing students to design their own course of study with faculty assistance. Some faculty sarcastically characterized the plan as the "smorgasbord approach" to education. Others praised the plan as an enlightened, student-centered curriculum, unfettered by dubious requirements that operated under principles of academic freedom for students supported by competent faculty advising.

Pollock also noted that an advantage to adopting the revised curriculum was that the reduction in the extensive Saint Mary's requirements would ease the transfer of students from community colleges. Transfer students would be able to delve more quickly into their major studies without having to invest time and tuition costs for making up the many requirements peculiar to the College. This latter argument was significantly persuasive to some on the Board, since an expansion of enrollment through transfer students would be welcomed by Board members and especially by those on the Finance Committee.

The revised curricular plan of seven required courses was later reduced to six when the state eliminated the American Institutions requirement. The approved 4-1-4 calendar did appear to manifest some sensitivity to an intellectual tradition that characterized Saint Mary's education since 1941, namely the World Classics (Great Books) Seminars, renamed *Collegiate Seminars* and the two courses in religious studies, which represented a significant reduction (from 16 units to seven units) in religious studies requirements.

In spite of complaints from Board members citing the haste and lack of planning, the Board of Trustees approved the changes in curriculum for the 1969-1970 academic year. The vote was 5 yeas, 3 abstentions, and 1 member absent. (Since the minutes indicate only one absent from among the 10 members who attended the meeting at the outset, some error in recording the final vote seems plausible.)

Unfortunately, the Collegiate Seminar Governing Board, appointed by the Academic Vice President, would soon manifest an appetite for the innovative trends pursued in the overall curriculum revision and would engage in a more than benign restructuring of the seminar program. A restructuring of the seminar with an accompanying rationale developed into a significantly controversial issue in light of the Great Books tradition of the College since 1941.

The assigning of themes for each seminar, rather than adhering to an historical chronological order, made the program vulnerable to invasion by various vested interests, especially those who saw the seminar program as an opportunity for promoting relevant or contemporary causes, rather than an objective, truly liberal, or free study of influential and exemplary texts from sequential periods of history. Introducing themes clearly prejudiced the seminar discussion, often cited as *The Great Conversation,* in favor of pre-conceived ideas rather than allowing themes, topics or pertinent questions to arise spontaneously, freely and naturally from the texts under discussion. The controversy became a reflection of what has been termed the *canon wars* in higher education, accentuating differing aims of education or loaded outcome expectations in the selection of texts, their arrangement or juxtaposition and the anticipated enlightenment of students. Inserting theme seminars is, in fact, antithetical to authentic liberal education, the thrill of discovery and the passionate discussion that arises from the serendipity that evolves from thoughtful reading. The "theme" proposal revealed that those posing the theme concept, more often than not, had an agenda in mind. Past attempts reveal agendas that are easily perceived in such proposed titles as "Domination and Submission; War; Gender Studies, i.e. Women's and Gay Studies; and Poverty."

The mission statement urges students who truly desire to learn (as opposed to students being told what to look for) to "look twice, ask why, seek not merely facts but fundamental principles." Students are asked to seek fundamental principles in freedom and on their own, without prompting by some predetermined interpretation (by an expert) or categorization of a text.

The Administrative Council, 1969-1973

As the faculty, student body, number of resident students, athletic program, administration and staff increased, the lines of communication, processes for planning and budgeting, and legal implications became more complex. Other concerns, such as governance; finances; facility planning; hiring of personnel; advancement/development; accreditation; athletic control; relations with national, state and local government; and public relations concerns with alumni and donors loomed large and were erratically time-consuming. To address this complexity, I formed a body of advisors called the Administrative Council.

The membership of the early Administrative Council was formed to include voices from the major areas of the College administration, but the initial attempts proved cumbersome, and by 1973 a smaller group composed of the vice presidents and a few key administrative officers was fixed at seven.

The Council met regularly on Friday mornings to discuss numerous issues facing the College, such as the annual budget, development (fundraising), facility renovation and new construction, the College mission as a liberal arts and Catholic institution, accreditation, minority student recruitment, on-campus minority issues, food-service evaluation, interior reports on student enrollment and public relations, cost and conduct of intercollegiate athletics, health services, search for administrative personnel. It also dealt with public relations with people and groups off campus, including neighbors, formal town and gown relationships, alumni, the Boards of Trustees and Board of Regents and, various associations such as The Association of Independent Colleges and Universities, the American Association of University Professors, the American Federation of Teachers, the West Coast Athletic Conference and the Western Association of Schools and Colleges. When the town of Moraga was incorporated in 1974, the college was compelled to interact with various town bureaucracies, such as the Town Council, Planning Commission, Design Review Board, police and fire services, and the anticipated and expensive demand for computerization. Federal government regulations which also required significant attention included directives on Affirmative Action; Equal Opportunity; Americans with Disabilities Act; gender equity, especially in athletics (Title IX); and the evaluation and submission of time-consuming government-mandated reports.

The first *emergency* meeting of the Administrative Council was convened on March 16, 1970, to discuss the cancellation of a basketball game with Brigham Young University in the face of threatened game disruption by some faculty and students over policies regarding African-Americans and the Church of Jesus Christ of Latter Day Saints (Mormons) which sponsors BYU.

The Athletic Director and head basketball coach, Michael Cimino, had signed a contract with Brigham Young University of Provo, Utah, to appear on the Saint Mary's basketball schedule. At that time the Mormon Church denied African-American members the opportunity to enjoy the fullness of the Mormon priesthood on earth, a status normally achieved by most other Mormons. African-Americans could, however, enjoy the fullness of priesthood in the afterlife as God saw fit. To change such a tenet of faith would require a revelation to the Chief Elder of the Church. Several faculty members, and particularly Alan Pollock, threatened to disrupt the game in protest of the Mormon Church's discriminatory policy regarding African-Americans. In order to avoid a confrontation and a potential melee with possible police involvement among athletes, students and the protestors, including several faculty members, I decided to cancel the game.

Authorities at Brigham Young were not pleased with the cancellation and immediately sent emissaries to the College to speak to me. The two representatives of Brigham Young University explained that the faith of the Mormon Church had little to do with policy regarding basketball, the basketball schedule or membership on a basketball team. The issue of the priesthood, they stated, was a matter of doctrine as defined by the Chief Elder, and noted that there were many *bona fide* African-American Mormons who led devoted lives as Mormons. It was not within the purview of the university or the BYU athletic department to alter Mormon doctrine. Cordial though the dialogue was, it was evident that legal action was among the possibilities the emissaries could invoke. I emphasized that I understood that the issue of membership of African-Americans in the Mormon priesthood in this life was a matter of Mormon Church doctrine and not a matter for university academic personnel or athletic policy *per se*. I had cancelled the game to avoid what might have become an ugly confrontation. The Brigham Young representatives seemed satisfied with the discussion but politely expressed the chagrin of those at the university that the game had to be cancelled because of possible violence.

Later in the spring semester when the Saint Mary's baseball team was about to play Brigham Young on the Saint Mary's campus, a student from Tasmania drove his car on the field, parked it on the pitcher's mound, locked the doors, and ran off. Though the game was delayed so that means could be taken to remove the vehicle, it was not cancelled, even though a small number of protestors milled around the baseball field. No confrontation occurred.

Several years later, the Chief Elder declared that African-Americans would be admitted to the priesthood in this life. The protests anticipated or realized at Saint Mary's were symptomatic of protests elsewhere. To those outside the LDS or the Mormon fold, it seemed that the divine revelation of the Chief Elder was the direct effect of the political activity of the protestors, but only the Chief Elder and perhaps his intimate confidants really knew.

Academic Applications

Implementing the New Calendar and Curriculum

Switching from a more flexible standard semester calendar to the 4-1-4 required some adjustment, since under the former calendar a number of courses, such as laboratory science and initial foreign language courses required five and four units respectively, and other courses seemed to be better served with meeting for only two or three standard 50-minute sessions each week. The January Term was publicized as an opportunity for both students and faculty to be creatively innovative. Most students were not allowed to pursue courses in their majors during January, so that they would be exposed to academic experiences different from their majors. Unfortunately, the first few January Term experiences turned out to be academically chaotic. Some faculty met with students only once a week, similar to the tutorial system in vogue at major British higher-educational institutions, while others attempted to teach classes using the standard *Carnegie* hours of 15 fifty-minute classes per unit. The disparity caused tension within the faculty, and residence-hall life was made difficult because too many students and some faculty failed to understand the peculiarities of the innovative January Term. Some residence hall directors complained that since too many students had time on their hands there was more self-indulgence than self-enlightenment.

Regulations for travel courses were not clarified, and the results were uneven, depending on how individual faculty members conducted their off-campus courses. Some monitored students conscientiously, hosted dinners in common and provided for various field events while others left students to fend for themselves (or theoretically, to engage in research and discovery) except for a few hours of class each day or each week or by gathering for some common activity, such as the theater or symphony, visiting a museum or appraising a noted architectural masterpiece. Complaints from both students and faculty were abundant. One major difficulty was that neither most of the faculty nor most of the student body were accustomed to tutorial-type education. Other complaints were that a number of faculty either lacked the imagination or were unwilling to invest the time for engaging in the innovative creativity heralded by the advance advertising. Since those in the upper classes had first choices in the selection of January Term courses, freshmen were left with few attractive options and, for good reason, were eventually excluded from travel courses. The initial quasi-structured and quasi-regulated nature of the January Term was of serious concern to me, other administrators and the College attorney who expressed concerns over travel-course liability and appropriate supervision. In fact, however, there were few, if any, liability problems regarding students and travel courses.

There were those who saw the January Term as an opportunity for developing creative courses that were aimed at intellectually stimulating both faculty and student interest in the some phase of the intellectual life. Some also found that an intense investigation of a single subject for an entire month was an academically fruitful experience for both faculty members and students. Scientific research, particularly laboratory work, and the ability for faculty to utilize the breadth and depth of their graduate studies provided opportunities for both faculty and students within the "J" Term.

Administrative concern prompted faculty to establish more significant means of oversight and to develop thoughtful academic structures which would eventually address the many initial January Term deficiencies without suppressing creative opportunities. One of the major changes in the administration of the January Term, and one that subsequently well served the program, was the appointment of a faculty member as Director of the January Term. The director's manifest enthusiasm for the creative aspects of the January Term caused the first director, Biology Professor George Hersch, PhD, to minimize the most pressing problems and faculty complaints. Within a year he bequeathed the direction of the "J" Term, as it became known, to Brother Ronald Isetti, PhD, an historian who viewed many aspects of life as weighty matters, including the academic life of the January Term. He emphasized that the quality of academic requirements and research, more than contact hours, should characterize the program, though it was not long before a minimum criterion for class hours was announced. Likewise he established guidelines for travel courses and requested advance course descriptions from faculty members. After hardly beginning, Brother Ronald relinquished the director's role to the able mind and hands of Brother Brendan Kneale, a long-term and respected member of the mathematics department. It was Brother Brendan's 12-year direction of the "J" Term that developed a common mind among both faculty and students and implemented basic workable procedures, thus preserving both the innovative character of the term and developing a warranty for its academic quality and respectability. Professor Ed Biglin, PhD, assumed direction following Brother Brendan's well-earned retirement in 1986. Biglin was able to fine tune the program and initiated a series of January lectures and other academic and cultural events complementing the term and providing students with additional "J" Term academic and cultural experiences.

Faculty Handbook

Early in the fall of 1969, I appointed Leo Oakes, among the first alumni to graduate from the Integrated Liberal Arts Program, as Assistant to the President because of his experience with personnel matters for his previous employer, De La Salle Institute, the central office for the Christian Brothers on the West Coast, and his ability as a clear and experienced writer and communicator. I then appointed Oakes and two faculty members, Professor Elmer Gelinas, PhD, of the philosophy department and Brother Dominic Ruegg, FSC, PhD, of the classics department, as a committee to update the *Faculty Handbook*, including the addition of governance structures and procedures that had been developed since the time that the handbook was published some nine years earlier.

Because the *Faculty Handbook* is regarded as an adjunct to the faculty contract, changes are perused by faculty with care, since changes would normally affect terms of employment, including remuneration. The updated edition of the *Faculty Handbook* was approved by the faculty in spring of 1971 and was published by the following August. After the formation of a Governance Committee composed of a majority of elected faculty members and chaired by myself, an updated *Faculty Handbook* was then scrutinized and published annually under the aegis of Valerie Gomez, PhD, who was appointed Dean of Academic Services.

Faculty Evaluations

In the waning days of the first semester of the 1969-1970 academic year, the student body president, James Wood, '70, joined with student leaders in other collegiate and university institutions to adopt a program in which students would formally evaluate their instructors. As expected it met with opposition from a majority of faculty, especially in light of the possible influence the evaluations might have on rank and tenure decisions. However, some faculty saw a value in providing consistent and organized student feedback. After some refinement of the evaluation forms, the Academic Vice President supported the concept, the results of which were conveyed to the Rank and Tenure Committee. Faculty are still formally and confidentially evaluated in each of their classes by their students.

Other Transitional Challenges

Accreditation and The Accreditation Visit of 1969

Accreditation is a process that evaluates the academic quality of an institution as well as the adequacy of academic support services as compared to the standards of academic quality and support established by a consortium of institutions in a particular region. Membership in a regional Accreditation Association is considered voluntary, but in actuality without regional or national accreditation an institution cannot receive federal or state funds or loans or support from many private foundations, corporations or even some individuals. Student transcripts from an institution not accredited may not be honored by other institutions. Accreditation is similar to a license to a profession, more analogously, it serves as an official stamp of approval by a consortium of peers. The approval guarantees academic integrity and quality to the general public, other educational institutions, parents, students, donors, various private organizations and governmental entities that would find it difficult on their own to evaluate academic standards among the diversity of educational enterprises both within and outside a region. Regional

53

Accreditation Associations must secure federal approval. Saint Mary's College became an early member (1949) of the Western Association of Schools and Colleges, which includes institutions in California, Hawaii and the U.S. Pacific Territories. Proprietary (for-profit) institutions of higher education in California that are not members of the Western Association of Schools and Colleges or an approved national accreditation association may apply for a license from the state bureau of Private Post-Secondary Education. Licensure status does not carry either the prestige or the influence of accreditation from a federally approved regional accreditation association or approved national accreditation organization.

My first experience with a regular collegiate WASC Visiting Team of eight evaluators to appear on the Saint Mary's Campus for purposes of reaffirmation of accreditation was on Oct. 22, 1969. The Visiting Team, chaired by Robert J. Wert, President of Mills College in Oakland, took special interest in the innovative 4-1-4 calendar. It also reviewed the modified requirements that were adopted by the Board of Trustees in July 1969 and implemented by the beginning of the subsequent fall semester.

Visiting-team members reported that they were impressed by the "spirit of experimentation, innovation and enthusiasm which permeates the Saint Mary's campus" and further noted that "Saint Mary's will shortly become co-educational." Some members of the team "perhaps envied," the team report noted, the ease with which members of one department crossed departmental lines in the spirit of cooperation and collaboration. "Saint Mary's College is blessed," the team observed, with a "healthy administrative climate." The Dean of the College, Alan Pollock, was cited as a "marvelous catalyst" and the new president as being "deeply committed to improving the educational program," an observation, "mentioned by several faculty members."

It appeared as if both the administration and the faculty were on their best behavior during the visit, for underneath what appeared to be a "blessed environment" were feelings of an abiding tension and elements of a latent resentment that divided the faculty. Concerns were voiced by more than a few sour grapes. Upon my arrival, appointments had been scheduled with me by several faculty members in order to apprise me of the tensions caused, they claimed, by an adversarial political climate among, and between, faculty and administration. The "blessedness" perceived by the Visiting Team was veneer rather than reality. The Academic Vice President Dean of the College, while justly recognized as intelligent, creative, well-informed and shrewd, was also considered by many as an active politician whose progressive political views affected his academic commitment.

While it was true, as the report noted, that I was strongly interested in fostering the intellectual life, I was skeptical of what I considered excessive changes in the curriculum, the inflexibility of the 4-1-4 calendar and the reduction of the faculty teaching load because of accommodation to the 4-1-4 calendar and what the changes meant in terms of liberal education, the Catholic mission of the College and, last but not least, an increasing budget deficit. It was clear just three months after the Visiting Team left the campus that adequate planning for the academic transition, a concern expressed by the Board of Trustees in June, had been overlooked by the accreditation team regarding the January Term.

The recommendations of a visiting team, as they usually do, reflect not only an overview of the institution in terms of Western Association of Schools and Colleges standards, but also the interests and backgrounds of individual visiting team members. In general, the majority of faculty in higher education in the United States at that time was politically liberal, and in an accreditation visiting-team, though objectivity is the goal, liberal bias was often reflected. Library holdings and the library budget came under criticism, even though a new library facility graced the campus. The *Great Books* seminar program required of all students "has tended," the observers noted, "to keep students from using the library as much as they might," since they must concentrate on, "basic texts and less upon supporting materials." Although this comment may appear as a benign observation, for more recognizable, but wrongheaded reasons, criticism of the Collegiate Seminar program would intensify with subsequent Visiting Teams. The seminar, as did former philosophy requirements, occupied curriculum space that several academic majors and the experts who taught in them sought to occupy. In general, greater investment in library holdings was recommended, a recommendation carried forward by subsequent visiting teams.

Commendation was bestowed upon student personnel services, including residence hall life, noting that the, "administration of the residence halls has been vastly improved in the last 10 years," an observation that was most likely based on reports that a more liberal residence hall governing policy had been recently enacted. Gone were the days of prefects, lights-out policies, campusing of students who misbehaved, curfew hours and compulsory Friday-morning mass for all resident students.

The Visiting Team report also observed that the minority program, an effort that had been in effect for several years to recruit minority students, needed more attention than any other. Simply increasing the number of minority students on campus was insufficient, as those involved in similar programs at other institutions soon discovered. *The Visiting Team observation proved prophetic*, since minority programs soon required costly efforts in terms of personnel, space, services and attention by experienced administrators to address special minority student needs and the introduction of a special program entitled the *High Potential Program*.

Minority and High Potential Programs

In the mid-to-late '60s Brother Michael Quinn and Academic Vice President and Dean Alan Pollock instructed the Office of Admissions to take means to increase the number of students from minority groups, primarily from the African-American and Chicano Communities. The Admissions Office has followed that directive ever since. Thus, as the College entered into the early '70s, the number of minority students enrolled at the College increased, in many cases because of what were considered suitable financial aid packages to such students. I soon discovered, after enduring several minor protests similar to those on other campuses, that a number of students identified as minority students suffered from various insufficiencies on campus. Measures were eventually instituted to address issues such as insufficient academic background, lack of proficiency in English language (especially in cases where English was a second language), insufficient financial support, difficulties relating to the majority and a lack of special counseling, tutoring and encouragement.

Almost everyone in administration soon realized that in spite of the pastoral and generally peaceful campus ambiance, minority students encountered misunderstanding, thoughtless jocose remarks and other insensitivities, sometimes not always intended, from some members of the dominant population. There was a need for personal adjustments in terms of the social and academic lives of minorities and the enlightenment of the majority. Incoming students were often bewildered, and minority students found it particularly difficult to find a faculty or staff member with whom they felt they could relate, even though most faculty were sympathetic to increasing the minority enrollment.

An initial solution was to appoint a faculty member or qualified advisors to provide guidance. Professor Lenneal Henderson, PhD, a an African-American, was the first appointment as an Assistant Dean for Special Programs (1969-1971). Henderson was well educated, bright and articulate, a man with whom the African-American students expressed their pleasure. Though the Chicano students respected Henderson, they believed that they required a Chicano advisor. The need for a Chicano advisor was critical to their identity, they stated, since the Chicano culture, was distinctively different from the culture of African-American students. The students requested a meeting with me. The ground rules for a meeting were set by the students with my agreement. The students wanted to speak for themselves without older adult (faculty or administration) participation. Unfortunately that did not happen, as one adult late comer to the meeting intervened in and disrupted the conversation with his own strident views. However, I did see the need and did make provision for a Chicano advisor, even though the addition placed a further financial strain on the College budget.

Professor Henderson was offered an attractive appointment elsewhere and a new African-American Assistant Dean for Special Programs was sought. Thomas Brown, a graduate of Saint Mary's College High School in Berkeley and the University of Southern California, was selected. He was energetic, highly articulate, bold and astute and had known me in the days when I was principal of his high school. A Chicano advisor, Steve Denlinger, was soon appointed to deal with the growing Chicano population. After less than a year, Denlinger resigned and Harry Acosta was hired in the role of Chicano Advisor. He was followed shortly by Inez Gomez-Clark. After a few years she was hired for a similar position at Santa Clara University and was followed by Margarita Santos and Brother Camillus Chavez., FSC. In the mid 1980s, the title of the Chicano advisor was altered to Coordinator of the Office of Hispanic, Chicano and Latino Student Programs. The position was assumed by Maria Hernandez, PhD, followed by Maria Sovall and Evelia Jimenez.

In 1973, Tom Brown was promoted to Associate Dean of Studies, and a Coordinator for the Black Student Program was appointed. Nate Carroll, '75, Toya Robinson, Wayne Kitchen and Pamela George were selected consecutively as coordinators.

Later, it became evident that the increasing number of students from Asian-Pacific backgrounds (Filipino, South Pacific and first-generation, low-income immigrants from Southeast Asia) also required special assistance in the person of a coordinator. Brother Dominic Berardelli, FSC, who had spent many years in the Philippines, was a strong advocate and participant in the Asia/Pacific Association and urged the appointment of a fulltime coordinator. The first person to be appointed as Asia-Pacific Coordinator was Grace Cardenas-Tolentino.

When interest in recruiting foreign students accelerated in 1978, Paul Larudee, PhD, a Georgetown University linguist was employed to conduct the Office of International Student Programs. After a short time Larudee was offered a "couldn't refuse" appointment elsewhere, and Louis Gecenok assumed the management of the Office of International Student Programs.

Concurrent with the minority and international student recruitment effort, a tutoring service was established in 1971 for all students, staffed at that time mostly by students. A few years later a full-time staff member was appointed to organize the tutoring program. Likewise, plans were formed to establish an English as a Foreign Language Program for foreign and Hispanic students whose English proficiency inhibited their ability to function well in the academic classroom, especially in seminar courses where articulation of ideas was essential. The services of Paul Larudee, PhD for the EFL program and guidance for foreign students in general proved to be the key to success for students requiring intensive English training. When Larudee left the College, Brother Timothy Rapa, FSC, followed by Nushi Safynia, assumed the direction of the program.

Shortly after Brown's appointment as Associate Dean of Studies in 1973, he developed a program for minority applicants who had the requisite potential for collegiate success, but because of a number of disadvantages such as a weak home environment, ineffective schooling, an ill-disciplined adolescent lifestyle, or because English was a second language, their academic potential had not matured. His program was approved and soon after, Brown sought out such students and inaugurated the *High Potential Program*. He limited the program to 20 students per year, since the special needs of such students required a significant investment of time by advisors and faculty members. New *High Potential* students would meet for three full weeks on campus during the summer in preparation for collegiate life and its attendant environment. Concentration on competent writing, learning how to approach both the lecture and seminar methods, and how to read assigned texts, especially the Great Books, occupied a major portion of the summer program. Advisors were fully available to students during the academic year, and a suite of rooms was provided for counseling and to serve as a meeting place. On average, close to two-thirds of the *High Potential* students graduated in four years, a figure that exceeded the national average and was attributed to the selection process and effective support services.

The creative mind of Dean Tom Brown also embarked on a plan for recruiting students from Asia and Europe. When the plan was approved, he personally visited Asia and parts of Europe with success, and as the students arrived he searched for someone who would likewise tend to their special needs. The foreign student recruitment model was based on what was learned from the initial attempt to increase minority students. Brown also instituted a program that brought law school recruiters to the campus and directly or indirectly encouraged all students to consider alternatives in advanced education or job opportunities once they received their baccalaureate degrees. He developed an extensive and effective new student advising program that was eventually assumed by faculty.

On the one hand, Brown was at times an aggressive, articulate contender with regard to his plans for advancing the minority and international student agenda as well as his other initiatives. His occasionally persistent lobbying improved the benefits and environment for all minority and international students who arrived and remained on campus. He also benefited students in general, for whom he served as advisor, especially for those seeking admission to law school. On the other hand, his personality, sense of humor, intelligence and concern earned him the respect of a diverse group of students, so much so that the seniors of 1998 requested that he be their commencement speaker. His address, as anticipated, was characteristically insightful and inspiring, and graduates were delighted with both his delivery and message.

Change in the Academic Vice President Position

After pondering the copious notes from hours of interviews with senior faculty and reflecting on the themes in Alan Pollock's addresses, *The Political Morality of the College* and *The Goals of the College*, as well as other statements and utterances, and taking into account the aura of suspicion and uneasiness that seemed to hold sway with a number of the faculty members, I informed Pollock that I had decided not to reappoint him as Academic Vice President and Dean of the College. Pollock retained tenure as a full professor and therefore would become a full-time member of the English Department faculty in the fall of 1971. A number of faculty, student disciples and recent alumni were sorely disappointed, but no one seemed more disappointed than Alan Pollock himself. He had worked assiduously and envisioned a College as a pacesetter in the promotion of his academic and social agenda. As a professional, however, he seemed to accept the nonrenewal in stride, but his underlying chagrin was discernable for many years, particularly during the following year when he came to the energetic defense of his colleague and friend, the Dean of Students, Odell Johnson, who was likewise not reappointed.

Changing Perspectives: The Search

The need for change in the office of Academic Vice President was in part prompted by a strong coterie of senior faculty who believed that the academic direction of the College had become overly politicized, less academically coherent and, as was the case with other Catholic institutions, more secular. A number of candidates were selected and interviewed by a search committee, the faculty-at-large and students. Prior to the search, I had flown to Santa Fe, N.M., with the intention of persuading Tom Slakey, '52, Ph.D, an outstanding classmate and practicing Catholic, to apply for the position. Slakey had been a faculty member at St. John's College in Annapolis, Md., and was currently on the faculty (a tutor) at the St. John's, Santa Fe, N.M., campus. (St. John's, though originally named after one of the Evangelists, had become a secular institution dedicated to rational education through the Great Books. The St. Mary's Integral Program is modeled on the St. John's curriculum and methodology.) After interviewing a number of qualified candidates, Tom Slakey was selected. He resigned his tenured position at St. John's in favor of assuming the post of Academic Vice President at his Alma Mater.

The Appointment: Thomas Slakey, PhD, '52

If ever there were a man of intelligence, integrity, generosity and idealism who was caught in a dilemma it was Thomas Slakey. He was an academic traditionalist, who sincerely believed in the importance of a liberal education for all students in the Western intellectual traditions as expressed in the Great Books and probed through the seminar method of instruction and desired to see a Saint Mary's reputation based on a vision paralleling the tradition of the heralded liberal arts colleges which dotted the nation. Yet, some faculty members were outspoken in opposition to his views and, to my surprise and shock, even questioned his integrity. Those dedicated to what many considered mainstream secular higher education saw the appointment of Slakey as a step backwards, yet Slakey was able to defend his views on liberal education with clarity and force. In the spring of 1974, facing some health problems and the anxieties occasioned by controversies and lack of finances, Tom decided not to accept another three-year contract and to step down as Academic Vice President and return to full-time teaching in the following academic year, 1974-1975. I accepted his resignation but not without significant regret. Yet I realized that Slakey's dedication to the College remaining a pure undergraduate liberal arts institution may have worked against what the College had to do to remain viable in growing Contra Costa County. After two years as a professor, he returned to St. John's, Annapolis, in the fall of 1976, and was later elected Dean of Instruction, the leadership position second to the President. He retired from St. John's in 1996. Slakey was truly an astute and loyal academician who appreciated the Saint Mary's College education that had inspired him to pursue his studies in philosophy, first at Laval University, Quebec, Canada and then at Cornell University, N.Y., where he was awarded his doctorate in philosophy.

New Focus on Education

Tradition vs. Change and the Great Books Seminars

One of the distinctive programs which marked Saint Mary's College for the 28 years prior to 1969 was the program in *Great Books*. While some students grumbled about having to grapple with difficult texts or with articulating their insights and defending positions in the seminar setting, the seminar program had been long touted by most alumni, old and young alike, as one of the authentic intellectually memorable and significant experiences of their collegiate years. The *Great Books* program began tentatively in the fall of 1941 under the direction of the late College Professor James L. Hagerty and "resembled John Erskine's Honors Course in great books, introduced at Columbia University in 1919." (*The Seminar at Saint Mary's College* by Edward Porcella, PhD, Page 1, *Distillations*, Oct. 5, 1992, Saint Mary's College Archives.) In 1942, *Seminar Studies* became a requirement for all freshmen, and the *College Bulletin* for 1942-1946 (spanning World War II) listed eight two-unit seminars, one each semester, for all students. In 1946, the seminars were renamed *World Classics* and were required of all students: for liberal arts majors, one course of two units each semester. For those in the Schools of Science and Economics and Business Administration only four two-unit World Classics seminars designed to cover the most salient works required of liberal arts majors were required. The readings, representing the most influential thinkers and writers of the Western intellectual heritage, were arranged in chronological order, beginning primarily with the Greek world and continuing to the Western moderns. Accompanying the *World Classics* were other requirements, noted previously, including religious studies, philosophy, classical or rational psychology, language, mathematics, science, logic and the history of Western civilization.

The Integrated or Integral Program

Led by James Hagerty and Brother Robert Smith, FSC, PhD in 1955 and 1956, and by Frank Keegan, PhD, in 1956-1957 under a grant from the Rosenberg Foundation of San Francisco, the College engaged in a two-year experiment, adopting as its premise that, "neither a course-based nor a Great Books curriculum was adequate for a liberal education." (Op. cit. *The Seminar at Saint Mary's College*, page 13) The Rosenberg Foundation experiment evolved into a program outline entitled *A New Venture in Liberal Arts*, to become known initially as the Integrated[1] Liberal Arts Program, or "The Program." It continues at the College as a distinct academic entity closely resembling the

---

1   The title of the program was changed from Integrated Liberal Arts to Integral Liberal Arts in 1971, because the word Integrated was too easily confused with programs under that title in other institutions that addressed ethnic and racial studies.

Great Books program at both campuses of Saint John's College, Annapolis, Md. and Santa Fe, N.M. and with some notable differences, of the program at Thomas Aquinas College, founded by former Saint Mary's faculty and alumni, and located between Santa Paula and Ojai, Calif.

Approach to Seminar and the Great Books

In 1967-1968 a plan was inaugurated to change the traditional World Classics, Great Books program by combining freshman English (with emphasis on developing writing skills) with an altered reading list combining both classics and modern or relevant works, but under the aegis of a *theme*. With the change in both calendar and curriculum in 1969-1970, the seminar program, by then renamed *Collegiate Seminar*, was redesigned under the theme motif for all four years. Professor Norman Springer, PhD, of the English Department directed the implementation of the new concept at the start, dispensing with the traditional chronological reading list and replacing it with, "an investigation as much into kinds of writing as kinds of thinking." (Op. cit. *The Seminar,* page 16)

Some faculty applauded the title change, claiming that *World Classics* was a misnomer, since the courses concentrated primarily on readings from the Western intellectual and cultural traditions. Ironically, for those faculty who sought the inclusion of nonwestern intellectual traditions in *Collegiate Seminar* the term *World Classics* would have been more appropriate.

The discussions on the formation of the new Collegiate Seminar requirement revealed the daunting issues that engulfed the Seminar Governing Board. Some members of the faculty thought that the quality of the reading should prevail over quantity, which meant reducing the number of texts that were to be read, so that each text could be read more reflectively. Some faculty favored the tradition of having students center on a text in order to to discover inherent concepts on their own and argued that this process was intellectually and pedagogically far preferable to having an instructor abstract from the text and lecture or provide "background," be it historical, cultural or critical, for each text prior to or during its being read. Some argued, as did the Governing Board, that seminar courses should be student centered rather than subject centered, but that view was countered by members who saw the purpose of seminar as developing student minds by engaging in dialectical investigation rather than to morph into a psychological group therapy session where phrases such as "I feel that ..." predominated. Progressives thought that the seminar should be more relevant rather than primarily classical, while others tempered such a view by urging the use of both classical and contemporary relevant readings with emphasis on the classical. Traditional voices, concerned that discussion could be eclipsed by concentrating on writing assignments, urged that writing assignments assume a lesser role in the Collegiate Seminar program, where the art of reading is cultivated and cogent, robust and articulate argumentation among the members of the seminar might prevail in the search for an understanding of the text and its revelations. The main focus of the seminar, they stated "is achieved by developing probing questions about a text, and then using one's imagination to discover the author's intent and culture by examining the author's use of language, logic and style as a medium for conveying insight."

The controversy over whether experts should enlighten students as to the meaning of the text prior to their reading it or at some juncture during the discussion was dramatically exemplified in the motion picture *Dead Poets Society* when a bright new instructor in a fashionable boys high school (played by actor Robin Williams) asked the students to open their great literature anthology text books to the introduction written by Dr. N. an expert in classical literature. The instructor then told the students to tear out the expert's analysis and discard it and at that point believed that he was ready to engage the students as they read and discussed the various literary works in the anthology without their having read a mind-bending analysis by some expert.

"The liberal arts verses the disciplines" controversies divided faculty members between those dedicated more to their respective disciplines (or major concentrations) and those who favored a strong general program in liberal arts education with a guiding philosophy. It was mainly the discipline-oriented, especially those in the English Department, who objected to the philosophy requirements prior to 1969. Some discipline-oriented faculty perceive collegiate education as the means for preparing students for graduate research or the professions in their respective disciplines as represented in an ever-expanding spectrum of a specific block of courses called academic majors. Some such faculty may engage in teaching only as a necessary hurdle to fulfilling their own desires to engage in research, their first love. Other faculty perceive undergraduate education primarily as a means for developing a comprehensive liberal education for all students with either no major, such as is the case in the Integral Program, or with majors limited mainly to the upper division and within a limited number of units, or with split-majors, that to a limited degree promote greater breadth. This latter group of faculty members perceives the liberal education of the person as the development of perception or critical thinking; an understanding of the principles of science and mathematics; the development of creative imagination, insightful writing, articulate verbal ability and forming a philosophical overview as being more fundamentally contributory to the broadly enlightened, mentally inquisitive, creative and intuitive person.

Another issue of contention, that between those dedicated to liberal education via the Great Books and the historians, is one of the more telling examples of the educational divergence that exists within the academy. Those examining the most influential texts of humankind are, they claim, leading students to develop the art of reading with care and perception, while acquiring an awareness of the development of thought. Some seminar advocates often do not include medieval or modern history on reading lists. History, they say, is an interpretation, replete with secondary assumptions and selected significant events of a certain time and place determined by the historian. The authentic seminar instructor prefers that students read time-honored influential texts in chronological order with the intent of probing each author's mind. Secondary assumptions and even fairly good guesses provided by the historian will encourage students to rely on such interpretations rather than, in unprejudiced freshness, to accost the text at hand. The historian will respond to being so rebuffed by first noting that the strict seminar advocate includes such ancient historical accounts as those by Herodotus and Thucydides, both of whom attempt to unravel the root causes of historical events. Secondly, the historian will contend that modern scientific historical methods have ameliorated the criticism of basing judgments on intuitive or imaginative speculation by an historian, thus reducing assumptions of an historian's bias or guesses in favor of rational scientific analysis. "History rightfully inhabits a place between art and science," one faculty historian observes, "and thus offers a valuable and indispensable contribution to one's intellectual journey." Some liberal arts faculty, while doubting the claims of the historian, will note that the liberal artist actually does history by reading the original seminar texts in chronological order, so that students may come to discover the development and effect of critical thought throughout history. "Students may read history as they please," they acknowledge, "but should understand what modern history is offering and exercise legitimate skepticism while reading it."

It was imperative that the newly appointed five-member Collegiate Seminar Governing Board begin the work of implementation on the Collegiate Seminar courses since they were among the few common requirements for all students. The Board organized the seminars under four major themes: The "nature of Self" for freshmen, "Nature of Mind" for sophomores, "Nature of Nature" for juniors and "Man and Government" for seniors. As Professor Ed Porcella observes, the theme approach was reminiscent of the Rosenberg

Foundation-funded experiment at the College in 1955-1956, that organized Great Books texts under the broad themes of Man, Nature and God, themes similar to the *"Great Books of the Western World,"* a 54-volume selection of Great Books, edited by Robert Hutchins of the University of Chicago and Mortimore J. Adler and published by Encyclopedia Britannica in 1952. The Rosenberg experiment soon evolved into the Integrated Liberal Arts curriculum, a comprehensive curriculum without themes, becoming a "college within a college," as noted earlier.

As for the theme approach, three core texts were selected for each theme (both classical and contemporary), and the remainder of the texts were to be selected by the instructor. "It was intended by this arrangement," wrote Professor Owen Carroll speaking for the committee, "to insure a wider introduction to the perennial and contemporary questions and avoid any reductionism to a particular discipline or thought style." The supplemental texts chosen by instructors would be from "psychology, economics, geography, philosophy, education, physics, literature, theology, law and sociology." (Op. Cit. *Seminar*, page 19.) By January 1970, the Liberal Arts Committee had been replaced by the Seminar Governing Board. Professor James Townsend, Jr., PhD, Chairman of the Governing Board reported in a reflectively damning summary of the past that "The aim is rather radically different from the one implicit in the World Classics program. There the student was asked to immerse himself in the text — an act of meaningful immolation, if possible; he could develop skills through the immersion, profitably if he escaped drowning and clung to a pattern meaningful on his own terms; he failed or drowned if the act of immersion ritualized itself and him into formula. The fundamental attempt now of instructors in the Collegiate Seminar is to catch students at the point where they are putting the world together and to get them to continue to put it together with the aid of a variety of materials close at hand and within reach. Eyes direct themselves not so much at the subtlety and perfection of materials themselves, as the work under construction — the students themselves, their world." (Op. Cit. *Seminar*, page 19.)

The problems that emerged during the first year of the newly designed seminar program elicited the following observations: "The Committee (Seminar Governing Board) characterized the Collegiate Seminar in its first year as a 'pluralistic structure in the process of defining itself.' Yet not all members of the faculty, or even of the seminar staff, believed that the 'lengthy and sometimes precarious exchange' of the first year was a good thing. Some diagnosed the discomforts as symptoms of disease rather than pains of growth." (Op. Cit. *Seminar*, page 21.) In response to criticism, new themes were concocted for the second year beginning with the 1970 fall semester. The freshman year theme was *Different Ways of Understanding* and sophomores were expected to encounter *Religious Experience.* For the two remaining seminars, upper division students were able to choose from among several titles: *Aims of Education, Art and Science, Poverty, Domination and Submission* and *War.* From the titles it was evident that current social or political issues had seriously affected the Collegiate Seminar program. However, in fall of 1971 the new Academic Vice President, Thomas J. Slakey, arrived from St. John's College in Santa Fe, N.M., with an in-depth understanding of the nature of a Great Books program as well as the seminar method, since St. John's had become nationally renowned through both its devotion to Great Books education and the intellectual quality and success of its graduates. Slakey took issue with the thematic or topical approach, demonstrating that themes skewed the conversation by imposing an agenda. He stated that "The topical arrangement of Seminar readings means that students simply don't confront authors and begin the difficult task of finding out what they have to say." Furthermore, he observed that the greater use of contemporary texts makes it "less likely that students will break out of the tangle of slogans, jargon and half-conscious assumptions in which we all find ourselves enmeshed." (Op. Cit. *Seminar,* page 21) With his arrival it was only a short time before the Collegiate Seminar program would revert to the time-honored, chronological approach, commencing with the ancient Greek World and ending with the moderns. Professor Frank Ellis, PhD of the Philosophy Department, by some fortuitous configuration of the stars, was selected chair of the Seminar Governing Board and was most willing to expedite the change to the model that had characterized the St. Mary's Great Books approach since 1942.

In an address to the Saint Mary's academic community on Nov. 8, 1990, Professor Eva T. H. Braun, Dean of Saint John's College, Annapolis, and friend of Slakey and Brother Robert Smith, addressed the issue of diversifying Collegiate Seminar texts: "Now what are the pressures we will, I would guess, have increasingly to deal with? Well, I can discern exactly the same two that everyone else sees: globalism and diversity … Globalism results in the call on our curricula to be broad enough to prepare students to deal with other cultures. We have on earth seven continents and about 140 countries. Almost all are accessible by telephone, television and electronic mail within the minute and by visit within less than a day: all equally are near-neighbors. Now which country, and its probably several cultures, are we going to teach our students about? Or are we going to devise an overarching subject called *Otherness*? I think that people who push for globalistic education are usually grinding a particular ax: They believe in the preeminence of some area and its relation to us — be it Pacific Rim, Third World countries, Eastern Europe, an African country, the Middle East. They are not, in fact, thinking of the whole globe at all.

"We have special responsibilities of understanding toward the world," Braun continued, "that has willy-nilly made us a cynosure. How do we best prepare to discharge them? My answer is the tried and true one: by knowing ourselves ...

"And here I come to the second pressure on liberal education, far more acute and, I think, dangerous: the cry for diversity at home. "The same goes for cultural and the consequently desired educational diversity. Black-, Asian-, Jewish-, Italian-American literature is flourishing. Many of these works seem to me rather good, a few really fine, none I have read seem to me so far to match the greatest the West has to offer. But then, of course, they <u>are</u> what the West has to offer at this moment, and from them will eventually come the continuation of the Great Tradition. In the meanwhile, which deserve representation on reading lists? It promises to be, and indeed already is, a curricular nightmare.

"I have a simple, though unpopular solution. Let us accustom ourselves and our students to reading everything we hear about, but let's keep our curriculum for the best and the hardest things we have in common. But, the cry goes, we do not have anything in common, certainly not a so-called Western tradition. It is in fact the enemy, the oppressor of the living, the nonwhite, the women.

"Let me characterize this claim as mildly as I can: It is false." Professor Braun then notes that those who make the claim rely upon the very elements, academic and cultural, found in common with the West: "They recognize history, and they believe in social change or even revolution. They advocate by means of argument. They operate with a notion of rights. They speak English. They read their predecessors critically and write books of their own. They use the telephone and go on television. They use courts of law. They are on university faculties. They raise consciousness and advocate self-consciousness ... In short, they are head over heels implicated in the tradition they want to set aside. And those sources are always the works of the Western tradition." (*Take No Thought for the Morrow*, Eva T. H. Braun, Dean, St. John's College, Colloquium on *Continuity and Change*, Saint Mary's College, Nov. 8, 1990, Saint Mary's College Archives.)

The Great Books program with its traditional nonlecture, *Great Conversation* approach had sufficient faculty adherents to withstand most political, cultural and experimental onslaughts of the late '60s and early '70s, although continued attempts to alter the seminar reading lists and guiding principles require continuous thoughtful defense.

Religious Studies, Philosophy and Requirements

There was little quarrel with establishing a two-course religious studies requirement in a Catholic institution, especially given the faculty appraisal by some that the Religious Studies Department avoided a doctrinaire approach. Yet, neither the religious studies curriculum nor its pedagogical approach was bereft of a diversity of opinion both within and outside the Religious Studies Department. Some in the department circled the wagons when outside opinion was voiced, citing their commitment to an immersion in Biblical studies. At least one faculty member, John C. Dwyer, PhD, made use of the "historical-critical method" as the "one effective path to Christian understanding of the intimate relationship between man and God." The historical-critical method subjects Scriptural studies to an intense scientific, rational analysis of the sources of Scripture, the historical documents of the Church Councils and the development of doctrine. As noted in the *Jerome Biblical Commentary* edited by Brown, Fitzmyer and Murphy (Prentice-Hall, 1968), the historical-critical method "faces the much more difficult task of discussing with scientific objectivity and in detail the New Testament exegesis that has vital dogmatic implications ..." Other members of the department preferred an emphasis on systematic theology as viewed through a scrutiny of the *Summa Theologica* of Saint Thomas Aquinas and modern commentaries in similar vein, e.g., the work of Karl Rahner, SJ. There were also differences of opinion expressed on how theology or religious studies courses should be taught and even whether the title of the courses should be *Theology* rather than *Religious Studies*. Religious Studies was the preferred title, since many public institutions included religious studies in their curriculums, and credit would be granted to students transferring from Saint Mary's or to graduates applying for graduate studies, if Saint Mary's courses approximated descriptions of courses in mainstream public institutions identified as *religious studies*.

The academic spirit of the Collegiate Seminar program to eschew textbooks in preference to reliance on the reading of original texts, followed by an engagement of students through their careful textual reading and analysis, was sometimes sidestepped by Religious Studies faculty not familiar with a methodology in vogue at the College since the 1940s. The particular pedagogical approach in which the text was the primary teacher was dependent on the academic attitude of the instructor in each course and tempered by discussion among faculty on the most effective educational method for quality education. Such a basic pedagogy was sometimes difficult to initiate or sustain. Some in Religious Studies, for example, preferred the lecture approach, (e.g., John Dwyer, STD and Brother James Lahey, STD) that is, the delivering of information from an informed source or expert, while acknowledging that the instructor be open to student questions that would prompt others to engage in dialogue. Some utilized textbooks or even wrote them (e.g. the late Professor Timothy McCarthy, PhD), including questions at the end of chapters. Other faculty members thought that students should develop their own questions from their reading and reflection and thus ridiculed the concept of tacking questions on to the end of textbook chapters. Those on the seminar side of the aisle believed that having students immerse themselves in the process of thinking through issues and difficulties after reading scriptures and other texts, such as *The Fathers of the Church*, the classical controversies of the early Church, and other classical texts including the various Councils in the history of Christianity as well as the documents of Vatican II, was more productive than having experts lecture students, urged by the necessity of covering much ground among the array of books and essays presently available.

The chair of the Religious Studies Department at the time of the curriculum changes, Brother Gabriel Murphy, FSC, STD, bemoaned the reduction of religious studies requirements from the former 16 Carnegie units to an equivalent seven Carnegie units under the 4-1-4 calendar.

Faculty who defended some of the pre-1969 curricular requirements came primarily from the philosophy, language and history departments, that is, those from which requirements were eliminated. Whereas the language and history departments were concerned with their respective viabilities, the majority of the philosophy faculty had to face the fact that its comprehensive influence on curriculum had been seriously undermined. What the Philosophy Department realized too late was that its longstanding conviction that it was preeminently responsible for the formation of the human mind and an understanding of the human person through its influence on curricular requirements was unacceptable to an increasing number of faculty, many of whom had been educated in secular undergraduate or graduate institutions. At least one member of the Philosophy Department favored the reduction of philosophy requirements because he believed, seemingly paradoxically, that the department was far too narrow in its philosophical perspective. Philosophy Department leaders did not seem to perceive that current political and major academic movements might well diminish or even eliminate philosophy requirements. No persuasive comprehensive philosophical vision that would affect the core curriculum set within contemporary culture was forthcoming at the time.

Given that the *Document on Catholic Education (Ex Corde Ecclesiae)* from His Holiness John Paul II that first appeared on Aug. 15, 1990, had recommended adaptations be made in higher education to respond to "contemporary culture, movements and discoveries," those concerned with preserving the essential formative intellectual elements that were represented in the pre-1969 curricular requirements had not been strategically alert. The culture of the College had evolved into a more collegial model rather than one where authority exercised ultimate command under the supposed aegis of Catholic thought. The ensuing avalanche of change allowed the disciplines or majors to predominate, with the English Department assuming the lead. The academic turf war between the leadership of the philosophers and that of the orators mirrored the perennial controversy over leadership within the wider academy. There was little doubt that most of the academic departments offered quality courses by proficient academic mentors, and that more often than not value-laden questions were posed either by faculty members, the texts or students during the four required Collegiate Seminars. Though students could choose to enroll in courses such as philosophy, ethics, language and history, they too often avoided encountering courses that grappled with philosophical or theological principles preferring to be engaged in discussing more tenuous and relevant issues seeking a solution. A new and imaginative John Henry Cardinal Newman (1801-1890), author of *The Idea of a University,* did not emerge at the time to urge the inclusion of comprehensive requirements guided by a compelling overarching philosophy, commonly viewed as the Catholic intellectual tradition.

In spite of what appears to be a lack of agreement on both religious studies and what it means to be a Catholic institution, historian Brother Ronald Isetti, PhD, noted in his 1994 address as *Professor of the Year*, that, "In a time and place when it is becoming increasingly difficult to achieve consensus among Catholics, not to mention non-Catholics, on important philosophical, moral and theological questions, the problem of defining the institution's Catholic character becomes all the more delicate and difficult."

Even without the former guidance of overarching comprehensive principles, certain requirements were reinserted in due time, as faculty rightly perceived gaps in the 1969 curriculum. Faculty soon realized, for example, that many entering students were unable to compose coherent and grammatically correct English compositions. A course entitled *Better Writing* soon became a requirement for all but a limited number who could convincingly demonstrate appropriate English writing skills. Other additions such as area requirements came later, as the rush for nondirective principles subsided, and some educational insufficiencies became apparent. Understandable social pressures resulted in one requirement identified as "diversity" which provided options either in ethnic or women's studies. It seemed expedient, in view of an increasingly diverse student body, to offer a limited number of courses that promoted the culture, self-esteem and understanding of significant groups of ethnic students and the majority of women, though there is an outstanding question as to whether women's studies fits within the definition of liberal arts. Such academic majors were seen as antithetical to the kind of comprehensive, liberal arts and Catholic education suited to developing an understanding of the dignity of the human person that would address issues common to all humankind, with some obvious emphasis on differences between men and women. Requirements in ethics and a philosophy of the human person were suggested, but not accepted, at least at that time.

The Liberal Arts Proposal for a New College — 1971

Between 1967 and 1971, Ronald McArthur, PhD, '49, professor of philosophy, several of his colleagues on the faculty and some alumni, produced a booklet that described what characteristics they believed an Integrated Liberal Arts Catholic college based on Great Books Seminars should manifest and proposed what initiatives might be taken to found such a college. Though the proposal for the new college resembled the College's Integral Program and the curriculum of Saint John's of Annapolis, Md., and Santa Fe, N.M., the proposal differed significantly inasmuch as it not only included ample readings and seminars in the Great Books but also included significant attention to theology and philosophy tutorials that utilized the *Summa Theologica* of Saint Thomas Aquinas as a major theological and philosophical lynchpin. Thomas Aquinas College, as the proposed college would be named, would emphasize its unwavering dedication to both reason and faith as verified by the *magisterium*, the teaching authority of the Church. McArthur, Valedictorian of the Class of 1949, was an articulate, dynamic, generous and convincing philosophy professor and a formidable, shrewd competitor when engaged in debate with both students and his faculty colleagues. He was a devout Catholic, who viewed his role as a bridge builder between faith and reason through an intense investigation of philosophical principles in relation to Divine Revelation and the Catholic intellectual tradition. Thus, Thomas Aquinas College, eventually located in a valley between Santa Paula and Ojai, Calif., came into being. Serving as the founding president of Thomas Aquinas College and enduring the skepticism of some accreditors regarding the Great Books approach to the intellectual life, McArthur developed a faculty and attracted a student body of astute quality, as well as acquired an attractive campus site in 1978. The campus was developed on the former Doheny summer estate. When McArthur retired from the presidency in 1991 he bequeathed direction of Thomas Aquinas College to another Saint Mary's graduate, Tom Dillon, '68, PhD. When Dillion was unfortunately killed in an automobile accident in Ireland in 2009, Peter DeLuca, '63, was named interim president until the fourth and current president Michael McLean, PhD, '68, was inaugurated in February 2010. All presidents up to this time have been Saint Mary's graduates.

Crucial Years

1971-1972

The year 1971-1972 was a crucial year. Since 1966 the College, as with most institutions of higher education, was in varying degrees of turmoil over United States involvement in the Vietnam War and the Civil Rights Movement. The proximity of the 30,000 students of the University of California, Berkeley, the notoriety of the free-speech, free-drug and "be-in" movements, the gassing of students in Sproul Plaza, and numerous Telegraph Avenue and People's Park disturbances, all had their effect upon collegiate campuses nationally, as well as neighboring Saint Mary's. It was in this atmosphere that I heard a number of complaints from Residence Hall Counselors/Directors about the management philosophy of the residence halls.

Since the appointment for the Dean of Students, Odell Johnson, extended to June 30, 1972, it was required that the Dean be notified before Dec. 31, 1971, whether he would be reappointed after June 30. I conducted interviews with each of the faculty counselors in the residence halls regarding the Dean of Students. The tenor of the interviews indicated that a change in philosophy was preferred. I was persuaded that differences in philosophy with the Dean of Students paralleled in many respects those of the faculty with the former Academic Vice President, Alan Pollock. Given the change in the direction and philosophy of the College that I saw as my mandate, along with the recent institution of coeducation, I concurred with my advisors that a new leadership appointment should be made so that a new philosophy could be instituted. None of the Resident Directors called for the pre-Johnson ways of management, such as requiring lights out at a certain time or the power of the Resident Prefect to campus students (not allow students off-campus) for a period of time who were guilty of rule infractions such as coming in after curfew. It became clear that developments on the national front and the resultant turmoil in higher education had made the former *in loco parentis* style of resident governance obsolete.

By Nov. 1974, a new federal law known as the *Buckley Amendment* mandated that collegiate students should be treated as adults, since they had become legally so at age 18, the age of most entering freshmen. The only exception to the recognition of adulthood at 18 was the liquor prohibition law, which set the minimum drinking age at 21, an exception that effectively weakened the concept that age 18 reckoned an achieving of majority, even though the minimum drinking age was established for apparent good reason. The mix of under 21 and drinking-age students in the collegiate setting posed, and still poses, a number of difficulties for those charged with student affairs. The *Buckley Amendment* also prohibited residence hall counselors or resident assistants from entering rooms without the permission of the inhabitants. Unless students signed a waiver, which was rare, the College was required to release academic grades and any notices of disciplinary action only to the students themselves and not to parents or guardians. (The disciplinary notification aspect of the law was later amended.)

Though the *Buckley Amendment* and its virtual abrogation of *in loco parentis* did not become effective until 1975, the Faculty Brothers and other Resident Directors believed that the residence halls should have been governed with more consultation and collaboration, and a different kind of philosophy, as well as with the provision of staff orientation programs. Though Johnson, an African-American and a well-known Saint Mary's student-athlete alumnus, was a respectable, reasonable and congenial personality and was generally liked by the Resident Assistants and the students, his appointment was not renewed.

The nonrenewal was considered anywhere from a latent to a blatant form of racism by many minority students and some others and led to a serious confrontation between students of color in union with a number of Caucasian students and some faculty against my decision and that of my advisors. Alan Pollock, who did not openly protest his own non-renewal as Academic Vice President, took a strongly aggressive role in the protest against the non-renewal of the Dean's appointment.

With the exception of the Christian Brothers, many of whom lived in the residence halls, faculty members had little or nothing to do with either student activities or the conduct of residence hall living. However, some faculty members became fellow travelers against an administrative decision far from their purview, justifying their stance by claiming that "any decision about residence living affected their instructional activities." While the contrary was more the case, that is, some students who were not academically challenged became a problem in the residence halls, these same faculty turned a deaf ear to complaints about there being insufficient academic work at times, particularly during the January Term. Their argument was, some stated, a smokescreen for the real agenda, namely, that Johnson was African-American and was considered an integral element in the progressive coalition's vision for the College. The late '60s and early '70s, was an era of incivility, and protests throughout the nation provided models for students to emulate. In keeping with the times, the Saint Mary's student protests over the nonrenewal were formed but did not generate significant notoriety until five African-American basketball players protested by refusing to return to the second half of a West Coast Conference basketball game with Santa Clara University. This one protest action made the headlines from coast to coast. The protest may not have reached the level it did, alledgedly had the basketball coach, Bruce Hale, exercised more rapport with his African-American athletes, a difficulty I heard about after the basketball protest incident. The basketball protest was followed shortly by a teach-in in the Madigan Gymnasium followed by a *sit-in* and so-called *fast* in the College Chapel, so-called because food and drink were secreted into the Chapel -- during the night. Unfortunately, members of the media descended upon the College and, as is the fallout in such circumstances, the tension was accentuated by giving protesting students a chance to state their message to a wider audience and to see their names and faces in the local newspapers and on television. There were minor acts of vandalism but nothing major. One of the more damaging incidents, however, was the distribution of negative literature during the January open house for prospective students. This action, in addition to the reports in the media, did have a significant negative effect upon the enrollment of new students for the following year, and the College endured a much higher attrition during the summer of 1972. Understandably, parents were not willing to send their sons and daughters to an institution in turmoil, regardless of the causes or whatever side had more justification, since one of the reasons why parents sent their sons and daughters to Saint Mary's was to avoid the kinds of confrontation occurring at Berkeley and on other campuses nationwide.

A few faculty and administrators recommended that the basketball protestors be expelled, but I was not inclined to take such action. I did not think that refusing to play in a basketball game was sufficient reason for terminating one's collegiate career, but I did believe that it revoked the right to continue playing on the team, if the coach or Athletic Director so decided. Arrangements were made so that all five of the basketball protestors could graduate on time. After graduation, all five went on to further education and/or worthy and productive careers. Nate Carroll had a 10 year career at the College in the office of Thomas Brown, Dean for Special Programs, and then at the University of California, Berkeley. Maurice Harper enjoyed a long career as counselor, teacher (particularly in the Advanced Placement Program) and basketball coach at Saint Mary's College High School in Berkeley and later became a principal of a Catholic grammar school in Oakland.

During the Chapel fast and sit-in, the new Academic Vice President, Thomas Slakey, and I engaged in prolonged negotiations with the 25 or 30 protesting

African-American and Chicano students involved. When the Bishop of Oakland, the Most Reverend Floyd Begin, read reports of the Chapel sit-in in the local newspaper he phoned me to state that if the students did not leave the Chapel he would excommunicate them. I convinced the Bishop that such an action, when it became public, would only increase the tension and might even prompt some students to travel to the Diocesan Chancery Office to protest. Many of the students were not Catholics, and either would not understand the sanction, or if they were Catholics would defy it in some uncomplimentary way. "Well," the Bishop said, "do your best." It became clear he wanted nothing more to do with the protest. The Academic Vice President and I heard the students' complaints, approximately 10 in all, and while most of them reiterated the themes of the day, several of their complaints seemed reasonable. An agreement was finally forged after both the President and the Academic Vice President refused to enter into further discussions. The press claimed a partial victory for the students over such issues as the need for orientation, academic advising, tutoring, and graduate and professional school counseling. These were reasonable academic requests, and the addition of such services for minority students was eventually extended to all students when funds became available. Many of the protestors were seniors and had graduated, and thus the following year began with little appetite for continued confrontation. Part of the agreement called for monthly meetings between the administration and a committee of African-American and Hispanic students. However, such meetings were soon discontinued as students became interested in other activities. Few protests were heard for many years afterward.

Following the sit-in and the tension created by it, William Niland, the Chairman of the Board of Trustees, who was also the President of Diablo Valley College, the community college in nearby Pleasant Hill, suggested that a man who had experience with resolving interpersonal relationships centered around minority student issues be hired as a consultant and mediator. Niland had himself contracted with a man named George Anderson, President of American Management Training Services, Inc. and recommended that he would serve the College well. George Anderson was an imposing African-American who had many of the qualities of a dynamic Baptist preacher. He wore a thick-brimmed leather hat and strode around the campus, his demeanor exuding command. What was effected within George Anderson's presence over several days in meeting with both large and small groups was a tempering of concerns, real and imagined, and a reduction in tension. His May 9, 1972, report, however, was a combination of opinion, fact and fiction. He was critical of administrative processes and operations, but given his time on campus he could not possibly have understood the governance or basic philosophy of the College in any significant way. While his intention may have been to encourage greater minority presence and interracial understanding, certainly worthy goals, his report was so filled with conjectures and inaccuracies that it could not serve in a serious way as a template for further action on the part of administration. George Anderson later sent his daughter, Hilary Anderson, to the College. She graduated in 1996.

Local television stations, the secular press and the *Catholic Voice*, the Diocesan newspaper, proffered opinions on the situation. Though the *Catholic Voice* attempted to be objective and quotations from well-meaning members of the clergy appeared, few understood either the cause, the people or the prevailing political positions affecting the campus. I restrained myself from stating some of the underlying causes for the protests, as well as from revealing the advice I received and my reasons for taking action. Since the *Catholic Voice* was distributed to all the parishioners in the Diocese of Oakland (Alameda and Contra Costa Counties) and was seen as the official voice of the Church in the Diocese, its incomplete reporting was troubling. Yet it was understandable that the *Catholic Voice* say something about protests that had appeared in the local media about a Catholic college in its Diocese.

In retrospect, it might have been more prudent to continue the Dean's appointment for an additional year, thus sending him the message that all was not well in his department and giving him, the administration and the faculty resident directors the time to reconsider, thus avoiding the confrontations which occurred at a difficult time in the history of both the College and the nation. To Johnson's credit, he remained in higher education and within a short time became the Dean of Instruction at the College of Alameda, in Alameda, Calif., and later rightfully earned laudatory respect as an 18-year President of Laney College, a large community college in downtown Oakland, Calif. Over the years, Odell Johnson and I met on a number of occasions at meetings and receptions, especially those sponsored by the Regional Association of East Bay Colleges and Universities. Johnson, always the gentleman, declared that he had moved on and held no bitterness toward the College. He returns to his *alma mater* from time to time to address and counsel students, particularly minority students. I considered myself honored to deliver the invocation at Johnson's Laney College retirement dinner in 1996. Though Johnson had officially retired, he was called from retirement by the Trustees of the Peralta Community College District to again serve as President of Laney College. He finally was able to retire in 2006, some 10 years after his first retirement attempt.

A search committee was established in the spring semester to interview for the position of Dean of Students. The committee included the President, Brother Counselors, Resident Assistants and students. William McLeod, an alumnus of the Class of '64 and Assistant Superintendent of Catholic Schools for the Diocese of Monterey/Fresno, was selected as Vice President for Student Affairs and assumed the position in the fall of 1972. McLeod was blessed with being free from protests or confrontations due primarily to the support from the Brothers who resided in the Residence Halls. Furthermore he did not encounter difficulties with any students because of the activities of the prior year. He did take definitive action against a few students who had been engaged in unlawful substance trade, thus indirectly informing all students that such activity would not be tolerated.

It was during this time that an activist faculty member decided to write a letter to the editor of the *San Francisco Chronicle*. The letter referenced a recent firebombing of a Bank of America facility by student protestors at the University of California Santa Barbara campus. The faculty member expressed his opinion that the firebombing was understandable, or even justifiable, given the complicity of Bank of America in supporting the Vietnam War. He signed the letter as a faculty member of the College. Shortly after the letter appeared in the *San Francisco Chronicle*, I was invited to attend an event at the Fairmont Hotel on San Francisco's Nob Hill. My host for the evening was intent on introducing me to various notable personages in attendance. As I was introduced to Mr. A. W. Clausen, President of the Bank of America, I mused, "I hope he hasn't read that faculty member's letter in the *Chronicle*." Mr. Clausen had read the letter and said almost immediately, "How can a faculty member be allowed to write such a letter? He should be fired.!" I apologized for any trouble the letter caused the bank, but at the same time noted that, as a member of the faculty, the writer had the right of free speech accorded any citizen. "The professor's one error," I noted, "was that he appeared to be speaking on behalf of the faculty or administration of the College." I also stated that the faculty member had tenure and that the express purpose of tenure was to protect faculty members from adverse reaction in voicing views in public that were not acceptable to others, provided they speak within their area of expertise or as ordinary citizens. "To dismiss a faculty member for his political or economic views," I observed, "would engage the College in litigation that would be both expensive and most likely unsuccessful." Mr. Clausen was not persuaded. However, when he was selected as the keynote speaker for the Executives' Symposium of Feb. 3, 1988, he was gracious, pleasant and seemed to have forgotten the incident. I did not remind him of it.

1972-1973

The high attrition rate occurring in the summer of 1972 and lower than expected enrollment in the fall 1972, was the basis for adding significantly to the already existing deficit by the summer of 1973. Both full-time and part-time positions were reduced as soon as possible, and budgets were trimmed. Such actions, often by fiat and regardless of their academic validity, tend to demoralize both faculty and staff. However, the attitude of a sufficient number of faculty and staff was able to overcome the anxiety of deficit spending by coming forth with positive ideas to resolve whatever difficulties the College faced. Creative discussions regarding the establishment of new programs, as well as increasing the traditional undergraduate enrollment, were conducted. One suggestion was to increase the Admissions Office staff in spite of financial restraints. Tom Slakey, Academic Vice President, favored improving the quality and reputation of the College as a liberal arts, undergraduate institution, thus making it attractive to a larger audience. Others, while not disagreeing with Slakey's advocacy of a quality undergraduate institution, were convinced that the addition of quality graduate programs, such as an MBA, and the expansion of the Department of Education or extension and continuing education courses for older adults would bring the College increased undergraduate applications as well. Both Moraga and the Contra Costa County area were rapidly growing, and many thought that practical wisdom behooved the College to grow along with them to become a positive influence in Contra Costa development. Offering programs that would appeal to the academic interests of older adults in the area would create a positive relationship with the community and also would encourage future enrollment of traditional undergraduates. Although appointing two admissions personnel in the Admissions Office was a financial risk, it did, in fact, have a significant positive impact on future enrollment and College financial health.

Frivolity Amidst the Darkness,

The **Butch Whacks and the Glass Packs** began as a duo, with Jerry Murphy and Julio Lopez, both of the class of '72, performing at a Straw Hat Pizza parlor in Berkeley on Tuesday nights. They thought that they were good enough to entertain their musically sophisticated friends at Saint Mary's with two others who joined them to make a foursome. Craig Martin and Bill Lazaretti merged with Jerry and Julio, followed shortly by Dan Ritzo on drums. Bruce Lopez heard a rehearsal session and offered to supply much-needed bass tones. Jim Dougherty and Michael Boele provided technical sound and special effects assistance. Their first campus performance would be in

79

the College amphitheater, now designated as Bertain Grove. A singer, Dee Dee Krueger, added a touch of colorful graciousness to the all-male Butch Whacks. Three vivacious freshmen women were also enlisted as Whackettes and thus Teri Godfrey, Teri Aguilar and Kerry O'Hara added a bevy of feminine enthusiasm and charm. While Butch Whacks' minds were focused on the first campus performance, a trial run at the Alpha Phi sorority house in Berkeley was deemed necessary. Feedback indicated success. The first performance under the Saint Mary's stars came after six months of practice and the prep at Alpha Phi. The St. Mary's performance was supposed to be the one-and-only. But it became the beginning of hundreds of performances in a multitude of places. More members were added: John Buick, Dennis Krueger, David Gonzales, Gary Murphy, (Jerry's younger brother), pianist Larry Strawther and comedian/commentator Bob Sarlatte. Gary Murphy was enlisted to write scripts for short skits between music sets and later went on to write for Johnny Carson and become executive producer for *Night Court* and *Malcolm in the Middle*. His movie script, *Without a Clue* was produced by Orion and starred Ben Kingsley and Michael Caine.

In the summer of 1971 the troupe performed throughout the Bay Area for high school and college dances. A stint in Guatemala made them international. They then accepted invitations across Canada from Vancouver, British Columbia, to Ontario. Performances in Colorado, southern Florida, Georgia, the Midwest, other parts of California and in other states followed. A few members dropped out of the group, and others joined, including Rob Birsinger, Morey G., Michael Moore, Tommy Tomassello and Karl Young. After hundreds of engagements and living out of suitcases for months at a time, members began to think of other careers and especially of family life. As a result, Butch Whacks and the Glass Packs slowed the pace and returned to the Bay Area. They reconvene on special occasions for special events and do an annual three-day *Final Farewell Performance* at Bimbo's 365 Club on Columbus Street in San Francisco. As of 2011, the Butch Whacks were in their 40 year and their 28 "final" Bimbo's performance.

Academic Initiatives

Graduate Programs — Historical Perspectives

The history of the College reveals early entry into graduate studies in the form of a Saint Mary's College School of Law (1924-1928). However, the Saint Mary's School of Law did not follow the move of the College from Oakland to Moraga in 1928. It remained in Oakland under another name. Graduate studies in education date back to 1926. Graduate summer programs in philosophy and theology were initiated in 1958 at the urging of the then Provincial and Chairman of the Board of Trustees, Brother Jerome West.

Graduate Theology, 1958-1987

Graduate Theology and Philosophy programs initiated in the summer of 1958 catered primarily to priests, brothers, sisters and some laymen engaged in ministries of education or other apostolic activities. Brother Dominic Ruegg, FSC, PhD, who was charged with directing the program, was pleasantly surprised when approximately 50 students entered the first class. The program attracted strong enrollment for nearly 25 years. However, as many priests, religious and laymen received their Master's Degrees, the numbers entering seminaries or religious orders declined. At the same time, many in religious life turned to apostolic vocations other than religious education. Thus, the need for Graduate Theology programs receded. The Saint Mary's program was discontinued in 1987, though no new students were accepted after 1984 due to declining enrollment. Because Brother Gabriel Murphy, who assumed the direction of the program from Brother Dominic Ruegg in 1966, had studied for his doctorate in theology at the Angelicum, the Dominican School of Theology in Rome, he became acquainted with a number of outstanding theologians and was thus instrumental in securing exceptional theological lights for one-week workshops offered prior to the regular summer session. Among these distinguished theologians were personalities such as Rev. Raymond O. Brown, noted Scripture scholar; Rev. Charles Curran, ethicist; Rev. Louis Bouyer, CO; Rev. Adrian Van Kam, CSSp; Rev. Bernard Haring, CSSR; Dr. Michael Novak; Dr. John Dillenberger; Rev. Roland Murphy, O Carm; Rev. Donald Goergen, OP; R.A.F. MacKenzie, SJ; Rev. Alfonso Nebreda, SJ; Rev. Anthony Schillaci, OP; Dr. James McClendon; Rev. Gregory Baum; Brother Gabriel Moran, FSC, PhD; Dr. David Moberey; John T. Noonan; Rev. John McKenzie, SJ; Rev. David Tracey; and Rev. Richard McCormick, SJ.

The regular summer six-week master's program began under the aegis of the Benedictines: Rev. Arnold Tkacik, OSB, Director; Rev. Emeric Fletcher,

OSB, Acting Director; Rev. Roderick Hindery, OSB; and Rev. James Solari, OSB. When the Benedictines withdrew from directing the program, other noted theologians were added to the faculty after the startup years, including John Dwyer, STD; Rev. Stephen Rowe, OFM; Rev. Kenan Osborne, OFM; Rev. Bernard Donahue, OSFS; Rev. James Reese, OSFS; Dr. Le Roy Moore, Jr.; Rev. Ignatius Hunt; Paul LeMaire; Rev. Jim O'Donoghue; Rev. Richard McBrien; and Francis Bauer.

The Program Directors were Brother Dominic Ruegg, FSC, PhD, 1958-1966; Brother Gabriel Murphy, FSC, STD, 1966-1978; Brother Timothy McCarthy, FSC, PhD, 1978-1987.

Graduate Philosophy, 1958-1962

The Master's program in philosophy was short-lived, since interest in the master's degree did not appeal to a wide audience at the time. The program, begun in 1958, ended in 1962 due to lack of enrollment. It was under the direction of former Jesuit, Professor John Wellmuth, PhD, who enlisted several philosophical experts on its summer faculty including Rev. Clifford Kossel, SJ; Rev. Bernard Lonergan, SJ., author of *Insight;* Brother Robert Smith, FSC, PhD; Rev. William Baumgaertner, PhD, of St. Thomas University, St. Paul, Minn.; and John Wellmuth himself. Its emphasis was on an analysis of postmodern philosophy.

Graduate Education—New Start, 1966

Devotion to teaching with both faith and zeal has been the spirit of the Christian Brothers since their founding in 1680, and given the large number of St. Mary's graduates, especially Christian Brothers, who have entered the teaching profession, the College has had a Department of Education with listings of courses in its catalogs since at least 1926. Though early catalogs spoke of a Credential program, it is doubtful that the so-called department was fully functional. Faculty lists indicate only one or two members as being part of the Education Department, and it seems unlikely that so few faculty could possibly mount a full-fledged department. Most likely, the courses were continually listed in the College Catalog to legitimatize credit for the courses in teacher training taken by the student Christian Brothers (Scholastics) in consecutive summer schools. In 1966 Brother Jerome West, who was both Provincial and Chairman of the Board proposed to both Brother Michael Quinn and the Board that a fully functional graduate Department of Education be instituted as being in keeping with the Lasallian or Christian Brothers mission of the College.

A revived Department of Education was instituted in 1966, under the direction of Hubert O. Brown. The program, not surprisingly, encountered some growing pains characteristic of most other new programs.

Opposition to the establishment of a graduate Department of Education was voiced by a number of faculty members who viewed graduate work as antithetical to what they envisioned as an institution focused on pristine undergraduate liberal arts education. Yet, given the tradition of the Christian Brothers' founder, Saint Jean Baptist De La Salle, and his institution of *Ecoles Normal* or teacher-training institutions in France and the presence of Schools of Education in other Christian Brothers institutions of higher education, its establishment at Saint Mary's was patently appropriate. Some faculty members considered the establishment of the graduate theology, philosophy and education programs as having been instituted through outside pressure. Outside pressure should be interpreted as any person or group outside of the current faculty or particular current faculty interests. It is not the case that new or reinstituted academic programs must emanate exclusively from the current faculty. The resistance of influential faculty members to graduate programs was expressed in a document prepared for the President's Subcommittee on the Goals of the College in the *Statement Concerning the Size and Undergraduate Character of Saint Mary's College*, Dec. 30, 1970, by Phil Leitner, PhD, Chair of the School of Science and Professor of Biology. (Saint Mary's College Archives.)

The second difficulty in the establishment of graduate education was also internal. Before being appointed President, I was a member of the Board of Trustees during which tenure I turned my attention to the graduate education program as far as it had developed by 1968. I had expressed my opinion as a Board member that the Education Department should be much more effective than it was in terms of teacher education and influence among the local school districts. I noted that Chairman Brown seemed intimately involved in the College politics of the moment, and I expressed doubt as to whether he was devoting sufficient time, imagination and effort to the development of the Department of Education. When the department was revitalized in 1966 it claimed an enrollment of 14 students. The next year the enrollment had dropped to three, and in 1968-1969 it began with 12 students but by the end of the year enrolled only 8. I was authorized as a member of the Board of Trustees to chair a committee to evaluate the Education Department and its director. The members of the Committee were myself, Professor Donald Hatfield of the School of Education at the University of California, Berkeley, and Brother Cassian Frye, FSC, Dean of Studies, and also a member of the Board. Our three-person committee met with Director Brown, Alan Pollock, Academic Vice President, and Brother Ronald Isetti, FSC, PhD, professor of history and an instructor in the Teacher Education Program. The team was immediately presented with a list of difficulties faced by the Education Department, including such issues as the need for part-time administrative assistance, insufficient faculty personnel, lack of equipment, and an incomplete curriculum. The needs list seemed plausible, but the team also discovered that Director Brown needed both prodding and colleague support in order to devote himself to the advancement of the department. After the committee visit, the members reported to the Board that the potential for Saint Mary's developing a quality Department of Education and attracting students from the growing Contra Costa County area was an opportunity that should be seized without delay. The major need, the team observed, was an enthusiastic and experienced leader with an informed and focused vision. Other needs included a plan for the future: increasing space; adding faculty, equipment and clerical assistance; establishing good relationships with other departments within the College and outside school districts; and investigating in-service opportunities, public relations activity and follow-up studies on graduates. The judgment of the Committee evaluation team was that the Department of Education had not been the beneficiary of sufficient administrative strength since Director Hubert O. Brown was allowed to function without much oversight, prodding or progress and had acquired an undue emotional attachment to campus politics. After my appointment as president I discussed the issue of the Department of Education with Alan Pollock, asking him to begin a process of easing Brown from the department and to begin a search for a new leader. The search for a new chair commenced in the spring of 1970, resulting in the selection of Joseph Beard, PhD, whose enthusiasm and selection of faculty increased the department from two full-time graduate students in Sept. 1970, to 28 within one year. Furthermore, he attracted several hundred students, mainly teachers in the Contra Costa County area, for short courses and workshops during academic year 1970-1971 and the summer of 1971. By 1975, the Accreditation Report observed: "Virtually non-existent at the time of the last report (1969), the Department of Education has flourished with imaginative leadership and a well-selected faculty. Because of its increased enrollment the Department is now one of the major contributors to the College general fund. This has occurred in spite of dire predictions about, and negative experience with the effective demand for teachers."

With the departure in 1974 of Beard, who was interested in new venues, Brother John O'Neill, FSC, Ed.D, agreed to assume the chairmanship for one year while he searched for a new leader. He was successful in discovering Paul Burke, who was an Associate Dean at City College of New York. He brought organization, imagination and growth to the department, which in 1985 it was named the School of Education with Paul Burke as its first Dean. When Burke retired in 1987, Peter Garcia, PhD was named his successor. His tenure was significantly short. Associate Dean Victoria Courtney assumed interim command in 1989 until Fannie Preston, who had been Associate Dean of Education at San Francisco State University, was selected Dean of the School in 1991 Dr. Preston was an astute and seasoned leader who had considerable experience with the state regulations and politics. Her guidance through accreditation and organizational changes were significant. The School annually enrolls some 850 students in diverse programs, including Credentials and Master's degrees, and Preston was the inspiration for the initiation of the doctoral program in education which commenced after she retired.

Master of Business Administration Proposal, 1970

I requested the late Brother Louis Civitello, FSC, MA, to investigate what could be done to establish other programs consistent with the traditional Schools of the College and its overall mission. As director of Continuing or In-Service Education, Brother Louis was able to bring the College into the technological age by instituting a modest program in computer education. He also promoted weekend travel courses for teachers who desired to widen their background in California history and engaged in research for the appointment of a replacement for H. O. Brown. He was successful in discovering a potential chair in the person of Joseph Beard, PhD, as mentioned above. Since Brother Louis held an MBA (Harvard) and had previously been involved with school finances, his interest in establishing a Masters in Business Administration program was on the top of his to- do list.

In the fall 1970, a group of faculty in the School of Economics and Business Administration under the leadership of Professor William Tauchar, PhD, Chairman of the School and Brother William Louis Civitello, FSC, formed a committee to develop a proposal for the institution of a standard model MBA program. The program proposal was brought to the Board of Trustees on Oct. 17, 1970, but the Faculty Representative to the Board, Professor Byron Bryant, PhD, of the English Department, requested that the proposal be submitted to the Academic Council and the Faculty Assembly before action was taken by the Board. The Board concurred and postponed its discussion.

A special meeting of the Faculty Assembly was convened to examine the MBA proposal on Oct. 14, 1970. Byron Bryant reported his intervention on the Board to the Special Faculty Assembly meeting which, in addition to many members of the faculty, was also attended by approximately 70 students, an unusually large contingent of so-called observers. Professor Bryant began by sarcastically stating that the Board of Trustees, composed of businessmen, had seemed favorable to an MBA program but consented to hearing from the faculty before a decision was made. It was important for me to note to the Faculty Assembly that membership on the Board included two college presidents (other than myself), six educators, two attorneys, one labor official and three business leaders.

As the meeting progressed, it became clear that the students, most of whom were enrolled in the School of Liberal Arts, had been urged by someone to attend the Faculty meeting to support faculty members opposed to the MBA proposal. They did so with groans, cheers and clapping, together with both spontaneous comments and formal remarks when recognized by Professor Bryant, who conducted the portion of the meeting devoted to the MBA proposal. The Academic Council, after considerable discussion, had earlier voted in favor of the MBA proposal by a vote of 6 to 2. However, Dean Alan Pollock rose to oppose the program on two grounds, the first being the usual deal killer, that insufficient research had been conducted to evaluate the program both within and outside the College, and secondly, stating the oft-heard redherring, that the "diversification of interest and energy occasioned by the program would be seriously distracting from the fundamentally undergraduate direction of the College." (Minutes, Faculty Assembly Meeting, Oct. 14, 1970, Saint Mary's College Archives.) Remarks from several faculty members opposed all master's degree programs. Professor Hersh presented a resolution submitted by "concerned faculty" (Owen Carroll, Joseph Lanigan, Dan Baedeker, M. Springer, N. Springer and George Hersh): "We the faculty of St. Mary's College recommend that the MBA program proposed for Feb. 1971 not be initiated." An amendment, "at that time" was quickly attached to the original motion.

A motion to poll the faculty by Friday, Oct. 16, (Cohen/Scovel) on the amended Hersh resolution noted above passed 33 to 11. However, in a memo to the faculty after the poll was taken, Brother Dominic Ruegg, Chairman of the Faculty Assembly called into doubt the results of the poll, since irregularities in voter eligibility by some who voted had surfaced. Given that information, a discussion on the MBA proposal was continued during the Faculty Assembly meeting of Nov. 11, 1970. Remarks during the meeting were essentially opposed to offering an MBA with reasons such as offering such a program would deflect attention from the undergraduate liberal arts character of the College, that financial difficulties should be solved through new fundraising techniques, that the financial benefits of the program are dubious, that the MBA market will soon evaporate, and so forth. A motion was made to accept the Academic Council's report of Oct. 12, with the exception of its approval of the MBA program. The motion carried.

The MBA proposal was again discussed by the Faculty Assembly on December 2. Arguments against the proposal, with some repetitions, were again heard. Other arguments intensified the rhetoric, calling the program a "radical new element," noting that making friends with the "mammon of iniquity" would not justify program income, that the MBA would not fit in with the Catholicity of the College, that the MBA was hostile to what Saint Mary's stands for, otherwise we (the faculty) would not be arguing defensively and be seeking to quarantine it." Reiterated were the deal killer and red herring arguments noted above. A motion was made to recommend to the Board of Trustees that the MBA not be initiated at the College. The motion passed, 33 to 10. The Board therefore postponed any action on initiating the MBA.

Four and a half years after this first attempt at establishing an MBA program, Brother Louis came into fortuitous contact with two young men who believed that a program tailored to both major and middle managers who desired an MBA would be appealing and successful. Brother Louis, Bob Ferguson, and Mike McCune, MA, spent the entire night of March 7, 1975, formulating plans for an Executive MBA program. When dawn broke, the plan was complete. Brother Dominic (John) Ruegg, FSC, PhD, who had assumed the mantle of Academic Vice President by this time, fully supported the introduction of the MBA. In recalling the incomplete pass to the faculty that occurred in 1970, Brother Dominic went directly to the Board of Trustees. Cognizant of the intransigence of some faculty members, not only regarding the MBA, but graduate programs in general, the Board reviewed the new MBA proposal with care and was impressed with its imaginative approach, possible support from corporations and the likely possibility of securing quality faculty in the area. The Board approved the institution of the MBA with the result being that it was beneficial not only to its older students but to the undergraduate business program and the College in general. Brother Louis assumed the position as director with Ferguson as Assistant Director, but following the first quarter he bequeathed direction to Mike McCune. McCune directed for the first two successful years after which his interests turned to other entrepreneurial enterprises. He selected faculty member Cliff Healy, Vice President of Crown Zellerbach, Inc., to take command of the program in 1977.

Physical Renewal — The Time Had Come

During the summer of 1969 the campus took on the appearance of a Vietnamese village under siege. The windows in Dante classroom building and De La Salle residence hall had been removed as both buildings underwent major renovation, including the fenestration replacement required by the Contra Costa County Uniform Building and Fire Codes. Large collection bins or dumpsters were placed in strategic locations to gather the refuse from the old interiors, and replacement materials were stacked outside awaiting installation. Open ditches and mounds of dirt dotted the campus as a new waterline required by the fire department to upgrade the pressure in hydrants was addressed. Trucks and equipment ran roughshod over what minimal landscaping, overgrown and untamed, still feigned at beautifying the campus. Construction crews sliced utility lines, wreaking havoc with outdated campus lighting, and telephone and irrigation lines. The frenetic activity and physical disruption that gave birth to much needed renovation was a symbolic parallel to the exceptional changes in calendar and curriculum which also had to be readied for the commencement of the new semester in September 1969.

The difference between the two different activities, however, was significant. While physical improvements would be welcomed by both students and faculty, the academic changes, their philosophical assumptions and how they were achieved would be a source of continuing controversy and tension. One of the more telling comments relative to the new academic direction of the College and what presaged the future was uttered by Brother Alfred Brousseau, FSC, PhD, former provincial, chair of the Mathematics Department and member of the Academic Council, who said to me one evening as we were on our way to the Brothers' Community dining room, "You know, Brother Mel, one benefit from this new calendar and change in curriculum is that the stranglehold of the Philosophy Department on the College has come to an end." The Academic Vice President (Alan Pollock), who was officially a member of the English Department, and several other members of that department were likened by some faculty as the "orators," and described by others of more cynical bent as the "sophists," who had achieved the ascendancy in guiding the College curriculum and its politics. The philosophical change in the academic direction of the College was a foreshadowing of what was to occur in many institutions of Catholic higher education over the decade of the '70s. In many ways Alan Pollock was a man both with and ahead of his time. Although he did perceive the direction that much of Catholic higher education was taking throughout the nation, what Alan

Pollock saw in his crystal ball unknowingly became his stumbling block in the minds of many Christian Brothers and a significant number of their lay colleagues as well.

Looking Ahead, New Physical Facilities

A number of Brothers and others associated with the residence halls were convinced that if students had a place for student activities, an adequate bookstore, a coffee shop, an entertainment center, student body offices and meeting rooms, an adequate place for the campus radio station and a theater, that pressure and tension on students, and subsequently on residence hall life, would be suitably reduced. Plans were drawn for the construction of a college union. Under Brother Jerome West's leadership, donations were sought from prominent members of the Board of Regents. At that time long-term, low-cost loans could be secured through the federal government for residence halls and college unions. The College availed itself of a government loan and was successful in securing support from donors, notably Regent and former Trustee Fred Ferroggiaro who, had been Chairman of the Board of Bank of America, and another donor who wished at the time to remain anonymous.

On the day of groundbreaking, a number of students from the School of Science engaged in a protest, because they felt that the needs of the science program were preempted by the need for student recreation. Without a doubt, the facilities for the School of Science were in ill repair, obsolete and inadequate. However, what neither students nor faculty members who encouraged them in their protestations understood was that government loans were close to impossible to secure for classroom and laboratory construction or renovation, whereas they were available for nonacademic student life, such as, for residence halls or the construction of a college union. It was fortuitous that the College took advantage of the low-cost government loan for the college union since such loans were drastically curtailed or discontinued but a few years later. A benefactor named Joseph McKenna had bequeathed the College an endowment to be used as collateral for a loan, as well as to provide interest to pay down the loan taken out for the construction of a college union. He stipulated that when the college union loan was amortized the interest on the amount of his endowment was then to be used for student financial aid. With the funding from this endowment, together with the donations of Fred Ferroggiaro and the anonymous donor, the college union, thenceforth to be known as Ferroggiaro Center, was given the go-ahead by the Board.

Fred A. Ferroggiaro, 1890-1982

Fred Ferroggiaro's connection with the College occurred during the presidency of a commanding leader, Brother Thomas Levi, FSC. An insightful Brother Thomas had invited the then president of the Bank of Amercia, Louis Giannini, to join the newly formed Board of Regents. Giannini, the son of the founder of Bank of America, was gratified to be considered for membership but confided in Brother Thomas that his physician had predicted he had less than a year to live. He therefore suggested that Brother Thomas invite Fred Ferroggiaro, a veteran employee of the bank who began his banking career under the founder, Amadeus. P. Giannini, and rose to become Chairman of the Board. He also served as Chairman of the Board of Lucky Stores, Inc. Ferroggiaro was thus invited to become a charter member of the Board of Regents. After gaining acquiescence from his spouse, Delphine, after whom Delphine Lounge is named, Fred became a staunch member of the Saint Mary's family. He served on the Board of Regents from 1952 to 1982 and on the Board of Trustees from 1958 to 1968. He was awarded an honorary Doctor of Laws degree, in 1955. Two of Fred's notable achievements on the Board of Trustees were his advocacy of establishing a faculty salary scale similar to that of the California State University System, and secondly, his strong support for the establishment of club football, and athletics in general. He later expressed his devotion to the students by providing half the funding for The Ferroggiaro Center which was dedicated in the 1973 spring semester.

Ferroggiaro became an affiliated member of the Christian Brothers, along with his compatriot friend Frank Filippi, in October 1994. A charter member of the President's Club and one of its faithful supporters, he was particularly effervescent during a club party at the old Trader Vic's in San Francisco and revealed to friends that he was going to marry Kathleen (Peggy) M. del Piano Wolf, a widow and longtime family friend. They were married in 1974. The marriage clearly brought new life to Fred. He died in December of 1982 at age 92. Socially an active livewire, Peggy continued to participate in both Saint Mary's and other organizations. She died in a retirement home in Oakland in December 1998.

Positioned on a prominent wall of Delphine Lounge in the new Ferroggiaro Center were two original oil portraits, executed by well-known Piedmont artist Bruce Wolff -- one of Fred Ferroggiaro and the other of his wife, Delphine. On a dark winter night the two portraits were purloined in advance of a West Coast Conference basketball game with rival Santa Clara University. The chief of campus security, John Ellis, a former Sausalito, Calif., police officer, exercising his skills as a veteran sleuth, located the portraits somewhere in Santa Clara County. After a short negotiation, the portraits were returned without further action and were firmly attached to the wall and covered with glass.

Residence Facilities, 1973

Augustine Hall, or Freshman Dorm as it was once called was, one of the three original 1928 residence halls that had not yet been renovated and had deteriorated to the point that only two of five floors were reasonably habitable. However, rather than secure funds for the renovation of Augustine Hall in 1973, and hearing the interest of both men and women juniors and seniors who desired housing where they could cook for themselves, a plan emerged to construct facilities similar to the existing More and Beckett Halls but with the addition of a small kitchen, lounge area and dining space in each of the units. Augustine Hall was renovated at a later date for lower division students.

Kazuo Goto, AIA, the campus architect developed the design for what were called *town houses* containing seven separate units for groups of four to six students per unit each unit was to have two to three bedrooms, a small kitchen, a lounge and bathroom facilities, and each of the townhouses would accommodate 40 students, and include private rooms for a resident assistant and a resident director or counselor. The concept created a type of living arrangement different from any other on campus, allowing students to exercise their culinary talents if they so desired. Government loans were still available for such facilities, and the College applied for a loan to construct four town houses. Donors were then sought to furnish them. Thus, Sabatte, Syufy, Thille and Freitas Halls came into being and were dedicated in 1973. Sabatte Hall was dedicated by the Sabatte Family in memory of John and Mary Sabatte, founders of Berkeley Farms; and Syufy Hall was named in honor of Pauline Syufy, mother of alumnus and late Trustee Raymond Syufy, Sr., of Century Theaters. Mary Thille named Thille Hall in honor of her brother, Andrew Thille, a longtime friend of the College who was impressed by the Christian Brothers and the College through his attendance at the Regents-sponsored Executive Symposia. Freitas Hall was named in honor of Edward W. Freitas by alumnus, the late Hon. Judge Carlos Freitas '25, and his spouse Earlda of San Rafael and Mrs. Frances O'Mara, sister of Carlos. Freitas Parkway in Terra Linda, Marin County, is named after the parents of Carlos and Frances.

Following the dedication ceremonies, Mary Thille was accompanied by

Brother Jerome West to a reception in Dryden Hall. Thille remarked that the area in front of De La Salle Hall was in serious need of both reconditioning and landscaping and asked how much such a project would cost. Brother Jerome quickly estimated that $100,000 would be adequate. Her additional gift of $100,000 allowed a needed project to become a reality. A few faculty members, upon hearing of her generosity, derisively called her the "flower lady," because they thought her gift could have been directed to something of benefit to the academic life of the College, or more particularly to faculty advancement of some kind.

During the townhouse construction, a group of students under cover of darkness made off with enough slump-stone bricks and mortar to wall up the door to the room of their second floor resident assistant, Christopher Sales, in the yet-to-be renovated Augustine Hall. When Chris awoke in the morning and opened his door on his way to the common shower, he was confronted with a wall of brick and mortar, which by morning had set fast. It was immovable. Since Chris lived on the second floor with the first and ground floors below him, escape without a ladder or a rope made the possibility of injury more than likely. He phoned the maintenance department from his room. Once the crew arrived, it took half an hour to remove the wall, releasing the fuming and frustrated Chris, who was late for both breakfast and his early morning class. His reaction was greater than what the wall builders had hoped. They were, to avoid detection, reservedly amused.

When the town houses were completed in 1973, Augustine Hall was closed until such time that it could be completely renovated. It was during this time of closure that a Contra Costa County Assessor's Office bureaucrat visited the campus and threatened to initiate a tax levy on the College for an empty Augustine Hall, since it was not being used for academic instructional or residential purposes, a threat which proved to be yet another annoyance in a time of financial stringency. Friends of the College serving as officials in Contra Costa County government intervened, and no assessment was forthcoming. Augustine Hall was completely renovated in 1977.

George R. McKeon, 1925-1976

Following in his father's footsteps as a developer of homes and commercial real estate, George R. McKeon, a San Francisco native and alumnus of Sacred Heart High School, was a member of the College Board of Trustees from 1970 to 1976. He was also an investor in the Sacramento Kings basketball team. George's older brother, Chris T. McKeon, also a Sacred Heart alumnus, attended Saint Mary's College in the '40s, but with the advent of World

War II entered the service and sacrificed his life in the European Theater. George served in the U. S. Navy, and at the close of hostilities assumed his father's business, joined with his vivacious wife Elaine, and developed McKeon Construction, Inc, into a successful enterprise. His success allowed him to exercise his and Elaine's exceptional generosity.

George was appointed a member of the Board of Trustees in 1970. I was asked by Brother Jerome sometime in 1971 or 1972 to visit George in his executive offices in Sacramento to determine his interest in supporting the construction of a College Union building, since the government was still granting loans and grants for such construction. We had already received a financial commitment from Fred Ferroggiaro, former member of the Board of Trustees. As Steve Camp, the Director for Development, and I drove to Sacramento we were speculating on how much we might request of McKeon for the project. "Do you think $25,000 might be a possible figure?" Steve asked. I pondered and thought that we might go a little higher. I believe that we settled on something between $30,000 and $50,000, depending on how he reacted to our proposal. We were greeted most cordially in his downtown Sacramento office, by George who dispensed with preambles by saying, "I know what you're here for. How much do you really need to finish this project?" I frankly responded that we needed a total of $250,000 to complete the funding. "You've got it," George said, "but I do not want my name mentioned. How about going to lunch?" And off to a most congenial and enjoyable lunch we went, on George. A day later I received one of those small household checks in the mail from George and Elaine McKeon for $250,000!

Since George was on the Board of Trustees he followed the various development projects and was well aware of the need for a new gymnasium to replace the 1929 Madigan Gymnasium bandbox. He offered to assist in funding some needy project and as he reviewed priorities he realized that a new gymnasium was a critical need. Unfortunately, George had contracted leukemia and knew that his life expectancy was short. Sometime after he had determined how he would support the gym project, he called Brother Jerome from his hospital bed and asked him to come to see him about his gift. That was a Friday, and Brother Jerome said he would be able to come on Monday. George asked if he could come earlier, perhaps on Sunday. Brother Jerome agreed and met with George and Elaine on Sunday. George, Elaine and Brother Jerome toasted the gift with a libation of Chivas Regal Scotch, on the rocks, joked a bit, and then George presented Brother Jerome with a deed to an apartment property and an admonition not to sell it for less than a certain price. As Brother Jerome was taking leave, Elaine spoke to him outside the hospital room and suggested that George's name be recognized in some way. Brother Jerome was more than pleased to do so, especially since George had refused be recognized as a donor for the Ferroggiaro College Union Center. George slipped into a coma on Monday and died on Tuesday, Nov. 13, 1976. He was but 51 years old.

The McKeon Pavilion was dedicated on Feb. 25, 1978 prior to a basketball game between the Gaels and the Stanford Cardinals (see pages 170-171). Elaine McKeon served on the Board of Trustees from 1980 to 1990 and as Chairman of the Board from 1983 to 1985. She also served as a member of the New Century Committee in 1996. Recognized in San Francisco society as a devotee of the arts, she was named Chairman of the Board of the new San Francisco Museum of Modern Art and served effectively and graciously in that capacity from 1995 to 2004.

Sichel Hall, 1976

The faculty in the School of Science had over the years provided quality undergraduate education for numerous members of the medical and dental professions, as well as science educators, researchers, inventors and technicians. Galileo Hall, constructed as a science facility in 1928, had become an outdated, deteriorating scientific relic. New facilities and the renovation of Galileo were needed, particularly if the curriculum required all students to experience a laboratory science as some faculty members rightly advocated. An appeal was made to Alfred Fromm, President of Fromm and Sichel, which was the national and international distributor of Christian Brothers wine and brandy products. Fromm, a German-Jewish immigrant who had come from a distinguished family (musicians, vintners and a famous psychologist) that had escaped the Nazi terror, agreed to support an appeal to the Sichel Foundation of which Alfred was chairman, for the construction of a new biology facility. The Sichel Foundation which was created through the largess of Franz Sichel who had passed away years earlier, normally supported Jewish causes. Concurrently with Alfred Fromm's intervention, the Development Office began an appeal to other foundations and alumni in science-related professions to solicit funds for the new facility. Alfred Fromm was able to persuade the Sichel Foundation to the support the project. In addition to the Sichel Foundation, 14 other foundations and 21 individual donors (including four dentists and seven medical doctors) contributed generously to the new facility. The facility, designed by Anshen and Allen, AIA, with associate Derrick Parker, AIA, in the lead, was dedicated on May 6, 1976.

Student Life

The Snowball Dance

There was nothing special about the Dec. 8, 1972 (or 1973) Snowball Dance at the Claremont Hotel in Oakland. It was after the dance that unexpected excitement merited a 2 a.m. phone call to me from some students who pleaded for help. I went to the hotel and heard the story. One attendee who, it was alleged, never drank alcoholic beverages, was persuaded to have a few drinks during the evening. When the dance ended sometime after midnight, the student climbed into his vehicle for the trip back to the College. Unfortunately, his unfamiliarity with the effects of alcohol dimmed the clarity of his thought. He put his car into forward rather than reverse and pressed the gas pedal. The car was located on one of the upper parking lots that surround the hotel and lurched forward over the curb of the lot and down an embankment. It sheared off a fire hydrant and rested on top of the spurting water, the position of the car directing part of the stream toward the hotel entrance. It flooded the entrance, as well as the road, and found its way down the stairs to the dance floor. As one hotel employee stated, "It was an unbelievable mess." The police were called and arrested the driver. Some friends told him to say that he was injured, hoping that this claim would allow him to be taken to a hospital rather than jail. "Oh, in that case," a policeman said, "if you injure anyone, even yourself, under the influence, you commit a felony offense." "Oh, I'm all right," he then repeated several times. He spent the night in jail.

A record cold spell froze the water that cascaded down the sloping driveway to the hotel, and the fire department found it difficult to drive its trucks up the sloping drive into the area where the hydrant was spewing. I returned to the College and in the morning was besieged by several students to loan them money for bail. That I did, and the young man was released. I suspect it was some time before the hotel was able to be reimbursed for damages. As far as I know, his career after graduation was in secondary education and coaching football, and, reports have it, he became an effective administrator.

Candlelight Elegance

Drawing upon his experience as a former student at Cambridge University, England, where he received his Master's, Brother Patrick Moore, FSC, PhD, returned to Saint Mary's in 1974 after earning a doctorate from the University of Leicester, England, and encouraged a group of students to sponsor a series of *Candlelight Dinners* in Dryden Hall. Reservations (limit 120) were required, and dress was semiformal. The dinners became popular, to the

95

amazement of many. The initial student organizers were Mark Broughton, Sylvia Marquis and Ceci Massetti. Bringing a touch of class to campus dining after the turmoil of the late '60s and early '70s was an imaginative, old world practice that students found to be chic. The *Candlelight Dinners* endured for several years until organizational enthusiasm waned. They were the talk of the campus while they lasted, but like many innovations, the project endured only as long as volunteers persevered in the face of turnover, and until the founders moved on to other projects. Student Sherie Swiess took the lead in forming a Candlelight Dinner Committee accompanied by such colleagues as Dennis Fuller, Frances Gordon, Harry Walker, Lezlee Ann Chun, Amy Chavez, Casey Brady, Dave Fregeau, Greg Bechelli, Michele Zipse, Kelly Keith, Kirk Trost, Anita Clinton, Greg Patterson, Jerry Powers, Steve Meyer. Gerry Browne, Brian Stevens, Moira Cooney, Mark Zipse, Chris Lewis, Bill Cherney, Jane Barnett and Brian Mahoney.

La Famiglia

Another attractive concept emerged from within a group of natural student leaders at about the same time as the *Candlelight Dinners.* That was the inauguration of *Casino Night* in 1975 by a group of students who chose an identity inspired by Francis Ford Coppola's *The Godfather* series. The inventive group who considered themselves a *Family,* designed a night that captured the imagination and interest of the campus for several years. Donning tuxedos, they assembled gaming tables in Oliver Hall, that were managed by appropriately costumed faculty, administrators and upper classmen. A large band from Reno, Nev., entertained those who wished to dance in adjoining Dryden Hall. *Casino Night* currency was non-negotiable, but those amassing the greatest number of points received prizes at the close of the evening. *Casino Night* continued for at least 14 years, until it lost its novelty and much of its original glamour. Administrators also became more concerned with liability because of alcohol consumption by underage students and state regulations on gambling. As casino night popularity filled the coffers of *The Family* account, the members decided to present to the student body of between 1,700 to 2,100 undergraduates, a subsidized celebration at the end of each academic year called *Mayfest,* featuring games, free victuals and drink on one of the playing fields. Members also dedicated part of their income to an endowed scholarship program, toward which many Family alumni continue to contribute. In 1977, when many of the original members were about to graduate they constructed a stage for commencement ceremonies that held the entire class of 1977. The stage was used for several successive years, until subsequent classes outgrew it, and the ceremonies were relocated to the College stadium. Original members of

The Family were the unassuming but highly organized leader Steve Meyer, Rob Regan, Ralph Verbogue, Steve Spiller, Kurt Bennett, Tom Wilson, Dan Lamb, Gerry Browne, Mike Felice, Thorpe Deakers, Matt O'Donnell, Mark Zipse and Keith Bernardi. As the years progressed, such names as *Friends of the Family* and *Family Affiliation* were used to designate the continuing tradition. Such members as Moira Cooney, Leslie Beddatto, Brian Stevens, Rick Hess, Reed Thompson, Michele Zipse, Bill Jones, Rick Rosario, Anne Agnew, Kelly Keith and many others joined the membership ranks over the years.

Financial Challenges
Finances, New Ideas, Same Old Intransigence
Financial Summary, 1969-1976
(See Appendices for Financial Accounting Charts. Page 350)

In 1969, the financial state of the College was clearly negative. Expenses exceeded income, and endowment was minimal in relation to the operating budget. The endowment is composed of funds invested according to the wishes of donors as an irrevocable trust in various financial forms for purposes of providing income for donor-designated uses. As a minimum, the rule of thumb at that time was that the endowment should be double the operating budget, and that approximately half the income from the endowment portfolio be normally reinvested as a hedge against inflation and approximately half be used to support such designated functions indicated by the donors as students in financial need, faculty chairs, building maintenance, support of the arts, and other academic or facility projects. The majority of the funds in the endowment have traditionally been designated for financial aid, or in popular jargon, scholarships. However, half the income from the endowment was appallingly far from covering the amount of financial aid offered to students.

There were other major factors that also placed stress on finances. The campus infrastructure was a major concern, namely, delivery systems for electrical and water services, fire protection, heating, telecommunications and disposal services. Most of the elements in the infrastructure were in dire need of repair, replacement, automation or extension. Electrical blackouts and floodings, for example, were frequent. Upgrading facilities, such as classrooms, residence halls, the gymnasium, a crumbling roof over the pool that was installed by the U. S. Navy Pre-Flight School in 1942, shower and locker rooms, the Chapel, antediluvian laboratories, potholed roads, parking space and sparse landscaping required serious attention. Within a few years additional facilities would be required to accommodate new programs and an increasing faculty and student body, as well as provide costly technological advances. Sincere efforts to address the financial and social needs of underrepresented students from ethnic minorities who would otherwise be excluded from a Saint Mary's education added to the overhead that included the employment of advisors to provide for the student's special academic and social needs.

Though the 1966 formula for faculty salaries was not followed during the time of financial difficulties, raises for faculty, administration and staff were

98

made as reasonably as possible. Unfortunately, there was little available for faculty or curriculum development, sabbaticals, research, or academic conference fees and travel to them.

The athletic program was barely able to compete with the universities most in competition with Saint Mary's in what was then the West Coast Athletic Conference (later renamed the West Coast Conference.) Given the size of the student body in 1969-1970, (under 1,000), the costs per student for athletics and some other services were higher per student for Saint Mary's than for our other, larger competitors. In 1970, Saint Mary's was the last of the comparable Catholic institutions on the West Coast to become coeducational, a recalcitrance that was unrealistic in view of modern American educational trends, dependent, as is usually the case, on which philosophy of education one adopts. When student-sponsored club football was unable to meet its fiscal responsibilities in 1970, the College assumed football obligations as one of its regular NCAA sports.

The College Development Office, coupled with Public Relations, Publications and Alumni Relations offices had barely come of age in the late '60s under the guidance of the late Brother Xavier Joy, FSC, Vice President for Development and Stan Skoog, Development Director. Some organizations and programs had begun to function more effectively in order to increase financial support, primarily, but not exclusively, to address student financial need. Organizations such as The Board of Regents, the College County Committee, the Saint Mary's Associates, the Saint Mary's East Bay Scholarship Fund, Inc., Alumni Annual Giving and The Saint Mary's College Guild were already in place, as was a modest fundraising campaign entitled *Partnership for Excellence*, designed to raise funds for faculty salaries, endowment and the construction of new facilities, including a new library and Beckett and More residence halls. Someone was needed to inspire the Development Staff and the numerous support organizations to move into fast forward. Former Provincial, Brother Jerome West, MA, appointed in 1969, was that someone.

De La Salle Institute, the corporation of the Christian Brothers and at that time the sole owners of Mont La Salle Vineyards, had contributed to the renovation of two 1928 buildings in the summer of 1969: Dante Hall, the main classroom facility, and the upper residence floors of De La Salle Hall. The Institute also contributed to the renovation of Aquinas Hall, also constructed in 1927-1928. That renovation was completed in the summer of 1970. In 1977 and 1978, the Christian Brothers provided a most welcome interest-free loan of $719,000 to reduce the deficit and the concurrent interest payments.

Shortly after Brother Jerome was appointed Development Director, he conferred with the newly appointed Campus Architect, Kazuo Goto, to develop a priority list of needed facilities, particularly residence halls and a College Union facility in view of increasing the traditional undergraduate enrollment, the mainstay of financial stability. The renovation and building program did not cease during the time of student protests and the consequent operational financial difficulty, since funding for such facilities came through solicitation from donors specifically for those facilities as requests to donors for the funding of new facilities was clearly more appealing than asking for funds to either avoid or retire a deficit. Ferroggiaro Center (College Union) and four student town houses accommodating 41 students each were constructed in 1973. Federal government loans for residence halls and student recreational facilities were still available in the early 1970s. As securing a federal government loan became much more competitive, the State of California eventually filled in for the Federal government by offering opportunities to secure California Educational Facilities Act Bonds that were utilized in the construction of the two Claeys and the first three Ageno residence halls.

Coeducation commenced modestly in the 1970-1971 academic year, and by the following year, 1971-1972, a significant increase in women students was seen as a promising development. However, student protests during that year resulted in a higher attrition rate than normal in the summer of 1972 and a lower number of entering students the following fall. A low enrollment in a particular freshman class will be a financial problem for four years. There were no reserve funds at that time to address unanticipated financial exigencies.

When a proposal was introduced by the Academic Council to the Faculty Assembly in Oct. of 1972 suggesting the College offer extension courses to the Contra Costa County community, the reaction was, as expected, disappointingly negative. Both liberal arts purists and the socially liberal commingled their protesting voices: "Mere skills courses are illiberal by nature! Such a program would demean the dignity of the College! The introduction of such a program might distract faculty from the special intellectual responsibilities of our time and place, and drain our energies!" Speculation added further concerns about faculty overload, the danger of having lower-paid extension faculty on a par with regular faculty, and whether such a scheme was financially feasible, even though no research was offered to suggest that such might be the case. Yet, there were faculty who believed College outreach important for several reasons, among them financial, political and academic. A few faculty members strongly believed that it would be wise for the College to be alert to the needs of the local community. (Minutes of Special Faculty

Meeting, Oct. 25, 1972, Saint Mary's College Archives.) Surprisingly a Sept. 1973 report to the faculty, noting that an invitation for local area residents to enroll in regular classes at a reduced rate, had netted 27 applicants, mostly women, with 18 already enrolled. The report merited a unanimous vote of thanks to Professor Carol Grabo who had promoted the program.

After the downturn in traditional undergraduate enrollment from 1,150 to 935 in September 1972, the Board of Trustees grew increasingly uneasy with the growing deficit and both the unresponsiveness and outright opposition of some faculty in considering proposed opportunities for developing new proposals or making effectively efficient changes in the status quo. During the Board meeting of Sept.1973, Board Members made several specific suggestions, including one that proposed an increase in the student-faculty ratio, though none became mandates at that time. Rather, the trustees requested a list of positive recommendations from the administration by Jan. 1974 directed to both curtailing expenses and increasing income.

Attached to the Faculty Assembly Minutes of Oct. 15, 1973 was an open letter to the faculty from Professor Mary Springer, PhD, of the English Department, opposing any increase in class size arguing that "we will move that much closer to losing the character of Saint Mary's College which has drawn students to us: namely, small classes, the seminar mode, and plenty of individual attention."

Though January 1974 was several months away, and the Board was not made aware of the Springer letter, the concern of the Board became more intense at the Nov. 1973, Board meeting when several members proposed that the student-faculty ratio be increased as soon as possible. Such was not uncommon procedure, since state legislatures normally set such ratios for budgeting purposes in dealing with public educational institutions. Discussion soon moved the Board to require a commitment from the administration and faculty that the student-faculty ratio would be set at 15 students per faculty member as soon as possible. A 15 to 1 student-faculty ratio would mean that class size, on average, would total 20 students, since faculty taught three courses per semester, and students enrolled in four. In order to achieve such a ratio and still accommodate smaller classes in such fields as foreign language, mathematics or chemistry, other institutions (both public and independent) balanced smaller classes with those of a larger, lecture-type format that could accommodate between 100 and 150 students or more. For approximately a dozen years, the College had for the most part abandoned the larger lecture classes in favor of those with smaller numbers, a policy that encouraged the conduct of classes as seminars rather than as lecture courses, allowing for greater student-faculty interaction.

In spite of the Trustees request for positive recommendations by Jan. 1974, that would address fiscal indebtedness, the faculty focused discussion primarily on the issue of student-faculty ratio until the end of the academic year. In November 1973, following the Trustees' motion of Nov. 1, 1973, a Faculty Assembly resolution requested that I ask the Trustees for a reconsideration of its proposal that a 15 to 1 student faculty ratio become the Saint Mary's standard. Passing without opposition in December was another Faculty Assembly resolution requesting that "no-nonreappointments of faculty or reductions of course offerings be made on the basis of student-faculty ratio until the budgetary and academic premises for such nonreappointments have been publicly justified." (Minutes of the Faculty Assembly, November and December 1973, Saint Mary's College Archives.)

With the student-faculty ratio standing at 13.5 to 1 in January 1974, Vice President Thomas Slakey, '52, presented an Academic Council report to the Faculty Assembly stating that "our own experience over the past 12 years indicates ratios from 11 to 1 to 15 to 1," and that, "a recent study of 48 liberal arts institutions recorded student-faculty ratios from 7.39 to 19.05 with a median of 12.68." "The Board (of Trustees)," Slakey noted, "had recently mandated a student-faculty ratio of 15 to 1, knowing that many other colleges operate with apparent success at ratios of 15 (to 1) or higher." Slakey then provided a detailed list of course deletions and suggested enrollment changes in various departmental offerings. He also stated that there were thoughtful and responsible faculty members on the Academic Council who viewed the 15 to 1 student-faculty ratio as an urgent necessity.

Vice President Slakey found himself in an almost untenable position. He was being pressured by the Board to increase the student-faculty ratio while being besieged by some faculty for retaining the status quo, though other faculty members acknowledged a necessity for an increase. The situation was not an unlikely scenario in higher education, where strong personalities (with doctorates and tenure, but without personal responsibility) uttered strong opinions on issues that required the Wisdom of Solomon to propose a reasonable solution.

The Board of Trustees listened to the plea of Academic Vice President Slakey on Feb. 20, 1974, that the student-faculty ratio be set at 13.5 to 1. However, the Board reiterated its stance that a 15 to 1 student faculty ratio "be effected as soon as possible." The Board moved "that the plan to attain a 15 to 1 student-faculty ratio be specific and that methods be devised by the April meeting (of the Board) which could effect this ratio for 1975-1976." (Minutes of the Board of Trustees, Feb. 20, 1974.)

While the Board continued to urge the implementation of a 15 to 1 ratio, a group of faculty, in a Special Faculty Meeting on April 3, 1974, passed several resolutions aimed at protecting as many faculty appointments as possible. Professor Mary Springer, speaking on behalf of an organized group of the more vocal faculty, presented a motion containing such phrases as "faculty cuts have reached the danger level," and "students are discouraged from returning for fear that some of their best teachers would be missing," and "students are already complaining of a lack of variety." The faculty voted in favor of a resolution that read: "… although the present judgment of the faculty after reviewing the alternatives so far presented is that the 15 to 1 ratio should be at most a long-term goal to be achieved principally through growth in enrollment rather than through reduction of curriculum and faculty, the faculty requests that if the Board should decide, after considering the alternatives presented and their consequences, that a 15 to 1 ratio is a necessity for the College in 1975-1976, the Board leave to the faculty and the administration of the College the responsibility of choosing among these alternatives."

The major faculty solution to achieving a 15 to 1 ratio was for the Admissions Office staff to recruit more students and to allow at least two years before the 15 to 1 goal was achieved. Academic Vice President Slakey attempted to both negotiate with and admonish the Board at the May meeting by reporting that the ratio for the coming year (1974-1975) would move from 13.5 to 1 to 13.8 to 1 and noted that increased enrollment could even push the ratio higher. He expressed optimistic hope that a 15 to 1 ratio could be reached by the 1975-1976 academic year and completed his report by stating that in his opinion he thought the Board to be in error by "focusing on the student-faculty ratio to effect budget reductions." The Board responded politely by stating that the 1974-1975 budget "must be balanced."

As I considered the dilemmas that faced the administration, there were some possible solutions if enough time were granted to realize results and draconian mandates could be avoided. The first part of the solution was to increase personnel in the Admissions Office, which I authorized to take effect immediately. I also insisted on tighter fiscal controls without damaging basic academic functions or alienating the majority of the faculty. The Administrative Council considered the institution of new income programs, such as programs for returning adults in Continuing Education, Extended Education and Master's programs in Education, Psychology and Business Administration. The Development Office, in unison with The Board of Regents and the offices of Public Relations, Publications and Alumni Affairs, was urged to increase, create and coordinate its funding activities. The Development plan, under the direction of Brother Jerome West, was to increase annual alumni giving, and establish a Planned Giving (bequests) Campaign, in addition to raising funds for needed facilities. The solution package, a four-pronged approach (admissions, fiscal controls, new programs, increased Development), was clearly a multiyear project based on the assumption that if enough of the anticipated creative proposals would prove to be fruitful, the pressures would ease.

The attempt by the Board to balance the budget by pursuing a student-faculty ratio of 15 to 1 (and later to move toward an 18 to 1 ratio) as a means for exercising fiscal stringency posed serious quality, and thus recruitment, problems. I was willing to support the 15 to 1 ratio at the Board meeting, but in discussing that ratio with Academic Vice President Slakey, I realized he had serious doubts about the achievability of a 15 to 1 ratio without negatively altering academic offerings and thus recruitment of students. His hope was to hold off enacting the 15 to 1 ratio while working to realize greater income through larger enrollment, attractive academic programs and the success of new and more energetic Development activities. While a 15 to 1 student-faculty ratio (with average class sizes of 20) was possible, I did not wish to see the critics persuade the majority of the faculty that the administration was intent on undermining the quality of the education offered to students.

Since I sincerely believed in the faculty and administration forming a community of scholars, a concept typical of classical English higher education, I did not want to prompt an adversarial relationship with the faculty at large. Yet it was clear that the Board was exercising its oversight responsibilities by demanding a balanced budget, and its suggesting, or even demanding, ways to do so. I was in agreement with the Board's broad objectives. With the unfortunate resignation of Vice President Slakey at the close of the academic year in the spring of 1974 and my appointment of Brother Dominic Ruegg in the summer of 1974, I anticipated an acceleration in developing new academic programs, since Brother Dominic was a staunch champion of educational ventures for older adults in the Contra Costa County community and strongly supported the concept of financial stability and independence from the financial support of De La Salle Institute, which in due time had to face its own financial concerns. The plan eventually proved effective, though not without some painful challenges. An enlarged Admissions Office did, in fact, increase undergraduate enrollment. New academic programs that focused on older adult enrollment and a more heightened annual giving program provided greater student financial aid. Faculty willingness to assume an additional course per year for two years, as well as assistance from the Christian

Brothers De La Salle Institute, all contributed to the elimination of the accumulated deficit and its interest payments within three years.

At the urging of Board member James Harvey, then President and CEO of Transamerica, Inc., the College began to build a prudent reserve equal to three months of operating expenses as a hedge against unforeseen eventualities, and under the guidance of Brother Jerome West, plans for the first major capital campaign in the history of the College began in earnest.

There were a number of external factors that affected the budget from time to time as well. The Cal Grant or State Scholarship program was subject to the vicissitudes of the ever-fluctuating State economy, especially when decisions were made late in the legislative year, usually out of synchronization with application and financial aid deadlines. The Federal government caused similar difficulties from time to time, and new Federal regulations regarding the disabled, while compassionate, increased the costs of building and retrofitting campus facilities with ramps and elevators. The Title IX Anti-discrimination laws in education favoring women's equal participation in interscholastic athletics, though clearly justified in intent, increased the athletic budget at a time when athletics in general were in the sights of many faculty critics from different faculty camps.

As the record will show, all of the above factors, from the previous deficit spending in 1969 to the institution of new programs in the mid '70s and the subsequent healthy growth of most of them, were pieces of a financial puzzle that ultimately fit together in a productive way and in turn had a salutary effect on campus governance, since a growing faculty required a different governance model to replace the more loosely organized, freewheeling Faculty Assembly. As with any vibrant and creative organization, there was much to be done, and plans were laid to accomplish a number of laudable goals. But like most human endeavors, however, some plans and programs were not without missteps, such as that, at least in part, with the relationship with the Institute for Professional Development, to be discussed later.

Power Struggle: The Appearance of the American Federation of Teachers

The minutes of the May 1974 meeting of the Faculty Assembly, identify Professor Ed Versluis as representing the newly formed chapter of the American Federation of Teachers. During the Dec. 6, 1974 Faculty Assembly meeting he declared that his remarks opposing any change in student-faculty ratio were supported by both the AFT and the American Association of University Professors campus chapter presidents.

The Administration had been tracking the activities of the newly established American Federation of Teachers chapter when it heard of its formation and had reckoned that a relatively small group were card-carrying members. A later revelation of the signers of the AFT Chapter Charter confirmed the original number to be 14. Only a small number of faculty seemed interested in supporting unionization. One longterm faculty member stated to me one afternoon that "with the current leadership in the AFT that it (unionization) would not evolve. Faculty are just not interested." His observation proved accurate. However, we knew that faculty interest could change if adversarial circumstances threatened normal faculty well-being.

Brother Dominic (John) Ruegg, FSC, PhD, Academic Vice President

With Tom Slakey's resignation I was forced to locate either a permanent or interim Academic Vice President in the summer of 1974. Brother Dominic Ruegg, PhD, FSC, had been engaged in an underwater archeological project off the coast of Mallorca, Spain but had ended his summer research and had traveled to Madrid for an International Meeting of Classicists. Brother Dominic's doctoral studies were in Classical Latin and Greek. I was able to locate his telephone number and asked him to assume the post of Academic Vice President. With some reluctance, Brother Dominic agreed to fill the assignment for a short time.

I was well aware of Brother Dominic's dedication to the intellectual life, but it so happened that Brother Dominic's earlier correspondence to me had suggested ways for the College to achieve financial stability by extending its influence in Contra Costa County. He felt that the so-called academic purists and progressive liberals held the College in bondage, and as long as efforts were not made to be creative and to open it to residents in the area the College would languish. He was also a strong advocate of financial independence from De La Salle Institute that had, from time to time, provided generous fiscal support in times of need. I was in agreement with Brother Dominic of the issues he raised and welcomed his acquiescence to assume the Vice Presidency, if only for a few years. Brother Dominic had reached his 56 birthday in early August, and his intention was to do what could be done within a limited time. He had held the highest elected faculty position, namely the chairman of the Faculty Assembly in 1970-1971, and I took his election as a sign that the faculty would support him.

As will be seen, Brother Dominic's four-year tenure as Academic Vice president had long-term, beneficial effects upon the future of the College, even more startling in some ways than the changes in calendar and curriculum which occurred in 1969. Adult education became a significant factor in the academic and financial life of the College. However, a few of the numerous endeavors undertaken by Brother Dominic, and they came quickly, were cause for faculty uneasiness and Accreditation Association criticism.

The Accreditation officers seemed inhibited from straightforward communication, perhaps for fear of legal action by the Institute for Professional Development, a group with which the College entered into contract. Similar to other institutions both within and outside of California, the College had contracted with the Institute for Professional Development, Inc. to offer, under College accreditation, baccalaureate degree programs for older adults who had at least two years of collegiate education. The relationship of any institution with the Institute for Professional Development within the WASC jurisdiction became the *bete noire* of both the Executive Director, Kay Andersen, and the Association. Andersen became aware of the contractual agreements between IPD and the College and considered it another incursion of IPD on WASC territory and, as both Brother Dominic and I later discovered, was intent on eliminating the Institute for Professional Development in California. In fairness, it must be said that there were a number of legitimate concerns as to whether the academic requirements of the Institute or IPD were as academically demanding as traditional undergraduate programs, or whether the IPD curriculum allowed for the distinctiveness found in the traditional undergraduate programs of each participating collegiate institution. Initial problems did appear in the Saint Mary's version of the joint Saint Mary's College-IPD program, such as an apparent too short a time for securing the baccalaureate degree and a more stringent review of prior learning, and there were also some continuing problems, most notably too many students with faulty English backgrounds, a widespread problem in higher education generally. Weaknesses with new academic endeavors, such as the inception of the January Term and the Collegiate Seminar Theme programs in 1969, could have been addressed regarding the IPD, primarily through clear and straightforward communication, without the high drama the Accreditation Executive Director and the Commission chose to stage. As it soon became apparent, the Accrediting Association had a much larger agenda than Saint Mary's relationship with IPD.

Brother Dominic was convinced that the College had to develop programs that would expand both enrollment and income, create stability and bring positive attention to the College, convincing the public that it was more than an obscure, outmoded quasi-seminary in the Moraga cul-de-sac. One of his primary tasks was to speak to the faculty, urging them to take part in a cost-reduction program of survival, necessitated by the economic effect of the student unrest in 1972 that had been encouraged by some faculty members. He suggested that each faculty member add another course to his or her schedule until the financial crisis eased. While many faculty accepted this additional academic burden as necessary for a time, others resisted, particularly those who did not wish to see the addition of graduate programs or new ventures over which they did not grant approval. This is not to say that faculty evaluations and recommendations should be taken lightly or ignored. However, the intransigence of some vocal and dominant faculty impeded movement toward financial stability and the opportunity of offering academic enrichment to a wider spectrum of students within the local community. It was this latter group that accused Brother Dominic of, "academic adventurism," describing the academic initiatives as "a series of unrelated activities held together by the plumbing system."

Even though the Faculty Handbook noted that qualified Christian Brothers could be assigned to positions in the College without a search, some faculty took umbrage with the fact that they were not consulted in the appointment of Brother Dominic, even though faculty are not readily available in the summer months. Following my opening address at the commencement of the 1974 fall semester Professor Norman Springer stated that he thought Brother Dominic should have been assigned the title of Acting Academic Vice President until a search process was initiated and completed. Though I was cognizant of the objections of some faculty as expressed by Professor Norman Springer, I seized the opportunity of Slakey's unexpected resignation just as the summer began to appoint a Christian Brother who had made shrewd and practical suggestions to me to overcome an unbalanced College budget and an increasing deficit.

On Oct. 16, 1974, Professor N. Springer invited Brother Dominic, as the new Academic Vice President, to a dinner with nine faculty members, among them a Christian Brother and the former Vice President, Alan Pollock. As Brother Dominic relates it, the dinner guests "spent several hours trying to convince me that I should set myself (with them) in opposition to the President, Brother Mel. I did not seem too cooperative. They were disappointed." (File note of May 6, 1978, Brother Dominic Ruegg's personal file.) Shortly thereafter Brother Dominic was invited to a picnic at the home of Professors Norman and Mary Springer in Stinson Beach in Marin County. As Brother

Dominic recounts the experience, the same group was assembled and again tried to persuade him to do what he could to see that I was removed from office. Brother Dominic's resistance to the overtures by the Springers was not appreciated, and they refrained from speaking to him for several years thereafter. (Op. Cit. Brother Dominic's personal file.)

In his first meeting with the Board of Trustees as Academic Vice President, Brother Dominic Ruegg notified the Board that both graduate and undergraduate enrollment had increased. However, the most significant issue Brother Dominic presented to the Board was his consideration of academic changes. While honoring the primary place of liberal arts education in the undergraduate college, he envisioned the possibility of instituting auxiliary programs, such as expanding both continuing education and graduate programs, as well as affiliating the College with other institutions to award the Associate of Arts degree awarded at completion of two years of college, as distinguished from the Bachelor of Arts degree awarded at the completion of four years of college. (Minutes of the Board of Trustees, Oct. 24, 1974, Saint Mary's College Archives.)

When this information was provided to the Faculty Assembly at its meeting of Nov. 15, 1974, Professor Norman Springer requested further information on auxiliary programs. He proposed that two members of the faculty attend the next Board meeting in order to enter into discussions on auxiliary programs, even though attendance at Board meetings is normally by invitation only. (Minutes of Faculty Assembly, Nov. 15, 1974, Saint Mary's College Archives.) Springer's concern was expressed by the faculty at large calling for a special Faculty Assembly meeting through obtaining a petition signed by 10 members of the faculty. The meeting was held on Nov. 21, 1974, to discuss Brother Dominic's proposed auxiliary programs. The meeting was prefaced by an open letter, dated Nov. 18, 1974, sent to all faculty, signed by Professors Norman Springer (English Department) and Joseph Lanigan (Philosophy Department) proposing that two faculty members frame a letter to be sent to the Board of Trustees prior to its Dec. 2, 1974 meeting, "pointing out the nature of the serious disadvantages raised by Brother Dominic's proposals."

An essay authored by Professor David Loomis was also sent to all faculty members extolling the virtues of liberal arts education as contrasted with programs "incompatible with liberal education." "The presence of students whose acknowledged concern is short-term credit accumulation for the sake of salary increment or advancement in programs elsewhere will militate against the enterprise of serious and accumulative acquaintance with a discipline ..." Though Professor Loomis' view of a traditional undergraduate liberal education, in principle, was the ideal of the exclusively liberal arts institution, there was no substantial argument why such an education could not exist side by side with more pragmatic or quasi-pragmatic educational activities. For decades the College had included a large School of Economics and Business Administration alongside the Schools of Liberal Arts and Science without compromising the liberal arts-science character of the College. In fact, the requirements of the Collegiate Seminars and Religious Studies for all students and, prior to 1969, the requirements in philosophy, language and history contributed to the liberal education of all students, including those in the School of Economics and Business Administration. Toward the end of his open letter Loomis also questioned, without evidence, whether the financial gain, if there were any, was worth the ultimate cost. (Essay of David Loomis, dated Nov. 1974, Saint Mary's College Archives) The question as to whether useful education and useless (non-pragmatic or theoretical) education could exist in the same institution had been debated for many years. There were faculty who would, if possible, gladly see the jettison of the business portion of the School of Economics and Business Administration.

During the Special Faculty Assembly meeting of Nov. 21, 1974, Brother Dominic proposed the following principles:

- The College is not realizing its full potential as an educational institution in Contra Costa County.
- Instituting new programs would not essentially affect the traditional undergraduate program.
- It is desirable that the College be open to the (local) community. The elitist atmosphere of the College does not attract increased participation in the educational opportunities Saint Mary's offers.
- Saint Mary's should stimulate interest among older adults in the community in its liberal arts education.
- Statistics show a decline in the number of traditional age students and an increased interest among older adults wishing to return to complete their education.
- An in-service and continuing education program would make Saint Mary's more visible in the area and attract interest from the community.
- The core program would be expanded to include various kinds of graduate work that would enliven and open up possibilities at the undergraduate level.

As expected, Professor Norman Springer, among the first to express his misgivings, reiterated his objection to Brother Dominic's proposals, speaking "about the ways in which the nature of the College might be changed by the addition of programs which conceivably could drain energy from the present staff precisely at a time when that staff is concerned with preserving and improving the fundamental educational thrust of a traditional liberal arts college." The objection was shallow. There was no evidence that an MBA program would drain energy from anyone except those engaged in it nor that it would preclude the liberal arts faculty from improving either itself or the liberal arts program. Brother Ronald Isetti and Alan Pollock both stated that the College should try to continue doing what it already does well and not enter fields where it has no expertise. Professor Norman Springer became the major gadfly in expressing his opposition to almost every proposal the Academic Vice President offered.

At the conclusion of the Special Faculty Assembly meeting of Nov. 21, the motion, as amended, read "that the four proposals of new programs (noted below) of the Academic Vice President be presented for action to the Board of Trustees after the faculty as a whole has voted on them by written ballot." The motion barely passed 13-12-0, but the written ballot submitted to the faculty as a whole yielded 47 yea and 15 nay votes with 6 abstentions, overwhelmingly and surprisingly supporting Brother Dominic's proposals, as cast in their final form as shown below:

"That the faculty approve,
1) the residential, liberal arts, Catholic College as the core of a program which recognizes other quality educational endeavors,
2) an increase in in-service and continuing education,
3) a separate Graduate Division (Theology, Education, MBA, Psychology),
4) affiliation with recognized educational institutes which want a liberal arts component, e.g., Music Conservatories, Art Institutes, Medical Technician schools, and so forth."

The Board of Trustees approved Brother Dominic's proposition on Dec. 2, 1974 by a vote of 10 in favor and 1 opposed

The Moraga Community

New Town — Old Gown, 1974

Groundbreaking ceremonies on the Moraga Campus on May 15, 1927, were followed by such an extraordinary pace of construction, that the College was able to open its Moraga doors in September 1928. While this was cause for the excitement that followed, within a little over a year the Stock Market Crash of October 1929 and subsequent major financial depression isolated the College in the Joaquin Moraga Valley cul-de-sac until several years after World War II, when the communities and towns or cities of Lafayette, Moraga, Orinda and Walnut Creek began to develop.

As Moraga gradually expanded, the local community and College relationships could be described as casual and friendly. Prior to 1970, though minimum expansion occurred on campus, approvals for the construction of new buildings were sought through a somewhat distant Contra Costa County Planning Department. However, in 1973-1974, several prominent citizens of Moraga actively engaged in seeking incorporation that would establish such civic governance entities as a Town Council, Planning Commission, Design Review Board, Park and Recreation Commission, Police Department, Fire Department, and other entities as needed. The aim of those favoring incorporation was to give Moraga citizens a stronger voice in their future, especially in supervising growth, aesthetics, architecture, landscaping, civic infrastructure, and police and fire security.

After careful planning and solicitation for support from citizens, those favoring incorporation submitted a ballot measure to Moraga voters. The Town of Moraga became official on Nov. 5, 1974, when 3,679 citizens voted in favor of incorporation and 2,537 opposed the plan. The dream for an incorporated Town of Moraga finally became a reality, a concept first considered in 1912, when the Moraga Land Company envisioned the development of a planned community. The incorporation celebration was held in Dryden Hall at Saint Mary's College. Members of the initial Town Council were Mike Cory, Sue McNulty, Merle Gilliland, Barry Gross and Bill Coombs. The position of mayor was rotated among Town Council members, with the late Mike Cory being honored as Moraga's first mayor. Since the College was within the official boundaries of the new town, the College was required to conform to the normal requirements of local governance. It was not long before the implications of incorporation required changes in both attitude and relationships with the civic body, now officially called the Town of Moraga and the various officers, committees and commissions within it. In addition to a mayor and Town Council incorporation meant a full-time Town Manager, Town Planner and Police and Fire Chiefs along with the various other governing bodies, all reporting to the Town Council. Almost all of the various civic entities, or the chairmen of them, had some interchange with the College administration from time to time. Dave Baker was the first Town Planner, and though congenial toward Saint Mary's, in his managerial capacity he was required, and had the appetite, to follow the book, which he did. All building projects had to be submitted to the Planning Commission and the Design Review Board. Since the College retained a competent architectural staff, there were few instances of difficulty with the supervising boards or commissions. The Fire Chief had access difficulties with haphazard campus parking that blocked easy access to residence halls, a problem that was resolved as soon as the College had sufficient funds to renovate or install new parking lots.

Shortly after the formation of the Moraga Police Department, some daring nocturnal students in need of off-campus transportation, ventured into the maintenance yard and unofficially borrowed a modified van that had been reduced to a makeshift flatbed truck used to transport furniture around campus. It consisted of a driver's seat, motor, steering wheel, gearshift, four wheels and little else. Someone had hand painted F-111 on what was left of a front panel. The modified van, such as it was, did not have lights, since it was used only during daytime working hours and only on campus. The students headed for the Rheem section of Moraga on their late-night journey seeking victuals and most likely some drink, and since the vehicle had no lights two students stretched out on the van floor, one on each side, each holding a flashlight. As the students headed up the Rheem Boulevard hill, a police patrol just happened to be cruising nearby and spotted the 10 or so students on the makeshift van with makeshift headlights and no rear lights. When the driver saw the police cruiser he headed the vehicle off the road and up an embankment so that students could bail out and escape. As the students abandoned ship, the van rolled backward into the cruiser. Though all but one of the students escaped capture, the one apprehended was forced to identify the group. Though the police cruiser had some modest damage, the event was handled with discretion and, the maintenance staff was urged to secure all its vehicles to prevent misuse by adventuresome and uninhibited students.

The F-111 painted on the modified van was a reference to an authentic F-111 aircraft that the U. S. Air Force had brought to campus a few years before (during the height of the Vietnam conflict) to encourage graduates

113

to consider joining. Some enterprising students in the dark of the night moved the authentic F-111 to an out-of-sight off-campus location much to the chagrin and embarrassment of Air Force personnel who arrived in the morning to begin their recruitment effort. Words like Federal Offense, Felony, Serious penalties, An F.B.I. matter, were uttered. However, the off-campus hiding site was discovered, and the aircraft was returned to its central place on campus. While the perpetrators and most of the student body were amused, the Air Force personnel were not. The strategy of the U. S. Air Force bringing an F-111 for display on campus as a recruiting device at an intense juncture in the Vietnam War left much political acuity to be desired, as Air Force personnel soon discovered.

For the most part, the relationship with Town personnel evolved amicably, but for many who had worked or lived at Saint Mary's for years prior to incorporation, the new order was seen as more intrusive bureaucratic interference in seeking approval for removing trees that the College had planted; for installing new tennis courts, playing fields and fences, especially those bordering on St. Mary's Road; for major renovation and construction projects; and for the submission of a Campus Master Plan with implications of controls such as enrollment, over the destiny of the College.

Numerous civic organizations were welcomed to the College, including the Kiwanis, Rotary and Lions Clubs and the Women Toastmasters. The College also housed the archives of the Moraga Historical Society, until such time as the citizens were able to raise funds to construct a Moraga Historical Society addition to the new Moraga Library. The first recruits for the new Police Department were interviewed at Saint Mary's, and Citizen-of- the-Year dinners were celebrated on campus, as were dinners and meetings of various civic and service organizations.

A positive outcome to a worrisome series of events was resolved with the help of a Moraga Police Department intern. In March and April 1983, the College was beset with a series of vandalisms beginning with the scratching of new classroom doors in Galileo Hall, the old science facility, by means of a beer opener. A short time later at about 9 p.m., at night a fire hose on the top floor of Dante Hall, a classroom building, was disconnected and the valve opened. Water flooded the hallway and was coursing down the stairways when a student entered the building to study in one of the classrooms. He alerted the nighttime janitorial staff who notified me. The janitorial staff and I armed ourselves with mops, buckets and squeegees and pushed the water out of the building. We opened doors and windows to dry out Dante Hall before morning classes. A few days later a similar form of vandalism occurred in De La Salle residence hall, flooding the first floor. At almost the same time, several small fires set in different places on campus, including a residence hall, pushed the vandalism to a level calling for police action. Toward the end of April a crude and despicable sort of vandalism occurred in one of the large restrooms in Dante Hall. Graffiti was written on the mirrors with fecal matter. Janitors found the task of removing it offensive. After, this act occurred several times, a Moraga Police intern offered to hide in a closet in the restroom in an attempt to discover the culprit. Within two days the intern identified and apprehended the vandal, a disgruntled premed major who had not received a positive recommendation for medical school admission by the School of Science advisory committee. Though the young man admitted to the flooding and door marring as well as the graffiti, he would not admit to the fires. He was dismissed from the College, and the vandalism, including the small fires, ceased.

A cooperative project aimed at beautifying the major vehicular corridors in the Town was arranged by the Former Mayor, Margaret DePriester, Mayor Barry Gross and myself. I agreed to participate in building a traffic island with a left-turn lane at the entrance to the College on St. Mary's Road. The College would then maintain the island and its landscaping. The task was accomplished, beautifying both a part of Moraga and the entry to the campus.

The Beginning of a Pre-Renaissance, 1976-1977

Brother Jerome West, FSC, 1918-2002

Brother Jerome West, FSC, a 1940 *Maxima Cum Laude* graduate of Saint Mary's College, was a native of Montana, born in 1918. Following commencement, he became an insightful, energetic teacher and basketball coach at Christian Brothers High School in Sacramento. Awarded an master's degree in economics from the University of California, Berkeley, in 1947, he was assigned to Saint Mary's College in the School of Economics and Business Administration where he became head of the department. In 1953 Brother Jerome was selected as Principal and Religious Superior of Saint Mary's College High Residence and Grammar schools in Berkeley. After six years he was then named Provincial Visitor of the Christian Brothers on the West Coast (1959-1968). His mother, Katherine Noonan West, parish organist and nonagenarian, had Irish roots and his father, William West, a butcher by trade and an octogenarian, was of German stock. One would not have to be a geneticist to conclude that ancestral genes had a profound influence on Brother Jerome's character. Intelligent, organized, neat, articulate, congenial and intense, he was competitive yet compassionate, purposeful but sensitive, steadfastly traditional but realistically adaptive.

In 1968 following his term as Provincial, he was assigned to be Secretary of Finance for the Christian Brothers Province and the following year was asked to serve as Vice President for Development at Saint Mary's College. His ability to charm College supporters, from Trustees and Regents to alumni and friends was an asset of extraordinary value. College alumni who enrolled in his classes in economics in the '40s and '50s will testify that he was demanding, incisive and intellectually astute in his role as economics professor, and alumni of the '70s through the '90s who resided in More or Guerrieri Halls will speak with fondness and appreciation for his wise counsel and friendship. It is true that a few may have groused when he insisted on quiet hours or on lowering the boom on some seniors who were given to sophomoric partying, but they all knew he was both the *boss* and a friend. In a position of authority, Brother Jerome set certain limits in his own mind and was uncomfortable with anyone who operated beyond them, be they students, colleagues, faculty, theologians or even close associates, such as myself. Yet he exercised his management skills with a shrewd assiduity. He controlled his domain, whatever it might be, so that it remained well within the purview of his practical judgment. As a member of the Administrative Council or

116

administrative team, he could be a strong voice in pursuit of ideals he held close to his heart.

Brother Jerome was clearly productive. His first major capital campaign was professionally planned with the assistance of fundraising consultants, Barnes and Roach, Inc. Members of the Boards of Regents and Trustees, Development Staff personnel, and alumni volunteered for solicitation tasks. Enthusiasm prevailed. When it became evident that the original goal of $31 million would be achieved a year prior to the estimated end of the campaign, the campaign leaders agreed to continue for the full five years which concluded with garnering over $50 million in cash and pledges.

Partial to athletics, Brother Jerome played golf and tennis regularly until arthritis limited him to tennis and hiking. A basketball coach in his early years as a secondary school teacher, he was an avid Gael basketball fan and supported other sports as well, becoming a worldwide traveler with the rugby team by accompanying parents and rugby fans. He supported with vigor the concept of appointing a full-time athletic director following the dismal 1969-1970 basketball season and was an outspoken advocate for the construction of a pavilion to replace the tired, ill-maintained, bandbox Madigan gymnasium built in 1929. A personal friend of George and Elaine McKeon, he was instrumental in securing funds for the construction of the McKeon Pavilion. With Ernie Kent as head basketball coach, Brother Jerome was invited to be the personal advisor to the players, a role he relished. He occupied a seat at the end of the bench for most home games. There is no doubt that Brother Jerome's advocacy of athletics contributed to the expansion and improvement of both the facilities and the program.

His Irish heritage bequeathed him a natural charm and personal concern for others that endeared him to many and his views on various topics became familiar, since his dedication to the mission of the College was paramount. Brother Jerome was profoundly committed to the Catholic nature of the College and frequently mentioned the need for a critical mass of dedicated Catholic faculty members. He was also concerned with securing endowment for student financial aid and expressed concern that the College was moving in the direction of secularism. Committed to maintaining a balance between male and female enrollment, he advocated a strong athletic program, especially football, to attract males, while at the same time acknowledging the value of the expanding women's athletic program.

Brother Jerome expressed his intention to retire from Development work early in 1992 as he had reached his 72-year mark. After nearly two years, when his replacement did not fit the needs of the College, he was asked to reassume the role of Vice President for Development until a successor could be named. With the appointment of Michael Ferrigno in 1994 as Vice President for Advancement (the *au courant* term for Development), Brother Jerome was able to relinquish the reins and relax with the title of Vice President for College Relations. A victim of cancer, he left the College for the Brothers' retirement center at Mont La Salle, Napa, in 2000 and was called to his eternal reward on Dec. 1, 2002, the 84th year of an energetically and productive academic and religious life.

Emerging from Poverty
Developing the Development Office

In addition to personnel dedicated to raising funds, the Development Office also included the Direction of the Alumni Association and the Public Relations and Publications Offices. The esteemed, articulate and debonair President Emeritus (1934-1940), Brother Albert Rahill, FSC, was an active, gracious and eloquent asset to the Development staff, especially for older alumni who recalled Brother Albert's leadership with abiding fondness.

Within a few years, the funding for many facilities, activities and the all-important College endowment was promoted through an expanding Development Office staff that grew to 13 by 1997. Working in tandem with the Development staff, the Publications and Public Relations offices, another six people, joined in the fundraising effort along with the Alumni Office through alumni annual fund and the alumni reunions.

Brother Jerome was assisted by a Development Director, who aided him in meeting with individual donors, be they members of the Boards of Trustees and Regents, alumni or friends of the College, in organizing Regents' meetings and a multitude of dinners, luncheons and special events. In succession, Steve Camp, Jim Pantera and, Michael Ferrigno served as Development Directors. When Brother Jerome retired as Vice President for Development in 1992 and his selected replacement did not fit the Saint Mary's environment, it became clear that Michael Ferrigno was best qualified to assume the office of Vice President for Advancement in 1994.

Mr. Dennis Koller, '66, MBA, headed the Planned Giving program; Jack McClenahan, '66, the President's Club; and Ron Turner, '79, Susan Collins, Kathy Barsi, '93, and Mark Roberts served as full-time members of the Development staff along with Maureen Allen, '77, and Kelly Pipes, who managed Gaelsports.

Brother Albert "The Prince" Rahill, FSC, 1900-1983

A native of Ireland, Brother Albert Rahill was blessed with a golden tongue enhanced by a cultivated vocabulary. He was associated with the College for more than 60 years, beginning with his freshman year at the Oakland Campus (The Brickpile). After serving in secondary schools in California and as principal at Saint Mary's High School in Berkeley, he was selected to be President of the College in 1935 and served in that position until 1941. His years as President were during the dark days of national depression, when Saint Mary's suffered foreclosure only to be spared by the Archbishop of San Francisco, Most Rev. John J. Mitty, DD. But they were also the glory days of Gael football under the legendary Edward P. "Slip" Madigan followed by coach "Red" Strader. After his Presidency, Brother Albert spent a year at Manhattan College in Riverdale, New York before returning to Saint Mary's. He served as Dean of Students for many years, as Admissions Director, and then as an active member of the Development Office, serving as spokesperson for the College at gatherings of alumni and other groups. His skill as a mellifluous orator was particularly evident when he spoke at the inauguration of the late Joseph L. Alioto, '38, as Mayor of San Francisco. Alioto had served as student-body president for his senior year during Brother Albert's presidency.

Brother Albert's appointment as President in March, 1935, made him the youngest college president in the nation. As President he inherited a nationally acclaimed football power; an unusually fine faculty; including the talented and renowned writer and orator, Brother Leo Meehan; a small, all-male student body; and an institution of singular architectural beauty-all on the threshold of insolvency. The formidable task facing this young Christian Brother would have been overwhelming to a man of lesser mettle. He weathered the threats, the bankruptcy, the criticism and the penury of the depressed '30s, but by the end of his term in office in 1941, the College had been stabilized.

Brother Albert was an ambassador *par excellence*. His love for the College, its students, Trustees, Regents, Alumni and friends burned with an unquenchable fire, as witnessed by his keen interest in a variety of student activities, alumni affairs, Regents and Trustees meetings; in the miles he traveled as ambassador and team moderator; and in the countless letters he wrote and phone calls he made to encourage, inspire, advise, beg and console.

He eschewed the crass, the crude and unseemly. If he attended an event that fell short of his standards, he would simply say that it was a "clodhopper affair." For him, every event, every publication, every activity the College sponsored should aim at raising the professional and cultural tone. Brother Albert was indeed an exponent of the great European tradition of culture, and he did pledge himself "to live as best as he could in harmony with the spirit and aims" of that tradition, a tradition he believed was at the heart of the College.

President Emeritus Brother Michael Quinn, speaking at Brother Albert's Golden Jubilee, observed that: "Style is difficult to define, but let me make just a few brief observations. Albert has been resolute without being arrogant; he has been patient without being timid; he has been compassionate without being maudlin; he has been proper without causing us pain. It is no accident that many of us called him The Prince."

It was Brother Albert's deep faith and his determination founded on faith that empowered him in his Presidency and in the many years that followed. While expressions of his faith were discreet, privately he was a man of prayer, with interest in religious life and the life of the Church and dedication to his religious community. He went to his eternal reward on April 23, 1983.

Spreading the Word

Intimately connected with both the Admissions Office and Development was the Public Relations - Publications Office. Relations with the media and publications for admissions, financial aid, alumni, athletics and fundraising were under the aegis of the Public Relations - Publications Office. Successively, Thomas F. O'Leary, S. E. Wright, Eric K. Wolff, Michael Vernetti, Michael Damer, Alan McKean and John Leykam managed the Public Relations-Publications Office. As the College expanded, the Publications Office was separated from Public Relations since the production of brochures, magazines, posters and other media for various departments required more considered planning and coordination with Development. The Public Relations Office was more concerned with current events, news releases and planning for receptions, dinners, celebrations and unexpected occurrences. Mary Lou Rudd was named the first Publications Director followed by Debbie Wambacher.

Extraordinary Factors of Support

The President's Club

During his first year as Vice President for Development, Brother Jerome attended a conference for Chief Development Officers and discovered a success story from another institution that had created a fundraising initiative know as the *President's Club*. He decided to do the same for Saint Mary's. In order to inspire donors, as well as recognize their generosity, those who had annually contributed $1,000 or more were enrolled as members of the *President's Club*. An annual thank-you black-tie dinner was held at the Fairmont Hotel in San Francisco for the couples or individuals who had supported the College during the previous year. The first *President's Club* event was hosted in the California Room of the Fairmont, honoring its first 28 members. While the Fairmont Hotel was usually the site for the event, the Trafalgar Room of Trader Vics was the one exception. That particular night William Niland, alumnus and member of the Board of Trustees and President of Diablo Valley College, delivered a fascinating minilecture on wine and wine making. Attending that evening were Mr. and Mrs. Ernest Gallo of E. and J. Gallo wines and brandy. When Earnest Gallo was informed that evening by phone that he was again a grandfather, he made an extra donation per ounce in honor of the new arrival to the Gallo family. Columnist Herb Caen spread the news the following Monday in his San Francisco Chronicle *Baghdad by the Bay* column As successive dinners were hosted, the number attending grew until the *President's Club* became one of the largest and most elegant dinner-dances conducted at the Fairmont Hotel.

The Grand Ballroom became the scene for exquisite cuisine and captivating décor. Trustee Elaine McKeon and Marcia Syufy, spouse of Trustee Ray Syufy, Sr., were particularly helpful to Brother Jerome in planning the menu and the décor. Elaine McKeon sponsored and selected the often awe-inspiring floral arrangements. Over the years the *President's Club* contributed millions of dollars to the welfare of the College and her students. Alumnus Jack McClenahan, a member of the Development staff, was assigned the responsibility for coordinating the President's Club and developing a list of potential members. In due time the minimum financial threshold for membership was increased, and by 1997 the club boasted of more than 500 members.

The Board of Regents

The Board of Regents was founded as an advisory and support group of 50 members (later increased to 55) from whom the College sought expertise, financial assistance or avenues to financial assistance (their wisdom and wealth). It was often from the Board of Regents that future Trustees were elected. The Board of Regents was established in 1952 by the then President, Brother W. Thomas Levi, FSC (1950-1956). When Brother Thomas proposed the introduction of a group such as the Board of Regents, the suspicion of some Brothers and other faculty members viewed the proposal as a subversive plot to replace the authority of the Board of Trustees. Though the term *Regent* is employed by the University of California to identify a member of the governing body of the University, there was no intention of creating a Saint Mary's Board of Regents to replace the Board of Trustees. The term *Regent*, however, did carry a prestigious aura. The Board of Trustees endorsed the concept, though Brother Alfred Brousseau, FSC, PhD, the Provincial at the time, was alleged to have expressed his concern that establishing a group such as a Board of Regents, with many business executives or people of means might be indicative of a lack of faith in God's Divine Providence. In consultation with L. M. Giannini, President of the Bank of America and the son of its founder, Brother Thomas was able to contact a number of potential Regents for the Board. One of those, Andrew Lynch, President of Marsh, McLennan & Cosgrove, Inc., Insurance Brokers, was elected as the first President of the Board of Regents. As the organization developed, the Board of Regents became a source of impressive financial support through the largess of such personalities as Fred Ferroggiaro, George McKeon, Raymond Syufy, Sr., Remond Sabbate, Carlos Freitas, Ed Ageno, Jerry Fitzpatrick, Frank Filippi, Silvio Garaventa, Peter Bedford, B.J. Cassin, Bernie Orsi, Hon. Arthur Latno, Jr., Linus Claeys, Alfred Fromm, Dean Lesher, Y. Charles "Chet" Soda, Ken Hofmann, Ross Yerby and Carlo Zocchi, to name but a few. The Regents were also responsible for various activities, among them the inauguration of the successful and impressive Executives' Symposium in 1958. The inspiration for the Board of Regents by the late Brother President Thomas Levi, FSC, was an extraordinary legacy bequeathed to the future of the College.

Presidents of the Board of Regents, 1968-1998: Carlos R. Freitas, JD, 1968-1970; Valentine Brookes, JD, 1970-1972; John J. Reilly, Jr., 1972-1974; Carson Magill; 1974-1975; Y. Charles Soda, 1975-1977; George R. Gordon, JD, 1977-1978; Albert E. Stevens, 1978-1980; Albert E. Maggio, 1980-1982; Thomas G. Kenney, 1982-1984; Hon. Arthur C. Latno, Jr., 1984-1986; Elaine McKeon, 1986-1988; Hon. Donald D. Doyle, 1988-1990; Maryellen B. Cattani, JD, 1990-1992; Giles Miller, MD, 1992-1994; Charles H. Shreve, 1994-1996; C. Joseph Crane, 1996-1998.

Executives Symposium

The Executives Symposium was originally designed as an overnight seminar, bringing Bay Area executives to the campus for discussions on salient business topics. The initial concept was to engage business leaders in seminars on the state of the economy as analyzed by speakers who were outstanding business or political leaders. The name *Symposium*, in keeping with the Liberal Arts traditions of the College, was taken from one of Plato's *Dialogues* on the nature of love. However, the Executives' Symposiums concentrated on the love of free enterprise rather than on the enterprise of free love. In the early days of the Symposiums participants resided overnight on campus in students' rooms, since they were held during a second semester break, usually before Easter or the week between the January Term and the second semester. The symposiums, with modifications in time and format, were conducted consecutively from 1958 to 1995. The format was eventually emulated in various forms by a number of institutions in the Bay Area, so much so that its effectiveness at Saint Mary's waned, because enrollment declined and noted speakers became more difficult to secure. Principal speakers for the Symposium were people from the business world, as well as environmentalists, statesmen, professors and authors.

Participants heard from personalities such as Walter Hoadley, Executive Vice President and Economist, Bank of America; Ben F. Biaggini, CEO, Southern Pacific Co; Otto Miller, Chairman of the Board, Standard Oil of California; General Lucius D. Clay, Board Chairman, Continental Can Co.; Charles Gould, Publisher, San Francisco Examiner; Jerome Hull, President, Pacific Telephone Co.; Paul Erdman, Author; John Gray, President, Standard Oil Co.; Casper Weinberger, Vice President, Bechtel Corp.; Ernest Arbuckle, Chairman, Wells Fargo; John Place, Chairman and CEO, Crocker Bank; S. Donley Ritchey, Chairman and CEO, Lucky Stores; Drew Lewis, Secretary, U. S. Dept. of Transportation; Hon. Ronald Reagan, Governor, State of California; Cornell Maier, Chairman, President and CEO, Kaiser Aluminum and Chemical; A.W. Clausen, Chairman and CEO, Bank of America; William R. Hearst III, Editor and Publisher, San Francisco Examiner; Hon. George R. Deukmejian, Governor, State of California; Paul Tagliabue, Commissioner, National Football League; Mervin D. Field, Field Research Institute; Michael D. Eisner, Chairman and CEO, Walt Disney Co.; Hon. Dick Cheney, Secretary of Defense; Condoleezza Rice, Provost, Stanford University; Lynn Martin, Former Secretary of Labor; and Stanley Skinner, President and CEO, PG&E. The complete list includes more than 170 speakers, since there were four to five speakers for each Symposium for 37 consecutive years.

Saint Mary's College Guild

During the gloomy days of the Great Depression, the late Nell West, spouse of alumnus Fred West, DDS, and colleagues such as Mrs. George McKeever, began one of the first development activities on the Saint Mary's Campus, primarily to aid students with financial need. Since 1939, the unassuming but unwavering devotion of the Saint Mary's College Guild has provided scholarship assistance, library funding and Chapel support through various fundraising enterprises. Annual rummage sales and fashion shows, monthly luncheons, occasional teas and similar events have contributed more than

$850,000 to student financial aid alone. If the figure were adjusted to reflect the value of dollars from the 1930s onward in current terms, the total figure would be significantly higher. In 1938-1939, tuition was $175 and room and board $550 per year, a total of $725. Tuition in 1996-1997 was $14,980 and room and board $6,909, a total of $21,889.

Realizing that the College library is an essential adjunct to offering quality education, the Guild has made consistent contributions to the library fund. The College Chapel has also been the recipient of Guild largess in terms of vestments and other liturgical accoutrements, notably through the late Marie (Jess) Hoeslick, past President (1953-1955), who personally created numerous liturgical vestments. This remarkable group of women, assisted from time to time by sons, daughters and spouses, has been a model of inventive projects, generous effort and dependable results.

Presidents of the Saint Mary's College Guild, from 1969 to 1998, were: Emily Tierney, 1969-1970; Rena Molinari, 1971-1973; Margaret Waters, 1973-1975; Virginia O'Farrell, 1975-1977; Helen Hildebrand, 1977-1978; Carmela Nilan, 1978-1979; Marion Gizzi, 1979-1981; Margaret Waters, 1981-1982; Lillian Whalen, 1982-1983; Mary Power, 1983-1984; Lois Demaria, 1984-1985; Helen Mury, 1985-1986; Barbara Garcia, 1986-1988; Eva Lopez, 1988-1989; Peggy Osuna, 1989-1990; Marjorie Banducci, 1990-1992; Jo Brown, 1992-1994; Barbara Molinelli, 1994-1996; and June Allen, 1996-1998.

Saint Mary's Associates

The Saint Mary's Associates, initiated under the guidance of Brother Xavier Joy, Vice President for Development in 1963, developed an ingenious program to support *Great Teachers Fund*. The purpose of the *Great Teachers Fund* was to enhance the academic quality of the College by recruiting and retaining quality professors. The fundraising dinner held in Oliver Hall, the stately student dining room, would feature selected Hollywood Stars who would be presented with an award for their contribution to American entertainment as well as their service to humanity. The award was named the Genesian Award in honor of Saint Genesius, the patron of actors and actresses. The President presented the award to the recipient celebrity and the celebrity responded with a short performance or remarks to the delight of the dinner guests. The man who was able to persuade Hollywood celebrities to travel to Saint Mary's to receive the honors was Mike Connolly, a syndicated columnist for the Hollywood Reporter.

The impressive array of Stars began in 1963 with Dennis Day, longtime Irish tenor for the Jack Benny Show, followed by Jerry Lewis in 1964 and Bob Hope in 1965. Ann Blythe was the 1966 recipient and the "Schnozz" Jimmy Durante in 1967. Danny Thomas charmed the audience in 1968 and Kaye Ballard in 1969. Connolly was honored during the 1965 event by being presented with the President's Award for his extraordinary service to the College. When he was called to his eternal reward in 1966, the Associates found it more difficult to secure further talent. Through the intervention of Regent Raymond Syufy, '40 (Century Theatres) and Regent Louis Lurie (Geary and Curran Theaters), the Associates were able to invite several other notable performers to participate. Comedian Milton Berle appeared in 1971 and singer/actor Tennessee Ernie Ford in 1972. Les Schult, an artist and designer of Rose Parade floats who then taught art at La Salle High School in Pasadena, introduced me to Dale Olson, an energetic and suave young agent for several cinema celebrities. He persuaded dancer, singer and actor Gene Kelly to appear in 1973.

Space in Oliver Hall was limited and similarly the audience. Given the investment of time and energy involved by the staff and a shift in priorities by the Development Office to the newly formed President's Club, a concept that promised greater development possibilities, as well as the continuing interest in the successful Executives' Symposium, the Genesian Award dinners were discontinued. With a larger venue, showbiz know-how, and TV exposure, the Genesian Award ceremonies could have become an exceptional public relations and fundraising event. However, the time and place were not advantageous in 1973, and the Associates were disbanded after the Gene Kelly event, as successful as it was. Perhaps at some other time the Genesian Award concept will be resurrected, and again the College could capitalize on its potential but in a more grandiose and dramatic way. The starting point is a contact in Hollywood with someone who has both felicitous relationships and strong bargaining power with the Hollywood celebrity world. Such a contact could begin the reintroduction of the event.

Regent Albert Maggio, John Murray, Campbell O'Neill, Michael Nelson and Linda Kavanaugh served as presidents of the Saint Mary's Associates from 1963 to 1973. An impressive Board of Directors was also listed, i.e., Karl Webber, John W Broad, Ed Ageno, Mario Ciampi, FAIA, John O'Leary, Francis Scarpulla, James Scatena, Henry Walker, Harold Williams and others.

Contra Costa County College Committee

Alumnus George Gordon, JD, President of the Contra Costa Community College Board and well known Contra Costa political personality, was pleased to lend his name and assistance to forming the College-County Scholarship

Committee in 1966. The Committee had two purposes; to create a community relations program between the College and its neighbors in Contra Costa County and to provide scholarship assistance to both current students and hopeful applicants with financial need from Contra Costa County. Antioch jeweler Ben Goldberger served as early chairman of the Committee with members Jack Amato, George Deeds, Anthony Dehaesus, Angelo and Fred Fagliano, Jerry Fitzpatrick, Art Fleuti, Major John Kennedy, Al Maggio, Jerry McCormick, Al Silva, Stan Skoog, Jack Snow and Karl Weber. Brother Albert served as liaison with the College. Additional members were recruited as the Committee gained more enthusiasm and attention. Gil Phelps of the Martinez Morning News-Gazette, Captain Russell Magill, USN, Al and Rita Compaglia, John and Patty Compaglia, Jerry and Dori Davi, Bob Ebert, Deputy District Attorney, John McTigue, Moraga Fire Chief Ed Lucas and his spouse Carol, Garry Grant, Binny Hindman, Jim and Carol Hatch, Susan Williamson who served as treasurer, Suzzane Hagin, Andy Chantri, Bert Peterson, Ted Schaefer, Ted Budach, California Highway Patrol Capt. Ed Jelich, Dr. Ray Kan, Doug Konig, Dan and Nilda Rego, John Leykam, Dwight Meadows, Joe Motta, Ted Schaefer, Frank and Virginia Wooten, Michelle Wright and Bill O'Malley, Jr. all played significant roles on the College-County Committee with its exceptional benefit to the students of Saint Mary's College.

The initial means for inspiring donors to support the program was an old-time barbeque and open house at the commencement of the academic year in September and a golf tournament in the fall. With the introduction of club football in 1967, a scrimmage was also open to participants. Barbeque master, Art Fleuti, part-owner and manager of the local Moraga Barn, baked tender barons of beef the old-fashioned way by burying them in the ground surrounded by glowing charcoal embers for many hours before the festive crowds lined up for succulent slices of his deft artistry. Though the scene was a clearly picnic, even a person with gourmet tastes would be gratified. Such activity required hard work by a group of devoted volunteers. Al Compaglia assumed the reins of the Committee in 1973 with William O'Malley heading the Annual Golf Tournament. While the barbecue was a successful venture, ticket sales leveled off by 1974, and a more venturesome event seemed to be in order. The Committee developed a concept for 1975 that anticipated greater revenue by encouraging wider participation from the sophisticated Contra Costa area, namely a College-County Wine Festival, raffle and wine auction. Committee members sold Festival and raffle tickets in advance of the event throughout the County and set up booths and tables on the campus Ferroggiaro Center for the expected turnout. The organizers were not disappointed. A story is told that future Sheriff Warren Rupf and

Deputy District Attorney John McTigue, College-County Wine Festival Vice President, vied for the honor of selling the most tickets in advance. He who sold the most was to be hosted at dinner by the other.

The College-County *Wine Festival* and eventually *The Wine and Food Festival* caught the attention of connoisseurs, epicures and gastronomes and those simply interested in cultivating their taste in near-divine nectars. Eight wineries participated in the first *Wine* Festival in 1975. By 1997, 39 wineries were involved, along with several restaurants and other food purveyors. The raffle and auction of cases of wine and select magnums was a significant source of scholarship funds. Many notable County figures, from judges and attorneys to the Sheriffs, Dick Rainey, (later a State Senator) and Warren Rupf, and the District Attorneys, Bill O'Malley and Gary Yancey, were volunteers as well as donors and patrons. Mike Verlander, then proprietor of *Prima Restaurant and Wine Shop* in Walnut Creek, served as advisor and then president of the Wine Festival. He also conducted a preview for selected guests the night before the main event. Both the Wine/Food Festival and the annual golf tournament garnered significant funds for the scholarship program, aiding numerous students from Contra Costa County.

The list of those contributing time and effort for the Wine Festivals and Golf Tournaments from 1967 to 2001 was extensive. The Festival was discontinued in 2002 in view of declining interest from volunteers who had invested years of work and increasing competition from others who emulated the Wine Festival, as well as increasing liability and insurance coverage requirements facing both organizers and the College.

An alphabetical List of Wine Festival and Golf Tournament Volunteers: Ed Ageno, Jack Amato, Ted Budach, Maureen Byrd, Hon. David Calfee, Sherman Carey, Mike Cleary (KNBR), Al and Rita Compaglia, Jack Danelovich, Jerry and Dori Davi, George Deeds, Harold DeFraga, Anthony Dehaesus, Lotus East, Capt. T. R. Eddy, USN, Hon. Nancy Fadden, Angelo Fagliano, Fred Fagliano, Joe and Phyllis Famiglietti, Jerry Fitzpatrick, Art Fleuti, Major James Gerard, Tim Gilmore, Ben Goldberger, Steve Gonsalves, George Gordon, Jim and Carol Hatch, June Harding, John Hesler, Ed Jelich, Dr. Raymond Kan, John M. Kennedy, California Highway Patrol Capt. Paul LaTour, Fire Chief Ed and Carole Lucas, California Highway Patrol Capt. Russell Magill, Al Maggio, Jerry McCormick, Sheriff Warren Rupf, John McTigue, Hon. William O'Malley, Jim Pantera, Bert Peterson, Gilbert Phelps, Virginia Ramelli, Connie Rusk, Henry Schulz, Tom Sheedy, Al Silva, Stan Skoog, Mike Sloan, Jack Snow, John B.Towne, Mike Verlander, Sam VonRajcs, Karl Weber, Susan Williamson, and Hon. Gary Yancy.

Chairs and Co-chairs of the Barbecues, Wine/Food Festivals and Golf Tournaments: Ben Goldberger, Al Compaglia, Michael Verlander, Hon.William O'Malley, Art Fleuti, Jerry McCormick, Jack Towne, Jerry Fitzpatrick, Bert Peterson, John Hesler, Jerry and Dori Davi, Jake O'Malley, Jim and Carol Hatch and Susan Williamson.

The National Alumni Association

The National Alumni Association includes graduates from any degree program offered by the College. Between 1969 and 1997 there were 26,297 baccalaureate degree, graduate degree, and paralegal certificate recipients from all programs conducted by the College. The Association is guided by a Board of Directors under the direction of the Alumni President, who is elected annually by the Alumni Board, and the Alumni Director and staff, who are employed by the College. The Alumni Office conducts the Annual Fund, a telephonic fundraising effort with alumni volunteers. Class reunions, usually convened for each class every five years, are conducted every summer. Other alumni activities either conducted or supervised by the Alumni Director and staff are: Alumni Chapter events in various venues, MBA and International Chapter events, Younger Alumni events, the annual Homecoming, Annual Alumni Awards, the Alumni-Faculty fellowship grants dinner, the alumni Great Books discussion groups, the Athletic Hall of Fame, post-basketball game socials, Alumni Wine Tasting, and whatever other kinds of social or fundraising events will bring alumni together to endow scholarships or to support other worthy College causes.

A list of Alumni Directors and Presidents, 1969-1997, can be found in the Appendix on page 353.

Saint Mary's East Bay Scholarship Fund, Inc.

Joseph Shally, '32, was a one-man wonder in his initiation of and consistent devotion to the Saint Mary's East Bay Scholarship Fund, Inc. The Fund began modestly in 1955, when invitations were sent mainly to alumni in the East Bay to attend a scholarship fundraising dinner at the Claremont Country Club in Oakland for $100 per person. The dinner, combined with the Treasurer's Report by long-term Treasurer Dick Logan, JD, and the pro forma election and reelection of Officers, is the only fundraising event conducted by the organization since its founding. At the insistence of some long-term members, attendees were presented with Planned Giving information that in a few cases encouraged the increase of the Fund endowment. President Joe Shally demonstrated a remarkable feat of memory year after year by introducing, without notes, each participant, together with his or her employment and position, a task that became more challenging as Joe aged and as the group expanded from the small Country Club dining room to the Lakeview Club atop the Kaiser Center on Lake Merritt, in Oakland, and then returning to the largest dining and reception room at the Claremont Country Club when the Lakeview Club suspended operations.

Saint Mary's East Bay Scholarship Fund, Inc., boasted $1,264,824 in its endowment portfolio in 1997 and contributed approximately $50,000 per year to provide financial aid to students from the East Bay. Only once did the organization deviate from funding scholarships, and that was when it sponsored the acquisition of the large brass bell that had called students to Chapel at the original Saint Mary's Mission Road Campus in San Francisco between 1870 and 1889. When the College moved to Oakland, it left both the Mission Road Campus and the bell to the Archdiocese of San Franciscio. The bell was purchased by the East Bay Scholarship Fund, Inc. from the Archdiocese in 1988 to commemorate the 125th anniversary of the founding of the College. Cast in 1870 at Troy, New York, the bell now rings on special occasions from a specially built tower over the passageway between the Chapel arcade and the courtyard on the west side of the Chapel.

When Joe Shally was called to his eternal reward in June 1993, the presidency was assumed by Lawrence Appel, JD, '64, who remained president until May 2003, when he was named Superior Court Judge for Alameda County. Attorney J. Randall Andrada, '72, a longtime member, assumed the reins from the Honorable Lawrence Appel. There have been many donors, large and small, to Saint Mary's College since its founding in 1863. Between 1969 and 1997 there was a continued increase of generous benefactors from among alumni, many of whom faithfully send an annual donation through the Alumni Annual Fund to support College projects and financial aid for needy students. Alumni, parents and friends have expressed their generosity by providing assistance, from the construction of needed facilities to enlarging the endowment for student financial aid and the establishment of faculty chairs. Assistance has been generously provided by both living donors and through estate planning.

Student Antics

Risky Business

At the break of dawn on a wintry Saturday morning in 1977 as I was walking across the campus in front of the Chapel in the semi-darkness, I discerned something unusual on the statue of Mary that stands in a niche at the top of the Chapel façade. As I came closer, I saw that a dark blue sweater was wrapped around her shoulders. That was surprising enough, but how the sweater happened there was astounding. A lad called D.J. and two of his friends found an abandoned sweater on a bench late one evening and thought that placing the sweater on Mary would be both a mystery and grist for local "who done it?" conversation. At about 2 a.m., and after alledgedly warding off the cold with a beer, the three climbed the roof of the Chapel. With his two friends aiding him, D.J. lowered himself down the façade, placed the sweater on Mary and was then hoisted back. The harrowing part of the story was the process of successfully accomplishing the task. The Moraga Fire Department removed the sweater a few weeks later by using its longest extension ladder on its largest fire truck during one of its regular practice runs on campus.

The Barn - A Major Watering Hole

Following a costume dance on Halloween in 1977, a group of students decided to enjoy a nightcap at the Moraga Barn, a former bar since closed and remodeled into offices. One of the revelers, a charming young coed who had attended the Halloween dance, was costumed in an authentic habit of a Dominican nun. An attractive Sister Jane (Jane Barnett from Bakersfield) still costumed, journeyed to the Barn with her colleagues. When she entered the building, a strange silence came over the crowd until she walked up to the bar and said, "A real cold beer, please!"

Barn Again!

An alumni event was held in Oakland one evening attended by Vice President Brother Jerome West and me. At the end of the gathering, several alumni urged both of us to drop in to an after-the-event party at the Moraga Barn. We both decided it would be interesting to drop by on the way home and did so. The Barn was crowded with Saint Mary's alumni and friends, and after making the usual greeting rounds, we both decided it was time to return to the College. As we left the Barn, three young men were entering. One seemed to be in no shape to be visiting a bar, since he fell into the flower bed just outside the entrance and had to be retrieved by the other two. Neither Brother Jerome nor I recognized them, and we went on our way. We had left just in time. The three arrivals, coming from a Cal game, went into the bar and discovered the large gathering of Gaels. One made disparaging remarks questioning the manhood of the Gaels and the confrontation was on. Police were called to quell the shindy, one police officer, a Saint Mary's alumnus, was injured in the melee. Brother Jerome and I concluded that deciding to leave when we did was Providential inspiration.

The Campus as a Work of Art, 1928

Kazuo Goto, Campus Architect, 1969-1997

Mr. Kazuo Goto, AIA, a resident of Berkeley and graduate of UC Berkeley, had extensive experience in building schools, churches and houses. I had met him in Madera, Calif., where he was completing finishing touches on a handsome new home. He had also been the architect of the well-appointed local Catholic church in city's downtown. I spoke to him about his architectural vision for the College and was impressed with his concepts. After consulting with a campus *ad hoc* committee I selected Goto, who immediately began work on renovation plans for Aquinas Residence Hall. He also took stock of the campus and realized that renovation, new construction, utility, drainage, parking and landscaping challenges faced by the College were long-term, requiring in-depth engineering and architectural planning. The commitment and stability of an on-campus architect working in tandem with effective fundraising efforts would be the key to fostering quality architectural standards in the spirit of the initial creative plan of John J. Donovan, AIA, the original architect for the College (1927-1928). The College was both a creative challenge and an opportunity for augmenting a unified work of art, similar to the building of the great cathedrals of Europe that required the coordination of successive architectural visions over a period of many years.

Following his graduation with a degree in architecture from the University of California Berkeley, Kazuo Goto engaged with a local architectural firm. However, his career plans were traumatically interrupted when he and his wife, Haru, (both native San Joaquin Valley Californians) were interned during the first portion of World War II. In the second half of World War II, they were not allowed to return to California, and he secured employment on the East Coast. Following the war he returned to California and worked for William Buckley, AIA & Associates before entering private practice. Goto was particularly sensitive to the original 1928 design by the Donovan Firm and thought that new buildings should capture the rhythm, scale and proportion of the initial award-winning concept.

Goto's principles, while not mimicking those of architect Frank Lloyd Wright, did resemble them in some respects. He believed that the residence halls should be scaled to make students comfortable in their home away from home, that new facilities should complement existing facilities as well as the natural terrain, and that there should be a dynamic balance within the campus. Every new building would shape the feeling of the campus for generations and thus lines of sight, walkways and coordinates, with the Chapel at the center, were considered with the care the original plan envisioned. He saw his role as creating a rational sense of proportion for an academic community. He believed in an honest simplicity and that each building should be subservient to the meaning and spirit of the whole campus and not to the self-image of an individual architect, which was an unusual attitude in the competitive world of modern architecture. Goto also believed it was crucial that he be present daily during the construction process to supervise both contractor and subcontractors and to provide architectural assistance as needed. In due time, Goto moved his architectural offices to campus to be available for supervision, discussions necessary for planning, the creation of architectural drawings, the interchange with city and county planning representatives, and the supervision required in revising campus infrastructure. He was assisted for 18 years by Gregory Collins, a talented, loyal and conscientious designer and a graduate of University of California, Davis, and whose four brothers, one his twin, are alumni of the College. Other assistants included Mitch Bolen, project supervisor and Ed Thorpe, who provided Computer Assisted Drawing expertise to the office. Goto retired in 1997 at the age of 81. Greg Collins, who was mentored by master architect Goto for more than 18 years and considered to be an excellent designer by him, assumed chief responsibility for the architectural and engineering services. He was assisted by Gary Ng, AIA.

The Moraga Campus

Brother Joseph Fenlon, FSC, was Provincial when the Moraga campus of Saint Mary's College was constructed between 1927 and 1928. He was fully cognizant of the significance of architectural quality, construction standards, choice of location and unity of design in a collegiate campus. The selection of John J. Donovan, AIA, as architect was an inspired choice, since he had designed a number of educational facilities in California and appreciated Brother Joseph's architectural instincts. In his address on the occasion of the blessing of the cornerstone by Archbishop Hanna, DD, of San Francisco, on Aug. 5, 1928, Brother Joseph asserted that "the principle of environment in education was of prime importance." He further observed that, "In harmony then with a first principle of pedagogy, and bearing the tradition of the age-old Church, the Brothers of Saint Mary's set about the selection of a site that might become a veritable thing of beauty, even of grandeur, for the students destined to their care." (*The Late Years of Saint Mary's College*, Matthew McDevitt, FSC, page 88, Saint Mary's College Archives.)

When the campus was opened on Sept. 13, 1928, an auditorium and library were yet to be constructed. A gymnasium and pool were added a year later. With the Stock Market Crash of Oct. 1929, completion of the Donovan Master Plan came to an end. It was not until the occupation of the campus by the U. S. Navy Pre-Flight program in 1942 that extensive new building occurred. However, the Navy buildings were starkly functional, and most were clearly temporary. With one exception, no Navy facility took into account the existing Donovan architecture or Master Plan. After the Navy left campus in 1945, most of the Navy structures were removed. Only two major Navy buildings were retained by the College. One of them was Assumption Hall, which underwent extensive renovation in order to be utilized by the Christian Brothers as a residence hall for the Scholasticate, that is, for the young Brothers being educated at the College. The second remaining facility is the building attached to Dryden Hall that was used following Navy occupation as an annex to the library housed in Dryden Hall, and subsequently as the College little theater and then the bookstore. It is now part of the Cassin Student Union. A small College bookstore built by the Navy was attached to De La Salle Hall but removed in 1970. What was once the Navy maintenance shop was converted into the U.S. Post Office, then a ticket office for athletics and a physical education classroom and eventually as a cultural center for both Hispanic and African-American students. This structure was removed in the late 1990s to make room for the new science facility.

The first permanent buildings added to the campus after World War II were Mitty Hall (1959), named after the late Archbishop of San Francisco John J. Mitty, DD, and Justin Hall (1961), named after Brother Justin McMahon, first Provincial-Visitor of the newly formed San Francisco District-Province and President of the College (1868). Architects selected for these facilities were on an *ad hoc* basis, and neither the architecture nor the construction standards were of a quality that matched either the comprehensive vision of the campus as a work of art or the distinctive architectural standards of the original Donovan concepts. Other facilities such as Beckett and More residence halls, the College library (St. Albert Hall) and 1965 additions to the kitchen were also designed by *ad hoc* architects, though the exterior design of both Beckett and More Halls resembled the original concept. Unfortunately, the architecture and construction standards failed to measure up to the 1928 facilities. The *work of art* that Donovan conceived as crucial to a comprehensive educational environment and a total aesthetic design was obscured, due in part to financial exigency but also to the absence of an imaginative overview and lack of awareness in astute architectural development on a collegiate campus.

Under the presidency of Brother Michael Quinn, a more imaginative campus development plan and a modest capital fundraising program had been initiated. A campus master plan was designed by well-known Bay Area architect Mario Ciampi, FAIA, the architect for the Holy Spirit Parish/Newman Center near UC, Berkeley, and the University of California Art Museum on Bancroft Way. The Ciampi plan represented numerous conversations with administrators as well as with Trustees, Regents, faculty and students. One salient suggestion emerging from the discussions was that the College become coeducational. In 1965 an addition to the dining areas by an *ad hoc* firm provided faculty, guest, and several other dining areas along with offices for the College food services, but these additions were not in keeping with the campus architectural scheme. They were removed in 2008, thankfully, to make way for an addition to the kitchen and a more appropriately designed faculty-staff dining area. With the assistance of federal loans and grants for College residence hall construction and library facilities, a new Saint Albert Library facility and two student residences were constructed, but they ignored the plan conceived by Ciampi. The residence halls, named after two English martyrs, Thomas Beckett and Thomas More, were erected in 1967 to accommodate a total of 86 students, appropriate for either men or women, with apartment-style living. Each unit contained three double occupancy bedroom/study rooms, restroom facilities and a too-small front room. A much needed three-story library facility was completed in 1967-1968, with an estimated service capability for 1,000 students. In the summer of 1969 two major renovation projects were commissioned under architect Jack P. Cochrane, AIA. Dante Hall, the major liberal arts classroom and the residence portion (top two floors and attic) of De La Salle Hall, often called Senior Dorm, were refurbished.

Shortly after arriving on Saint Mary's, I invited several architects to campus to consider an appointment as the permanent campus architect in order to design needed facilities. I sought candidates who viewed the campus in terms of a comprehensive artistic plan in keeping with the original vision and spirit of the 1928 masterpiece. A campus architect would also control the architectural appetites of other architects who may be commissioned to do certain facilities, such as a theater or athletic facilities, so that any new construction would conform to an architectural plan consistent with, or complementary to, the original Spanish Mediterranean architecture and quality building standards.

It was critical that the Development Office work closely with the Architecture and Engineering Office, so that coordination in terms of needs, costs and timing could be effectively achieved. Upholding the architectural standards consistent with a vision of the campus as a work of art was often difficult.

With a campus architect on hand, agreement was usually achievable and projects were so designed and managed to conform to projected estimates.

The extraordinary effort of both the Development and the Architectural and Engineering Offices resulted in the completion of the following projects between 1969 and 1997:

Renovations:
- Dante Hall Classroom facility, 1969
- De La Salle Hall residence, 1969
- Aquinas Hall residence, 1970
- De La Salle Quadrangle, 1974
- Augustine Hall residence, 1977
- Galileo Science facility, floors 1 & 2, 1980
- Galileo offices, top floor, 1982
- Pool enclosure and Madigan gym showers, 1984 (also listed under athletic facilities)
- Dante Hall offices , top floor, 1984
- Graduate business offices in Assumption Hall
- East Wing of the Chapel arcade, 1992
- Central heating plant decentralized, facility turned into exercise room, 1992
- West Wing of the Chapel arcade, 1996
- Chapel remodel, three phases, one each summer, 1995-1997
- Chapel organ, 1996-1998

New Facilities:
- Ferroggiaro Center, LeFevre Theater and Quad, 1973
- Sabatte, Syufy, Thille and Freitas Townhouse residence halls, 1973
- Sichel Hall, biology facility, 1976
- Hearst Art Gallery, 1977
- Albert Rahill Athletic Center, 1978 (also listed under athletic facilities)
- Brother Cornelius art classrooms, 1979
- Guerrieri East and West Townhouse residences, 1980
- Claeys Hall, North, residence, 1984
- Claeys Hall, South, residence, 1987
- Michael Ageno Hall, residence, 1988
- Soda Center, Claeys Lounge, 1989
- Tim Korth Tennis Courts and Club house, 1990 (also listed under athletic facilities)
- Majorie David Ageno Hall, residence, 1990
- Ferdinand and Camille Hall, residence, 1990

- Frank and Olivia Filippi Hall, administration, 1991
- Brother Jerome West Hall, administration, 1991
- Mary Candida Garaventa Hall, high-tech classroom facility, 1996
- Chapel quadrangle and statue of Saint La Salle, 1997

Athletic facilities:
- Football stadium, 1972
- Practice field, 1972
- George McKeon Pavilion and Brother Albert Rahill Athletic Center, 1978 (noted above)
- Renovation of pool and showers, 1984 (noted above)
- Timothy Korth Tennis Courts and Clubhouse, 1990 (noted above)
- Silvio Garaventa, Sr. soccer field, 1990
- Patrick Vincent rugby field, 1991
- Renovation of central heating plant as an exercise room, 1992 (noted above)
- Stadium expansion, 1996

Projects in Planning, 1997

Several projects were in midconstruction, renovation or planning by June 1997. The Chapel and organ projects were in the last summer of a three-year cycle. Since the Chapel was needed during the academic year, the renovation project was confined to summers. The project (including organ) was completed in the 1997-1998 academic year. Brother Dominic Berardelli, in conjunction with the Architectural Office guided the fundraising effort for Chapel renovation and redesign. Brother William Woeger, FSC, from the Diocese of Omaha, Neb., and a nationally recognized liturgical artist, inspired the redesign for the most part. Plans were on the drawing boards for new science facilities, not only to provide state-of-the-art facilities for science majors, but to provide liberal arts and business and economics majors with the opportunity to experience hands-on laboratory science and an understanding of the scientific method so prevalent in almost every facet of life. Also on the drawing boards was a performing arts facility, suitable for collegiate theater and dance, to be located opposite the Soda Center and designed by both Kazuo Goto, AIA, and Borra, Inc., AIA, of Portland, Ore., experts at designing performing arts facilities, including the Robert and Margrit Mondavi Center for the Performing Arts at UC, Davis. The construction of a new performing arts facility would then allow the Le Fevre Theater in the Ferroggiaro Center to accommodate an orchestra, ensembles or a chorale, assuming the plans for a music instruction and practice facilities were completed nearby. Two additional town house residence halls were also in the design process through a gift from Ed Ageno to be named in his honor.

Schematic drawings for additions and alterations adjoining the Ferroggiaro Center were generously funded by Brendan J. and Bebe Cassin. Mr. Cassin was chairman of the Board of Trustees and his son, Jonathan, an alumnus. A new music and dance instruction facility near LeFevre Theater and an Economics and Business Administration facility, a computer center, Communications Department classrooms, TV Studio, editing rooms, and so forth were also in the design stages. The computer center and communications facilities were to be funded through a pledge granted by the three-member Kalmanovitz Foundation Board of Directors, one of whom, alumnus Bernie Orsi, '65, was a member of the Board of Trustees. Drawings for a physical fitness center as well as expanded athletic facilities, including a new swimming pool, were also to be funded in part by the Hofmann Foundation. The relocation of the baseball field to a space not far from the existing football practice field was termed a *dream* athletic facility by the local press. An advisory council formed by Dean Edwin Epstein, JD, for the School of Economics and Business Administration developed schematics and elevation drawings for a proposed new facility for both graduate and undergraduate divisions of the School to be located between Filippi and Galileo Halls. An agreement was reached between the College and the Town of Moraga to remove the power, telephone and TV cable lines from the front of the campus, considered by the Town as part of the Moraga Scenic Corridor. The costs for placing utility lines underground during the summer of 1997 were shared equally by the College and the Town, the latter having received a grant from Pacific Gas and Electric, Inc. The project was completed under budget.

The Fine and Performing Arts, 1969-1997

The fine and performing arts in the history of the College resembled that of the often neglected and yet at times acclaimed stepchild. The apparent stepchild's fortunes were usually dependent on the strong interest of an individual faculty member and/or the fluctuating interest and patronage of chief administrators. Although the fine arts, including the performing arts, are different from the liberal arts in their transmission of impressions and ideas, there is an interrelationship based on an evocation of wonder and perception within the two kinds of arts. Some philosophers who view the College as a medium for developing the intellectual life tend to be Platonic in judging the fine and performing arts as distant from developing the life of the mind. For those few, juxtaposing intellectual cultivation alongside the fine and performing arts evokes a haunting fear that intellectual purity is somehow compromised. On the contrary, the intuitive element in the lives of all men and women alike is one effective means that moves one toward both emotional and intellectual integration and even toward an insight of religious faith as well. Pope John Paul II in his *Letter to Artists,* April 1999, observes: "Every genuine art form in its own way is a path to the inmost reality of man and of the world. It is therefore a wholly valid approach to the realm of faith, which gives human experience its ultimate meaning." The power of fine and performing arts, thoughtfully and expertly exercised, cannot be undervalued in creating a sense of awe, insight and wonder. Cultivating the intuitive powers may well move and inspire many students to discover profound truths about reality, themselves and their personal relationships. Participation in creating an artwork such as a play, performing in a musical ensemble or a dance troupe may well bring satisfaction and a sense of what it means to be an authentic professional by devoting oneself to achieving quality results.

Some faculty have objected to expanding the fine and performing arts, with the rationale that the College should not become a fine and performing arts conservatory. Developing a conservatory, however, had not been a consideration in expanding a basic, but quality, academic program in the fine and performing arts. To paraphrase John Henry Cardinal Newman in his discourse on liberal education, I can say that the College is not engaged in training fine and performing arts students to be professional actors, dancers or musicians, but should one or more emerge from the College, faculty can rejoice in such individual accomplishment and likewise rejoice that while students pursued fine and performing arts, they had the opportunity to drink heartily from the intellectually formative fountain of the liberal arts.

The fine and performing arts should occupy an essential educational place in cultivating the perceptions and disclosing the "hidden meaning of things," as Pope John Paul II notes in his letter. "As a director and actor," Professor Dan Cawthon observes: "I am keenly aware of a process that all who are involved with theatre must undergo in order to give birth to the production of a play. It involves grappling with and overcoming darkness. For long weeks, the director, actors, designers and technicians are challenged to surrender themselves to the demands of the play, to discover and enter into its action, its characters, its world. One of my favorite moments in theater occurs when, immediately before a performance, the house goes black. Wonder reigns. The actors backstage, the technician in the booth, and the audience in the auditorium, for a second, are united silently in a darkness charged with the promise of splendid life. As the lights go up, that which is new and unique appears, quickening the hearts and spirit of all who perceive it.

"I am suggesting that the process of creating a new work of art is similar to the experience of faith. For the pivotal decision of faith is whether to trust the unknown darkness which engulfs our being. The primary teaching of Christianity is that the mystery which surrounds us and underlies our entrances and exists on the stage of life is *life giving*, though it is perceived as indifferent and arbitrary. It is loving, though hatred and evil abound within our midst. Faith invites us to trust the darkness we fear - including death. As we do, our spirits are quickened into authentic life, grounded in the transcendent mystery which has us in its grasp. Our blindness falls away. We see. We understand the world and ourselves in a new way." (Dan Cawthon, *Art, Its Role in Catholic Higher Education,* Update Magazine, Vol. 20, no. 4, Summer 1999.)

Music

Early historical reports on the fine and performing arts at Saint Mary's name Frederick Scborcht (1845-1936) as the conductor of the Saint Mary's Orchestra and band for three and a half decades (1869-1904). (The Late Years, Brother Matthew McDevitt, page 118) Faculty members Abbe Jean Ribeyron (choral Director) and Roberto Sangiorgi (Glee Club director) organized a tribute to Giovanni Pierluigi de Palestrina in 1931 with Father Ribeyron's San Francisco Cantoria singing Palestrina's *Mass of Pope Marcellus* in the College Chapel. Father Ribeyron also directed the Student Brothers choir with remarkable success. Mr. Joseph McTigue (bandmaster 1934 – 1951) gained notoriety as leader of the silver helmeted Saint Mary's College band, composed of both students and Gael enthusiasts who played for athletic events, commencements and other occasions until McTigue retired from the position shortly after the discontinuance of major football competition in 1951. Monroe Kanouse directed a Saint Mary's all-male chorus from 1962 to 1968. The chorus produced a respectable 33 inch recording of selected works. When Kanouse was named Director of the San Francisco Opera Chorus, Edward Lowman accepted the baton as music director for two years. Greater depth and versatility was added to the Gael choruses when the College became coeducational in 1970. Peter Gaffney, AKA Juan Pedro Gaffney, '62, who later became director of the impressive San Francisco Coro Hispanico, directed the glee club from 1972 to 1975. Computerized music and a crustacean instrument were introduced by Ed Tywoniak, EdD, MA, Mus. to the music program beginning in 1977. The music program, however, required monitoring by a seasoned academic, namely, Brother Carl Lyons, FSC, who chaired the program from 1979 to 1987, at which time the music program was combined with dance and theater. The music program expanded gradually as other musicians were appointed. Pianist Nancy Rude joined the faculty in 1979. Frank Ryken arrived in 1981 to direct choral music, and Scott Connolly took the reigns in 1989, forming a new choral group with the moniker, the NightenGaels. Mori Achen, classical guitarist, joined the faculty in 1982, and composer Martin D. Rokeach, PhD, became a strongly influential member and music director in 1984. Rokeach has acquired distinctive honors for his compositions and has had his work performed at numerous national conferences and festivals. He has also been awarded several commissions to compose music for diverse instruments. His works have been both published and recorded. Brother Martin Yribarren, FSC, PhD (music with emphasis on organ) joined his music confreres in 1995. The major reconstruction and renewal of the College organ in 1997 was meticulously supervised by Brother Martin. The renewed instrument was the cover feature story of the November 1999 issue of American Organist, and since that time several concerts co-sponsored by Saint Mary's College and the local chapter of The American Guild of Organists have graced the College Chapel. Brother Martin has composed and published works for both choir and organ, and because of the acoustical attributes of the Chapel and the quality of the organ, several acclaimed organists have cut recordings in the Saint Mary's Chapel.

Theater

Newspaper reviews in 1921 praised the work of the famous lecturer, Brother Leo Meehan, FSC, who wrote and directed *Dante, the Wing Bearer*. He continued to direct other dramatic works well into the 1930s, as did Professor

Louis LeFevre (1892-1948) of the History Department who wrote, directed and acted in numerous dramatic productions. Yale Meyer assumed the reins of dramatics director after World War II until 1954. One of his productions, *Behind These Doors* (1950), was authored by a young Saint Mary's English Professor, George P. Elliott, whose short stories appeared for several years in *The Best American Short Stories*. He also authored a novel whose cast of characters resembled many Saint Mary's personalities. Entitled *Parktilden Village*, it entered both the hardcover and paperback markets. Brother Matthew Benney, FSC, was intensely interested in dramatics and dramatic criticism and in 1954 became the "drama" portion of the English and Drama Department appellation when he assumed direction of dramatics from 1954 to 1976. Ill health, the result of an auto accident, forced Brother Matthew to retire from directing dramatics in 1976, when Brother Charles Marin, FSC, was presented with the keys to the theater, but under the aegis of the Communications Department, not English.

Though both Brother Matthew and Brother Charles were committed to theater arts and produced some collegiate quality work, it was not until Professor Dan Cawthon became a member of the College faculty in 1980 that a greater depth and breadth informed the College stage, and progress was made in combining the disparate performing arts activities and courses. Brother Carl Lyons, a member of the Religious Studies Department who had significant interest in music, was influential in combining music, dance and theater into a single academic entity. When he stepped down as chair of the program in 1987, Dan Cawthon assumed direction. Rebecca Engle was appointed to the theater faculty in 1983, and Frank Murray joined the performing arts faculty in 1989, directing *You Can't Take it With You*, by Kaufman and Hart, and *The Life of Galileo*, by Bertolt Brecht. Michael Cook came to the performing arts stage in 1991 as set designer for many productions as well as directing *Little Women* by Marion DeForrest and several January Term productions for local children. The January Term productions initiated Saint Mary's students to the complexities of staging a play. Cook also has written a one-man play on the life of St. John Baptist De La Salle that he has performed for a number of Christian Brothers' institutions.

It was not until 1993 that the Music, Dance and Theater Program was granted full departmental status as the Performing Arts Department with Dan Cawthon as chair. Professor Dan Cawthon's doctoral studies encompassed both theology and literature. Because of his various ventures in radio and on stage as drama critic and actor, he holds membership in Actor's Equity Association. A talented addition to the faculty as well as the Performing

Arts Department, Cawthon performed for the Berkeley Repertory Theater, the San Jose Repertory and the Berkeley Shakespeare Company. He also starred in a compelling one-man play, *Damien*, the story of the leper-priest, Father Damien de Veuster of Molokai, Hawaii, performing it over 60 times from San Francisco to Edinburgh, Scotland. Cawthon brought an appreciated professionalism to the Saint Mary's theater program. He directed such titles as *Antigone, Man From La Mancha, Joseph and The Amazing Technicolor Dreamcoat, The Importance of Being Earnest* and Brian Friel's *Philadelphia, Here I Come*. He has also been concentrating his literary efforts on Irishman Brian Friel's extensive dramatic work, as well as that of Irish-American playwright Eugene O'Neill, and his doctoral thesis featured an analysis of O'Neill's work, especially *A Moon for the Misbegotton*. Cawthon serves as Vice President of the Eugene O'Neill Foundation and has directed a dozen plays at Tao House, O'Neill's former home in Danville, Calif. He was also the author of the text for the tribute to O'Neill embodied in stone markers near the Danville community theater. Dan has taught in Religious Studies, Performing Arts and Extended Education, and for years has shepherded his January Term students to the Sundance Film Festival in Dark City, Utah. He has had a profound and effective influence on the academic quality of the liberal arts, performing arts, Extended Education, the Master's Program in Liberal Studies and the Catholic and Lasallian mission of the College.

Some of the notable plays and performances on the St. Mary's stage under Brother Matthew Benney, FSC, were *Tartuffe*, by Moliere, in 1970; *Man for All Seasons*, by Robert Bolt, in 1971; and *Hadrian VII*, by Peter Luke, in 1974. Under the direction of Brother Charles Marin, FSC, the highlights were *Waiting for Godot*, by Samuel Beckett, in 1976; *Grease*, by Jim Jacobs and Warren Casey, in 1977; *One Flew Over the Cuckoo's Nest*, by Dale Wasserman, in 1978; and *Equus*, by Peter Shaffer, in 1980. Director Dan Cawthon produced *Carnival*, by Bob Merrfill and Michael Stewart, in 1982; *Sweet Charity*, by Neil Simon, Cy Coleman and Dorothy Fields, in 1984; *The Importance of Being Earnest*, by Oscar Wilde, in 1987; *The Crucible*, by Arthur Miller, in 1988; *Joseph and the Amazing Technicolor Dreamcoat*, by Andrew Lloyd Webber, in 1990 and *Man From La Mancha*, by Wasserman, Leigh and Darion, in 1997. Assistant Director Rebecca Engle also directed several notable performances such as *Miracle Worker*, by William Gibson, in 1983; *Winners*, by Brian Friel, in 1985; and *House of Blue Leaves*, by John Guare, in 1994. For a complete list of directors and productions 1969-1997, see the appendix, page 357-358.

Prominent student thespians (1969-1997): Norman Denning, '70; James Reedy, '70; Stephanie Jennel, Holy Names College, '70; Coralee Blewett,

HNC, '70; Bob Schiffler, '70; Randal King, '71; Will Gesilbracht, '72; Frank Ditullio, '73; Adrienne Lamb, HNC, '71; Michael Sullivan, '72; Mary Chamberlain, HNC, '71; Maureen Grabill, HNC, '71; Leonard DeFilippis, '74; Kirk Trost, '78; Julie Paris; Joseph Kutyla, '78; Gregory Patterson, '78; Kelly Keith, '78; Roberta Corning, '79; Jose Valera, '79; Steve Kubicki, '78; Stephen "Bucky" Herron, '79; Silvia Burgos; Lorna Lynch, '89; Roy Disney, 79; Maggie Hernandez; Steve Caruso, '79; Joseph Girillo, '80; Kerry Gallagher, '80; Beth McBrien, '80; Kevin McKenna, '81; Jorge Sierra, '81; Phil Nash, '81; Kathy McKenna, '81; John Housen, '82; Kelly Young, '81; Mary Donovan, '81; Louis Lotorto, '83; Janet Martinez, '83; Ann Batko, '83; Sharon Healey, '83; Alison Ehlers, '84; Alisa Becerra, '85; Eric Casanave, '85; Louis Desmond, '87; John DeBernard, '87; Teresa Arriaga, '88; Florence Howard, '88; Bill Fahrner, '90; Michael Ball, '91; Lorien Schmidt, '92; Paul Rickey, '92; Michelle Jones, '93; Chris Brennan, '93; Mahershala Gilmore, '96; Saudia Davis, '96; and Jennifer Moore, '97.

In the early '90s, student Paul Ripple, '93, formed a group of students to present several plays in both LeFevre Theater and Delphine Ferroggiaro Lounge. Ripple surmounted several obstacles to fulfill his spontaneous effort and demonstrated his organizational leadership. As of 2004 he was employed by a motion picture/TV production company in Hollywood, Calif.

Dance

With the advent of coeducation, Claire Sheridan, MFA, was appointed to develop a dance program in 1977, but facilities for such an art form were not yet available. When McKeon Pavilion was constructed in 1978 an appropriate dance studio was included in the new facility, thus alleviating the use of makeshift accommodations. Sheridan joined with theater-arts in training students for the choreography required for musicals and plays, as well as staging independent dance such performances as *The Rites of Spring*. Her pioneering work at Saint Mary's was a first step in developing a comprehensive performing arts program and Department. Her efforts were at times frustrating, since novice material and initial lack of facilities required an enduring patience. The dance program was at first placed under the Department of Health, Physical Education and Recreation since there was no performing arts umbrella. Brother Carl Lyons, FSC, seized the opportunity to persuade the Academic Council to combine the various performing arts into a single entity in 1983 under his direction. Cooperation among the three performing arts was thus facilitated, with Sheridan providing the necessary dance expertise. In the fall of 1996 Sheridan relinquished direction of dance activities to Catherine Marie Davalos, MFA. Sheridan was instrumental in

143

establishing in Saint Mary's School of Extended Education, Liberal Education for Arts Professionals (LEAP) Program for San Francisco, Los Angeles and New York Ballet performers who wished to complete their baccalaureate degrees in anticipation of that time when their dancing careers came to an end and new career opportunities had to be found.

Fine Arts (Sculpture and Painting)

Brother F. Cornelius Braeg (1877-1962) single-handedly promoted the existence of the Art Department with courses leading to an art major. He also sought funds to develop an art gallery, and with the reduction of construction costs in mind, began a program of molding adobe bricks himself with the help of both students and friends. Brother Cornelius envisioned a gallery that would hold a distinctive College collection, with particular emphasis on the works of early California artist William Keith (1838-1911), a close friend of naturalist John Muir (1838-1914). He also authored a 600-page biography entitled, *Keith, Old Master of California* (1942) and a second volume that included correspondence, notes and other details (1956). Though the handmade bricks mounted, the grandeur of Brother Cornelius' vision loomed too large for practical and financial implementation. A gallery was temporarily installed in one of the remaining U. S. Navy buildings (later named Assumption Hall) but was moved when the College administration remodeled the facility in 1949 as a House of Studies (called the Scholasticate) for the young Christian Brothers attending classes at the College. Brother Cornelius then moved the gallery to a large room (now called the Kyran Room) that had been a tailor shop and was located behind the Chapel. There it remained, first under the supervision of Brother Cornelius until his accidental death in 1962 at age 85, then under the aegis of the Art Department chairman and faculty, and later under the joint administration of both the Art Department and volunteers from the Oakland Art Association. A modest, but exclusive, gallery and art center were constructed in 1977 without, however, the use of handmade adobe bricks. The gallery was named in honor of William R. Hearst, since major funding for the project was gifted by the Hearst Foundation, but current art center, including the gallery, art studios and faculty offices, carries the name of Brother Cornelius.

Hearst Art Gallery

From the time of the death of Brother Cornelius in 1962 to 1972, the College art gallery was supervised by the chairman and faculty members. From 1972 to 1977, the supervision of the gallery was shared with volunteers from the Oakland Art Association.

In 1977, a new Gallery, named after William R. Hearst, came about primarily through the intervention of Charles Gould, a member of the Board of Regents and Publisher of the San Francisco Examiner, a Hearst newspaper. Gould also served as Executive Director of the Hearst Foundation and was a dynamic and gracious personality, with a quick-witted sense of humor. During World War II he served as Commanding Officer of a destroyer escort for the U.S. Navy and received both the Bronze Star and the Distinguished Service Medal. Gould delivered an eloquent and inspiring address at the dedication of the Hearst Gallery on Nov. 6, 1977, reflecting his exceptional ability to deliver thoughtful and exuberant remarks, as was well acknowledged among participants of the Executives' Symposium on the campus. As a newspaper publisher he was on the cutting edge of San Francisco and California politics, and he was not bashful in disclosing his thoughts, though with cogent and often inspirational vigor. In addition, Gould was clearly dedicated to the cause of education and participated in numerous charitable organizations in the San Francisco area.

With the establishment of the new gallery, the arrangement between the College and the Oakland Art Association came to an end, and Janice Parakilas Alvarez was hired as its first full-time official curator from 1977 to 1981. Michael Damer, Director of Public Relations assumed Interim Director status until Ann Harlow was selected as regular curator/director. She served between 1982 and 1998. During her tenure a permanent Keith room was designated for gallery viewing, and both a video and booklet on William Keith were produced, as well as many other publications for the exhibits occurring in the gallery. A program featuring outstanding area artists called *Great Artists' Tributes* was instituted that included a dinner-dance and exhibits of the honored artists' works in the gallery. An administrative reorganization named Head Librarian Stephanie Bangert as overseer of the Hearst Gallery in 1993 as a logical ordering of College resource preservation. Marvin Schenk joined Ann as curator in 1986 and remained until 1999, when he was named director and curator of the Grace Hudson Gallery in Ukiah, Calif. Carrie Brewster assumed the director's role in the fall of 1999.

The Hearst Art Gallery has made its mark in the Moraga, Orinda and Lafayette area, since it offers exhibits open to Saint Mary's faculty, staff and students as well as the general public. Between 1977 and 1997 there were over 141,200 visitors to the gallery, an average of 7,062 per year, and from 1994 to 1997 the average increased to more than over 11,000 visitors per year. The gallery preserves a collection of Keith paintings numbering over 150, a few of which are regularly on display. Other exhibits, in addition to those of William Keith, have been, "Collection of Henry and Gertrude Schaefer-Simmern," 1978; "Landscapes of Linda K. Smith and Portraits by Carole Peel," 1980; "Painted Silk by Mia Kodani and Burnished Clay by Miriam Licht," 1981; "Japanese Folk Arts and Crafts," 1983; "Poseidon's Realm: Ancient Greek Art from the Lowie Museum," 1983; "Two Faces of India: Rajput Miniatures and Tribal Paintings," 1984; "Hidden Splendors: Chinese Textiles of the Quig Dynasty," 1985; "The MA Circle: Budapest and Vienna, 1916-1925," 1986; "Architectural Inspirations: Venice and Rome," 1987; "Armin Hansen: A Centennial Salute," 1987; "Vestments East and West: Japanese Kesa and European Chasubles," 1988; "Six Bay Area Women Sculptors," 1988; "Art of Our Time: Works on Paper from the Olga Hirshhorn Collection," 1989; "Rupert Garcia: Jose Guadalupe Posada," 1990; "A Collection of California Paintings," 1990; "Wayne Thiebaud at Seventy," 1991; "Maurice Logan, Artist and Designer," 1992; "Nathan Oliveira: Figurative Works, 1958-1992," 1993; "Wonderful Colors! The Paintings of August F. Gay," 1994; "Fascination with Trains," 1994; "Art for the Healing of African Societies," 1995; "Manuel Neri: A Sculptor's Drawings," 1995; "Puppets of the World," 1996; "Mark Rothko, The Spirit of Myth, Early Paintings," 1997; "Ruth Bernard, Photography," 1997; and many others.

The Gallery has sponsored two traveling exhibits from the Keith Collection, the first traveled from November 1992 to May 1995, starting in Flint, Mich. and ending in Anchorage Ala., and included such sites as Ventura, Calif., Palm Springs, Calif., Palm Beach, Flo, Baton Rouge, La, Scottsdale, Ariz., and Manitowoc, Wis. The second exhibit made the rounds of galleries between 2003 and 2005.

The gallery also celebrated distinguished local artists with exhibitions known as Master Artist Tributes. Master artists included Wayne Thiebaud, 1991; Nathan Olivera, 1993; Manuel Neri, 1995; Ruth Bernhard, 1997; and Frank Lobdell, 1999.

On the occasion of the 20th Anniversary of the opening of the Hearst Gallery, a gala formal event on Saturday, Oct. 4, 1997, featured an address from I. Michael Heyman, Secretary of the Smithsonian Institution, former Chancellor at U.C, Berkeley (1980-1990), and Boalt Hall Professor. Delivered in his characteristically dynamic and gracious manner, he discussed the importance of preserving history in its art and artifacts in museums and particularly in the critical efforts of the Smithsonian Institution and the 16 galleries and museums, the National Zoological Park, and the scientific and cultural research facilities under his supervision.

Collection acquisitions from 1969 to 1997 increased significantly in number, quality and worth. Among the more valued acquisitions on paper are 19 Morris Graves works; *Manet and the Sacred Heart,* by Rupert Garcia; 37 Roi Patridge works and 20 works by Helen Hyde. Two Emile Bernard paintings, V*enise - Campodelle Gatte* and *Femmes sur un banc;* 20 oils and watercolors by Maurice Logan; 25 additional William Keith paintings; *Resting Fleet* by Armin Hansen and *Old Adobes, Monterey* by August Gay. Art works from the Master Artist Tribute series are: *Hill Street* by Wayne Thiebaud (drypoint and color woodcut); *Figure 89* by Nathan Oliveira (photolithography); *Jollen No. 12* by Manuel Neri (oil paint stick, dry pigment charcoal); *Draped Torso* by Ruth Bernhard (photograph); *8.10.91 III* and *9.13.93* by Frank Lobdell. The galley also holds approximately 600 photographs from the Stanley Truman photography collection documenting California and including the gold country, the missions and other state sites.

One afternoon, Alan Holloway, Chief Financial Officer, was looking over a number of files that contained bequests to the College. He recalled one that had been on file for some time, and in looking over the bequest he noticed that the donors, a husband and wife, had bequeathed an Emil Bernard painting, *Femmes sur un banc,* to the College on their demise. He made a phone call and discovered that the couple had died a few years apart a number of years previously. The College had received neither notification nor the Bernard painting and several others listed in the bequest. Another phone call disclosed that the paintings were in the possession of one of the heirs to the estate. The heir acknowledged the bequest and Chief Budget Officer John Rengel was dispatched to Los Angeles to claim the paintings.

The Gallery published 27 booklets on galley exhibits between 1977 and 1996 (some of which are now out-of-print). A hardcover volume on William Keith by Alfred C. Harrison and edited by Ann Harlow was published in 1988, and a video in 1995 was entitled, *William Keith, the Artist and His Times.* The 23-minute video offers a review of some of Keith's major works, reflecting an important period in California history -- 1859 to 1911.

The Hearst Gallery was accredited by the American Association of Museums in 1990, the only art museum in Contra Costa County so certified at that time.

Artists in the Arts
Brother Kyran (Ernest) Aviani, 1929-1969
A young man who was a native of San Francisco from a Slavic background, a graduate of Abraham Lincoln High School and who then attended San

Francisco City College in 1947, Brother Kyran Aviani was drawn to the fine arts, teaching and the idea of the religious life. Encouraged by a high school friend, he entered the Christian Brothers Novitiate in 1947 and received the religious habit in 1949, taking the religious name of Kyran, not a commonly known saint's name. But the choice was consistent with an artist's creative instincts. Handsome, sharp-featured, robust, athletic, competitive and perceptive, he discovered an inner compatibility with Saint Mary's and the Great Books curriculum. Brother Kyran Aviani graduated from Saint Mary's in 1952 and within a few years was assigned to Saint Mary's College and the Art Department. He completed his Master's of Arts degree at UC Berkeley in 1957 and a Master of Fine Arts from the University of Notre Dame, Indiana, in 1961. Named chair of the Art Department, Brother Kyran represented a divergent view in both art education and artistic creativity from that of his predecessor, Brother Cornelius. With the arrival of Henry Schaefer-Simmern in 1961 as a visiting professor of art, Brother Kyran found a kindred colleague. Rewarded with a grant, he studied at Oxford in 1963. Brother Kyran was planning to travel to Ostende, Belgium in 1969-1970 to study the art of creating stained-glass windows. A drunk driver who entered Highway 101 in Marin County in a camper truck going the wrong way at night with his lights out, however, ended Brother Kyran's talented and influential life in May 1969 by colliding head-on with Brother Kyran's vehicle in the fast lane. The Christian Brothers, students and faculty were visibly saddened by Brother Kyran's untimely death. The tastefully and appropriately celebrated funeral was conducted in the Chapel filled with family, faculty and students.

Henry Schaefer-Simmern, 1896-1978

The friendship between Henry Schaefer-Simmern, an unusual and dynamic personality, and Brother Kyran Aviani, FSC, MA, MFA, chair of the department, was that of like vision in viewing the world of art and education. Brother Robert Smith, PhD, of the Philosophy Department also considered Henry a valued and close associate. Both of these Christian Brothers in their devotion to the principles of Great Books education found in Henry a compatible colleague with similar philosophical and art education principles. Henry likewise found the spirit and pedagogy of the campus for the most part in tune with his own educational perspective.

During my first year as President, Brother Robert Smith approached me regarding a Professor Schaefer-Simmern acquisition of a 15th century, almost life-sized corpus of Christ constructed with a wood base wrapped with leather. The corpus came from a small town near Lake Como in Italy. In order to ship the artwork, it was necessary, probably for economic reasons, to sever the outstretched arms from the body and package the corpus and severed arms in a wooden, coffin-like box. Since Brother Robert knew that I had experience with woodworking, he asked me to reattach the arms. I did so, but knowing full well that a practicing artisan would be more adept. However, Henry was pleased to see the corpus again in one piece and gave directions for its being mounted in the Chapel. He was also pleased to learn that I was interested in quality art for the campus and approached me with a proposal that captured my attention.

Henry proposed that on his next journey to Europe he would acquire a series of prints from the ancients to the moderns that could be mounted in the halls and stairways of Dante Hall, the main academic building. The students would thus encounter well-duplicated prints of time-honored art, paralleling their experience in the Great Books, both arranged in chronological order. I concurred with Henry in the project, and within a year he was busy with local metal artist Victor Reis, mounting the prints throughout Dante Hall. Henry then approached me with another idea, namely, that each classroom be dedicated to a certain artistic epoch. He proposed mounting the artworks, along with lists of significant achievements and discoveries, each from a distinct era, their authors and inventors in science, literature, philosophy and government. "Students," Henry claimed, "would thus learn, almost by osmosis, the history of art, the names of inventors and their inventions, significant authors and historical landmarks, as they sat in classes discussing the Great Books." Unfortunately, at the time the College was in the throes of extricating itself from financial difficulties, and Henry was able to complete only part of one room, and to fill one hallway display case with small models of early sculptures. In that first classroom, he mounted exceptional reproductions of primitive cave drawings found in the French caves of Lascaux, etched on simulated-stone backgrounds.

Henry Schaefer-Simmern was a man of intellectual principle and pragmatic application. His unbending (some have said, "undiplomatic") views on art education were reason for his termination after three years as a visiting professor of art education at UC, Berkeley. He ran afoul of the art faculty, who would have nothing to do with Henry's concept of art education. But through selected excerpts, Henry can speak for himself:

"I believe that education is not a question of putting in or stuffing in, but rather a question of drawing out." (*His Figure and His Ground: An Art Educational Biography of Henry Schaefer-Simmern*, Vol. 1, page 116, Brother Raymond C. Berta, FSC, PhD) Henry was convinced that development in visual art would also induce improvement in the human psyche. He was awarded the honorary degree, Doctor of Humane Letters at the 1975 Commencement, at which he delivered some acceptance remarks, that seem to embody a touch of Socrates:

"It seems to me that a college education cannot dismiss, first of all, an education which belongs to the mental nature of man, namely, the formation of the intuitive forces of vision … Students in a college which fosters such an education may obtain a visual judgment and, with this, the ability to transform the outside world according to a visual order built upon the relationships of form. Such a superior mental attitude is far beyond any democratically allowed permissiveness of taste. That means that in the visual shaping of this world, a democracy will rest upon an aristocracy of conscience." (Op. Cit., Vol. I, page 3).

He strongly opposed the trend of "self-expressionism," and its excesses he typified as "indulgent self-expressionism" in current art. *"Self-expression* is not a result of artistic visual conceiving in the orderly mind of man. Rather, it is the result of the other part of our existence - the devilish chaos within us…" (Op. Cit. Vol. I, page 149.)

He was particularly critical of "picture-postcard paintings," into which category he consigned those by early California artist William Keith, and advocated selling the extensive College Keith Collection in order to "purchase some worthy works of art." Henry's attitude toward Keith was clearly opposed to that of the College gallery founder, the late Brother Cornelius Bragg, FSC. Even though I admired Henry, I was not inclined to follow his advice regarding the Keith Collection, since Keith was one of the notable California landscape artists. Further I did not deem it prudential policy to allow the sale of either recognized collections or individual works of art bequeathed by benefactors, since donors assign works to the College gallery because they believe that they will be retained, cared for and exhibited from time to time. I did not wish to shake the confidence of future donors, since once an institution accepts a work of art, it is understood that the work merits retention, unless an agreement at the time of procurement would allow for its sale at some later time for certain purposes, such as the acquisition of a more critically noteworthy piece or to expand an existing and recognized College collection.

As various works of art were placed in strategic areas of the College, from the classroom and Chapel to gardens and courtyards, it became clear that the insights of Henry Schaefer-Simmern (1896-1978) and architect Kazuo Goto (retired 1997), were beginning to transform the College environment.

It is a legacy that remains in various ways, in tribute to stalwart artists of vision and optimism. Their legacy beckons others of insightful stature, authentically dedicated to cultivating the natural wonder and intelligence of students who will transform the world in creative ways because they have cultivated their intuitive perception, intellectual acumen and an aristocracy of conscience. Such are elements, among others, essential to authentic compassionate and cultivated leadership.

Artist and professor Roy Schmaltz, MFA, has chaired the Art Department since 1969. He inherited and attracted notable artists, including Victor Reis (metal sculpture), Margrit Schurman, and E. Maria Neumeyer. Schmaltz developed his own creative style and has exhibited his works in local galleries and exhibits.

Athletics: They Did it Every Time, 1969-1997

They Did It Every Time is the title of the story of Saint Mary's football authored by Randy Andrada, '73, an Oakland attorney. The title he adopted was inspired by Jimmy Hatlo, the cartoonist for the defunct San Francisco Call-Bulletin whose weekly cartoons on local football contenders was titled, *They Did It Every Time*. Hatlo's characters depicted each of the San Francisco Bay Area football teams by mascots, such as the Saint Mary's *Senior Moraga*, the San Francisco *Don*, the Cal *Bear* and Santa Clara *Bronco*. After the weekend games his follow-up cartoon would depict the fate that each team met through the posture and facial expressions of his characters.

Pig-Skins vs. Sheep-Skins

Athletics had been a source of controversy at Saint Mary's from the very commencement of intercollegiate athletics, particularly in the heyday of big-time football. During the '20s and '30s in a 400 to 900 all-male student institution, the percentage of those participating in football was significant. Some members of the faculty resented the football notoriety they viewed as over-emphasis for, they believed, the College should have been known for its academic achievements. Brother Leo Meehan had made his mark as a lecturer on English literature and other pertinent topics in the greater Bay Area, spoke on national radio for the *Catholic Hour,* was a Commencement Speaker at UC Berkeley and the University of Washington, taught summer classes at UC Berkeley, and was the author of a widely adopted collegiate textbook on English literature. He was appointed Chancellor of the College in 1931 but resigned after two years, because, some claimed, he believed that big-time football on the Moraga campus overshadowed its academic achievements. But alumnus, former member of the F.B.I. and attorney William Simon '38, who as a student drove Brother Leo to many of his speaking engagements and became one of Leo's closest friends, averred that such was not the case (*Called to the Pacific,* Brother Ronald Isetti, pages 338-339.) No one really knows Brother Leo's reasons for stepping down. His abiding academic interest in literature, poetry, writing, teaching and speaking engagements are among the more plausible surmises for his decision to relinquish the Chancellor's role. Furthermore, the sometimes unbending restraints on a person in religious life at the time may have been another impetus for seeking the freedom necessary to pursue his well recognized talents.

Yet, other strong academic personalities on campus, such as philosopher James L. Hagerty and historian Louis LeFevre, participated in the big-time football mystique, Hagerty by sitting on the sidelines as the official game timekeeper and LeFevre as former graduate manager and assistant to coach Edward P. "Slip" Madigan. Many of the Christian Brothers who were teaching in the Christian Brothers High Schools in the state considered athletics as crucial to the interests and manly maturation of the boys they taught or even coached. Though a number of the Brothers and faculty colleagues at the College were critical of what they viewed as a misguided emphasis on athletics as well as its costs, others tolerated or even accepted athletics, and football in particular, as a necessary appendage of the times, as well as a public relations, recruitment and financial income advantage. Controversy never ended on whether big-time football was, on average, a financial boon or bust to the College.

Many faculty members rejoiced when big-time football had run its course and was officially abandoned in 1951, along with baseball, though baseball did not carry with it the same misgivings as football. Some faculty members feared that the reintroduction of club football in 1967 was tantamount to the camel's nose under the tent and that it would expand as an official college sport with its attendant costs and distractions to the detriment of academic life for both athletes and faculty members who had to contend with travel, practice and game schedules, as well as other related distractions. In one sense, the reintroduction of football did require the College to assume its financial burden, as well as NCAA regulations regarding its status and conduct. It did not develop into the kind of competition that characterized Saint Mary's football prior to its discontinuance in 1951,

At the Starting Block

Saint Mary's devotion to athletics began in 1872 with baseball. From 1890 to 1997 the Saint Mary's *Phoenix* contributed a surprising 54 major league players, four of whom were starters (two on each team) in the World Series clubs of 1915. The name of Harry Bartholomew Hooper, Class '07, (Red Sox and White Sox) is inscribed in the Baseball Hall of Fame in Cooperstown, NY. Baseball between 1969 and 1997 continued to send players to the majors: Von Hayes (Indians and Phillies), Tom Candiotti (Indians, Brewers, Dodgers, Blue Jays, Athletics), James Mouton (Astros, Brewers, Expos), Joe Millette, (Phillies), Broderick Perkins (Padres), Steve Senteney (Blue Jays) and MikeYoung, (Orioles).

Football took to the gridiron in 1892, but because of excessive injuries the sport was discontinued in favor of what was assumed to be more civilized encounters on the rugby pitch. Football returned in 1915, and two years later, under the coaching of Russell "Babe" Wilson, Saint Mary's posted an 8-1-1 record.

With the advent of the draft for World War I, the College lost two-thirds of its all-male student body. After the armistice, many of the returning veterans (absent any G. I. benefits) sought whatever work they could find, and the College was left with a miniscule student body of 71 students and the task of building for the future. The Saint Mary's athletic program was unable to measure up to its competition, and the annual football game in 1920 with its crosstown rival, UC Berkeley, ended in shambles. The score: UC, 127; SMC, 0. The remainder of the Saint Mary's season was canceled. In spite of this postwar athletic fiasco, football soon became the captivating sport that brought Saint Mary's national notoriety under the colorful, determined and imaginative coaching of Edward Patrick, "Slip," Madigan, a University of Notre Dame graduate and Knute Rockne protégé, who was hired in December 1920, after describing himself to Brother President Gregory Mallon, as the, "Christmas present Saint Mary's was looking for." Following years of extraordinary success and national acclaim, Madigan's greatest triumph came on New Year's Day, 1939, with a 20 to 13 win over Texas Tech in the Cotton Bowl.

Following the Madigan era, which ended with the 1939 season and bowl game, there were other dynamic contests and two bowl games (Sugar Bowl, 1945, Oil Bowl, 1946) and such noteworthy coaches as Red Strader, (1940-1941), Jimmy Phelan (1942-1947) and his whiz kids (including the late All-American Herman Wedemeyer), Joe Verducci (1948-1949), and Notre Dame graduate Joe Reutz, PhD (1950), who a short time later became long-term athletic director at Stanford University. In addition to Wedemeyer, there were other Saint Mary's football All-Americans including Larry Betancourt, George Ackerman, Ike Frankian and Red Strader. John Henry Johnson, installed in the Professional Football Hall of Fame, was an exceptional fullback star on the 1950 team.

With the end of World War II, professional football expanded because of greater public interest and the potential income associated with growing TV coverage. Both professional and collegiate football adopted the free substitution rule enacted in 1948, replacing the old rule that prevented a player who was removed from the lineup in one quarter from returning to the game until the next quarter. The free substitution rule was at first named the platoon system by sports reporters, because it allowed the whole team to be replaced for offence or defense, thus increasing the size of the entire football team. Free substitution also allowed for specialists such as field-goal kickers. Fielding free substitution football teams moved football financing to a new level. Many smaller institutions found the costs to be insurmountable. With the Korean War (1950-1953) the Selective Service Draft was reactivated, and again the all-male Saint Mary's student body would be depleted by as much as 50 percent. It became impossible under such circumstances to continue to field both intercollegiate football and baseball and thus the Board of Trustees issued the following press release on Jan. 5, 1951: "Saint Mary's College will continue basketball as the only major intercollegiate sport, while the minor and intramural athletic programs will be reorganized to satisfy the needs of all of the students of the College." (*They Did It Every Time*, Randy Andrada, page 226.) Such institutions as the University of San Francisco, Santa Clara University Loyola University, in Los Angeles, Georgetown University in Washington, D.C. and Fordham University in New York, to name a few, discontinued big-time football a few years after the Saint Mary's decision to withdraw from competition.

In the heady days of big-time football, faculty' and coaches' complaints, at odds with one another, were voiced with increasing passion. Some coaches whined about admissions requirements, academic standards and the absence of a physical education major, factors they claimed excluded many exceptional athletes who would have been obvious assets to Saint Mary's athletic programs. They also complained that athletic scholarships and recruiting support did not keep pace with competitors, and thus promising athletes interested in Saint Mary's were lost to other institutions. Faculty members observed that student-athletes missed classes or examinations because of travel (a perennial complaint), and that some were inattentive or failed to turn in assignments on time during the athletic season because of exhausting practice, game and travel schedules. A number of faculty claimed that the academic malaise characterizing a number of student-athletes was rooted in an attitude that attendance at college was a hurdle to be endured for the sake of engaging in athletics and possibly a profitable career as professionals. Many student-athletes, however, took full advantage of the opportunity that athletic financial aid provided them to earn a Saint Mary's education. They later profited from both the education and the character formation that athletics could reinforce. Some of these student-athletes became devotedly active members of the Alumni Association, and the many who entered the ranks of teachers, coaches and public school administrators became advocates and recruiters for the College, primarily through their example, though their words of encouragement and devotion to the College were an added positive factor.

Naïve Enthusiasm—New-Era Football

In the mid-'60, student Greg Aloia became fascinated with the glories of Gael football history as found in the voluminous clippings in the College library archives and sought to regain a small part of that tradition by establishing club football. His advisor John Parziale, the Dean of Students at that time, soon became the moderator of the football club. Though some administrators and many faculty members were not supportive of this student initiative, many students were, particularly in the face of successive years of dismal performance in basketball and the absence of athletic competition during the first semester. They expressed their approval and support by allocating student-body funds to initiate the club. With encouragement from Parziale, Greg Aloia requested and was granted an opportunity to present his club football proposal to the Board of Trustees in Oct. 1966. Heartened by his interview with the Board, and with promises in hand for donated operating funds from elsewhere, a tentative schedule and team roster were formed, and a search was initiated for a coach. Aloia again appeared before the Board on Feb. 25, 1967. After Aloia's presentation, Brother President Michael Quinn uttered a Delphic-like prophesy that program expansion could not be restrained and would creep to the proportions of a major sport. Countering such speculation, Brother Jerome West, the Provincial of the Christian Brothers, and at the time an *ex officio* Board member, stated that the Board could control the level of competition, which was partially accurate, but, as it turned out, unlikely. Board member Brother Kyran Aviani, FSC, a strong advocate of rugby, opined that the program would fail, since there would not be a winning season, and thus the effort would "die of its own weight." Member Fred Ferroggiaro was of the view that the project, with Board encouragement, had gone too far to abandon. Conditions were attached as amendments to gain approval by the Board. The conditions required that the program be *completely self-supporting*, that it provide liability insurance covering itself and the College, and that no compulsory football tax be imposed on the student body by the administration. Under these conditions the Board approved the initiation of club football with a vote of 7 yea and 2 nay. The first season of resurrected Saint Mary's football was scheduled for the fall of 1967.

The faculty in general did not greet the *Football Club Initiative* favorably. Comments made during the General Faculty Meeting of January 1967 regarded Aloia's proposed football club with skeptical criticism. Some faculty considered the reinstitution of football as "step one in a program of endless expansion." Others claimed that football would cause "irreparable damage to the image of the College." Yet others were suspicious that members of the Board were pressured into approving club football by influential alumni or donors, though there is little or no evidence to support such pressure.

As anticipated, the club football program could not support itself. When the enthusiastic initiators graduated, both their enthusiasm and promises of financial support were graduated with them. Though the initial football fervor continued, the quest for funding waned. The successors to the initiators were unable or did not have the enthusiasm to secure increased funding from the student body or to generate a larger donor base for supporting the club. Shortly after the end of the third club football season in 1969, I received an invoice with penalty from the Internal Revenue Service claiming that the withholding taxes on the salary for the club football coach, George Galli, had not been paid. Investigation into club football finances revealed that the program had been operating on a shoestring, accompanied with a surmise by team members that the coach and his assistants had, like the Brothers, taken the vow of poverty. I discussed the problem of the unpaid taxes with College legal counsel, John W. Broad. The problem was brought to the Board before whom John Broad stated that if football were to continue, that College would have to assume direct control, not only in view of the IRS, but in consideration of inevitable liability issues. The team was composed of Saint Mary's students, used Saint Mary's facilities and called itself the Saint Mary's Galloping Gaels. Any attempt before a court to claim that the College was not responsible for the team or the payment of payroll taxes or would not be liable should an accident occur, was indefensible. The Board voted to assume control of the club as an NCAA sport in Division III and to settle accounts with the IRS.

The Athletic Director, a Full-Time Task

For several years the Board of Trustees had discussed the need for hiring a full-time athletic director who would not be distracted with personal coaching duties, but no action had been taken since funds were so scarce. In 1969, Elwood "China" Lang, '35, George Canrinus, '34, and Bill Fischer, '32, alumni who had spent long careers in San Francisco public education following their graduation from the College, and Dr. Louis "Dutch" Conlon, '26, retired president of San Francisco City College, made an appointment with me to express the unhappiness of many alumni with the decaying facilities and the decline and ineptitude of the athletic program, particularly intercollegiate basketball and baseball. Their casual investigation concluded that the College seemed to have assumed a principle of benign neglect toward athletics in both athletic performance and facilities. They again called for the hiring of a noncoaching full-time athletic director as the only way to begin addressing the deficiencies in a failing athletic program short of dismantling it and withdrawing from the West Coast Athletic Conference. Convinced by their arguments and bolstered by their assurances and, with Board approval,

I formed a search-and-screening committee to find a new athletic director. Some interpreted this move as a return to the days of alleged athleticism, but that was not my intention. Yet I was sensitive to the interests of students and alumni who appreciated a well-organized sports program and saw the management of athletics by a competent professional as imperative if the College was to recover from its doormat status in the WCAC, a source of demoralization throughout segments of the College, both on and off- campus.

To discontinue athletics in 1970, or to ignore its deficiencies in the face of competitive athletic programs being offered at neighboring Catholic institutions could well signal to the public that Saint Mary's had become a second- or third-tier Catholic institution that was in dire straits and would further weaken the confidence and support of the public, parents of potential students, donors and alumni, many of whom basked in the glories of past athletic prowess. Some members of the faculty suggested that improving academic quality by reducing its commitment to athletics would strengthen the attractiveness of the College as a selective academic institution, a proposal they believed had not been fully investigated. I estimated that a substantial modification in the long-term athletic tradition of the College would have required a major internal and external public relations effort necessitating the infusion of significant capital that the College did not have. A hurried, underfunded change carried no guarantee that the College would in a short time assume the image of a distinctive academic powerhouse in the Bay Area was a worthy aspiration, but such aspirations require thoughtful and patient planning, particularly in the hiring of faculty. In my view, the College had to expand its student body, facilities and an astute faculty in order to both survive and then flourish. There were those who thought that athletics played an important role in the development of character and applauded an anticipated improvement under an Athletic Director who would control the excesses of athleticism and yet provide student-athletes with the encouragement and means necessary to fulfill themselves as students.

I realized that activities with as high a profile as intercollegiate athletics should be conducted with professional skill, regardless of the level of competition but always commensurate with the mission of the College. In view of the athletic history of the College and the probable importance of recruiting males to maintain a gender balance in a future coeducational student body, the option of discontinuing or downsizing intercollegiate athletics seemed unwise, at least at the time. Moving to a lower level of National Collegiate Athletic Association (NCAA) competition, that is, from Division I to Division II or III or to the National Association of Intercollegiate Athletics would be nearly as costly as remaining in the WCAC, unless the nonscholarship option of Division III were selected. Lower level athletics would still require significant financial support with fewer redeeming benefits in terms of cost, alumni enthusiasm, the ability to recruit male and minority students, and to sustain a positive public relations image in comparison with other California Catholic collegiate and university institutions. My ultimate goal was to see the College achieve wide acclaim as an institution of indisputable intellectual quality and at the same time operate an athletic program that would bring student-athletes to the College who were interested in a quality education as they took advantage of the opportunity to participate in well-conducted athletics. Such lofty hopes, however, required planning, adequate facilities, sufficient endowment, a reasonable modicum of faculty acceptance, enduring patience and significant cooperation among administration, faculty, alumni, donors and students.

The search and selection committee for the new athletic director, otherwise known as "the AD," was composed of myself and alumni Elwood "China" Lang, George Canrinus and "Dutch" Conlan. Saint Mary's was the smallest institution in the West Coast Athletic Conference (other members in 1969-1970 were the University of San Francisco, Santa Clara University, Loyola University, University of the Pacific, Pepperdine College, the University of Nevada at Las Vegas and its counterpart in Reno, UNR) and thus to compete with its larger members, the student body per-capita cost of conducting the program was higher. The addition of club football in 1967 and its subsequent reclassification under NCAA Division III in 1969, as well as the resignation of football coach George Galli, added to the cost and personnel complexity of the athletic program and made the selection of an Athletic Director more compelling.

Following interviews of five potential candidates selected from among a much longer list of applicants, the search committee recommended that Donald J. McKillip, EdD, Assistant Athletic Director at Adams State College in Alamosa, Colo. be appointed. McKillip carried an impressive record of successful football coaching, as well as administrative assignments. He also held an earned doctorate, ideal for heading an improved Health, Physical Education and Recreation academic program. He would not act as coach but rather as administrator and faculty member. During the interview, McKillip made clear his commitment to the priority of academic life for the student-athlete. What he inherited in the fall of 1970 was a weak interscholastic program, hobbled by lack of funding, limited physical education offerings, an underfunded intramural program, insufficient staff, disinterest on the part of both alumni and local residents, and physical facilities that were in dire need of repair, replacement or expansion. His first task as Athletic Director was to appoint both a football and a basketball coach for the forthcoming academic year. Doc McKillip, as the students called him, was faced with a formidable task, compounded by disinterest among a majority of the faculty. A faculty vote in the 1972 spring semester made front page headlines of the *Oakland Tribune* on March 1, 1972. It read: *Faculty Move to Drop Sports at St. Mary's.* The student newspaper, *The Saint Mary's Collegian* responded boldly with a headline in the March 3, 1972 issue *Student Group Votes to Drop Faculty.* A student poll conducted during the following week revealed that 275 students, or 54 percent of those polled, refused to support the negative faculty vote regarding the athletic program. (*Collegian,* March 10, 1972.) Some faculty viewed the funding of athletics, perhaps appropriate for an all-male institution of the past, as restraining similar funding for programs that would enhance the academic and cultural life of the College, such as debating, summer science research for students, the hiring of needed faculty and staff, expanding academic offerings, the publication of a faculty journal and a student literary magazine as well as the development of choral and instrumental ensembles, dramatics, and the other fine and performing arts for both men and women. The faculty view concerning the use of funds for academic enhancement had merit, but the administrative response was not to downgrade an already meager athletic program but rather to emphasize the need for an aggressive, but measured, expansion of a coeducational student body and to inspire a Development Office effort leading to the addition or urgent upgrading of academic, residence hall and recreational facilities.

Don McKillip sought a football coach who was the product of an institution committed to both quality football and academic achievement. He discovered that his younger brother, Leo McKillip, a graduate of the University of Notre Dame who had played football for the Fighting Irish and held a PhD from the University of Utah, was open to accepting the head football coaching assignment at Saint Mary's. Leo McKillip's availability coincided with the move from club football to NCAA Division III. By the 1970 season, the upgraded football program was placed under the full control of the Athletic Director.

Since the role of Athletic Director also carried an appointment as chair of the academic physical education department that in 1971 consisted of seven upper-division courses, Don McKillip began planning for an improved program, including a major in Health, Physical Education and Recreation. Because Leo McKillip also held a doctoral degree, he was enlisted to serve in the Physical Education Department in addition to his football assignment. Both Don and Leo McKillip appeared several times before the Academic Council to plead for the approval of an undergraduate physical education major, since so many alumni entered the teaching and coaching professions in both public and private education. The major, first introduced in Dec. 1971, was finally approved by the Council and the Faculty Assembly on Feb. 13, 1975 (Faculty Assembly Minutes, Feb. 17, 1975). As an adjunct to the undergraduate program, Don McKillip later proposed a Masters Degree in health, physical education and recreation that was approved by the Graduate Council in 1977. The graduate program, that included the production of a thesis eventually enrolled approximately 60 part-time students in courses taken over a three-year period, mainly during summers.

When Don McKillip arrived on campus in the summer of 1970, he had an opportunity to observe the athletic summer camps being conducted on campus for grammar, junior high and high school students. The summer camps were operated by athletic entrepreneurs outside the College who rented such College facilities as residence halls and food services. The summer camp attendees lived on campus five days of each week of attendance. Approximately 78 youngsters were then enrolled in the athletic summer camp. McKillip presented me with an athletic summer camp plan to commence in 1971 that would be conducted by the College athletic department and its coaching personnel. When Don relinquished his role as Athletic Director in 1990, the program annually enrolled between 1,000 and 1,400 boys and girls each summer in such sports as football, basketball, soccer, volleyball, baseball, softball and, for a time, courses in computer science. Summer camp youngsters were instructed by the professional collegiate coaching staff, and the computer instruction was conducted by regular departmental faculty. The revenue from the summer camps provided coaches and faculty with additional income and contributed to both College residence hall operations and support of the athletic program. Partial funding for renovations of the athletic facilities and athletic stadium, built in 1973, came from the summer camp program.

A welcome addition to collegiate life, namely the entry of women into regular interscholastic athletics, complicated the role of Athletic Directors everywhere. In June 1972, reacting to the demands of women for equal opportunity in collegiate athletics, Congress amended the Educational code to bar discrimination toward women in competitive collegiate athletics. The new regulations were adopted under what has become known as *Title IX*, the common jargon that identifies the legislation banning sex discrimination in academic, residential and athletic opportunities for all students. Thus, women would have equal opportunities in terms of athletic financial support and the option to participate in a number of women's sports comparable to those offered men. The ambiguities in applying Title IX regulations led to numerous legal cases nationwide and nearly doubled the responsibilities of Athletic Directors to include the hiring of a women's Associate Athletic Director. Saint Mary's avoided legal challenges by offering women athletic opportunities and financial support required by the new laws since, both Don McKillip and the Vice President for Student Affairs, William McLeod, monitored the application of the Title IX laws with care.

When Don McKillip retired as the Athletic Director in 1989 he was replaced by Mr. Rick Mazzuto, MA, who had served as Athletic Director for Iona College in New Rochelle, NY, an institution sponsored by the Irish Christian Brothers. Don McKillip continued as chair of both the graduate and undergraduate programs in Health, Physical Education and Recreation until 1994 and taught in the department to the end of the spring 1998 semester. He also participated in fundraising activities for Gaelsports and remained a member of the President's Club. The innumerable assets bequeathed to Rick Mazzuto allowed him to plan for the future without having to begin from ground zero. Given the increase in the athletic interests of women, Mazzuto appointed Shari Otto as Associate Athletic Director with the responsibility for monitoring the requirements of Title IX and the women's athletic program and to encourage the participation of women as student-athletes.

Football Expansion

Division III meant that the football program was a nonscholarship sport. That is, student-athletes could not receive financial aid for athletic participation. The reason that Saint Mary's football moved from Division III to a higher division was that the NCAA demanded an upgrading of the football program if it were to continue in conjunction with the maintenance of basketball as an NCAA-IAA sport. The NCAA mandate was beyond the control of the Board. Changes in National Collegiate Athletic Association football status occurred through legislation enacted by the organization during its annual meetings. Saint Mary's scheduled several Division III team competitions in Southern California, but a Division III Gael team too often overwhelmed its Division III competitors which included California Institute of Technology and Claremont-McKenna College. Such institutions soon refused to schedule the Gaels. However, the State Universities, Santa Clara University, Loyola University and University of San Francisco, Division II football institutions were eager to schedule the Gaels and did so. It was therefore required that Saint Mary's declare itself a Division II institution, since it engaged mostly Division II institutions on its schedule. Being placed in Division II allowed for the awarding of financial aid to student-athletes who played football. A change from Division II to Division I-AA was mandated in 1979 by the NCAA if the other major sports sponsored by an institution were in the Division I category, which was the case with Saint Mary's basketball and baseball. Thus, the observations offered by some faculty and former President Brother Michael Quinn's speculative prophecy in 1967 were fulfilled. Though the Board had the, option of controlling,or even discontinuing the football program, as Brother Jerome stated, the arguments favoring football were persuasive enough to encourage the Board to support it in spite of its heightened ranking. The major arguments favoring football were that it would help maintain the male and ethnic minority numbers in the student body and would provide students interested in athletics with a major first semester sport, not unlike other collegiate or university institutions in the area at that time. Football would also satisfy a significant number of alumni and donors, as well as give note to the general public that Saint Mary's was competitive with its counterparts, especially in the Bay Area.

Football, 1967-1997				
Coach	Years	Won	Lost	NCAA Status
George Galli	1967-1969	12	10 (T 1)	Club
Leo McKillip	1970-1973	17	17 (T 1)	NCAA III
Jim McDonald	1974-1976	9	20	NCAA III
Dick Mannini	1977-1983	45	24 (T 1)	NCAA II
Joseph DeLuca	1984-1985	8	14	NCAA II
Craig Rundle	1986-1989	29	12	NCAA II
Mike Rasmussen	1990-1999	52 (incl. 1999 season)	46 (T 1) incl. 1999 season	NCAA I AA

Outstanding members of the football club and NCAA teams were QB Pete Kelly '67; Bob Vallon, '69; QB Jim '68, and Greg Huarte '70, (brothers to John Huarte of Notre Dame); John Blackstock, '71; Julio Lopez, '72; QB Jerry Murphy, '72; Randy Nelson, '74; James Datrice, '74, named "Little All-American;" John Crockett, '75; Oliver Hillmon, '80; QB Mark Drazba; '81; QB Tim Rosencranz, '90; kicker Kevin Shea, '79, (played in the East-West Shrine Game and a short-lived new professional league); Terry Cottle, '80; Fran McDermott, '80 (became Canadian FBL Rookie of the Year); John Arnaudon, '81; Scott Ruiz,

'82; Bryan White, '83; Marti Storti, '84; Kevin Will, '84; Andre Hardy, '85, (NFL Philadelphia Eagles and Seattle Seahawks); Warren Parker, '88; Brian Richey, '88; kicker Doug Beuerlein, '89; (Brother to Steve Beuerlein of Notre Dame and NFL); Jon Braff, '88; James Javier, '89; Frank Cavalier, '88; Cassidy O'Hara, '88; Daryl Rogers, '90; Scott Wood, '91; Miles Freeman, '91; Cree Morris, '93; Mike Estrella, '93; Peter Baichtal, '94; Lavelle Townsend, '94; Coley Connely, '94; Bonner Cummings, '95; Ricky Ellis, '96; Blake Tuiffli, '96; Tom Antongiovanni, '96; Ed Williams, '97; Sean Laird, '97; and Brandin Young, '99.

In 1988, the football team under Coach Craig Rundel enjoyed an undefeated season with a final cliff-hanger score of 27-24, against archrival Santa Clara University in the Saint Mary's stadium. In the stands was Ron Fimrite, a feature writer for *Sports Illustrated*, who praised Gaels' Coach Rundle and Quarterback Tim Rosencrantz in a colorful feature article. (*Sports Illustrated*, Nov. 28, 1988.) Fimrite also authored a major feature article on the glories of the "Slip" Madigan football era for *Sports Illustrated, Special, Fall Issue, 1992. (Vol. 77, No. 17.)* [2]

Rev. William Rewak, SJ, President of Santa Clara University, representing a group of institutions that sponsored football and a football conference (Cal Poly, San Luis Obisbo; Santa Clara University; Portland State University; California State University, Northridge; andCalifornia Lutheran College, Thousand Oaks) invited Saint Mary's College to become a member of the conference, known as the Western Football Conference. After considerable discussion among the Athletic Advisory Board, the Athletic Director and Vice President William McLeod, a report from McLeod recommended that the invitation be declined, because entry into the WFC would be too costly in terms of tuition waivers, added personnel and other financial factors to meet the competition of the conference, composed mostly of larger institutions, both public and independent. I responded to Father Rewak on March 20, 1982, thanking him for the invitation but declining the offer. (Letter of Brother Mel Anderson, FSC, to Rev. William Rewak, SJ, March 20, 1982, Administrative Council minutes and notes, Saint Mary's College Archives.)

Over the next several years, more overtures were made to entice the College to become a member of the Western Football Conference. An Oct. 12, 1983 memo to the Administrative Council by Vice President McLeod

---

[2] For an extensive and captivating history of Saint Mary's football from 1872 to 1996, see *They Did it Every Time*, by Randall J. Andrada, '73, usually available in the College bookstore (operated by Barnes and Noble, Inc.), or it can be ordered online at www Gaels.com.

noted that the Athletic Director, Don McKillip, appeared to have changed his original position on the football conference issue. McLeod's memorandum to McKillip questioned him on the extra costs, need for added personnel and the necessary change of image and spirit in the existing College football program, originally designed as a low-key program open to many students. He further questioned what effect the higher level of competition and its attendant costs would have on the status of women's athletics if equal opportunity were to be the guideline. In October 1984, further requests were made for Saint Mary's to become a member of the WFC, and on Nov. 1, 1984, the Administrative Council again discussed the invitation to WFC membership and again advised me to decline the invitation. A Nov. 13, 1984 memorandum from McLeod to the Board of Trustees reported the consensus among the members of the Administrative Council and myself that the College not join the Western Football Conference. The Board concurred. In full agreement with the Administrative Council, I thanked the members of the WFC for considering Saint Mary's, but reported that the College did not believe that it was in its best interests to join the conference.

Another plan for a conference was discussed in the Chancellor's Office at the University of California, Davis, a little later. Both Saint Mary's and the University of Santa Clara were invited to join this other new football conference. The then President of Santa Clara, Rev. Paul Locatelli, SJ, was interested in the conference and urged me to consider entering it. I was reluctant however, to join a conference with public institutions. The athletic financial aid disparity between public and independent institutions was significantly wide, since the tuition for students at public institutions is subsidized by the State. The College did not grant athletic full rides for football (room, board, books and tuition) nor did it even grant full tuition waivers to all football players.

The complaint from coaches and some alumni was that the College did not spend enough on football to field a consistently competitive team. Yet, given the record of the team from the early 1970s through 1996, the football program could be considered competitively respectable, and in a few peak years, exceptional, doing what it could in terms of financial aid and without a conference membership.

Every Football Team Needs a Stadium

Mr. Ken Hofmann (founder of The Hofmann Company, Inc.) had enrolled at Saint Mary's as a freshman to play with the Galloping Gaels, in part because of the celebrity status of the coach, "Slip" Madigan. However, he transferred to the United States Merchant Marine Academy as World War II unfolded and served with the merchant marines upon graduation from the Academy. Yet, his interest in the College persisted and when talk of building a new football stadium on campus reached his ears, he generously and personally assisted in its construction. I recall the day that Hofmann and I were on our knees rolling out the new turf for the stadium. He later served as a member of both the College Board of Regents and the Board of Trustees. Alumni, under the leadership of Bill Fischer, George Canrinus, "Dutch" Conlon, Elwood "China" Lang, Al Cinelli, Jack Bannister and non-alumnus Y. Charles "Chet" Soda, also raised funds for the project. The stadium was dedicated on Sept. 22, 1973 when the Gael season opened with a 35-0 win against Southern Oregon.

In 1996, Joe Kehoe, 77, JD, Executive Director of Campus Facilities, served on a major committee for the Pleasant Hill School Board. Since the closure of Pleasant Hill High School, the steel and wooden spectator stands stood idle and deteriorating for some seven years. The School Board was willing to donate them to St. Mary's if Joe Kehoe would remove them as soon as possible. Joe and Rich Meier, '64, planned the move. Kehoe moved the steel frames to the Saint Mary's Stadium, installed new seats and provided stairs, walkways and access ramps with the help of Ron Fadelli and Ron Fadelli, Jr., of Berkeley Cement Inc. who contributed both foundations and stairways. The stadium capacity was doubled to approximately 5,500 seats.

When for budgetary reasons, Hayward State, San Francisco State, Sonoma State and Chico State University all discontinued football between 1993 and 1998, and Santa Clara University dropped the sport in 1992, Saint Mary's was forced to schedule games at greater distances and with greater cost, though guarantees defrayed some expenses. The discontinuance of football at Santa Clara had a perceptible effect on student interest in football at Saint Mary's.

Perspective, 1997: The Future of Football at Saint Mary's

At the time of the return of club football to Saint Mary's in 1967, the University of San Francisco, Santa Clara University, San Diego University and Loyola University all fielded similar football teams. However the University of San Francisco discontinued its revived football program in 1972, Loyola University in 1974 and Santa Clara University, the major institutional crosstown rival, in 1992. San Diego remained in a lower category of NCAA competition. Santa Clara President, Rev. Paul Locatelli, SJ, observed that there were no negative effects on the recruitment of either males or minority students at Santa Clara after the discontinuance of football.

Discussions on the future of Saint Mary's football in 1995-1997 were conducted with the recommendation that close scrutiny by the Administrative Council be exercised to ascertain student interest and actual costs of conducting the
program, as well as such factors as public relations value, enrollment gender
balance, financial support from alumni and other donors, influence on admissions, and overall image with and without football. "What would happen," the
question was posed, "should St. Mary's follow the route of Santa Clara and the
State Universities in the area?" The penultimate answer was to see how the
sport and all attendant concerns, especially finances, would play out over the
next several years, leaving the ultimate decision to be based on what the best
option for the future would be for the entire athletic program and the College
in general. Football was again discontinued in 2004.

The National Collegiate Athletics Association (NCAA) Athletics Certification Experience

Abuses in athletics, especially in a number of major football institutions,
elicited criticism from members of faculties, students, administrators, the
general public, the press and even the liberal motion picture industry. Inter-
nally, there were issues raised by smaller institutions regarding the tendency
of some major athletic powers, especially those with major football teams, to
foster legislation favoring themselves in such areas as schedules, recruitment,
inducements, national tournaments and TV coverage. NCAA officials and
institutional executives were persuaded to address the issues of national concern and to develop a process for correcting abuses and certifying compliance
with operating principles applicable to all institutions in four major areas,
namely, a) institutional athletic governance and rules compliance, b) academic integrity, c) fiscal integrity, and d) equity and student-athlete welfare.

Under NCAA governance stipulations, the certification process examines issues such as whether athletics are fully under the control of the chief executive officer and the Board, whether appropriate campus constituencies such
as faculties have had the opportunity to provide input into the formulation
of policies and effective review processes, and whether outside groups, e.g.,
boosters clubs, were properly controlled. Academic integrity would include
conformity on such items as whether those student-athletes accepted for admission have a reasonable chance of graduating, that student-athletes follow
normal attendance requirements, normal grade point standards for participation, and whether graduation rates of student-athletes compare favorably
with graduation rates for the student body in general. The principle of fiscal
integrity would require scrutiny as to whether athletic grants-in-aid follow
NCAA principles; whether the influence and contributions of individuals or

boosters organizations are effectively controlled by the institution; whether operating expenses for travel, facilities, and equipment are reasonable and equitable for men and women; and whether inappropriate inducements are involved in recruitment. Equity and student-athlete welfare would include issues such as gender equity; prohibition of discrimination and provision of opportunities for minority students, coaches and staff; the fair treatment of student-athletes, especially in their academic role as students; and whether policies and practices are communicated through written materials or some other effective means; whether exit interviews are conducted; and whether grievance or appeals procedures are in place.

Federal government Title IX mandates on gender equity seriously affected the conduct of NCAA member institutions and the responsibilities of administration, athletic directors, coaches and conferences in the use of facilities, allocating finances, remuneration of coaches, financial aid, equitable scheduling and services to both men and women. In 1987, six men's and six women's sports were required of every WCAC conference member. For men, Saint Mary's sponsored basketball, baseball, soccer, golf, tennis and cross-country. For women, it was volleyball, basketball, soccer, tennis, cross-country and rowing (crew.) In 1987 only three WCAC institutions, namely, Saint Mary's, the University of San Diego and Santa Clara University, sponsored football, and thus football was not considered a conference sport.

Saint Mary's College was selected to be among the first Division I institutions to enter into the first round of the new NCAA Certification process. Saint Mary's appointed a diverse committee to begin work on a comprehensive self-study in 1993-1994. The peer-review team, chaired by Michael Ferrari, President of Drake University in Iowa, was conducted from Oct. 24 to the 27, 1994. The official notification from the NCAA stated that the College was in substantial conformity with the Operating Principles of the NCAA, citing praise for careful attention to both academic and fiscal integrity. However, Certification was delayed until the College submitted a written plan for gender equity and minority opportunities. The plan was submitted and Certification was granted on March 6, 1995.

Men's Basketball, 1969-1997

The basketball program between 1962 and 1970 was conducted under the direction of alumnus, Head Coach and Athletic Director Michael Cimino, and a series of assistant coaches, including Les Edwards, Pat Curran and Bill Van Gundy. Since some West Coach Athletic Conference teams refused to play in the dilapidated Saint Mary's bandbox gymnasium which had been construct-

Standing: Brother Albert Rahill, FSC, Assistant to the President 1962–83, President, 1935–41. Seated: Jack Brennan, contractor, restauranteur, farmer and builder of Saint Mary's College, 1927–28. Fred A. Ferroggiaro, retired chairman of Bank of America's Board of Directors, and member of SMC Board of Trustees, 1958–68.

1

2

Gesian Awards, Executives Symposiums
1. Tennessee, Ernie Ford, 1972.
2. Brother Jerome West and Milton Berle, 1971. (Not pictured, Gene Kelly, 1973.)
3. Executives Symposium: 1985, Elaine McKeon, Pres. of the Board of Regents, James Lockhart, luncheon chairman, Hon. George Deukmejian, Governor.
4. Executives Symposium, 1990: Welcoming Mr. and Mrs. Michael Eisner, CEO of Walt Disney Corp. and Mr. and Mrs. Roy E. Disney.

3

4

Facility Dedications 1. Mary Candida Garaventa Hall, 1996; Louisa Garaventa Binswanger, '77 at the podium, Mr. and Mrs. Silvio Garaventa seated on right.

2. Sichel Hall, 1976, Representative from Sichel Foundation, Mr. Alfred Fromm, President of Fromm and Sichel, Mr. Y. Charles "Chet" Soda, Pres. Board of Regents. 3. Claeys Hall South, Rev. Michael Sweeney, OP, Mrs. Ruth Claeys, Mr. and Mrs. Dean Lesher, publisher of *Contra Costa Times*. 4. Majorie David Ageno and Ferdinand and Camille Ageno Halls, 1992; Michael Ageno Hall was dedicated in 1988.

1. "Carnival," 1982, Alison Ehlers and Rob Halligan '84. 2. "Equus," 1980, John B. Housen '82. 3. "Carnival," 1982, Professor Ben Frankel and Ann Batko '84.
4. "She Stoops to Conquer," '91.

1. "Imaginary Invalid," 1983, Ann Batko '84 and Louis Lotorto '83.
2. "Man of La Mancha," 1997, Chris Olson '98, Mark Palacios '97, Jennifer Moore '97, Chris Pearl '98.
3. "The Fantasticks," 1980, Kathy Bishop and Mark Clarke.
4. "Man of La Mancha," 1997, on stairway: Michael Neward '99, Bill Frey (faculty), Paul Marvold (lead professional), Stage floor: Jennifer Moore, muleteers and cast.

1. Terri Rubenstein, womens' basketball coach, 1983–97. 2. Men's Basketball, vs. Loyola-Marymount, 1979, Coach Frank LaPorte. 3. Portrait of George McKeon, (developer and donor, 1925–76) by Bruce Leslie Wolfe

PERFECT ENDING

ST. MARY'S COLLEGE football players hoist coach Craig Rundle onto their shoulders Saturday after the team defeated Santa Clara University.

St. Mary's wins them all

4

5

4. Football, 1988, a perfect ending winning all 10 games with the final cliffhanger, 27–24 against Santa Clara at St. Mary's Stadium; Craig Rundle, coach, and Tim Rosencrantz, QB.
5. Court of Princesses, Homecoming, 1982.

1. Parodi sisters, Christopher Major, and Paul Tiernan. 2. Senior Ball, 1983, Jenine Toomey '83 and Richard Barry. 3. 1988, Richard Martin, '88 ASSMC President, and Anne Wagner, '88, Homecoming Queen. 4. Casino Night, 1979, Roy Disney '79 and friend. 5. Halloween, 1984, John Krpan '85.

ed in 1929 and had aged well beyond its spectator-friendly years, games with anticipated large attendance, as well as with those teams that declined playing at Saint Mary's, were scheduled in the Richmond Civic Center, a cross-county site. Losing seasons, distance and limited security in the Richmond area discouraged attendance. The conference basketball win-loss record between 1962 and 1970 was 30 wins and 78 losses. The Gaels were unable to win one conference game in the 1969-1970 season and only won a total of 12 out of 56 or a cumulative 21 percent for the four preceding Conference seasons.

By 1970, Saint Mary's was both a basketball and WCAC embarrassment. Poor basketball performance could be attributed to four key factors, depending on who was offering the attribution. The first was an alleged administrative disinterest in athletics, the second, financial stringency, the third, inadequate athletic facilities, and the fourth had something to do with the attitude of the coach, Michael Cimino. Cimino was a principled man who knew the sport well. For some reason though, it seemed that he had difficulty relating to student-athletes who came from financially successful families or who asked pointed questions about strategy, especially if there were any suspicion of hubris in their questions. He was a disciplinarian who did not tolerate misconduct or player arrogance on or off the court, yet, in general, he was personally caring towards his players and appreciated the priority of academic achievement. Following the 1970 season he knew that his time as basketball coach had come to an end, and when the advertisement seeking a full-time athletic director was posted, he applied for the position. Though he was articulate, candid, a gentleman and knew more than most others about both the College and the problems of the athletic department, he was not selected and subsequently resigned and entered the business world.

One of the first tasks of the new Athletic Director was to hire a basketball coach for the 1970-1971 season. After interviewing potential coach candidates, McKillip, who had coached basketball himself, was beset by a number of lobbyists favoring individual candidates. He decided on a person with age, experience and a number of successful seasons, namely, Bruce Hale, a coach well-known in the Bay Area (Bishop O'Dowd High School, University of Miami, Golden State Warriors). After three seasons, the last one including a protest by African-American players over a nonbasketball issue, Hale retired. He was succeeded by alumnus Frank LaPorte, '56 who improved Hale's 33 percent wins by 10 percent. Bill Oates, following LaPorte, came to Saint Mary's from Christian Athletes in Action and achieved a 41 percent winning record and one conference championship in 1980 that he shared with the University of San Francisco during his seven year tenure.

169

In 1989, the West Coast Athletic Conference deleted the word "Athletic" from the conference title and became known as the West Coast Conference or the WCC. Basketball fortunes further improved under a demanding Lynn Nance with 66 percent wins, a West Coast Conference championship and a place in the NCAA Tournament in 1989, the first since 1959. However, the Gaels did not advance beyond the first tournament game, losing to Clemson University. Lynn Nance was lured away by his Alma Mater, the University of Washington, following the 1989 season. Paul Landreau was hired to guide the Gaels in 1989. However, during the 1990-1991 season, Assistant Coach Dave Fehte inherited the team after Paul Landreau resigned for personal reasons. Fehte amazingly brought the team to within one game of the NCAA tournament. Some thought that Fehte should be named head coach, but Ernie Kent, who had greater experience and notoriety, was hired for the 1991-'92 season. The Gaels achieved 53 percent wins, including the championship in the 1997 West Coast Conference Tournament and a place in the NCAA Tournament, only to lose the first game to Wake Forrest. Kent was hired by his Alma Mater, the University of Oregon, at the close of the 1997 season. Assistant Coach Dave Bollwinkel was elevated to Head Coach for the 1998 to 2001 seasons, which soon became a disappointment.

The persuasive and coaching ability of the basketball mentors, the financial investment by the College, the cooperation and enthusiastic interest of alumni, the aura of the College, its academic reputation, standing in the community, adequacy of facilities and the previous win-loss record had much to do with the attraction of many student-athletes and nonathlete students to the Saint Mary's campus. A shrewd, enthusiastic coach with an outstanding record both and at the College elsewhere speaks well to prospective student-athletes. Beginning with the early 1970s several seasons and numerous contests have been acutely competitive and even thrilling. The fact that most student-athletes complete their baccalaureate degrees and venture into productive lives is a significant achievement not usually touted in media headlines. Alumni, faculty and students understand that the majority of student-athletes who came to the College would never have been able to avail themselves of a Saint Mary's education had it not been for athletic financial aid. The program is thus a fulfillment of one Lasallian ideal of granting assistance where it would truly benefit students in need.

The vitality and aspirations of the basketball program encouraged donors such as George and Elaine McKeon, Ken and Jean Hofmann and many others to contribute to the building of the McKeon Pavilion at a time when needs for College facilities were numerous and funds were not. The completion of the modest McKeon Pavilion in 1978 brought the basketball program into a competitive stance with other institutions in the area. The dedicatory game in the McKeon Pavilion, Feb. 25, 1978, hosted the Stanford University Cardinals. Though the Gaels lost the memorable and exciting McKeon Pavilion opener 62-61, the closing words in the pregame dedication by the former President, the revered Brother Albert Rahill, after whom the entire athletic complex was named, electrified the student body. "Remember," Brother Albert announced to the excitable crowd, "God is a Gael!" It was a symbolic phrase that caught the imagination of students and fans but may have caused local theologians some scruples. The fact that the phrase appeared on T-shirts, badges, caps, stickers, in the newspapers and on a large sign that was unfurled from the Tower of Pisa by students in Italy for a January course Term only accentuated the concern of some that the appealing phrase could be considered terribly irreverent.

Men's Basketball				
Coach	Year	Won	Lost	NCAA Status
Mike Cimino	1969-1970	3	22	Division I
Bruce Hale	1970-1973	26	52	Division I
Frank LaPorte	1973-1979	69	93	Division I
Bill Oates	1979-1986	86	103	Division I ^
Lynn Nance	1986-1989	61	27	Division I **
M. Landreau/ Dave Fehte	1989-1991 1991	20	37	Division I
Ernie Kent	1991-1997	90	80	Division I **
David Bollwinkle	1997-2001	35	80	Division I

**   NCAA Tournament participation, 1989, 1997

^   In 1980, Saint Mary's shared the WCAC title with the University of San Francisco.

Outstanding players identified as members of All Conference Teams were: Maurice Harper, '74 and '75; Ralph Baker, '76; Nick Pappgorge, '77 and '78; Ken Jones, '78 and '79; David Vann, '80, '81 and '82; Peter Thibeaux, '82 and '83; Paul Pickett, '83 and '84; David Boone, '84; David Cooke, '85; Eric Cooks, '85; Paul Robertson, '86; Robert Haugen, '87, '88 and '89; Erick Newman, '89; Dan Curry, '89; Erick Bamberger, '91 and '92; Brian Brazier, '93; Chris Johnson, '94; Brent Farris, '95; Jumoke Horton, '95 and '96; Brad Millard '97; and David Sivulich, '97;

Ted Wood, Team Captain, '80, Brandon Bennett, '83 and David Sivulich, '98 were named West Coast Conference Scholar-Athletes of their respec-tiveyears. Ted Wood, '80, and Mark Sulek, '83, were selected GTE/Verizon Academic All-Americans. Ted Wood was selected by his class colleagues as Valedictorian for the Class of 1980. Named to the WCC All-Academic Teams were: Brian Driscoll, '95; Eric Schraeder '96, '97, '98; and David Sivulich, '96; '97, '98. Ted Wood is now a medical doctor.

The Saint Mary's vs. Santa Clara University rivalry incites the interest and peaks the emotions of many students and alumni, as well as some faculty and administrators. Yet, relationships have been most cordial and coopera-tive. When I first came into office in 1969, Santa Clara President Rev. Thom-as Terry, SJ, was most helpful with advice and counsel. For College admin-istrators, the relationship between the College and Santa Clara University was also most cordially productive and friendly. For several years the Col-lege administration and the Santa Clara administration under Rev. Thomas Terry, SJ, President, and his successor, Rev. William Rewak, SJ, traded off with Saint Marys to put on pregame basketball dinners. The presidents, vice presidents, Development officers, athletic directors, chief financial officers and their spouses enjoyed the reciprocal hospitality, as well as mutual benefi-cial relationships on various topics throughout the years. As the institutions grew and schedules became more complex, the dinners were discontinued. However, the cordial and helpful relationship between the two institutions remained steadfast.

Baseball, 1969-1997

The Saint Mary's Phoenix baseball program enjoyed two episodes of rising from the ashes after the 1951 Board announcement. One year after the of-ficial discontinuance of intercollegiate football and baseball, the March 7, 1952, edition of *The Collegian* carried the headline, *Phoenix Arises as New Semipro Nine*. Louis Guisto, alumnus, former major leaguer and manager of the on-campus student coffee shop, *The Brickpile*, gathered together 35 hopeful players who agreed to the formation of a semipro team wearing Saint Mary's uniforms and playing top flight semi-pro and college aggrega-tions in the Bay Area. After 12 years as a semipro or club sport, alumni Bill Fischer, George "Icehouse" Wilson and Louis Guisto petitioned that baseball be restored as a regular College sport under the direction of the Athletic Department. Receiving approval in 1964, the Phoenix thus rose a second time, albeit feebly, from the 1951 Board-mandated cessation of the sport. However, the Athletic Department budget did not allow for the hiring of a full-time coach.

In 1968, baseball, by then an official College sport, suffered from budgetary constraints allowing only the hiring of part-time personnel to coach the team. Odell Youngblood (1968-1970), Floyd Baker (1970-1971) and Doug Weiss (1971-1972) stated that they could not coach, scout, recruit and personally cultivate the baseball diamond under part-time status. I agreed with them and expressed my gratitude for their devotion, but noted that I was unable to dedicate more funding to baseball and athletics in general at the time.

However, after the baseball season of 1972, it became clear that conducting the baseball program as a West Coast Athletic Conference sport required the commitment of a full-time coach. Baseball professional and graduate of UC, Berkeley, Miles McAfee, MA, was hired as full-time baseball coach in 1972. He remained head coach until the close of the 1980 season. Since that time the position of baseball coach remained full-time.

A staunch Gael alumnus who played both football and baseball and later became a referee for collegiate football contests on the West Coast, Bill Fischer, '32, was instrumental in securing funds for baseball for many years from other alumni and friends.

Coach	Year	Won	Lost	NCAA Status
Odell Youngblood	1969	9	32	Division I
Floyd Baker	1970-1971	33	49 T-2	Division I
Doug Weiss	1971-1972	21	22	Division I
Miles McAfee	1972-1980	230	189 T-7	Division I
Tom Wheeler	1981-1985	141	126 T-4	Division I
Jim Jones	1986-1989	84	142	Division I
Don Jamerson	1990-1995	133	189	Division I
Rod Ingram	1996-1998	46	101	Division I

Players named to WCC All Conference Teams were: Chris McKinnie, '71 and '72; Larrry Digliantoni, '72; Bill Kooyman, '72; Xavier Dixson, '74; Broderick Perkins, '75; Terry Van Hook, '76; Albert Richmond, '77; Tom Candiotti, '77 and '79; Rick Lewis, '82; Jeff Peterson, '82 and '83; Mark Homen, '83; Matt Castello, '83; Dave Velez, '83; Greg Redmond, '84; Ed Capozzo, '84; Ken Riensche, '85; Dan Ward, '87; Deron Johnson, '88; James Mouton, '89 and '91; Toby Freeman, '91; Chris Koeper, '91; Ryan Haley, '91; Demerius Pittman, '92; Brian Oliver, '93.

Broderick Perkins was named Player of the Year in '75

Members of the WCC All Academic Team: Kelly Asan, '92 and '94; Robert Barelli, '94; Olin Cohan, '96 and '98; Jeff Hebert, '98; Mike Waugh, '98.

Those interested in Saint Mary's baseball history may wish to read *Harry Hooper, an American Baseball Life* by Paul J. Zingg, PhD, University of Illinois Press, 1993.

Men's Soccer

Coach	Years	Wins	Losses	Ties	NCAA Div.
Matt McGhee	1967-1970				Club
George Roussakis	1971-1977				Club
J.F. Villarroel	1978	0	8		NCAA
Randy Farris	1979-1982	11	49	2	NCAA
Bob Martin	1983-1996	92	154	28	'92, Div. I
Mark Talan	1997-2000	28	46	3	Division I

As soccer became more of a national sport, Saint Mary's began fielding a soccer team in 1967 with students who were interested in the game but had minimal talent. Matt McGhee, coach 1967-1969, set forth ambitious schedules, but aspirations were soon tempered. The soccer team, or "booters" as they were called, lost its first three games in the 1969 season, but, as reported in the Collegian in November, "lost only one game in their last six. That loss came at the feet of San Jose State." Joe Blell from Sierra Leone was a standout player, as was Suphot Charenthongtrakul. Others on the team were Jack Kleinbach, Chuck Burnham, Gary Lyons, Dan Leary and Jesse Casteneda. The Gaels defeated Santa Clara 3-2 in midseason but closed the 1969 season with losses to Stanford and the Naval Postgraduate School in Monterey. Unfortunately, records were not systematically kept in the early years of Gael soccer. The 1970 season began with a loss to Santa Clara, followed by a mediocre season. Though a midseason loss to Stanford was a downer, a win over UC Santa Cruz bolstered spirits, but the Gaels lost the final game of the season to UC, Berkeley, 5-2. Joe Blell, Will Gesselbracht and Guy Kuhn were Saint Mary's College stars.

George Roussakis assumed command as head coach in 1971, facing a tough schedule with teams such as San Jose State, University of San Francisco, Stanford, and UC Berkeley. At the close of the season, Joseph Blell was named All West Coast Athletic Conference selection and also earned the Most Valuable

Player distinction. Roussakis led the Soccer Gaels through the 1977 season, when J.F. Villaraoel was named head coach for the 1978 season. It was in 1978 that soccer became an NCAA Division I sport at Saint Mary's. The soccer team was aligned with the Pacific Coast Conference until 1988, when it moved into the West Coast Conference.

Named to the West Coast Conference All-Academic team were Shawn Fitzgerald, 1996 and 1997; Ben Froelich, 1997; Scott Regier, 1990, 1991 and 1992; Jeff Yoos, 1990, 1991 and 1992; and Scott Mossman, 1990.

Randy Farris assumed the head coach mantle from 1979 to 1982. With few financial-aid incentives, the team was able to win 11 contests but lost 49 and tied two over the four-year period. Though an improvement over the 1978 record, the male Gael soccer team neither achieved the sort of notice that attracted student-athletes dedicated to soccer and greater financial aid for soccer student-athletes or even many interested spectators. After four years as men's coach, Randy Farris stated that he could manage only one team and preferred to concentrate his efforts on the women's Gael soccer team. Bob Martin accepted the reins of men's soccer in 1983, guiding the team for 13 years. The record again improved from 18 percent wins in four years to 33 percent wins in 13 years. There were notable team highlights and players in particular years that garnered attention. Bob Martin cites the 1983-1984 seasons as the turn-around time for the program, with a 3-2 win over San Jose State, in a torrential Moraga rainstorm. Randall Smith, Joey Bilotta, and Carlos Azevedo were notable booters. Mike Foy and Mike Foscalina were also standout Gaels in the early years. Greg Busch, considered a soccer iron man, Kevin Talan, Adam Bliss, and Mike Gable were vital participants. Saint Mary's participated in a Winston-Salem Tournament in 1990 and surprised No. 14 North Carolina until late in the game with a 2-1 loss and then tied No. 13 ranked Wake Forest 1-1. Juan Guarda was identified by *Soccer America* as the top freshman of the year in 1991. Saint Mary's College achieved ranking in the top 20 in 1992 by defeating No. 9 Seton Hall 2-0. Juan Guarda and John Ashworth were among the standouts. When Saint Mary's College entered Division I in the NCAA, Coach Martin considered the schedule one of the most challenging in the nation. In 1995, the Saint Mary's College Classic hosted No. 1 teams in the country with the Gaels playing the University of Virginia in an overtime game before 4,000 spectators in the Saint Mary's College stadium. "The Gaels eventually lost" said Bob Martin, "to a great team." Goalkeeper Rob McDonald was instrumental in forwarding Gael prowess that day. The Gaels earned national respect, and the West Coast Conference was acknowledged as one of the country's top soccer conferences.

Former male Gael soccer talent, Mark Talan assumed coaching duties in 1997, following Martin's reign as the Saint Mary's coach. Talan was able to increase wins by 35 percent during in his four years as mentor.

Men's Tennis

Men's tennis was a nonscholarship sport until 1980, when Coach Ted Collins was allowed one partial scholarship. Tennis also became one of the Saint Mary's men's NCAA sports in 1979. Between 1969 and 1997 men's tennis attained a kind of cottage-sport popularity among both players and spectators within the Saint Mary's campus. Its coaches, especially among the players, were both respected and, in some cases, admired. However, tennis (as well as golf) did not attain widespread campus notoriety, if one is to judge by meager coverage in *The Collegian,* the student newspaper.

Ted Collins, who guided the team from 1978 until he retired in 1994 because of failing health, succumbed to cancer on March 30, 1995. A well-attended memorial service was conducted in the Saint Mary's College Chapel. A congenial and devoted coach as well as a cultured gentleman, Ted Collins, was well-respected and admired by his players. Men's tennis coaches from 1969 to 1997 were: Vic Gill 1969-1970, (student captain and coach); Lynne Rolley, 1971-1972; Ron Noon, 1973-1975; Gerry Cotter, 1976-1978; Ted Collins, 1979-1995 (NCAA Division I sport in 1979); and Michael Wayman, 1995-.

As an NCAA, Division I sport under Coach Ted Collins, the Gaels were able to garner a .529 winning average. Collins guided the team to 220 wins over 196 losses during the 15 years he coached the team, with a 12-9 record in 1993 and 17-6 in 1994. (Coach Collins died in March 1995)

Tennis standouts were: Roland Sexhauer, 1969; Mike Oden, 1969; Brother Ronald Gallagher, 1969; Steve Tool, 1970; Vic Gill, 1971; Don Byrd, 1971; Roland Sexhauer, 1972; Rueben Hunter, 1973; Ed LaCava, 1973; Mark Bechelli, 1975; Bob Manalo, 1976; Terry Gong, 1978; Andrew Crawford, 1980; Brandt Rossi, 1980; Bob Bellerose, 1982; Greg Orrell, 1983; Kirk Giberson, 1983; Matt Glasgow, 1984; Craig Kerr, 1984; David O'Neill, 1984; Rob Pardi, 1984; Sergio Mendoza, 1984; Jon Storm, 1984; Todd Murphy, 1986; Mark Kanapeaux, 1987; Ed Ashman, 1987; Steve Finden, 1987; Mark Trapin, 1988; Mike Sindel, 1988; Dean Pournaras, 1988; Mo Gotterup, 1989;.Ole Hofelmann, 1990; Greg Kobayashi, 1991; Alex Green, 1992; Tony Pett, 1992; Santiago Tintore, 1992; Chris Sindel, 1994;. Steve Noel, 1994; Mark Aizenberg, 1994; Ronnie Campana, 1995; Saburo Waki, 1995; Brian Topping, 1996; Mike Morgan, 1996; Dirk Vlicks, 1996; Matt Grintsaig, 1996 and; Keith

Awisawa, 1996. West Coast Conference All-Academic tennis members were: Keita Arisawa, 1993 to 1996; Chris Sindel, 1992 to 1995; Stephen Noel, 1992 to 1994; and Alex Green, 1992 and Ken Parker, 1982, both of whom returned to Saint Mary's as English professors.

Saint Mary's best finish was third place in 1969, and from 1987 to 1996. Through the generosity of Howard and Geri Korth, 12 new tennis courts replaced the four aging courts alongside Augustine Residence Hall. The new courts and club house, named after their deceased son, Timothy, a University of Notre Dame graduate, were located not far from the Townhouse Residence Halls. This new facility allowed the Gaels to host West Coast Conference tournaments and provided high-quality courts six with night lights to the Gaels, together with conveniently located tennis offices. It also provided other students and local neighbors with lighted courts for night tennis. Saint Mary's had planned to light all of its courts, but restrictions were imposed by the Moraga Planning Commission, because neighbors were afraid that the lights would encroach upon their property or would obscure their night-time views, even though the lights selected had been developed to avoid illumination beyond the courts. Power to the lights was automatically cut at 9:30 p.m.

Men's Golf

Men's golf was considered an NCAA Division I sport in the West Coast conference since 1969. While individuals gained some stature in the Conference, Saint Mary's was not a serious contender. Since WCC records were maintained starting in 1968, Saint Mary's never achieved championship status. Erin Meichtry was an individual top finisher in 1993 and John Pirotte in 1984. Other Gaels who were cited as low scorers were Brian Ruiz, 1985 & 1986; Brett Langley, 1986; John Bajek, 1993. The team standing ranged from a low of eighth in 1975 to a high of third in 1982, and 1993. The average team standing over the 26-year period from 1971 to 1997 was between fifth and sixth place or 5.8 among 8 teams, a respectable position, but below the midpoint.

Cross Country, Men and Women

Both men's and women's Cross Country teams were entered into the West Coast Conference, the men's in 1975 and the women's in 1988. For the men, only once, in 1979 did Saint Mary's College gain fourth place out of eight teams. By 1997, the Gaels had achieve six fifth places, five sixth places, one seventh and six last places. It was evident that Cross County was not considered a major sport, even though it was an NCAA Division I effort.

177

The women fared better, finishing first in 1990, five times in second, once in third, twice in fourth and once in fifth. Anne Wedum achieved notice in 1990 and Arpan Melwani in 1992. Named to the West Coast Conference All-Academic Team: Michael Gagnon, 1992 and 1995; Bernard Darcy, 1994; Rodrigo Flores, 1991; Stephanie Hovanick, 1996; Molly Lawrence, 1996; Jennifer Michaels, 1994 and 1995; Christen O'Brien, 1994; Aimee Tolan, 1991 and 1992; and Jill Moore, 1991.

Men's Club Sports

Club sports were not officially recorded by the athletic department. However, an effort was made in the summer of 2005 to archive records of the various club sports, wherever obtainable. Thanks go to Katherine Gernhardt, Director of Club Sports, for establishing a club-sports archive gathered from *The Collegian, The Gael,* local newspapers and several other sports information sources, including the *All Sports Media Guide* published by the West Coast Conference, *The Collegian* and *Gael Yearbooks,* and individuals such as Marti Storti and Brother Martin Ash for Rugby, Randy Farris for Soccer, and former Athletic Director Don McKillip for various sports.

Water Polo and Swim Team

Since Water Polo was not an NCAA sport and its genesis was student inspired, consistent and accurate records in the athletic department archives were not kept. The student newspaper is one source of information. The Water Polo team seems to have been formed in the fall of 1968 and continued through the fall of 1969. In 1968 and 1969 coach George Sanders led the team that included Rich Stocks, John Smead, Mel Herman, Jay Conroy, Mal Jester, Matt Morris and co-captains Mike Meys and Dan Delaney (MVP). The water polo enthusiasts boasted a 20-game schedule with such teams as Diablo Valley College, Cal State Hayward, University of Santa Clara, San Francisco State, UC Berkeley, Occidental College and the California Maritime Academy.

An editorial by student Peter Detwiler in *The Collegian* on March 19, 1971 bemoaned the possible extinction of some minor sports because the Athletic Department budget could no longer support the number of sports in the department portfolio in the face of funding the major sports and the resurrected football program. An article in *The Collegian* on Jan. 30, 1970 disclosed plans for the 1970-1971 Water Polo season. However, since no word of water polo appears after the fall of 1969 season, the assumption is made that the sport was discontinued.

The Collegian carried an article on Sept. 28, 1972, announcing an organizational meeting for a swim team with William Radley as coach. A later article on Oct. 26, 1972, described the expertise of the coach and the first workouts for the potential swim team. No further information on the proposed swim team appears in either *The Collegian* or the *Gael Yearbook*, for 1973.

When the U. S. Navy Pre-flight School occupied the campus during World War II, walls and a roof were constructed to enclose the pool so that it could be utilized year-round for as long as the Navy occupied the campus. The structure, temporary in nature, was a wood frame and stucco building. Evaporation from the pool accelerated the deterioration of the wooden roof and walls, normally called *dry rot,* though in this case would be more aptly termed *wet-rot.* Mention was made in a Nov. 1974 *Collegian* article that the deterioration of the pool roof put "swimmers in the cold," since the pool could not be used until the roof was removed. Coach Radley's name appeared a year later as using the pool for training Amateur Athletic Union swimmers. No further mention was made of a swimming team in *The Collegian.*

Rugby Club

The initiation of rugby, considered a more civilized sport, occurred after football was banished from the campus in 1899 because of its "brutality," as related by Randy Andrada in *They Did It Every Time.* Student historian Jamie Fernandez, 1994, relying on an article in *The Collegian* of October 1907, records rugby being played on the Saint Mary's campus from 1888 to 1890 and again between 1907 and 1915, just prior to the reinstatement of football in 1915. Modern rugby returned to the rugby pitch on the Saint Mary's campus in 1956, during the gap between big-time football that was discontinued in 1951 and its modest return in 1967. The Rugby team sought as its faculty advisor Brother Kyran Aviani, FSC, who was both young and athletic. He accepted the invitation, assuming his post as advisor with eagerness. It has been alleged that Brother Kyran sometimes even played with the team, but regardless he established a strong bond with the players as a faculty advisor and continued as an avid rugby advocate.

Patrick Vincent came to Saint Mary's in the fall of 1967 to coach the rugby team and had an outstanding reputation in the rugby world, in particular as a captain of the New Zealand All Blacks. Though he was an enthusiastic sportsman, he was also a graduate of the University of New Zealand and earned his master's degree in history at the University of California, Berkeley. Vincent's leadership, passion for and knowledge of the game raised the sport to an improved level on the Saint Mary's campus, giving the team an impetus to earn both reputation and respect. Vincent was returning with the team on a flight from France in 1983, when he suffered a fatal heart attack. The coaching reins were then assumed by Dan Noecker (1983-1986), Brian Sherin (1987-1991), and Marti Storti (1992-1997). Headed by alumnus John Henning 1939, Director of the state AFL-CIO and former U. S. Ambassador to New Zealand, the Pat Vincent Memorial Fund was established, and contributions from team members, rugby alumni, fans and friends, along with a bequest from the Pat Vincent Estate, made possible the construction of the Pat Vincent Memorial Rugby Field (or Pitch) at the entrance to the campus. It was dedicated in 1991.

One special feature of Gael Rugby was its travel schedule, and from 1972 onward, the team adopted the slogan, *Follow Gael Rugby Around the World*. Brother Martin Ash, FSC, was instrumental in promoting rugby world travel. Every year from 1969 through 1997, during the Easter recess, the team traveled the globe, playing in such locations as the U.S. East Coast, Hawaii, England, Wales, British Columbia, Ireland, the Bahamas, New Zealand, Scotland, New Orleans, and Nashville, France, Singapore, Italy, Argentina, Washington, D.C., Australia, Portugal, the Caribbean, Thailand, China, Hong Kong, Florida and Bermuda. Not only did the team make the junkets, but interested parents and fans also made the tours after 1972, with Ireland, New Zealand and Hawaii being the most popular destinations.

Pebble Beach was the venue for the annual Monterey Rugby Tournament normally held in March. The Gaels played against many of the top collegiate teams in the nation. Jerry Kelleher was selected on the All World Rugby Team, a distinctive honor in the eyes of rugby enthusiasts. Chris Casey, 1989, was named All-American by the U. S. Rugby Association. Other Gaels cited as distinguished Monterey Tournament participants were Greg Schneeweis, Brad Andrews, John Hincken, Aurelio Perez, Mike Fanucchi and Eric Whitaker.

The Hawaiian House of Representatives (with the Honorable Herman Wedemeyer as a member) commended Saint Mary's College and the Gael Rugby Team with House Resolution 338 when the team visited Hawaii in 1971. Fifty-one legislators personally signed the Resolution which began: "Whereas, the personal bonds between the people of the State of Hawaii and Saint Mary's College have been affectionate and near ..." On the Wales-English tour in 1989, His Eminence Basil Cardinal Hume, Archbishop of Westminster, a former rugby player and coach himself, invited the team to his residence for tea. He graciously posed for photographs and exercised his inventive wit with the team in the residence reception room. When the team arrived at the Cathedral on Easter morning for the Cardinal's Pontifical Easter Liturgy, the entourage was escorted to the front row. Father Patrick LaBelle, OP, Director of Campus Ministry and chaplain to the team, concelebrated the Easter Mass with His Eminence. Cardinal Hume graciously thanked the team for presenting him with a Gael rugby jersey, though he could not, he said, "envisage an occasion when it will be an entirely appropriate garment to wear. But one never knows."

From 1971 to 1997 Brother Martin Ash, FSC, arranged the travel schedule and was the official College moderator for the team.

Lacrosse Club

Men's Lacrosse on the Saint Mary's campus came into being in 1985 when student Peter Krawiec, '89 spoke to potential lacrosse players, urging them to join him in initiating a team. He gathered 10 players (two short of a full team) for the 1986-1987 season. The first season was clearly a building year as is often said of young and inexperienced teams. Student Terry McNiff, '88, assumed coaching duties for the 1987-1988 season, a still-building year. NcNiff, Gagan, Burns, Nagle, Osmer, Petersen and Jelso weathered the building traumas well. The coaching services of Tom Dalryumple as head coach and Phil Tagimi as assistant coach were secured for the 1988-1989 year, a year in transition, as the team entered the West Coast Lacrosse League and recorded its first win, 12-6 against Chapman College in Orange, Calif. The season record: 5-4. Ken Nussbaum was named Gael of the Week. By 1989-1990 the team had matured sufficiently to earn a place in the WCLL playoffs. Season record: 7-3. By 1990-1991, with 31 players, the Gaels garnered the WCLL championship in the Northern Conference, Division II. Four Gaels, Damon Foss, '92; Tom Grywczuynski, '91; Mark Gagan, '91; and Eric Hayes, '92; were named to the WCLL All-Star Team. Goalkeeper Hayes became a three-time WCLL All-Star. In 1993-1994, with a 6-5 record, J. D. Lanigan, '93, and Jack Radisch, '93 were named All-Stars and Ryan Nordyke, Mike Burkart and Kevin Daly were singled out by other conference coaches for their quality performances. Spirited John O'Keefe made for good copy in Lacrosse reports. In 1994, Joseph Ianora, '88, was named assistant coach, and Eric Burns, president of the team. The 1995-1996 season (5-8) was the last for coach Tom Dalryumple Goalee Matt Kaminski was named to the All-Stars, and the team garnered a win against UCLA, 12-7 in the playoffs. Senior standouts were Bryan Holmes, Mark Hollenback, Josh Weiler and Dan Dick. In 1996-1997 (5-9); Joe Ianora assumed head-coaching duties. Mike Jensen and Matt Kaminski were named co-captains and Mike Lickiss president. Mike Jensen, Matt Kaminski and Mike Lickiss made senior honors.

Volleyball Club

With Susan Pantos as coach, men's volleyball commenced in 1981. Leading the team were Chris Morris, '83 and Bob Krueger, '81 as the 1981 member team looked to possible competition from UC Berkeley, Fresno State, Stanford and Humboldt State. The team played in two tournaments, but inexperience worked against a winning season.

The next information on men's volleyball came in 1983 with Joey O'Connor, '86 as captain and experienced Russian immigrant Skerven Glazenberg as coach. John Schunk, Barry Kester, Paul Bearden, Jim Clamfielder, Don Reynolds, Kevin McQuire and Andy Solari joined the team. The schedule was "patched together" as one member observed, and included such teams as Stanford, Pepperdine, Long Beach State, and UC Santa Barbara. As with any novice team, scheduling against established teams was inherently difficult and frustrating, since the opposition was consistently taller and more experienced. The season record was not impressive. Interest waned, the coach resigned, and the sport was suspended after the 1985-1986 season.

A short resurrection occurred in 1992 when Oscar Crespo became head coach and Jake Chow assistant coach. Two games were recorded with University of San Francisco and Fresno State. Mark Trinidad, Jeff Waldrop, Tracey Hubbord, Matt Navdagopol, John Hasset and Bob Roney were team members

Crew Club

Crew at Saint Mary's began in 1965 under the voluntary leadership of Ed Lickiss, coach of the Lake Merritt Rowing Club. The crew club required commitment and determination in that members had to rise at the crack of dawn, to make practices on local lakes and reservoirs before classes began at 8 a.m. The first opponents were Santa Clara, Stanford, UC Berkeley and the University of Southern California. The experience whetted appetites, and the schedule was expanded. By 1968-1969 the schedule included Stanford, UC Santa Barbara, UC Berkeley, Loyola, Oregon State, University of Oregon, Long Beach State and Santa Clara. The team posted 3 wins, 2 losses and 1 tie for the 1969-1970 season. In the spring of 1970, the team purchased a new shell (boat) through a fundraising effort by crew enthusiasts. Former President, the revered Brother Albert Rahill, was called upon to christen the new shell, named *Kyran* in tribute to Brother Kyran Aviani, FSC. Given the light construction of the shell, champagne was temperately poured on its prow by Brother Albert with the words, "We cannot afford to waste too much champagne in these difficult economic times." There was sufficient champagne for the celebration that followed how ever, later in the year Brother Albert was honored with the naming of the next new shell the *Albert*. There are no quotations from that christening, but photos disclose a full bottle of champagne that was certainly consumed with delight. Mark Brast, '71, and Ralph Galluci, '70, were named captains with Peter Detwiler, '71, as coxswain.

In 1971-1972 crew practice sessions under coach Ed Lickiss and team captains Mark Brast, Ralph Gallucci and Lee Jones were moved to such lakes closer to the College as Briones, Upper San Leandro and San Pablo reservoirs. Eventually the Briones Reservoir became the Gaels "home lake," and with the permission of the East Bay Municipal Utility District, a storage shed was constructed on its banks, to house equipment and shells. Given the early morning practice sessions and meager financial support the crew teams endured, a special spirit and enthusiasm was required to sustain the sport. Team co-captains such as Bob Rota and John Crvarich, Stephen Williams and Paul Opel were instrumental in maintaining fervor in the early 1970s. By 1975 coach Ed Lickiss felt that he had done all he could and resigned. Mike Bennett assumed the coaching reins for the 1976 and 1977 seasons. Tom Wilson was selected captain.

For the 1978 season, the Gaels secured the services of Giancarlo Trevisan, a colorful and enthusiastic native Italian, as coach. Trevisan's dynamic flair inspired both the team and team benefactors. Though Trevisan dreamed of having a rowing tank on campus some day, his anticipation of such a facility did not dampen his enthusiasm as both coach and fundraiser. He had good reason to express his satisfaction with the 1980 season performance. By 1981, six of the crew members he coached as freshmen were now seniors. Crew members in 1981 were Joe Bertain, Dean Ongaro, Scott Sweiss, Mike Martell, Vic Bruni Mike Lahey, Joe Motta, Frank Mello and most inspirational, Brooks Bruett. The McGunagle men, Tim and Kirk, were stalwarts for the next few seasons, along with Greg Gonsalves, Mike Magnani, Chris Emerick, Mike Tressel, and Greg Dohlen, and Mary Hutcheson and Karena Zakhour as coxswains. The Gael crew was clearly a contender, with wins over such diverse teams as UC Berkeley, University of San Diego, Santa Clara University, San Diego State., Humboldt State, UC Davis, University of the Pacific, and others. In 1986 the lightweight four won the Pacific Coast Rowing Championship over USC, UCLA and University of the Pacific. In the summer of 1986 a group took a shell to Europe to sharpen their skills. In 1990 the team celebrated a win over UC Berkeley by 1.3 seconds. By 1991 Coach Trevisan boasted 100 crew-team members. Six Saint Mary's College shells entered the Corvallis Invitational Regatta. Matt Brennan, Jason Bateman,

Tom Dierkes, Carlos Aguilar and Erin Burke, along with coxswains Bandy Hernandez and Christy Baiko, were cited for their performance. Padraic McGovern was listed as most valuable rower and Robert Rodriguez as most inspirational in 1993. In March 1995, the year of the 30th reunion of crew members, the team brought home the Blue Heron Trophy from the Blue Heron Sprints in Eureka, Calif. The men's and women's crew teams carried home two gold, two silver and two bronze medals in the 1996-1997 season in four separate regattas that included gold medals for a single-sculling race won by Jonathan Young. Robert Rodriguez, Mark Maubarrett, Brandon Parrett and Zane Doyle were the other men's standouts. Giancarlo Trevisan coached the men, and Don Cedarborg and Shannon Hancock shared coaching duties for the women.

Women's Athletics

The male tradition at Saint Mary's was definitively altered in the fall of 1970, when the first women entered the College as full-time undergraduate students. At the time, there was little or no thought given to the concept of a women's athletic program, small or large. The long male athletic tradition remained intact until 1978. The passage of Title IX anti-discrimination laws in education in June 1972 was clearly the major impetus for establishing a full-fledged women's athletic program. However, it required several years for higher education institutions to understand and apply the Title IX prescriptions. It also required time for the women to understand what to seek in terms of formal athletic participations.

Since 1977 women have gradually become an integral, and, as much as possible, an equal part of the Gael athletic tradition, though women's athletic history is, by comparison, obviously short. Basketball and volleyball were the first sports that women found attractive, and they first participated in those sports under the aegis of the National Association of Intercollegiate Athletics, a national athletic organization that is geared to smaller collegiate institutions. It was not until a Moraga resident, an energetic women's basketball coach by the name of Terri Rubenstein, arrived on the court that women's basketball began to come of age. With her team's success, a natural shift from the NAIA to the NCAA placed the women's program theoretically on a par with the men's, though it would take time for women's athletics on the whole to fully mature. Other sports were added as interest by women was expressed and other institutions in the West Coast Conference began to field an increasing number of women's athletics. In due time, the Conference began scheduling women's Conference contests and tournaments. As of this writing, the West Coast Conference schedules contests and tournaments for women in basketball, soccer, volleyball, tennis, rowing (crew), and cross country. Lacrosse and softball are also NCAA sports offered for women at Saint Mary's, but are conducted by organizations other than the West Coast Conference.

Women's Basketball, 1978 – 1997

	Year	Won	Lost	Status
Annette Chiara	1978-1979	19	9	NAIA
Craig Johnson	1979-1982	28	43	NAIA
Brown/Koury	1982-1983	20	9	NAIA
T. Rubenstein	1983-1997	235	158	NAIA-NCAA I

Women's basketball holds membership in the West Coast Conference and is positioned in Division IA in the National Collegiate Athletic Association. Terri Rubenstein was selected as *Coach of the Year* in 1989. Outstanding players cited on WCC All Conference Teams were: Anja Bordt 1989, 1990 and 1991; Cheree Tappin, 1991; Fran Fabien, 1992; Natalie Rynn, 1992; Christina Marshall, 1993; Joy Durand, 1994 and 1996; Shannon O'Brien, 1995; Liz Wilkinson, 1997; Anja Bordt, 1991 and Mollie Flint, 1997 who were both named as Scholar-Athletes of the Year, and Anja Bordt 1991 who was named GTE/Verizon Academic All-American. The All Academic Team Rosters cited the following: Kim Rubenstein 1995; Melissa Schreiner, 1995; Joy Durand, 1996; Mollie Flint, 1996 and 1997; and Liz Wilkerson, 1997.

Women's Soccer

	Year	Won	Lost		Status
Randy Farris	1982-1986	W 33	L 48	T 12	NAIA
Randy Farris	1987-1997	W 106	L 100	T 12	NCAA I

A women's soccer team was the offspring of a coed Physical Education activity class taught by Randy Farris in 1981. The women in the class inquired why women's soccer was not included in the athletic offerings for women. Farris discussed the inquiry with the Athletic Director, who called for a meeting of women interested in soccer. Fifty showed up and a team was established in 1982 under the banner of the National Association of Interscholastic Athletics. The Gael women won the first championship sponsored by the NAIA two years later, in 1984, and defender Kathleen Jones was named the NAIA National Player of the Year. The Championship All-Tournament Team included Beth Litell, Sue Caporicci, Marcie Champie, Kathleen Jones, Mary Jane Laster, Lisa Del Fiugo and Kathy D'Avolio.

When women's soccer was introduced, the athletic budget did not include such items as women's uniforms. During the first year, the men's uniforms had to serve double duty. As soon as the men's games were completed, the uniforms were washed and readied for the women's games, often on the same day. Parents came to the rescue in 1983 and secured uniforms for the women's team.

The Women's Soccer Team defeated Westmont College of Montecito, Calif. in 1984, thus qualifying for the Western Regional. Athletic Director, Don McKillip, Vice President for Student Affairs McLeod and Coach Randy Ferris discussed whether the team should be allowed to participate in the national finals, given the austere athletic budget and doubts about the ability of the team to perform at a higher level. "If we're allowed to participate, we'll do our best," Farris stated. The team was allowed to participate and won the 1984 National Association of Intercollegiate Athletics Championship. The women again rejoiced in an NAIA National Championship in 1986. That team included Beth Litell, Christy Baird, Desi Engle, Kathleen Jones, and Georgeann Wharton. Desi Engle was named to the All-Freshman Team for all collegiate institutions. The women Gaels hold a place in the National Soccer Hall of Fame in Oneonta, N.Y. for the national championship wins. Kathleen Jones' jersey is retired in Oneonta.

In 1987, the Women's Soccer Team was placed under the National Collegiate Athletic Association, since all of the other teams, with the exception of club sports, were associated with the NCAA. Though in the first year under NCAA rules, the women Gaels compiled one of the best national win-loss records, the strength-of-schedule was deemed insufficient, and Saint Mary's was not invited to participate in the playoff contests. From then on, Saint Mary's annually formed a rigorous strength-of-schedule program and participated in NCAA post-season tournaments in 1988 and 1994. Women named in WCC All Conference Teams were: Kim Donohue 1992, 1993, 1994 and 1995; Lori Hokerson, 1992, 1993 and 1994; Monica Larsson, 1994; Val Williams, 1996 and 1997; and Amy Hood, 1996. Lori Hokerson was named Soccer All-American for 1992. Named to All-Conference Teams were Lori Hokerson and Kim Donahue in 1992, 1993 and 1994; Kim Donahue in 1995; and Val Williams in 1996 and 1997. WCC All Academic Teams listed Wendi Ashworth, 1992; Dee Dee Robertson, 1992; Michele Michelotti, 1992; Erin McDonald, 1993 and 1995; Monica Larsson, 1994; Leslie Smith, 1995; Julie Brady, 1995; Amy Hood, 1996; and Lauren Weaver, 1997.

Women's Softball

	Year	Won	Lost	Status
Milt Pangotaios	1989-1990	W 41	L. 89 T-2	NCAA IA
Stephanie Papas	1991-1995	W 103	L. 163 T-1	NCAA IA
Dan Ward	1996-1997	W 39	L 69	NCAA IA

Outstanding softball athletes: Batting averages: .418, Kellie Hogue, 1984; .396, Stephanie Bush, 1986; .373, Claire Lammerding, 1986 and .346, 1987; .349, Yvonne Millette, 1984; .348, Trisha Dean, 1996; Games pitched: 34, Kristi Delaplain, 1994; 32 Michelle St. Pierre, 1995; 32 Michelle Wierschem, 1989; 31, Cindy Waterman, 1995; 29, Rae Paulson, 1997; 29, and Jean Pick, 1997. Strikeouts: 119, Kristi Delaplain, 1994; 101, Jenn Pick, 1998; 90, 98, Cindy Waterman, 1994,1995; Shutouts: 15, Cindy Waterman, 1993-1996; 15, Kristi Delaplain, 1991-1994; 41, Cindy Waterman, 1993-1996; 39, Raw Paulson, 1996-1999; 39, Kristi Deane, 1987-1990; 26, Michelle Wierschem, 1986-1989; Homeruns: 6, Molly McClenahan, 1994-1997; 4, Trisha Dean, 1996-2000; 4, Gina Javier, 1997-2000; 4, Staci Zierman, 1986-1988; 4, Kellie Hogue, 1984; 3, Trinchy Floro, 1995-1997; 3, Alicia McLelland, 1993-1994; 3, Kim McAtee, 1984; 3, Yvonne Millette, 1984.

Women's Volleyball

	Year	Won	Lost	Status
Loretta Monaco	1978	12	16	
Sue Pantos	1979-1980	19	26	
Glenda Guilliams	1981	6	10	
Joan Tamblin	1982-1987	139	63	NCAA IA '87
Jim Cherniss	1988-1995	82	161	NCAA IA
Ron Twomey	1996-2001	50	112	NCAA IA

Few individual records for the early years (1977 – 1984) were kept. Most matches: 40, 1983 and 1985; most games, 129, 1991; most wins: 38, 1983; most losses, 24, 1987 and 1992. NCAA Division I: 1987, 4-24, WCC 1-13; 1988, 5-22, WCC 2-12; 1989, 18-12, WCC 8-6; 1990, 13-19, WCC 2-12; 1991, 8-23, WCC 1-13; 1992, 7-24, WCC 3-11; 1993, 12-19, WCC, 5-9; 1994, 11-21, WCC 4-10; 1995, 8-21, WCC 3-11; 1996, 7-21, WCC 2-12, 1997, 9-21, WCC 4-10.

Greatest number of games played in a season: 129, Melissa Margala, 1991; in
a career: 460, Tracie Hajudokovich 1988-1991. Greatest number of matches
played in a season: 38, Lisa Bertaccini and Anne Cooper, 1984; in a career:
121, Leslie McKinley, 1990-1993. Women's Volleyball began in 1978 under
Loretta Monaco. Some outstanding volleyball athletes were: Lisa Betanccini,
1984; Michelle Neely, 1984; Ana Robles, 1985; Anne Cooper, 1985; Jackie
Banks, 1986; Gina Miller, 1986; Theresa Hanks, 1988; Angela Yzsunsa 1988;
Terry Miller, 1989; Julie Sinclair, 1990; Kirsten George, 1990; Tracie Haydu-
kovich, 1991; Wendy Dumbolton, 1992; Trudi Herber 1993; Jennifer Haney,
1993; Leslie McKinley, 1993; Shannon Davenport, 1994; Kiel Murray, 1994;
Alisa Vasys, 1994; Julie Dare, 1994; Melissa Margala 1994; Rebecca Gehlke,
1995; Meredth Guevara 1995; Vanessa Dahl, 1996; Kara McKeown, 1996;
Kara McKeown, 1996; Zoa Armstrong, 1996; Julie Grieve, 1997; Whitney
Hoover, 1997; and Merideth Guevara, 1998; Jim Cherniss was named Coach
of the Year in 1989.

Women listed in All WCC Teams were: Julie Sinclair, 1988 & 1989; Kirsten
George, 1989; Leslie McKinley, 1993; Kiel Murray, 1994; and Vanessa Dahl,
1995. Women appearing on the WCC All-Academic Team in volleyball were:
Tracie Hadjukovich, 1991; Melissa Margala, 1992 and 1993; Laurie Griffith,
1992; Kiel Murray, 1993 and 1994; Shannon Davenport, 1994; Nicole Pen-
nington, 1995; Rebecca Gehlke, 1995; Rachel Parker, 1996; Abby Waller, 1996
and 1997; Molly Horan, 1997; and Julie Grieve, 1997.

Guiding Student Life

The Dean of Student Life

The Reverend Patrick LaBelle, OP, '61, Ph.B., came to the College as a member of the Campus Ministry in 1973. After a year he joined the Residence Life staff and lived in De La Salle Hall as a Resident Director. He was named President of the Dominican School of Philosophy and Theology in Berkeley from 1975 to 1980, but for several years continued to serve as a Resident Director. A few years after his term as President of the Dominican School of Philosophy and Theology, he returned to the College and was named Dean of Student Life from 1984 to 1997. Although his role included that of maintaining good order within the student body, he was beloved by the students. His well-known *Graduation Chair Committee* was recruited from among those who incurred minor infractions during the year. Their task was to set up the several thousand chairs for the commencement ceremonies. His perceptive sense of humor allowed him to relate stories encountered in his role as disciplinarian with a touch of both suspense and jocosity. Students knew that he was not to be challenged or deceived. His balance and common sense were trusted characteristics, even among those eligible for the graduation chair committee.

In the fall of 1979 Father LaBelle attended a meeting in Seattle and was absent from the campus for a few days. The students discovered the date and time of his return trip to San Francisco International Airport. They enlisted the help of Brother Raphael Patton of the Mathematics Department and devised a plan to greet Father LaBelle as he deplaned. Students dressed in suits and ties and some were equipped with flash cameras, while others had a wire running from beneath their coats to a small earphone in one of their ears. Several wore Sheriff's Department badges, courtesy of the toy section of Long's Drugstore. Erich Weber, '79, dressed in a military uniform and had handcuffed a briefcase to his wrist. Still others either lined up as greeters or formed a crowd of eager onlookers, some with small American flags. Interest from travelers in the waiting room peaked, since they believed a celebrity of national importance must be arriving. Some retrieved their cameras from their carry-on luggage and stood to view the scene. Brother Raphael, dressed incognito, held a medallion attached to a red ribbon in the ready to place around Father LaBelle's neck as soon as he entered the waiting room. Roy P. Disney, '79, waited at curbside (with the permission of the Airport Police) in a large BMW with small flags attached to each front fender to accommodate the "ambassador" and lead the entourage back to the College.

189

By chance the flight was full, and when Father LaBelle entered the aircraft in Seattle the only seat left was in first class which he gladly accepted. He removed his clerical collar to relax on the flight to SFO. He was one of the first to deplane. The greeting entourage lined up. Cameras flashed, Brother Raphael, accompanied by the students with the earphones, greeted Father LaBelle, the "Ambassador," as he emerged from the gangway. Prior planning had determined that if Father LaBelle were still attired in his clerical garb he would be called "Cardinal," if not, he would be identified as "Ambassador." Brother Raphael bowed and placed the pectoral medallion with ribbon around his neck. Travelers in the waiting room joined in the celebration asking, "Who is this? What's this all about?" Some took flash photos. "Ambassador" LaBelle, an imposing figure, was both astonished and perplexed, but quickly rose to the occasion, accepting the vigorous adulation in all his dignified glory, as the greeters made their way through the airport crowd in haste to the waiting car. The talk on the campus went the rounds for days. (Post 9/11, such a prank would never be permitted under subsequent airport security restrictions.)

After 13 years as Dean of Student Life at Saint Mary's, Father LaBelle was named Catholic Chaplain to the students of Stanford University in 1997 and served in that position until 2008 -- a role in which was eminently successful.

Parents as Gaels — Sister Clare Wagstaffe, OP, 1921-2007

Sister Clare Wagstaffe, who was a graduate of Stanford University and held a doctorate in Philosophy from the Catholic University of America, had joined the College staff in 1980 after serving as a campus minister at the University of Washington (1972-1977) and then in a special ministry program in Denver. She served one year as a member of the College Campus Ministry staff, but her abundant talent was tapped by Student Affairs and she was appointed Dean of Student Services in 1981. Her academic background and extensive experience with college-age students was a godsend to the College in her role as both counselor and instructor. Sister Clare was a residence hall Director during her many years of service to the students of the College. Her reputation as a wise counselor for both men and women was widespread, and she was a champion in encouraging the success of women, without the stridency that has often characterized the agendas of some women's movements in recent times. The Alumni Association named her an Honorary Alumna in 1986, and the Christian Brothers conferred upon her their highest honor, that of Affiliation to the Institute of the Christian Brothers on May 4, 2001. She deeply appreciated that honor.

In her abundant contacts with students Sister Clare realized that the College could benefit from some kind of official liaison between the College and parents. She convinced the administration that an Office of Parent Relations would serve as a resource for parent-College interchange and would provide an opportunity to recruit parent volunteers eager to support various programs. Sister Clare was appointed Director of Parent Relations in 1994 and within a year had instituted an active Parents' Advisory Council. The wisdom of such a program was soon manifest in encouraging parental participation and support and in its ability to respond to numerous inquiries, especially for new parents, and in providing parents with information they might request in view of resolving difficulties a son or daughter may have related to an instructor, other students, housing, health, the curriculum or even problems with his or her own parents. At the time, because of the *Buckley Amendment* the College was not allowed to contact parents regarding grades, personal or disciplinary matters without a student's knowledge and consent, making Sister Clare's assignment one that required delicacy and discretion. Her graciousness and wisdom was a significant resource for parents interested in supporting the academic and cultural life of both the College in general and their offspring in particular. After a lifetime of wise service, Sister Clare retired in July 2004. She was diagnosed with cancer and confined to a rest home for several years before she succumbed on Jan. 1, 2007. Both the Wagstaffe family and the Christian Brothers celebrated liturgies of Christian Burial. As an Affiliated Member of the Christian Brothers she was interred at the Christian Brothers cemetery at Mont La Salle, Napa on Jan. 17, 2007.

Associated Students of Saint Mary's College (ASSMC)

The official organization representing the student body of the College went under the title of *The Associated Students of Saint Mary's College* with its officers elected by the student body. The Student Body President, Vice-President, Secretary and Treasurer campaigned for office toward the end of the Spring semester. They assumed office during the final month of the academic year (as was the custom then) to allow for some transitional interchange between incoming and outgoing officers. The post of Social Chairman, appointed by a Selection Committee, was almost as significant as that of the president, since he or she assumed the responsibility for providing campus social life, an element of considerable concern to many students. The treasurer held a position of unusual responsibility, because at that time he/she received $100 per student in student-body fees, amounting to more than $115,000 per semester to be distributed to *The Collegian, The Gael* (student yearbook), student body social events (via the Social Chairman) and various student clubs and organizations. The Student Body President was assisted by the Senate that met almost weekly to discuss various issues and approve various appointments and the finances. The Senate could override a president's decision by a two-thirds vote. The Executive Council of the Senate was composed of the four student body officers. Collegian and Gael editors, and the manager of KSMC-FM were selected by the prior editor or manager and the student body president with final approval resting with the Senate. The Senate was composed of 21 senators, including the student body officers, class presidents and 12 representatives. The Senate appointed a parliamentarian, and formed a finance committee to allocate funds and a judicial board, akin to a supreme court. It funded the intramural athletic program, some minor sports, Gaelforce (cheering section), and numerous organizations. The Social Chairperson, Yearbook editor, Collegian editor and Intramural manager were modestly salaried by the Senate.

In general, the student body officers and the members of the Senate were among the most creative, focused and ambitious students.

Undergraduate Student Body Presidents

James M. Wood, 1969-1970; John Blackstock, 1970-1971; Joseph Blell, 1971-1972; Sam Camacho, 1972-1973; Michael J. Lee, 1974-1975; Paul Andrew, 1975-1976; Matthew O'Donnell, 1976-1977; Mary Mejorado, 1977 (resigned due to illness); Rocky Lucia, 1977-1978; Garth Collins, 1978-1979; Richard "Ric" Rosario, 1979-1980; Daniel Nerney, 1980-1981; Victoria Murray, 1981-1982; Mark R. Murray, 1982-1983; Michael Brisbin, 1983-1984; Steven Dondanville, 1984-1985; Shawn P. Pynes, 1985-1986; Victoria Verber, 1986-1987; Richard Martin, 1987-1988; William Gaffney, 1988-89; Kenneth Mooney, 1989-1990; Frank Lonergan, 1990-1991; John Fistolera, 1992-1993; Chris Lamson, 1993-1994; Julie Parkin, 1994-1995; Carolyn Busselmaier, 1995-1996; and David Perry, 1996-1997.

Professions of former student body presidents:: Attorneys, 6; Education, 3 (1 PhD); Public Relations, 1; Dentist, 1; Government, 2; C.E.O, Business, 4; Accountant, 1; Business, 6; Entrepreneur 1.

Joseph Blell, '72, an international student from Sierra Leone, West Africa is in Sierra Leone Government; Mary Mejorado, '78, first female Student Body President, resigned after a short time in office because of health issues. She now holds both an MA and a PhD. Victoria Murray, '82, second woman Student Body President and Mark Murray, '83, are sister and brother, and both are attorneys. (Their father, Al, '61, is also an attorney.)

Campus Fourth Estate

The Collegian

The Collegian, the official newspaper of the Associated Student Body since 1903, had over the years chronicled campus events, featured student -- and occasionally faculty -- essays, poetry and editorials. Students developed a tradition of quality collegiate journalism, selecting essays with care and vying with one another over style and accuracy. Creative headlines became a hallmark. Securing a place on The Collegian staff was a sign of distinction. However, by the mid '60s The Collegian had thrown journalistic quality to the winds, a significant departure from 60 years of taste and student pride in respectable journalism. It energetically entered the discourse on the anticipated change in calendar and requirements, as well as political issues both on and off campus. "The Collegian," one observer noted, "took on the appearance of the Berkeley Barb," by mimicking its layout and tone, as well as its vulgar and strident language. The Berkeley Barb was a popular liberal tabloid devoted to revolutionary activism, capturing the spirit of the Free Speech Movement inspired by Mario Savio and other radical students and hangers-on who roamed UC Berkeley's Sproul Plaza, Telegraph Avenue and what became known as People's Park. The Admissions Office had distributed The Collegian as one means of inspiring high school seniors to attend Saint Mary's but discontinued its distribution among the secondary schools as it lost its quality journalistic luster. The Public Relations Office had sent The Collegian to Trustees, Regents and potential donors but no longer did so and justifiably eliminated its financial subsidy to the paper.

On April 14, 1970, the Executive Council of the Student Body heard claims that characterized the value of The Collegian on campus as being "nil," and that students had "concern over lack of journalistic credence in various articles." The Council approved a proposal to publish The Collegian only every three weeks as a, "means of community expression" and "where meaningful problems and solutions will be discussed." The Council was persuaded that another publication entitled Applejuice would bring weekly bulletins, important announcements, news on athletics and Executive Council Minutes to the student body. Applejuice appeared for only three months, March through May 1970. The proposal that The Collegian would appear every third week with Bob Peacock as editor, assisted by Mike Genovese, Richard Anderson, Mark Ferrari and faculty advisors Professors Susan Tanaka and Bryon Bryant, did not materialize. The Collegian resumed regular publication with the 1970-1971 academic year. Journalistic maturing from that time onward became evident, though not without occasional columns, headlines and themes of

193

unseemly taste. Sometime in the mid '70s *The Collegian* began to regain a semblance of its former respectability. *The Collegian* celebrated its 100th Anniversary in 2003 under the editorship of energetic Josh Farley, '03.

Collegian Editors, 1969-1997: Michael Duda, fall 1969; Bob Haine, Jan. and Feb. 1970; *Applejuice* with John Blackstock, March, April, May, 1970; *Collegian Editors*: Peter Detwiler, September 1970 to February 1971; Co-editors Algene Nash and John H. Love, March, April, May, 1971; Michael Riley, 1971-1972; John H. Love, 1972-1973; Richard J. Kern, fall 1973; Michael Connolly, spring 1974 through spring 1975; Patrice Power, 1975-1976; Chip Gathright and Sue Kavaloski, 1976-1977; Chip Gathright, fall 1977, Steve Caruso, spring 1978; James Whittaker, 1978-1979; David Richardson, fall 1979; Maria T. Grocholski, spring 1980 and 1980 – 1981; Kirk Giberson, fall 1981; Joseph Enos November 1981 - January 1982; Mary Kavanaugh, February 1982 - December 1982; Moria G. Reynolds February 1983 - December 1983; Diane Kipley, spring 1984; June Ahearn, fall 1984 Eamon Murphy, spring 1985 through fall 1986; Andrew M. Solari, 1986-1987; Kathleen Hurley, 1987-1988; Jeff Angell, 1988-1989; Timothy J. Moore, 1989-1990 and 1990-1991; Corrine C. Clement, 1991-1992; David Martindale, 1992-1993; Courtney Atwood, 1993-1994; Brian Thomas, 1994-1995; Chad Dunnigan, 1995-1996; and Jonathan Randall, 1996-1997.

The Gael

The College yearbook (Annual) has been published regularly since 1906. An unusual breach occurred in 1973 when the 1973 *The Gael* failed to appear. In 1974 *Gael* was titled *The Lost Gael, 1973-1974* and included as best it could both the 1972-1973 and the 1973-1974 academic years. For several years in the late '80s, *The Gael* was published through deficit spending until the Student Council Media Board decided that a senior only book would be forthcoming in 1988 in order to eliminate the accumulated yearbook deficits. Several enterprising seniors pooled both voluntary services and solicited financial resources to publish with success *The 1988 Independent Yearbook*. The *Independent Yearbook* included College history and an imaginative layout as well as a strong senior section in spite of administrative skepticism and various obstacles. Tom Shephard, Editor, Bruce Inman, Mark Bedford, Leda Zukowski, Margie Shephard, Angela Maniaci, Katrina Baer and Maria Ray were the 1988 yearbook volunteers. Other students as well as some administrators and faculty also contributed to the volume. A gratifying element in the *Independent Yearbook* was the amount of text that accompanied the photos of club activities, various events, sports, the class and history of the College, celebrating its 125th year. A colorful seniors - only Gael yearbook entitled, *A Coming of Age,* celebrating the 125th year since the founding of the College and edited by Douglas Schroeder appeared under Media Board auspices.

For the most part, *Gael* yearbooks followed the common editorial and layout practices in vogue in many collegiate institutions, but there were exceptions. The 1970 *Gael* was bisected so that it had two front covers, that is, one could open the yearbook from either cover, and the text to the halfway point would read as if the first page were the beginning of the book. In 1971 the yearbook publication was boxed, enclosing two volumes with the second volume concentrating on the seniors and commencement. Imaginative John C. Blackstock, '71 was Editor-in-Chief and Jim Quandt, '71 served as Business Manager for both the 1970 and 1971 innovative publications. In 1972 an enthusiastic young student named Lawrence E. Brennan convinced his peers in the Student Council that all student publications should be centralized in one office entitled *Gael Publications* while assuring the Council that efficient cost savings would result. The Student Council polled the student body. In view of the cost savings the students accepted the proposal. Brennan's proposal also included a plan to separate *Gael Publications* from Student Council oversight and have the yearbook become independent, but only partially so. Independent meant that the Student Council would only provide a certain sum to support the yearbook. The umbrella organization, *Gael Publications,* would search for additional funds required for an exceptional yearbook publication. Brennan's first act was to transform his office into something becoming for an aspiring entrepreneur in the publishing business. Toward year's end when various kinds of fudging prevailed in response to numerous inquiries as to when the 1973 yearbook would appear, suspicions grew. Calls to the printer revealed that the 1973 yearbook had never gone to press. An official audit of *Gael Publications* told a tale of mismanagement. The problem was naivete, accompanied by misguided ambition, rather than knavery or chicanery. The 1973 events that would have appeared in the '73 Gael were incorporated into the two-year year, 1973 and 1974 yearbook.

Over time there have been controversial attitudes expressed about the need for publishing yearbooks or annuals. Some faculty and students did not think that either the expense or the investment of student and faculty moderator time to publish what is, for the most part, a photo album is worth the cost and time. Yet, students, and especially seniors, seem to appreciate the annual publications once they appear, and those who respect the gathering of history consider the yearbook a valuable record. A mandatory student-body assessment at one time covered the cost of publishing the yearbook, if budgets were observed. But as publication costs and the student body increased, a charge was made for the yearbook. There are usually abundant candid photos depicting campus personalities, scenes, and various events, a few academically oriented but mostly athletic and social. At times a clever sense of humor in depicting events prevailed. Some books carefully identify photos and offer some well-crafted literary commentary to remind readers in their more nostalgic years what took place and why.

Yearbook editors, 1970-1997: John Blackstock, '71, 1970 and 1971; Danny L. Bernstein, '72, 1972; Patrick Joyce, '75, 1973-1974 and 1975; Co-editors Laurie Stephens and Wynne Lum, '78, 1976; Co-editors Cheryl Hoefler and Wynne Lum, '78, 1977; David Duncan, 1978; Stephen "Bucky" Herron, 1979 and friends, 1979; Harold Wong, '81, 1980; James Ozanich '83, 1981 and 1982; Jennifer Brazil, '85, 1983; Patti Wall, '84, 1984; Eric J. Ipsen, '85, 1985; Chris Christman, '87, 1986; Scott Kahl, '87, 1987; Tom Shepherd, '88; Independent Yearbook, 1988; Douglas Schroeder, '88, Senior Gael, 1988; David Farinella, '89, 1989; Wendy Brown, '91, 1990; Co-editors, Maggie Ruddy '91 and Eric LaBonte, '93, 1991; Co-editors Kathy Greve, '92 and Jennifer Colton, '92, 1992; Co-editors Rosa Novello, '95 and Suzanne Exberger, '95, 1993; Neeley M. Wells, '95, 1994; Samantha Sargent, '96, 1995 and 1996; and Nick Bowles II, '98; 1997.

Student Literary Magazines

In recent history, Saint Mary's literary magazines seemed to rise with the enthusiasm of inspired individuals and then fade away when leadership waned. *The Phoenix,* the same name used by the baseball team symbolizing a rising from the ashes of a previous life, was one appellation for the student literary magazine. *The Phoenix* was published from 1956 to 1969. Former United States Poet Laureate Robert Hass, Superior Court Judges Peter Spinetta and Lawrence Appel, Marin County Supervisor Gary Giacomini, musician Peter (Juan Pedro) Gaffney, authors Armando Rendon, Bob San Souci and Denis Kelly were among the student contributors to that journal. A subsequent literary magazine made its appearance in 1982, but the editor, Robert Thompson, and his staff thought that a new title congruent with the spirit of a noted literary giant would be both symbolic and attractive. Thus *riverrun,* the first word in *Finnegan's Wake* by James Joyce was selected. The chosen title had a number of meanings for James Joyce, from a river in Dublin, Ireland, that flowed near the Church of Adam and Eve to the Tigris and Euphrates rivers, the alleged site of the Garden of Eden. Among other meanings, the word also symbolized the flow of literary vocabulary in the stream-of-consciousness format devoid of punctuation that characterized Joyce's unconventional text. The astute choice of the magazine title was considered a minor victory for culture.

The faculty moderator and a major architect for reestablishing the publication was Professor Phyllis Stowell of the English Department. The purpose of the magazine, similar to its predecessor, was to publish the best essays, poetry, short stories and plays, photography, drawings and paintings from literarily and artistically talented students. The publication in terms of layout, stock, cover and binding made it evident that someone with good taste was influential and that adequate funding had become available. The contents, as to be expected, varied in imagination, insight, style of expression and literary prudence. For the most part *riverrun* represented the current and choice issues of the times merged with both the educational and cultural backgrounds of insightful student writers and artists. That the opinions and tenor of the majority of articles and poems exhibited a leftward bent is no surprise. Over the 15 years of its publication, the magazine maintained a reasonable vision of its mission with tasteful expression.

Editors of *riverrun* were: 1982, Robert Thompson; 1983 and 1984, Alicia Payne; 1985 Jeanne E. Negley and Brother Kevin Michael Slate; 1986 Ann Marie Menkal; 1987, Ed Robertson; 1988, Aaron Walburg; 1989, Maria Ray; 1990, Julianne K. Crisholm; 1991, Mark Weyland; 1992, Alex Green; 1993, Aimee Tolan and Jody Hill; 1994, John Kyle; 1995, Erik Thornquist; and 1996, Dave Johnson.

Faculty, who encouraged good taste and guided, but did not dictate, publication policies, were: 1982-1985, Phyllis Stowell; 1986, Carol Beran and Robert Gorsch; 1987-1988, Robert Gorsch; 1989, Chester Aaron and Barry Horwitz; 1990, Barry Horwitz; 1991, Barry Horwitz and Brenda Hillman; 1992, Brenda Hillman (SMC Poet in Residence); 1993-1997, Lou Berney.

Though *The Phoenix* was funded by the Associated Students, the resurrected literary publication required more diverse funding sources. The editors, with some assistance from faculty moderators, solicited support from such sources as the English Department, the Associated Student Body, the President's Office, the Better Writing Program and the Committee for Lectures, Art and Music.

Campus Ministry, 1969-1997

The celebration of the Mass of the Holy Spirit in the fall of 1969 that was intended to inspire the entire academic community at the commencement of the new academic year was an ominous reflection of both the indifference and cynicism of the times. Over the previous several years, the College community had endured the disheartening departure of several priests and Christian

Brothers from the ministry and was enmeshed in divergent opinions as to how the Church, through the publications and declarations of Vatican II, would adapt to what it identified as the signs of the times. As is the case with politics and law where there are various shades of interpretation, so too, there were liberal to conservative interpretations of the documents of Vatican II.

Aside from the Church and Vatican II, students of every persuasion had to confront moral issues related to war, the draft, civil rights, the role and status of women, sexual ethics, homosexuality, AIDS, abortion, marriage, in-vitro conception, stem cell research, priestly celibacy and abuse, clericalism, poverty, various Papal Encylicals and so forth. These were increasingly complex times where theology and spirituality met head on with the scientific skepticism and relativism of the secular world as well as the psychological and moral confusion of the times. Students who come to Saint Mary's from secular schools, and even from some Catholic secondary institutions, have been influenced both by materialism, an unstable moral compass and the secular doctrine that truth is unattainable. Many are not only unfamiliar with the concepts of spirituality and faith but the language that expresses them, as found in such words as "soul" and "spirit." On the one hand, the task of priests and other members of a Campus Ministry Team is to enlighten and mentor young Catholics who look to the Church for guidance, example and strength, and on the other hand it is to encourage those who live outside the Church to investigate the enlightenment the Church offers in finding their way through the chaos they encounter in their daily lives. The task is daunting.

Rev. Paul Feyen, a young diocesan priest, was decent and straightforward. One of his salient gifts was his congeniality and honesty toward students, faculty and staff. Whether he was appropriately prepared for the issues he was to encounter among college-age students was doubted by a number of the Resident Directors and others who worked closely with students. He was appointed as chaplain to the College by the Bishop of Oakland, The Most Rev. Floyd Begin, DD, in 1968. Father Feyen and his successor were the last priests to fill the office of chaplain, the long-term title of the priest who was charged with the the pastoral guidance of students and who occupied a suite of rooms (outfitted with a confessional with access from the hallway) in the so-called Senior Dorm, otherwise known as De La Salle Hall. Adapting the Sunday liturgies to address the confusion and tensions of the times shrewdly, but without compromise, required both a commitment to fundamental theological principles and an insightful, experienced ability to speak to the authentic yearnings of the spirit within the student body. These were not irenic times. Seemingly faced with his own doubts about the efficacy of his priestly role, Rev. Paul Feyen resigned his position before the summer of 1970.

Paul Feyen was followed by Rev. Edward Martin, graciously sent to the College by the religious order of the Oblates of Mary Immaculate. Father Martin arrived at a time when continued turmoil over the war in Vietnam and other major controversies prevailed, and in addition to the campus issues and protests over the nonrenewal of appointments for both an Academic Vice President and a Dean of Students, both admired liberal leaders to many. Father Martin, whose views of the Church could be considered traditional, was an attractive personality and a conscientious priest who seemed to relate well to students. He engaged students positively both as Chaplain and pastoral counselor and attempted with some success to attract more students to Sunday liturgies. On one occasion, for example, the cast of the musical *Godspell*, which was playing on the professional stage in San Francisco, was invited to sing for the Mass on Sunday, Nov. 12, 1972. This special addition to the liturgy was announced publicly in advance and was allegedly disapproved by a conservative group known as Catholics United for the Faith. The cast only sang parts of the Mass normally assigned to music and followed the appropriate biblical and liturgical language. Located to the side of the sanctuary, they were clearly more flamboyant and the music more dramatic that than a Gregorian Chant choir. Several attendees who were said to belong to CUF marched out of the Chapel muttering "blasphemy" to whomever would listen.

However good his intentions, Father Martin's background did not seem to have prepared him for the theological and emotional difficulties a priest in the early '70s would encounter with a confused group of 18-to 22-year-olds, as well as the peculiar tensions encountered at the College during his tenure as College chaplain. Differences of opinion among articulate and politically astute faculty contenders often evoked strong rhetoric that caused both intellectual and emotional confusion, not only among students but among others as well. There is no doubt that Father Martin tried to provide some balance to ameliorate tensions, to establish understanding, and to address the serious emotional issues among students. However, personal reasons intervened. He, too, resigned toward the end of his third full year in 1973.

Seeking a new direction for the former chaplaincy, I sought help from a venerable religious order that was founded in the 13th Century and had significant experience with Newman Club ministries at the collegiate level. The Dominicans were thus well aware of collegiate students, their attitudes, aspirations, motivations and confusion. Founded in Spain by Domingo de Guz-man in 1215 to confront various unorthodox groups, especially the dualism of the Albigensians plaguing the Church at the time, the Order of Preachers, as the Dominicans are officially known, can boast of a history of intellectual luminaries, beginning with Albertus Magnus or St. Albert the Great (1200-1280) and St. Thomas Aquinas (1224-1272) and in more recent times, with luminaries such as the Rev. Ives Congar, OP, Rev. Murphy O'Connor, OP, and Rev. Eduard Schillebeeckx, OP. The hope was that the Dominican intellectual, spiritual and communicative tradition would be a strong suit in a complex and competitive academic setting. Furthermore, the Dominicans have had a lengthy relationship with both the Christian Brothers and the College, founded by Dominican Archbishop Joseph Alemany, OP, in 1863. Over the years the Dominican Provincial had generously assisted the College by providing either chaplains or Directors of Campus Ministry, as well as additional priests for Campus Ministry and such other roles as members of the faculty, administration or as Dean of Student Life.

Dominican Sister Clare Wagstaffe, OP, first came to Saint Mary's in 1980 as an associate Campus Minister. It was during that time that she initiated a creative *Saint Mary's Alive* week that brought members of various religious congregations and Diocesan priests to campus to promote vocations to the priesthood and religious life. Students seemed interested, and many participated in the events of the week, but the times were not conducive to inspiring young people to offer themselves to serve in religious orders or to prepare for the priesthood in a diocesan seminary.

Numerous Dominicans and the Rev. Basil De Pinto, a former Benedictine who had become a diocesan priest for the Diocese of Oakland, fulfilled the role of Campus Ministry Director from 1973 to 1997. Though alumnus Rev. Patrick L. LaBelle, OP, only served for one year as Director of Campus Ministry, he was present on campus for many years in other capacities and was able to assist the Campus Ministry Team in numerous ways. His ability to deliver creative homilies (sermons) and to oversee various student activities was inspirational to many students. Other Dominicans, including Cassian Lewinski, Jerry Milizia, Michael Morris, Bruno Gibson, Michael Carey, JD, John Morris, Jude Eli, John McDonough and Michael Sweeney, were likewise able to deliver poignant homilies, as well as to teach classes and counsel. The late Rev. John Fearon, OP, chaplain to the Brothers in the '70s, was admired for his ability to deliver a cogent and insightful daily homily in three to four minutes. The impact of the Dominican community on the campus was deeply appreciated. The Dominicans found it necessary to withdraw from Campus Ministry in

1997 because of other commitments, especially those at Newman Centers in other collegiate settings. The last Dominican to serve as Campus Ministry Director was Rev. John McDonough, OP, who was admired for his distinctive, compelling and well-crafted homilies. Father Basil De Pinto, who was also an arts-and-entertainment critic for the Diocesan newspaper, *The Voice*, and other publications, contributed an eminently consistent liturgical celebration and provided insightful homilies as well. He left the College in 1987 and later became a pastor of a parish in the Oakland Diocese. The Rev. David Diebel, a diocesan priest and also both a canon and civil lawyer, served in Campus Ministry from 1995 to 1997. He then became legal counsel for the Diocese of Sacramento and served as the chaplain for the Christian Brothers at Mont La Salle, Napa. The Rev. Salvatore Ragusa, SDS (Salvatorian), as well as Brother Ronald Roggenback, FSC, PhD, Brother Michael Murphy, FSC, MA, Brother John Moriarity, FSC, Brother Norbert Finn, OP, Brother Gary Hough, FSC, Sister Clare Wagstaffe, OP, PhD, Sister Judith Rinek, SNJM, Sister Bernice Bittick, OP, Sister Ingred Clemenson, OP, Sister Timothy Gatto, OSU (Ursline) and several lay persons also served at different times as associates in Campus Ministry. Father Salvatore Ragusa, SDS, who served as Director from 1997 to 2000, still serves in the Campus Ministry as of 2011.

Under the pastoral guidance of the Most Reverend John S. Cummins, DD, Bishop of the Diocese of Oakland, and with the generous agreement of the Presbyteral Council of priests in the Diocese, the College was granted permission to celebrate the Sacrament of Matrimony in the College Chapel in 1978 for students, faculty, staff and alumni of the College. Marriages, as well as baptisms and confirmations, are officially recorded at Saint Monica Catholic Church in Moraga, though the Campus Ministry Office retains unofficial files on various sacraments administered in the College Chapel. Given the number of alumni who wished to be married in the College Chapel, it was necessary to employ a wedding coordinator to schedule and guide couples in planning the ceremony. Melissa Logan of St. Monica Church, was the first coordinator, followed by Maida Pearson of St. Giles Episcopal Church. Both women were graciously effective and considerate, and both were appreciated by the Campus Ministry and the alumni who chose to be married in the Chapel of their Alma Mater. The required premarriage counseling sessions were conducted by the Campus Ministry.

Though not directly related to the Campus Ministry, the College administration engaged in an ecumenical outreach with the St. Giles Episcopal Church community in the Moraga-Orinda area. With the approval of The Most Reverend John S. Cummins, Roman Catholic Bishop of Oakland and the Right

Reverend Bishop William E. Swing, Episcopal Bishop of California, Saint Giles Episcopal Parish began celebrating Sunday Eucharistic Services in the College Chapel in the Advent of 1982. The congregation has continued utilizing the Chapel. Saint Giles parishioners and the Campus Ministry cooperate in numerous ways, such as providing Chapel decorations for Easter and Christmas. The Rev. Lois Pinneo (who later became Rev. Lois Pinneo Hoy) was named the permanent Rector for St. Giles shortly after the parish was established at the College. The President received letters of gratitude from both the Right Rev. William Swing and the Archbishop of Canturbury, the Most Rev. George Leonard Carey, on the occasion of the 15th Anniversary of the relocation of St. Giles to the Saint Mary's College Chapel. The presence of St. Giles parish offers students who are Episcopalians (Anglicans), Anglo-Catholics or others who are not in union with Rome an on-campus alternative religious tradition.

In addition to preparing for and celebrating Sunday liturgies during the academic year, the Campus Ministry was also responsible for conducting retreats. The Rite of Christian Initiation for Adults, marriage preparation counseling, the Sacrament of Reconciliation (Confessions), daily Mass for the Christian Brothers and other attendees, Masses for special occasions such as the Mass of the Holy Spirit, and funeral services for Christian Brothers and members of the faculty and staff, managed weddings and worked with student leaders in organizing various Christian service outreach programs for those with various needs. In 1997-1998 funds were secured to develop a more aggressive outreach program under the acronym CILSA (Catholic Institute for Lasallian Social Action) that allowed the Campus Ministry staff to devote itself to more pastoral duties while encouraging students to participate in charitable works under the auspices of CILSA. Some members of the Campus Ministry staff have taught classes, and others have lived in the residence halls as Resident Directors.

In the late '70s to the early '80s, the Dominican Fathers were able to secure the services of Bay Area organist David Farr to provide supportive music for various liturgical events. The most notable were several Advent services in preparation for the Feast of Christmas. Candlelight processions, grand organ music, an echo organ in the side Chapel, and a trained student choir added to the inspiration of the homily and sacredness of the Eucharistic celebration. The Advent ceremonies were celebrated in preparation for the Christmas liturgies that students would attend in their own parishes during the Christmas holidays.

The files on Campus Ministry housed in the College archives are filled with leaflets and brochures, liturgical music and photographs of numerous activities sponsored by Campus Ministry. The archives also contain a number of historical accounts written from time to time outlining successes and activities, observations for improvement and expressions of frustration regarding the support of the Ministry. Several Campus Ministers expressed the need for a Christian Brother as a full-time member of the Ministry team who would, among other benefits, provide a direct link between the Campus Ministry and the Brothers' communities. I acknowledged that more direct communication between the Brothers and the Ministry would be beneficial, since the communication between the Campus Ministry Team and the Christian Brothers waxed and waned over the years. In considering the elegant and inspirational moments and those more *tres ordinaire,* as well as the few ineptly conducted celebrations, one must view the total effect as one does sage investments in the stock market. Over a 28-year period one would have to admit that, all fluctuations considered, the Campus Ministry has maintained a reasonable and stable effectiveness in a particularly difficult time in Church history in the United States. For indications of the efficacious impact the Ministry has had on numerous students one must note the large number of alumni who return to be married in the College Chapel. The College administration, the priests and the Christian Brothers have reason to be eternally grateful.

On reflection, I stated that had I the means to do so I would have provided more funding for enhancing liturgical celebrations, so that a consistently impressive student choir with accompaniment would be available for Sunday Mass and special occasional liturgies. Raising the intellectual and cultural tone of the student body is one function of collegiate life, and thus raising the qualitative tone of liturgical life would complement and enhance the College Mission. Since the College enjoys an unusual relationship to God though the Real Presence of Christ in the sacrament of the Eucharist as a gift of God's love, the presence of the Eucharistic sacrament provides an emphatic meaning to the Lasallian phrase, "Let us remember that we are in the Holy Presence of God!"

Though Campus Ministry did sponsor lectures and colloquia, more funding could have provided additional debates and events on current issues, perhaps in conjunction with the Religious Studies Department. Educational awareness programs and seminars would have been particularly relevant to students' needs.

A listing of chaplains, directors and associate directors of the Campus Ministry program is located in the Appendix, page 357.

Academic Life, 1975-1997

New Academic Programs, 1975

Executive MBA, an Inspired Concept, 1975

In 1975, two young men, Bob Ferguson and Michael McCune, asked for an appointment with the late Brother Louis Civitello, who was at that time the Financial Vice President and one of the administrators who had proposed an MBA program a few years earlier. Bob Ferguson, Vice President of Shannon Research, Inc., had reflected on MBA programs and proposed the institution of an MBA program that contained an appealing requirement, thus making it different from any other MBA program in the area at the time. He suggested the formation of an Executive MBA program that would limit acceptance of students to those who had at least five years of business experience. Not only would the students be learning from their professors, he claimed, but they would be learning from each other as well.

Plans were generated for the MBA program, with both the usual requirements in terms of credits and time required, but also with its distinctive element. Corporate sponsors were enlisted to fund the new venture in Contra Costa County. The initial sponsors, generous in their support, were Bank of America, Marsh-McLennan Insurance, Safeway Stores, Standard Oil of California, Wells Fargo Bank, Newman Construction Co., American Building and Maintenance and the Khashoggi Institute. The Clorox Company, Frank B. Hall, John R. Cahill and Richard Wall were later donors.

Brothers Louis and Dominic both viewed the plan with enthusiasm. I was likewise intrigued. On the contrary, Brother Robert Smith, FSC, PhD, the Director of the undergraduate Integral Program spoke to me urging me not to approve the establishment of an MBA program because, he argued, Saint Mary's could not match the quality of the Haas Graduate School of Business at the University of California, Berkeley, or the MBA program at Stanford. "Saint Mary's would only be second or third tier," he opined, "and could become a source of embarrassment for the College in the business community."

After carefully reviewing the proposal and discussing the concept with my administrators, I thought Brother Robert had underestimated what Saint Mary's could do to offer a quality program to the citizens of Contra Costa County. I also realized that public relations intensity and creativity would be required to promote an MBA that differed significantly from other institutions of higher education in the Bay Area. The public relations firm of Vilas, Inc. was commissioned to do just that. It delivered an intriguing advertising program that proved to be attractive to potential students. We were off to a good start.

The ability of a graduate business program to compete with other graduate business programs in the area would have to be in terms of faculty academic background and expertise, the theoretical quality and practical application of its curriculum and the efficacy of its five-year experience requirement for all students. I approved the MBA concept in principle and agreed to submit the MBA proposal directly to the Board of Trustees for approval, since the Faculty Assembly had turned down the concept but a few years before in the circus-like atmosphere of its meeting on that occasion. Brother Dominic, the Academic Vice President, proposed to divide the College into two major academic groups, namely graduate and undergraduate, with a separate faculty council for the graduate division. The Board readily approved the MBA concept and the academic division, if only temporarily. The program would operate on a conventional quarter system, be conducted on campus four nights per week from 6:00 p.m. to 10:00 p.m. and would span 21 months for completion and the awarding of the degree. MBA students would attend four-hour classes twice a week. Within the first year the program exceeded all expectations primarily because of the quality of management, students and faculty, several of whom also taught at the Haas School of Business at U.C Berkeley.

The program commenced in September 1975, with Brother Louis Civitello, FSC, as Director and Robert Ferguson as Assistant Director. Within the first quarter of the fall semester 1975, for personal reasons, Brother Louis relinquished the direction of the program to Michael McCune, the energetic, imaginative and capable entrepreneur who worked with Brother Louis and Bob Ferguson on the program design. However, as an entrepreneur, McCune soon found other opportunities for his varied organizational talents and appetites and in 1977 placed the direction of the program in the hands of one of its faculty members, Clifton Healey, who served as Vice President for Crown Zellerbach, Inc. Healey directed the program from 1977 to 1979, when he relinquished the leadership to another faculty member, Eric Hansen, PhD, who had joined the faculty in 1977. Hansen successfully served as director for 10 years, 1979-1989, returning to faculty status after having had sufficient fill of administration. Nelson Shelton, who was a graduate of the Saint Mary's MBA program and who held a doctorate from UC Berkeley, headed the program commencing in 1989. The earliest faculty members (1975-1979), all part-time at the outset, were David Bowen, PhD, Leonard Auerbach, PhD, and Roger Lamm, PhD, Eric Hansen, Ph.D, Thomas McCullough, PhD, Lionel Chan, PhD, JD, CPA; and Tom Herman, PhD. The first faculty placed on the tenure track in 1983 were David Bowen, Leonard Auerbach, Roger Lamm and George Fletcher. Barry Eckhouse was placed on the tenure track in 1988.

The Graduate Business Program engaged in a creative advertising program with posters in BART Trains and advertising in local newspapers. In due time, not only did competing institutions engage in advertising, but they also established Executive MBA programs. The Graduate Business Program earned a reputation as a pacesetter in terms of promotion and academic quality, its ability to translate theory into practice and its attractiveness to upwardly mobile students engaged in full-time management.

The success of the program was predicated on the power of good ideas being born of conceptual and creative thinking, and not unlike Plato's insistence that the educated creative intellectual return to aid his fellow citizens, the MBA student is challenged to bring rational order to the often disjointed reality of the workplace. Sophisticated insight and criticism is preferred to mere information or technique, and yet while intellect is paramount, it must not be too removed from corporate activities beyond the boardroom.

In 1984 a non-executive, part-time MBA program was added to serve a capable, but less experienced, group of students with an average age of 27.

Nelson Shelton, a graduate of Stanford, earned his MA in Political Science from Northwestern University and his Doctorate in Business Administration from UC Berkeley in 1991. He continued to direct the MBA programs well into the new millennium.

After 1989, the Graduate Business Programs added a significant complement of full-time tenure-track faculty. The tradition of recruiting faculty with outstanding academic credentials continued with the hiring of Andrew Williams and Phil Perry, both Stanford PhDs; Deepah Sainanee, PhD (University of Chicago); Yung Jae Lee, PhD (UC Irvine); James Hawley, PhD (McGill University); Ted Tsukahara, '62, PhD (Claremont Graduate School); and Jose Blanco, PhD (Utah State). Many among the MBA faculty have had considerable business experience, reflecting the balance between theory and practice, one of the notable marks of the Saint Mary's College Graduate Business Programs from the start.

I saw the MBA program as a means of supporting the College, of offering a program of benefit to the people of Alameda and Contra Costa Counties, and as a natural extension of the undergraduate School of Economics and Business Administration. Assuming that the program would characterize itself as one of quality, I conjectured that its public relations value would be a positive advantage within the educational and business community of the County, which it became.

Accounting

A proposal presented to the Faculty Assembly on Jan. 10, 1975, that an accounting major be instituted in the undergraduate institution in the fall of 1975, evoked apprehensive remarks about such a major from some liberal arts faculty. "However, among vocationally oriented programs," one faculty member declared, "the accounting major would be the most acceptable and would, in fact, improve the academic climate of the School of Economics and Business Administration." No reasons were offered as to why the accounting major would, "improve the academic climate of the School," unless the comment was an acknowledgement that the study of mathematics (albeit, theoretical rather than applied) was one of the Quadrivium, the four major scientific academic areas among the liberal arts. Nor were any clarifications offered as to why the academic climate in the School of Economics and Business Administration required improvement. Another faculty member stated that the selection of new programs should *not* be governed by their ability to be, "a boon financially." The motion to approve the accounting major passed with a vote of 14 yea and 7 nay, with 3 abstentions. The accounting major became an exceptionally popular and successful major, especially in terms of employment opportunities.

Division of College into Schools

In 1928, with the move from Oakland to Moraga, the College Catalog (of Courses) identified three Schools: *Arts and Letters, Commerce* and *Civil Engineering.* However, the School titles for various curricular programs do not appear again in the annual catalog until 1934. Between 1929 and 1934 various programs were identified as professional programs; the Pre-Dental Curriculum, the Pre-Legal Curriculum or the Economics and Commerce Curriculum. The *School* of Economics and Business Administration was listed in the 1934 Catalog, and was the sole *School* listed. The following year the *School of Arts and Letters* and the *School of Science* were also given the title of School, thus forming an academic triumvirate.

That the economics and business administration curriculum was the first to be named a School in the new listing of Saint Mary's curricula in the 1934-1935 catalog may be indicative of widespread student interest in preparing for career opportunities in a time of grave national depression. Or it may have been so designated to clearly distinguish it from the liberal arts which comprised the main academic emphasis of the institution. It may also explain the use of earlier career titles, such as pre-dental, pre-legal and pre-medical to encourage students to follow their professional aspirations through normal courses in the sciences and arts and letters. The fact that athletics, especially the apparently successful big-time football program, attracted students to an all-male student body may have also had a bearing on highlighting offerings in career opportunities upon graduation. The administration was undoubtedly seeking enrollment at a time of serious financial stringency.

The legacy of the Christian Brothers to attend to students in need would be an ingrained prompt to offer pragmatic career programs to the young men of immigrant families -- many of whom were Catholics -- who comprised a significant percentage of the population of the greater Bay Area between the two great wars. The Brothers, particularly in religious men like Brothers Leo Meehan, Edmund Dolan, Robert Smith, Virgil Eastham and Alfred Brousseau, also well understood the importance of comprehensive studies that would not only provide opportunity for professional advancement, but would also provide insight for living a respectable life. Thus, requirements were developed for all students in all Schools. Philosophy and religious studies requirements provided all students with a comprehensive understanding of ethics, the natural law and the philosophical principles of wonder and discovery. Graduates would thus be able to form their own philosophy of life, hopefully in light of the Catholic intellectual tradition.

Within recent memory, corporate practices have become exceedingly more sophisticated as they absorbed the rapid advances in technology, statistical studies, marketing techniques, business ethics, psychology, accounting practices, leadership training and strategic management, the complexity of organizational structures and the exigencies of globalization. An institution such as Saint Mary's has continued its long-term tradition of offering selected career-oriented programs in conjunction with what it deems essential components in liberal arts education for living a fulfilling life.

When Dean C. J. "Mike" Walter assumed leadership of the School of Economics and Business Administration in 1984, he was quietly chagrined to discover that the School was carrying a higher student-faculty ratio than the School of Liberal Arts, and slowly moved toward a program of equalization. Walter worked tirelessly to enhance the professionalism of his faculty. He became a man in the midst of controversy when the Accreditation Team of 1985 recommended that both graduate and undergraduate faculties by placed under the Dean of the School of Economics and Business Administration, something the heretofore independent graduate faculty opposed. Whether such a move was necessary is debatable, but there was some trickle down, as well as some trickle up, advantage to having graduate and undergraduate faculty interchange ideas, along with the fact that graduate faculty were being placed on the tenure track and thus assuming roles on various College-wide committees.

Health, Physical Education and Recreation

Football coach Leo McKillip, EdD, representing the Physical Education Department, appeared before the Faculty Assembly on Feb. 13, 1975, to propose establishing a major in Health, Physical Education and Recreation, a program that would draw heavily from the School of Science for necessary courses to fulfill the major. Professor Chester Aaron seemed skeptical and wondered whether the major would be detrimental to other classes since its students would be prone to cut classes or do incomplete work as did some athletes. Professor Norman Springer stated that it was "injudicious to devote money, time and energy to developing an Health, Physical Education and Recreation major when liberal arts programs are being cut back ..." Alan Pollock cited program as, "one more element in the proliferation of courses, that in his opinion are moving Saint Mary's away from her position as a good liberal arts college." The motion to approve the H., P.E. and R. program passed by a vote of 21 yea, 3 nay, with 3 abstentions.

Given the lopsided vote in favor of the H.,P.E. and R. Major, lingering questions with regard to adding certain major studies to the College curriculum in view of the overriding philosophy of the College. That philosophy must take into account the students that come to Saint Mary's College, as well as those we may wish to attract. Questions that come to the fore are: What kind of education should be offered to all students, and what kinds of major areas in principle should be added to the comprehensive curriculum? What are the best majors for a quality liberal arts education? What are the weakest majors in terms of a quality liberal education? Are there majors that are fundamentally opposed to a good liberal arts education? Secondly, which majors and general requirements would be supportive of a quality liberal eduation and which would not? One must ask whether a major like H., P.E. and R. will most likely detract from what is philosophically considered a good liberal arts education? What are the principles that define "quality" and "liberal arts," and are these principles generally agreed upon by the majority of the faculty and administration in light of the College Mission statement?

While it seems that the addition of Health, Physical Education and Recreation did not in any way affect what are called Liberal Arts majors or the Collegiate Seminar program, does it provide the students with a major bereft of serious academic and Liberal Arts mettle? Are there other majors that have been added to the curriculum in similar stance to questions about H., P.E. and R.? Is Women's Studies, for example, moving Saint Mary's away from her position as a good liberal arts college? While one cannot ignore Alan Pollock's question about "one more element in the proliferation of courses, etc ..." did his own vision of the changes of 1969 contribute to what he now questioned?

Education Master of Arts and Nursing Proposals

Following two victories in establishing additional academic programs in spite of opposition, a report to the Faculty Assembly meeting in March on the Board of Trustees Meeting of February by Valerie Gomez, Ph.D, the faculty representative to the Board, evoked some strong reactions. Norman Springer asked, "How it had come about that a graduate program leading to an MA in Education had been approved without consultation with the faculty, considering that the faculty had, on Oct. 11, 1973, tabled a motion proposing an MA in Education indefinitely." Professor Gomez stated that "no plan had gone beyond the talking stage and that when matters are ready to present to the faculty they will be presented." She also cited the fact that the written ballot of the faculty on Nov. 27, 1974, as well as the action taken by the Board of Trustees on Dec. 2, 1974, both approved the proposal by the Academic Vice President that he should proceed to "develop other quality educational endeavors," including a graduate division, thus superseding the faculty vote of Oct. 11, 1973.

Professor Gomez' report did not satisfy some members of the faculty. Confusion seemed to reign. Some thought that the Board had approved what were being presented to faculty as progress reports on proposals. Springer voiced his view that "faculty should always participate in the give-and-take discussion concerning changes in curriculum," as did Ed Versluis and some others, one of whom thought that the Academic Vice President had committed an "outrageous affront." The Assembly attempted to mollify the discussion by passing a resolution that "the Academic Vice President consult with faculty and the Academic Council before taking to the Trustees any final program proposals for adoption." The vote was 18 yea, 3 nay, with 4 abstentions. (March 1975.)

The Academic Council's governance proposal advocated three divisions -- undergraduate, graduate and extended education -- but with the proviso that there be an academic senate to coordinate and monitor them. Brother Dominic did not favor an Academic Senate at this time, stating that it was too premature.

Three faculty members (Professors Larson, Isetti and Loome) petitioned to speak to the Board at its meeting of April 30, 1975, to urge the acceptance of the Academic Council proposal. The Board, noting its Dec. 2nd 1974, meeting, clearly separated graduate from undergraduate, and extended education from the other two. However, the Board also required that the Academic Vice President consult with appropriate committees and urged the Governance Committee to prepare models of governance to oversee the functioning and coordination of the three major divisions. It also added that the guidelines of the Western Association of Schools and Colleges, the official name for the area Accrediting Commission, be followed in establishing external degree programs.

The Board also approved the proposal for the establishment of an Executive MBA Program as outlined by Robert Ferguson, in accordance with the guidelines for other proposed programs, and with the added admonition that initial start-up funding would not be drawn from the College operational budget.

While I favored certain of the proposed programs and the separation of the College into three divisions with the provision that the Governance Committee be charged with establishing a governance structure for appropriate oversight, I had two concerns: one was the establishment of programs without acknowledging the old adage that "the devil is in the details," and the other that faculty morale would suffer if oversight were not satisfactory. I assumed that the Accrediting Commission's guidelines would be considered seriously. Unfortunately, this was not a valid assumption, as later events would reveal.

The wisdom of the Board regarding academic politics and policies drew particularly upon three members: Dr. William P. Niland, an alumnus, who had been Academic Vice President at the College in the late 1940s and was at that time President of Diablo Valley Community College in Pleasant Hill, and Chairman of the Saint Mary's College Board; George R. Gordon, JD, an alumnus of the College and President of the Contra Costa Community College Board; and Sister Ambrose Devereux, SNJM, PhD, President of Holy Names College in Oakland. These Board members were keenly aware of faculty politics, management protocol and the responsibility of both the Board and administration to manage prudently. The elements contained in the Board action reflected this awareness as well as the frustration of the Board in seeking full faculty cooperation in a time of both crisis and opportunity.

Academic Crises

The administration is expected to lead the institution out of any crisis, financial crises in particular. However, there is a protective hook buried in the expectation that the administration work its magic, namely that it does so through what often becomes almost endless consultation with both individuals and groups of faculty members. It must be admitted that at times a discussion in a faculty community, acting as a genuine community of scholars, produces quality productivity. Though practical concerns, some quite legitimate, heighten anxiety, some research and detail-oriented faculty tend to speculate broadly, and at times endlessly, on the myriad possibilities that financial exigency may have, not only on their personal pocketbooks but on their academic ideals as well, especially when new ventures are suggested. Understandably, internecine conflicts can have a deleterious effect on morale and thus high-drama conflicts if possible, should be avoided. During the financial crisis, increases in salary, though modest, were granted and essential budgetary elements were preserved. Fiscal reductions in certain areas were a cause for reasonable concern. Yet, there was an element among more outspoken faculty that seemed to relish stirring up the witches' brew, since their rhetoric continued to heat the boiling cauldron.

The abrupt Tom Slakey resignation as Academic Vice President in June 1974 and his hurried replacement by Brother Dominic Ruegg, FSC, PhD, left some faculty members reeling. Brother Dominic did not tarry in seeking ways to promote new programs which would provide financial support, ameliorate financial exigency and enhance the reputation of the College in the County. In view of the financial strain, he asked faculty members to take on one extra course for a limited time so that the financial crisis could be eased. His publicly suggesting at a faculty meeting that the faculty "get off their posteriors and help resolve the problem" did not sit well with the more outspoken members of the so-called progressive or liberal old guard. I surmised that an increase in the student body, not only in traditional undergraduates but in graduate and certificate programs as well, would be a major factor in resolving financial difficulties, as would a prudential restraint on spending, especially since the budget was already uncomfortably thin.

With these issues in the minds of both administrators and faculty members, the College received notice that the regular visit of the Accreditation Association, the Western Association of Schools and Colleges was due in the fall of 1975.

The Accreditation Visit of 1975

The WASC Accreditation Team arrived on campus a month after the commencement of the 1975-1976 Academic Year. Its report was not surprising given the dissatisfaction caused by fiscal anxiety among the faculty, the administration and the Board of Trustees, as well as the opposition among a group of faculty members to both Brother Dominic's appointment and his proposals for expanding the offerings of the College. The Official Visit of an Accreditation Team was seen by some faculty as an opportunity to sway the Team to support the claims of a dissident faculty group that the administration, supported by the Board of Trustees, had gone terribly wrong. In fact, it was the hope of some that the report of the Visiting Team would be so strong that the administration would be forced to resign. The Visiting Team did not perceive that under the leadership of a few articulate and influential faculty members, a relatively small, but well-orchestrated effort was alleged to be underway. The Team, even after being informed of such an attempt, denied that any such effort was evident, which to them might have been the case. Letters to the Team from two tenured and normally non-politcally involved faculty members were seemingly ignored.

The Visiting Team of 1975, chaired by David Cole of Occidental College in Los Angeles, took alarming note of current heightened faculty tensions, something that the Team of 1969 did not detect during its visit. He exercised a dramatic flair not usually found in accreditation reports. "The financial difficulties are intensified, and in our opinion sometimes increased by a state of interpersonal tension which pervades faculty-administration relations, and influences relations not only between those two sectors, but within each sector as well. The committee was left with the profound impression that these tensions have reached such a destructive level and that it is they, fully as much or perhaps more than the financial crisis, which threaten the institution." (Accreditation Report, David L. Cole, Chair, Oct. 15-17, 1975, Saint Mary's College Archives.) No doubt the Visiting Team was faced with a perplexing array of conundrums that focussed upon major administrative changes, a developing financial crisis that the Board of Trustees was intent on reversing, proposed academic expansion with or without full faculty approbation and the alleged coordination of a variety of seemingly rehearsed faculty complaints. This particular faculty coalition was described by John C. Dwyer, STD, professor of religious studies as making "the entertainment of the committee almost a full-time job during the visitation." (Letter of John C. Dwyer to Brother Mel Anderson, Jan. 26, 1976.)

Some recommendations of the 1975 Visiting Team belabored the obvious, since they couldn't have been said in jest, such as, "The College should move at once away from the recent plan of deficit budgeting." I had clearly stated to the Board of Trustees in 1975 that I would be most gratified "if there were but a $1 surplus by the end of the year."

Recommendations such as those critical of the Collegiate Seminar program were viewed by both myself and a representative number of faculty members as meddling with the sacrosanct core of the traditional liberal arts curriculum. The Report caustically states: "That any literate teacher or student is capable of extracting from one of the classics some great idea that is transformed effortlessly or magically into compelling personal principles is an unwarranted assumption. A quiet recognition of prevailing student academic capabilities might lead the College to reduce the number of mandatory seminars and schedule this smaller number in the junior and senior years."

The Visiting Team observations on the Seminar program reflected a not uncommon view of those immersed in mainstream higher education often characterized by departmental autonomy and the adaptation of the scientific method within all departments, the use of lectures and textbooks, and the mentality that the most honorable task of any department is to prepare stellar students for graduate research. To encourage all members of the Saint Mary's faculty to engage in conducting Collegiate Seminars was anathema to certain members of the professoriate, who believe that only experts in a particular discipline should be allowed access to classes that discuss the texts from a particular discipline. The unwarranted criticism of the Accreditation Team, however, did prompt the inauguration of faculty seminars so that involved faculty could become better versed in conducting them for students, a creative means to foil what was considered glib criticism.

Unfortunately, the Visiting Team either did not understand the principles governing the Collegiate Seminar program or did not agree with the principles as understood by a representative group of faculty. Conducting seminars on the classics or Great Books, as they are often called, demands considerable professorial talent to lead students to read carefully, to raise significant questions from their reading and then engage in focused dialogue with classmates and their instructor in seeking understanding. Great Books seminars are often called *The Great Conversation,* and the seminar itself is symbolized as a *Community of Learners.* There is no effortless magic involved, unless the dawning of the light in certain students at inspired moments is considered magical, as it sometimes seems. Under normal circumstances the seminar process is neither effortless nor magical. Though it is true that older, more experienced students will often see the light sooner than younger ones, an accomplished seminar instructor can evoke within younger, idealistic students the wonder necessary to pursue thoughtful questions raised through reading the likes of Plato, Aristotle, Sophocles, Augustine, Dante, Shakespeare, Locke, Kant and Marx, not only upon the first reading, but upon reflection and some late night discussion in the residence halls. An obvious pragmatic advantage of the seminar is that students learn to express themselves among their peers and, in due time, argue their positions with both force and clarity. Writing cogent papers on various Great Books topics requires students to think through their ideas as they compose a literate assignment.

Faculty members who inaugurated the Collegiate Seminar program were both talented and appropriately educated.. They had thought seriously about its principles and methodology and had evaluated its effects for many years. One wonders whether the critics of the seminar program are contending that a literate person could not read a classical text unless some expert were available who could explain it and demonstrate how its insights would be applicable or how the concepts in one text related to earlier ones. There is a rationale as to why texts are arranged in chronological sequence, just as there is nothing magical about engaging faculty across the disciplines to read, reflect and discuss the greatest books ever written. Having faculty members not previously acquainted with the Great Books read them and engage in faculty and student seminars produced, over time, a more liberally educated faculty, something that many other institutions without an organized liberal arts curriculum that crosses disciplinary lines cannot enjoy.

The report of the Visiting Team was less critical than the so-called detractors had hoped, but much more critical than the administration and many other faculty members had anticipated. The Visitors of 1975 acknowledged that several new programs such as the MBA and an Associate of Arts program in financial planning (that was eventually shelved) showed signs of promise, both academically and financially.

The Visiting Team also noted that the Accreditation report of 1969 had stated:"During a short period of time, Saint Mary's has changed from a paternalistic method of administration to one with greater and greater participation in important decisions by the entire college community. The Committee believes that this increasing participation, particularly on the part of the faculty, has contributed immeasurably to the high morale which pervades the campus." The 1975 report, reflecting on the 1969 report states, "Against this backdrop, the circumstances encountered by the committee reflect an unfortunate change." (Op. Cit. Report, Oct. Pages 15-17, 1975.)

Ironically one major reason for the change in academic leadership in 1971 was that many faculty alleged that the Academic Vice President was, authoritarian and domineering. While there was a change from what could be deemed paternalism in some areas prior to the 1969 report, many faculty claimed that the academic administration in the Pollock era manifested the *appearances* of democracy; while the tension mounted within the faculty as the Pollock years progressed. I had been appointed to attempt a reconsideration of the so-called progress under Alan Pollock, and even to reverse efforts that he and his associates had achieved by inserting into the institution a philosophy that differed from the time-honored intellectual traditions of Catholic higher education. The 1969 Visiting Team was naïve in assuming that faculty morale was generally positive and uniform. I discovered within a short time that the contrary was clearly the case. My experience with the so-called progressive mentality I encountered was that it was an uncompromising, determined, one-way attitudinal street, an observation one could also make of the far right.

After having read the 1975 Accreditation Report, Professor Frank Ellis, a member of the Philosophy Department, stated in a letter to me, dated Dec. 1, 1975, that "the report's adverse comments about the administration are unbalanced. The administration does have the support of a majority of the faculty. It seems to me that the recent (Visiting) Committee got a rather one-sided view of things." (Letter of Frank Ellis to Brother Mel Anderson, Dec. 1, 1975 .)

Professor John C. Dwyer of the Religious Studies Department, stated in his letter to me that: "I have come to a conclusion that I believe can be verified by any impartial observer: the majority of our faculty are happy with the direction which the College has taken during the last five years. Unfortunately, this majority did not bother to inform the accreditors of this fact. Perhaps in this we all made a mistake: it did not occur to us that the accreditors would be quite as naïve as they were, nor did we believe that the dissident faculty members (including one or two of your own community) would be willing to compromise the College to give vent to the irritation they feel at the reassertion of the authority of the administration and the Board of Trustees." (Letter of John C. Dwyer to Brother Mel Anderson, Nov. 26, 1975.)

Though the Accreditation Report was unflattering and underscored its perceived difficulties in dire terms, it did not accomplish what the dissident group desired. Neither I nor my staff resigned nor did we lose heart. The improvement of the campus physical Master Plan was not deterred, and both my administrative staff and I were confident that new programs, a vigorous admissions staff and careful budget management would reverse the negative financial situation. The Board of Trustees was also confident that a financial plan envisioned a positive balance and noted with satisfaction that the building and renovation program continued unabated. The new Provincial, Brother Raphael Willeke, was well aware of the motivations that prompted the initiative the dissident group had undertaken. He was negatively impressed by the seemingly uniform statements from a number of faculty who requested a meeting with him, urging him to act at once on their proposal to appoint a new administration.

On the advice of my Administrative Council, I responded to the Accreditation Commission's Report of 1975, indicating that the report was unbalanced for two reasons, the first being that an organized effort was made to discredit the administration and the second, that the Visiting Team made judgments without input from an objective cross-section of faculty representing all Schools of the College. Not only did the members of the Council receive written documents from faculty members, but several faculty members voiced or wrote objections to the one-sidedness of the Report. However, the College was fully accredited.

The budget deficit, which had reached a high of $1.32 million in 1976, had been reduced by over half a million dollars by 1977, and by 1979 it was eliminated. But the road to financial solvency contained troublesome bumps, including some missteps and misgivings.

The Institute for Professional Development, 1975

Toward the end of Brother Dominic's first year as Academic Vice President (1975) he was contacted by John Sperling, PhD, then president of an academic services organization creatively titled *The Institute for Professional Development* located in Santa Clara County. John Sperling, an academic entrepreneur and former professor at San Jose State University, had designed a baccalaureate program for older adults who had accumulated two years of collegiate work and had for personal reasons interrupted their collegiate education. Since many older adults had acquired certain skills and insight through their employment, Sperling was of the view that they could be awarded limited academic credit for what he described as work experience. For example, if a potential student had worked as a computer technician for several years, would not his work experience be worthy of credit for basic computer courses in a collegiate setting? A potential student's two-year academic program at an accredited collegiate institution, combined with credit for courses taken at other colleges, as well as limited credit for his/her work experience which matched descriptions of courses in college catalogs from accredited institutions, would give him/her a limited number of units required toward a baccalaureate degree. The claim was made that an academic program for completing the degree in an accredited institution utilizing the techniques designed especially for the adult learner by The Institute for Professional Development would be both attractive to, and advantageous for, the adult learner.

The baccalaureate degree would be awarded by the accredited institution once the student had acquired the requisite number of units required by the state and/or the institution and had completed a major. Majors were predominantly in business administration, management or health services. Since the California State University system had devised its own program for older adults taught in more conventional ways with existing faculty, Sperling's innovative program and in particular the concept of credit for work experience was not acceptable to the State University system. Brimming over with imagination, determination and shrewdness, Sperling had faith in his ideas and took leave of the State University system to develop his program through existing independent institutions. He approached Brother Dominic and convinced him that the program would be suitable for Saint Mary's, noting that other institutions such as the University of San Francisco, San Francisco College for Women (Lone Mountain), Redlands University and Regis College in Denver had contracts with IPD to what seemed to be the mutual benefit of the students, the institutions and IPD. However, what Brother Dominic and the officers of various colleges learned in due time was that the officers of the Accrediting Association, the Western Association of School and Colleges, viewed Sperling's academic venture with profound skepticism, and harbored serious doubts as to whether the IPD program met the Association's academic standards. As a result of its displeasure with the Institute for Professional Development, the Accreditation Association was most cautious in its dealings with both IPD and the institutions which had signed agreements with it to form joint programs, most likely fearing the possibility of litigation initiated by IPD or by one or more of the independent institutions.

Brother Dominic's enthusiasm for the program was two-fold. First, the program would bring many adults the benefits of higher education, an opportunity many could not enjoy earlier in their lives for any number of reasons, such as financial inability to pursue higher education, marriage and the responsibilities of family life, service in the armed forces or personal deficiencies associated with being young adults, such as academic disinterest, the lure of earning a living and its consequent independence, personal instability, lack of academic focus and so forth. Secondly, Brother Dominic saw the program as a means to increase the financial base of the College by adding students without adding more facilities or the necessity of providing certain services, such as residential housing or athletics, to the older adult group. He was also inspired by the concept of linking older adult needs with the spirit of St. John Baptist De La Salle, the founder of the Christian Brothers, who in 1680 had reached out to those with limited or no opportunity for securing an education by establishing both grammar schools and teacher training institutions (*Ecoles Normal*). In the 19th Century, the French Brothers conducted many successful academic programs for older adults in need of adapting themselves to the industrial revolution and new ventures in Europe. Of course, in 19th Century France there were no accrediting agencies. Student satisfaction was the best measure of general approval as identified by full enrollment.

Though many older adults who had not completed their collegiate education soon realized the importance of completing the baccalaureate degree, they found that most of higher education was not flexible in its scheduling or offerings so that their needs could be served in a manner that accommodated their family and/or work schedules. I heard Brother Dominic's petition that the program be established and accompanied him to the Institute for Professional Studies headquarters in Santa Clara to conduct a preliminary investigation. The Institute was housed in a large, clean modern facility, which was well-appointed, organized and manned with apparently competent and sufficient personnel. John Sperling presented a step-by-step overview of the process and was specific as to the role the College would play in a Saint Mary's - IPD liaison. The College would have on-campus program administrators who were full-time College employees answerable to the Academic Vice President. Furthermore, faculty members who were attuned to teaching returning adults would be offered the opportunity to teach in the program.

Though I was hesitant to adopt IPD programs wholesale, on Brother Dominic's advice, I agreed to sign a contract, provided the Board of Trustees would approve it. After Trustee approval, a contract was signed on Oct. 10, 1975 for one year, with the provision that it would extend for four more years if it were not terminated by the end of the first year. Contained in the contract were clauses regarding curriculum, mutual financial agreements and responsibilities toward students. Some of these clauses proved to be significant escape hatches at a later date. The program was placed in the hands of faculty member Robert Terrell, but before it commenced he resigned in favor of a full-time appointment elsewhere. The program began in the fall of 1975, under the direction of Nancy Dyar, MA, as the chair of the Saint Mary's Department of Extended Education. One usually anticipates that a new program will encounter difficulties requiring adjustments, as was the case with the January Term, the new curriculum of 1969, the Master's programs in psychology and the Department of Education. As anticipated, the joint Saint Mary's/IPD program was no exception. The unusual nature of a joint program, with one partner not holding official accreditation, was a concept new to Saint Mary's but not to the WASC Accrediting Commission for Schools. Sperling and his associates had created a system and techniques particularly designed for the teaching of older adults, the majority beyond their mid-30s, who required a certain kind of sensitivity and perception not always possessed by every undergraduate professor. Had it not been for the carefully conceived processes on screening both students and instructors, the fledgling Extended Education program would not have functioned as well as it seemed to do.

Brother Dominic learned from colleagues that IPD and its relationship with institutions other than Saint Mary's were under severe scrutiny from WASC and reported this fact to me. Brother Dominic's view, which coincided with that of John Sperling, was that the Accreditation Association was dominated by people who could not accept the possibility that there were ways of conducting an educational program, particularly one for older, returning, working adults, that could be as effective as the traditional undergraduate experience offered to 18- to 22-year old collegians. Not only did Brother Dominic support IPD and John Sperling with enthusiasm, he also became an adversary of what he considered an overly conservative and unhelpful accrediting body, often dominated, he claimed, by the California State University system. Brother Dominic was later asked to become a member of John Sperling's Advisory Council, an invitation he accepted and on which he served for several years. However, it must be said that *the Accrediting Association did have some legitimate concerns* with the innovative program. The WASC Accreditating Commission for Schools concerns were unfortunately couched more in terms of governance issues than in academic ones, though academic concerns were based on whether the regular full-time faculty of an institution had oversight and control over all of the institutional academic endeavors. In the view of the Accrediting Association, the IPD arrangement compromised the independence and control of the accredited institution and its faculty. It is generally accepted academic wisdom that a qualified faculty will exhibit instructional quality, and that academic reputation and ultimate academic viability is thus its charge.

It was at this time that Kay Andersen, the Association's Executive Director, proposed a new sanction to all members that could be imposed on any member deemed wanting in whatever way the Association so judged. The proposal was accepted. The sanction of "probation," that did not remove or deny accreditation, was added to the others, namely, "show cause" and "withdrawal of accreditation." When the Accreditation Association became aware of Saint Mary's formal involvement with IPD, it was determined to curtail further IPD joint programs in the California higher educational arena, though this intention was never openly stated. WASC determined that any institution could hire consultants for the development of an academic program, provided the institution and its faculty were in full control of the program and that the role of the consultant was limited to suggesting concepts and methods for practical application to the faculty and the administration, but that the full responsibility for accepting suggestions rested with the accredited institution.

The intent of Kay Andersen and his associates to remove IPD programs from California eventually backfired when IPD moved to Arizona, named itself the University of Phoenix and received full accreditation from the North Central Accrediting Association. The University of Phoenix returned to California by establishing satellite campuses throughout the state and beyond. In fact, it became the largest institution of higher education in the United States. Eventually, as will be noted below, the College divested itself of IPD (the University of Phoenix) and significantly improved upon its fundamental concept, thus gaining not only approbation but commendation from the Accrediting organization for its School of Extended Education.

Expansion and Tension

A Proposal for a Communications Major, 1976

A proposal for the institution of a major in Communications was officially introduced to the Faculty Assembly on Dec. 9, 1976. Professor Stuart Kaplan from the Communications Department at the University of California, Davis, had been invited to explain the value of the major and its attractiveness to students and to answer any pertinent questions. Kaplan was clear and astute, but many members of the Assembly in attendance were not to be persuaded. A memorandum to the faculty dated Nov. 15, 1976, stated arguments against the establishment of such a major, including "the lack of clear focus, the risk that the major might dilute the quality of some present departments." Professor Mary Springer spoke against the major as an undesirable and risky venture without appropriate personnel to staff it. She also felt that its establishment would weaken the strength of the English Department by drawing students to an unknown and untried major. "Fragmentation of a traditionally strong department should be avoided," she said. Professor Paul Burke spoke in favor, noting interest by students. "Its ability to draw students would justify its existence," he stated. Professor Norman Springer, in speaking against the proposal, stated that priority rights (in financing) should go to developing basic reading and writing skills and doubted whether the major could produce "knowledgeably critical" students. He also objected to "dividing the College with yet another program."

Professor El Gelinas proposed a trial period of a year and a half or more to see how the major would fit in, but Professor Pollock noted that the idea of having a tentative major would be unfair to students. Professor Waddell repeated the notion that the College should not imitate other institutions but rather continue to do what it does well. Success of the major elsewhere, he added, did not in itself justify having it at Saint Mary's. Professor Mary Springer challenged the wisdom of setting up a new major when the English Department had difficulty staffing Better Writing courses.

Brother Raphael, PhD, suggested retaining courses in communications and the media but did not favor the proposal as it stood. Though I did not voice my view at the Assembly meeting, I was inclined to welcome the major since I believed that having liberally educated graduates with a moral compass in the media and entertainment industries would improve the media and uplift what I thought had reached near nadir in the entertainment and news reporting industries. In my mind, I was hopeful that the Communications major would, in its foundational courses, be as close to a rhetoric major as possible, since rhetoric was one of the three great liberal arts of the classical *trivium*. I was hopeful that students educated in the great liberal arts tradition and who made a career of communications might be able to overcome the vapid superficiality associated with much of modern media, and deliver insightful, reflective and balanced views of the world they encountered. A motion to establish the Communications major failed with a vote of 9 yea, 10 nay, and one abstention.

Shortly after the December Faculty Assembly meeting, reports to various faculty members from the Dean of Admissions noted that a communications major would be a recruitment asset since Admissions Officers had encountered significant interest from potential students regarding the major. Dean of Admissions Peter Mohorko, expressed his disappointment to the Assembly that the major was not approved. A written faculty poll instituted by the Academic Council on Feb. 11, 1977, supported the major, as well as did a random student poll administered by Student Body President Matthew O'Donnell that indicated 123 students in favor and 10 opposed. The Academic Council suggested that the Academic Vice President proceed with establishing the major if the Faculty Assembly approved the concept on February 17th. In spite of objections from Norman and Mary Springer of the English Department (Mary Springer suggested that a communications program be merged with the English Department), the Faculty Assembly approved the Academic Council's recommendation of pursuing the development of the Communications Major, by a vote of 15 yea, 2 nay, with 0 abstentions. (Minutes of the Faculty Assembly, Feb. 17, 1977.)

International Institute for Banking and Finance, 1976

The International Institute for Banking and Finance began in 1976 at the suggestion and with the support of Regent John Thompson, who at that time was President of Security National Bank (later merged with Hibernia Bank) in downtown Walnut Creek. The bank was supported by capital from Adnan Khashoggi, an international businessman with Saudi Arabian roots. The International Institute was first named the Khashoggi Institute to honor its major benefactor. However, after the press reported that the United States government sought the appearance of Khashoggi in a United States court with respect to some of his commercial activities, those organizing the institute, namely Robert Cox of Security National Bank, Violette Yacoub, a native of Iraq and well-versed in counseling students from the Middle East, and the on-campus Executive Director, Max Forster, thought it best to rename the project the International Institute of Banking and Finance. Its initial purpose was to conduct a Master of International Business Program for international students, particularly for students from the Middle East, though students from any nation could attend, if qualified.

One of the prerequisites was an ability to read, write and converse in English, a requirement that those charged with conducting the program soon discovered had to be addressed by offering English as a Foreign Language to those lacking English proficiency. The Special Accrediting Team of 1977 applied the same principle to the Institute as it did to any cooperative program, namely that the College, being the accredited institution, was required to take the lead in conducting the program with its own faculty and administration. The Master's program in the International Institute of Banking and Finance was thus assumed by the Graduate Business program. In 1979 the program was altered to a Master of Science Degree in International Business, with Carolinda Lee as its Coordinator. By 1989 the Program was again altered as a consequence of the U. S. conflict with the new Iranian government and the depletion of applicants from the Middle East.

The program was replaced by an MBA in International Business, open to domestic students as well as those from overseas. However, since Saint Mary's was not well recognized internationally, and with the word "college" in its title, recruitment of foreign students was difficult, because the term "college" normally meant a secondary school in Central and South America, Europe and the Middle-East. The problems associated with recruiting, registration and housing of international students, as well as student proficiency in English, were extensive. Since the Graduate Business faculty was concentrating on developing a highly competitive MBA, the International Business feature of Graduate Business was discontinued in 1997. The programs in English as a Foreign Language, open to both graduate and undergraduate students, were placed under the supervision of the undergraduate faculty and the Academic Vice President.

The Master's Degree in Psychology, 1976

When the eight-course load was instituted in 1976-1977, Brother Michael Quinn, FSC, PhD, former president and subsequently chair of the Psychology Department, developed a proposal whereby members of his department would teach their eighth course in graduate psychology, thus enabling the department to offer a Master of Science Degree in Psychology. The entire faculty of the Psychology Department held degrees that would enable them to offer advanced academic degrees. Approved by the Academic Vice President, the department began offering the Master's Degree in the following semester. After the eight-course load was rescinded in 1978, the psychology faculty continued offering the MS Degree and approximately 350 graduate students in psychology had earned that degree by 1997.

The Paralegal Professionals Program, 1977

In 1975, faculty member Mary Ann Mason, who held a doctorate in history (University of Rochester), as well as a doctorate in law (University of San Francisco), and Michael Tonsing, '65, an admissions officer, alumnus and law student at the University of San Francisco, came forward with a proposal that the College establish a program for paralegal assistants. Mason had recently completed her law degree, and Tonsing was close to completing his. The purpose of establishing a program for paralegal assistants was to provide the legal profession with certified personnel who had engaged in an academic program conducted primarily by teaching attorneys that would prepare students with understanding and expertise for service in legal firms.

The availability of paralegal program graduates would provide law firms with a group of candidates who had a common and current background for assisting in legal matters, as well as relieve law firms of the necessity for conducting their own educational programs. The presence of paralegal professionals in law offices would result in lower costs for legal services for clients. Brother Dominic proposed to the President's Council that the program be instituted.

Since a paralegal assistants program was not a degree-granting program nor was it connected to any department of the College, it did not seem necessary to secure the advice of the Faculty Assembly. Mary Ann Mason, PhD, JD, was selected to direct the Paralegal Professional's Program, officially inaugurated in 1977. Expecting that the enrollment would begin modestly, both Mason and Mike Tonsing were surprised that after an announcement in local papers, more than 300 enquiries regarding the program were recorded the first week. Mary Ann Mason formed an advisory board composed of attorneys from the area and persuaded several to teach courses. The program proved to be more popular than anticipated and enrolled so many students that accommodations were sought off-campus for conducting classes during the day, since space on campus during prime academic hours was at a premium. Off-campus classes were held on the second floor of the new Clorox Building at City Center, Broadway and 12th Street, in Oakland, conveniently located over a BART (Bay Area Rapid Transit) station. One feature assuring success of the program was a quality placement service directed in the initial years by Guyla Cashell. The American Bar Association approved the program in 1981 after the preparation of an institutional self-study, customary evaluation and a site visit by an ABA evaluation team. Between 1978 and 1997 Paralegal Certificates were granted to 1,821 paralegal professionals.

After establishing the program and authoring two books, Mary Ann Mason entered a new career at UC Berkeley as an assistant professor of law and social welfare. She rose to the rank of full professor while writing several books and articles on family law and children's rights. In 2000 she became Dean of the UC Berkeley School Graduate with its 8,000 students.

Michael Tonsing, after completing his law studies, was named administrative law judge for the Public Employees Retirement Board and was then awarded a coveted Fellowship in the United States Supreme Court in Washington D.C. under Chief Justice Warren Berger. Tonsing then served for more than three years as a United States Attorney for the Federal Government in San Francisco before entering private practice in Oakland, Calif., in 1984. Tonsing taught in the paralegal program for 20 years.

The Cooperative Nursing Program Proposal, 1977

An alumnus, the late James Turre, MD, was a neighbor to the College, his home resting on the hillside along Bollinger Canyon Road on the east side of the campus. His gynecology and obstetrics offices were in Lafayette. Since Dr. Turre served many of his patients through Merritt Hospital in Oakland, he was conversant with the aspirations of Samuel Merritt Hospital College of Nursing. The National League of Nursing an organization which is dedicated to nursing education and located in New York, had promulgated its strong interest in schools of nursing making arrangements to provide nursing students with an education leading to the baccalaureate degree. In the past, most schools of nursing offered the RN, the registered nursing certificate with the nursing pin, and, in some cases, in conjunction with a community college, the associate of arts degree, signifying the completion of two years of collegiate work. Samuel Merritt Hospital College of Nursing had made arrangements with a local community college to share curriculum, so that its students could earn the associate degree. But officials at Samuel Merritt were seeking an appropriate partner, so that the baccalaureate degree could be offered to its nursing graduates.

Samuel Merritt Hospital School of Nursing had approached Vice President Slakey in the early '70s, but Slakey was not interested in pursuing a joint baccalaureate program at that time. When Brother Dominic became Vice President upon Slakey's resignation, he received several suggestions that Saint Mary's consider offering a nursing program and engaged in some preliminary investigation. Research indicated that the student-faculty ratio for the clinical component of a nursing program was exceptionally low and therefore might be prohibitively expensive. Finding the appropriate venue for conducting the clinical component would also be a formidable hurdle. Brother Dominic spoke to Dr. Turre about his interest in a nursing program, and it was not long before Brothers Dominic and I were enjoying a delightful repast at Dr. Turre's home at the expert hand of his wife, Carmen. The conversation focussed on establishing a nursing program at Saint Mary's.

Dr. Turre spoke to the administrators of Samuel Merritt Hospital College of Nursing and discovered a strong mutual interest in establishing a baccalaureate program in nursing. A meeting was arranged for Brother Dominic and the College of Nursing administration, represented by S. Richard Wickel, Merritt Hospital Administrator; Clem Long; Laurie Howes, RN, Director of the Hospital College of Nursing and Sharon Diaz, RN, Assistant Director. Following the meeting, Brother Dominic was pleased to report that the concept of a joint intercollegiate program was viewed with favor. He saw the education of nurses as contributing to the development of a caring profession, in keeping with a long Saint Mary's tradition of preparing numerous students for entry into the medical and dental professions. The nursing program would also increase the number of students enrolled in courses in the School of Science, which offered a number of required, but underenrolled courses.

The faculty in the School of Science was both constructive, and cooperative and on March 15, 1977, Brother Dominic presented the proposal for the cooperative program to the Academic Council, which unanimously approved the concept. On April 19, 1977, the Board of Trustees was presented with the Samuel Merritt - Saint Mary's joint-program concept. A letter of intent had been signed by Brother Dominic and Samuel Merritt College of Nursing on April 12, 1977. At the Faculty Assembly meeting of April 21, after Brother Dominic brought what he considered positive news to the Assembly, Professor Mary Springer expressed her dissatisfaction with the signing of the letter of intent prior to the Faculty Assembly meeting. Brother Dominic replied that "the moment was propitious" and that a recent Faculty Assembly approval for a program in respiratory therapy was taken as an encouraging sign that the faculty would have no objection to a joint intercollegiate nursing program. Professor Norman Springer rose to complain that it was not appropriate for Saint Mary's to engage in a nursing program, because it was technical in nature and not in keeping with a liberal arts tradition. "We don't want those technical people in our classes at Saint Mary's," Springer snarled. The Faculty Assembly, however, endorsed the concept by a vote of 15 yea, 3 nay, with 3 abstentions. Once the nursing program was established and professors Mary and Norman Springer discovered that nursing students, most being women, who enrolled in their classes were conscientious, well-prepared and articulate, a change of heart occurred. Norman and Mary Springer, to their credit, became strong advocates of the cooperative or joint nursing program.

Though Saint Mary's offered a strong program in science, it did not offer an applied or so-called practical science program. Nursing was considered by some faculty as a how-to-do-it program and not compatible with traditional theoretical science programs, but, since Samuel Merritt College of Nursing was responsible for the clinical portion of the program and Saint Mary's for the basic science courses, the issue was resolved. However, it was essential that the College seek a qualified person with a recognized nursing background, as well as bona fide academic credentials, to represent the College in the joint baccalaureate effort. On July 9, 1978, Abby Heydman, RN, who was completing her doctorate at the University of California Berkeley, was appointed to oversee the Saint Mary's portion of the Nursing Program. Her appointment was a fortuitous decision by Brother Dominic's successor, Brother William Beatie, FSC, PhD, since her intellectual commitment, nursing credentials, administrative ability and congeniality proved to be a major factor in creating an amicable and mutually beneficial relationship.

Once the program was established, the Merritt administration was convinced that accreditation by the National League of Nursing was essential. Sharon Diaz, RN, who had assumed the position of President of Samuel Merritt College of Nursing, and I flew to New York as the final step in the tedious process of self-evaluation, self-study documentation and the hosting of visits by National League of Nursing personnel for ultimate NLN accreditation. Since an intercollegiate program was a new concept, a minor glitch in the proceeding was the cause for some apprehension, chagrin and a few quizzical smiles.

The National League of Nursing had little experience with a baccalaureate program conducted by two independent institutions, and its regulations did not allow for more than one representative for a nursing program to appear before its Accrediting Board. But since Saint Mary's and Merritt were each responsible for half the credits toward the baccalaureate degree, it only seemed appropriate that both presidents appear before the Board. After some hurried discussion behind closed doors, the Board consented to waive what had been a hard-and-fast rule and admitted both presidents to the proceedings. Nothing out of the ordinary seemed to occur in the meeting that the presence of two representatives of a joint program would have disturbed or disrupted. National League of Nursing accreditation was granted.

Brother Dominic relinquished the office of Academic Vice President to Brother William Beatie, FSC, PhD, in the fall of 1978, and thus Brother William completed the contractual negotiations with Samuel Merritt Hospital School of Nursing leading to the awarding of the innovative joint baccalaureate degree awarded by both institutions.

Stringency and Anxiety

As financial difficulties increased, many faculty members became alarmed when stringency seemed to require eliminating or cycling some course offerings, increasing the teaching load and the possibility of reducing some faculty positions, if not by attrition, then by non-reappointment. A resolution submitted to the Faculty Assembly by the local chapter of the American Association of University Professors listed the primary concerns of faculty, one of which claimed that Saint Mary's professors were "teaching larger classes at salaries considerably lower than those at state and other independent colleges and universities." Former Vice President Slakey took issue with the claim that faculty members are "teaching larger classes at considerably lower salaries" by noting that the claim was not entirely accurate. Alan Pollock moved to table the resolution to permit further discussion. The resolution was tabled without opposition. (Minutes of the Faculty Assembly, Oct. 22, 1975, Saint Mary's College Archives.)

A month later the revised resolution proposed cycling courses rather than increasing the teaching load. The resolution passed by a vote of 8 yea, 5 nay, with 2 abstentions. (Minutes of the Faculty Assembly, Nov. 20, 1975, Saint Mary's College Archives.)

The Eight Course Teaching Load

By Dec. 11, 1975. the Faculty Assembly began to realize that financial necessity would require more aggressive faculty action. The Assembly asked the Academic Council to study the effects of moving from a seven to an eight course teaching load and to report the results of the study to the Assembly no later than Feb. 12, 1976. Though no formal motions were made, several faculty members expressed interest in curtailing expenses for athletics and administrative overhead.

In response to disclosure on athletic and administrative expenses, memos to the faculty from Leo Oakes, Personnel Director, and Stanford White, Professor in the Department of Economics and Business Administration to the Academic Council, noted that criticism of athletic and administrative expenses were unfounded and that, in fact, the athletic and administrative budgets had been streamlined effectively. (Memoranda by Leo Oakes, Jan. 29, 1976, and Professor Stanford White, Feb. 2, 1976, to the Academic Council.) Numerous new government regulations such as Title IX on gender equity in athletics, were causes for some unavoidable increases. Arguments against a drastic reduction in athletic participation, such as the discontinuance of intercollegiate competition or a change to a lower rank of conference membership, were weighed against the risk of reducing public visibility; losing student, alumni, donor, Regents and Trustees interest and support; and the negative effect on recruiting both men and women students.

An extensive report from the Academic Vice President on administrative and athletic expenses and income complemented the Leo Oakes and Stanford

White reports, dispelling much of the suspicion and misinformation that affected faculty understanding of the financial status of the College.

On Feb. 12, 1976 the faculty proposed four ways to achieve a balanced budget. While it cited the possibility that the academic quality of the College might be adversely affected, the faculty also noted that the budget should not only be balanced but return a surplus in order to reduce the deficit that had accrued. And lastly the faculty approved a motion to reduce the instructional budget by increasing the faculty teaching load to eight courses per academic year. By a vote of 16 yea, 10 nay, with 1 abstention. (Minutes of the Faculty Assembly, Feb. 12, 1976, Saint Mary's College Archives.)

New academic programs then underway (MBA and a program for older adults returning to complete their baccalaureate degrees) would accelerate the reduction of the deficit and allow a return to the seven-course load sooner rather than later.

In the course of the Board of Trustees meeting of Feb. 26, 1976, the Board commended the faculty for its cooperation in meeting the financial crisis facing the College by accepting the eight course teaching load. (Minutes, Board of Trustees, Feb. 26, 1976, Saint Mary's College Archives.)

The faculty assumed the eight-course teaching load for the 1976-1977 academic year. During that time there were occasional complaints similar to those made when the eight-course load was first discussed. The objections registered prior to adopting the eight-course load claimed that quality would suffer because faculty had reached the limit with a seven-course load, and that institutions with reputations for quality often required less than seven courses per year for faculty. Toward the end of the first year with the eight-course load, (May 14, 1977) the Faculty Assembly heard a report from Professor John Correia, PhD, of the Chemistry Department and chairman of the Faculty Committee on Teaching Load proposing a Committee recommendation that full-time faculty teach 15 courses over a two-year period, that is from 1977 through the 1979 spring term. However, the proposal was tabled, with thanks to the Committee.

Alan Pollock and Norman Springer then moved that the College return to the regular seven-course load for the forthcoming year, namely the 1977-1978 academic year, commencing in September. Correia defended the proposal that had been tabled, observing that hiring part-time faculty to accommodate the seven-course load would not be in the best interests of the College, especially in view of the shortness of time. Norman Springer stated that other collegiate institutions had less than a seven-course load, noting that an eight-course load was not widely accepted, and said that many of his colleagues could already see that academic quality suffered. Professors White and Waddell attempted a motion advocating a return to the seven-course load in the fall of 1978 rather than the fall of 1977. An amended Pollock/Springer motion to return to the seven course teaching load for 1977-1978 academic year, included the addition, "that there be an extensive study made of the proper teaching load of the faculty by a committee appointed by the faculty chairperson." The motion passed by a vote of 18-0 with one abstention. (Minutes of the Faculty Assembly, May 14, 1977, Saint Mary's College Archives.)

I responded to the Assembly motion through a letter to all faculty members on July 8, 1977 stating that May 14, 1977 was much too late in the scholastic year to consult with the Academic Council to alter the approved budget for 1977-1978, to secure and hire (especially during the summer) necessary instructors that a return to a seven-course load would require, and to revise all returning and new student schedules that had been completed in preregistration. I stated that the eight-course load would be retained for the 1977-1978 academic year, but I said nothing about when a seven-course load would return. (President's file, letter of July 8, 1977.)

The change to an eight-course teaching load (three courses in one semester, one in January and four in the other semester) is more complex than it appears at the outset. Most institutions reckon the teaching load in terms of Carnegie units, not on courses *per se*. A Carnegie unit represents 15, 50-minute classes in a 15-week semester, thus a three-unit course would meet three times per week for fifty-minutes each for a 15-week semester. In 1976-1977 the State University System required undergraduate faculty to teach 24 units per year or 12 units in a normal semester. If courses were normally three units, a faculty member at a California State University would be teaching eight courses per year. Yet there could be two-unit courses as well as four-and five-unit courses, thus changing the number of courses but not the number of units. The student/faculty ratio also has a significant bearing on the teaching load. Professors in graduate programs or research universities (such as the University of California System, Stanford or University of Southern California) normally teach fewer units or courses because of the intensity required for graduate work and time required for research and publication. But research institutions usually have access to government subsidies and possess extensive endowments.

In the fall of 1977, because of the complexity of assessing an appropriate teaching load, Brother William Beatie, PhD, the Undergraduate Dean, expressed his plan to study, along with the members of the Academic Council, what an appropriate teaching load for the College might be. Undoubtedly, such a study had political and financial implications. Following the study, the Academic Council recommended that the College return to the seven-course load in September 1978. The concept, Brother William noted, was "approved by the President, given the early timing of the proposal and assuming that the details could be worked out in the following few months." I officially agreed to end the eight-course teaching load by the end of the 1977-1978 academic year.

Committee on Interpersonal Relationships, 1976

It was dubbed the *Love Committee* by a wag and became the tag by which it was known throughout the campus. After the Accreditation Visit of 1975, Brother Dominic Ruegg, instituted the *Committee on Interpersonal Relationships* to determine what the root causes of discontent might be, even though most of the administration already knew. Brother Dominic selected Vice President for Student Affairs William McLeod as Chair of the Committee with other members being: Brother Edward Behan, Director of Counseling; Lawrence Cory, Professor of Biology; Brother Brendan Kneale, Dean of Studies; Katherine Larson, Professor of History and Faculty Chairman; Brother Michael Quinn, Professor of Psychology and former President; and Patti Winkler, Assistant Registrar. I was, without doubt, skeptical regarding the objectivity and effectiveness of such a committee, since its formation was so close to the Accreditation Visit of 1975. I opined that the Committee would simply hear what was already known from the previous Visit. I was both right and wrong. The *Love Committee* did hear many of the complaints heard but a year and a half earlier, yet provided some statistics on those interviewed, enabling the reader to make a broad assessment of the credibility of the Accreditation Committee report. As for solutions that were sought by the Committee, that on governance revealed a serious concern that all academic entities functioning at the College were not granted full citizenship. What was required, opined several faculty members, was a radical change in academic governance, namely that a fully representative Academic Senate be established.

However, the opposition to the formation of an Academic Senate by the more vocal and politically involved members of the Faculty Assembly delayed the formation of a Senate for a decade. It was clear that the opposition had a vested interest in the Faculty Assembly, though other faculty members found the freewheeling nature of the Assembly, while often fascinating, was frequently frustrating in spite of its amusing moments.

As was expected, both myself and the Academic Vice President were the objects of strong criticism by a number of those interviewed. Approximately a third claimed that the president should not be president, stating that, "he often appeared more interested in that which is peripheral to the College rather than that which is central to its academic function, and has being unwilling to listen to the faculty except for a favored few, and *diluting that which was best in the previous administration.*" (Interpersonal Relations Committee Report, page 11, May 1977, Saint Mary's College Archives.) The section entitled *The Faculty* noted that "the faculty received much less criticism from the administration than the administration received from them." (IRC Report, Op.Cit., page 13.)

Criticism about certain faculty from both faculty members and administrators did have an effect upon some hypercritical, vocal and politically active faculty members, an observation that benefited the entire academic community when the outspoken critics realized their tactics were not appreciated by many members. "Though it was generally agreed that most faculty members are temperate, there were among the interviewees from both the administration and the faculty those who felt that some faculty hold extreme views or are self-serving. They felt some faculty use the students in their campaigns against the administration, for example, airing their personal grievances and complaints to the students at the expense of teaching class. It was pointed out that some faculty fail to recognize that the administration, in its attempt to guarantee the survival of the College, are at the same time securing the faculty's future. It was also asserted that frequently, both in and out of faculty meetings, some faculty members act in an unprofessional manner: disrespectful, gossiping and insulting to the administration in public." (IRC, page 13.) These observations were significantly contributory to the reduction of acrimonious discourse and consequent tension. I had to agree that a redeeming result of the Love Committee inquiries was the improvement in civility.

Western Association of Schools and Colleges and the Institute for Professional Development

Special Accreditation Visit I, 1977

The officers of the Western Association of Schools and Colleges were determined to exercise surveillance (some considered it harassment) of the College, for the most part on the grounds that there was grave concern in the Accrediting Association regarding joint programs between any California institution and the Institute for Professional Development. The WASC Accrediting Commission for Schools was determined to halt further IPD incursions within the

Accreditation region (California, Hawaii and the U.S. Pacific Territories.). A small Interim Visiting Team of two members and a WASC representative visited the College on May 12th and 13th, 1977, to engage in fact-finding, primarily regarding contracts with non-accredited contractors, specifically IPD and a smaller organization called California/American Field Studies that provided two-unit nondegree travel enrichment courses on California and American history. The Visiting Team (Leon Levitt, Dean of Continuing Education at Loyola Marymount, and George McCabe of the Consortium of California State Universities accompanied by Leo Cain, a WASC representative and retired president of California State University, Dominguez Hills) was charged with "investigating new and proposed graduate degree programs conducted solely by the College, as well as those conducted in association with nonaccredited organizations." The Team found few or no difficulties with the programs operated entirely by the College, namely the new MBA program and the Master of Teaching programs in the School of Education. However, they viewed those operated in conjunction with nonaccredited education contractors as not being in compliance with existing WASC standards, and they were correct. They did not, in fact, engage in much fact-finding, since their report was written before they arrived. Their appearance was merely another page in a formal paper trail.

Discussions with senior faculty did raise a number of legitimate questions regarding the relationship between Saint Mary's and IPD and the comparison of the regular undergraduate degree requirements with those of the joint venture with IPD, such as the requirement that all Saint Mary's undergraduates be exposed to the Great Books or Collegiate Seminars and religious studies. Cain argued that IPD programs had no distinctive quality that represented Saint Mary's or any other institution with whom it was associated. "They peddle this same program everywhere," he critically observed. It became clear that the external-degree concept required more serious and meticulous scrutiny, as well as incorporating a significant Saint Mary's academic distinctiveness so that the academic value of the Saint Mary's diploma would not be compromised. Brother Dominic held fast to the idea that an external-degree program was meritorious for both the College and the older-adult students and believed that the Accrediting Association and its Executive Director, Kay Andersen, did not seem willing to negotiate in achieving reasonable academic standards, since they alleged that the IPD program lowered academic standards within the Western Association of Schools and Colleges. They also knew that IPD and John Sperling were formidable opponents and were unwilling to adopt the California State University model for adult education. The truth was most likely somewhere in between. In the final analysis, the education of older adults had merit, and it was accurate to say that the education of older adults required an approach different from that of the traditional undergraduate.

Brother Dominic argued that older adults who entered the program were much like transfer students from a community college, which was a fair appraisal. But even so, the Saint Mary's requirements for transfer students included courses in both religious studies and the Great Books seminars, neither of which were required of those in the older-adult program. Furthermore, other courses did not have the number of hours required that were required of traditional undergraduates. Omitting such requirements did not reflect the character and universal stamp of a Saint Mary's undergraduate program and supported the Leo Cain view that the IPD program did not adapt to the institutions with which it had teamed to deliver a baccalaureate degree. There was a serious concern of not burdening working students with weighty requirements, or, as is often the case, with requirements that did not seem to potential students to address career improvement and corresponding financial remuneration. This latter concern was clearly an issue with the traditional liberal arts faculty. However, older students, if judiciously screened, more often than not will respond to serious academic demands in a more timely and effective manner than many traditional 18- to 22-year-old undergraduates. By the time that Saint Mary's signed a contract with IPD, the Accreditation Association Commission believed it had ample evidence from other institutions concerning the weaknesses it perceived in the IPD program and had already decided to pressure any institution associated with IPD or a similar relationship with any other contractor to assume full institutional control of such programs, leaving IPD or any other outside contractor with a reduced, clearly secondary role, if any role at all. The uneasiness I experienced at the initiation of the IPD agreement grew to be outright troublesome. I heard from presidents and deans of other institutions who strongly supported the IPD concept of offering programs to older adults. I also spoke to the Executive Director of the North Central Accreditation Association, and even a few members of the state legislature who had been lobbied personally by IPD's John Sperling.

The objections lodged against the two-unit nondegree travel courses offered in conjunction with California and American Field Studies seemed as if that program was caught in the blanket disapproval of the much larger IPD issue over institutional control. Since the programs were academically more difficult to monitor and raised questions in the minds of those devoted to more traditional formats about their academic timbre, and even though they did

235

provide some helpful remuneration to the College, as well as future students for graduate programs in education, they were discontinued in short order.

Special Accreditation Visit II, 1977

Within five weeks after classes resumed in the fall of 1977, the major Interim Visiting Team of seven members arrived on campus on Oct. 13-14, 1977, two academic months since the smaller May 1977 so-called fact-finding visit. Heading the Visiting Committee or *Visiting Team* was Ann M. Heiss, a retired Associate Research Educator from the Education Department at the University of California, Berkeley. The Committee was to review the College on three fronts, namely, 1) On all programs and all contractual agreements for programs that had been instituted since September 1975; 2) on the financial stability of the institution; and 3) on interpersonal relations on the campus." (Accreditation Report, 1977, Ann M. Heiss, Chairman). Because the financial situation had improved considerably since 1975 with the deficit having been reduced by $521,300 -- from $1,320,190 to $798,890 by 1977 -- and with expectations of reducing the deficit to $578,361 by the 1977-1978 academic year, the issue of financial stability was no longer a critical one. The primary focus of the Accrediting Association, was the contractual relationship of the College with the Institute for Professional Development. Calls to other independent institutions in California that had contractual agreements with the IPD revealed that they were also under pressure to either drastically alter or sever relations with the Institute as well.

When the Interim Visiting Team appeared in 1977, morale had improved noticeably, though it was still considered a difficulty especially in the view of Professor Norman Springer, who had assumed leadership of the local chapter of the American Federation of Teachers, a subsidiary of the AFL-CIO. The administration kept close watch on the unionization attempt, and it did not appear to be a major cause for alarm since the majority of the faculty was not inclined to join in the effort. When the union effort sounded strongest, information garnered by the administration indicated an AFT card-carrying membership of less than 15. By 1980 the unionization effort became moot.

The major issue with the Accrediting Association was the relationship between the Institute for Professional Development and the College, because the College was perceived as not having full, or nearly full, control of the external degree program. The Institute had recently changed both its location and its name to the University of Phoenix, since it was now headquartered in Phoenix, Ariz. The subsequent *Visiting Team Report* of the regular 1980 visit clearly confirmed that the relationship between the College and IPD was the major concern of the Accrediting body. "Since the decision by WASC to place Saint Mary's College on probation was based on the 1977 team's concerns over the External Degree programs, the present team chose to look at this activity with considerable care." (*Visiting Team Report* of 1980, Paul E. Hadley, Chairman, page 163.)

The Accreditation Association most likely realized that John Sperling would be a formidable opponent in a lawsuit and thus approached IPD, its administration and colleagues gingerly. The major WASC argument utilized in opposing both IPD and the two-unit travel courses not under IPD was that Saint Mary's used its accreditation to grant degrees or academic credit for programs over which the College did not exercise full quality control since they were designed by others and offered on any campus that would sponsor them. The College did have its own overseers for both the administration and conduct of the program, however, it was WASC's view that little or nothing in the IPD program characterized the distinctive academic spirit or quality of any of the degree-granting institutions in California. As a matter of policy, if the WASC Accrediting Commission found a major deficiency in the conduct of any program sponsored by a college or university, it would exercise its authority to sanction the entire institution rather than single out an individual program which it determined to be deficient. In principle, WASC does not accredit or withdraw accreditation from programs, only institutions.

I could readily see that the WASC Commission was not going to tolerate relationships with IPD or any other academic contractor. The College had to assume full control of any so-called cooperative program. Yet, the Academic Vice President, himself a classical academic scholar (Latin and Greek), entrepreneur, innovator and dedicated academic supported IPD in the face of WASC disapproval and what he considered intrusive interference rather than helpful counsel in the development of an innovative or experimental program designed to assist older students in need.

Brother Dominic was so appalled with the way the WASC visiting Team investigated the IPD-Saint Mary's relationship, I thought it prudent to appear alone before the WASC Accrediting Commission in the spring of 1978, prior to its making a decision regarding the status of the Saint Mary's accreditation. The meeting was a difficult one, since it was clear that the Visiting Team Chair, Dr. Ann Heiss, and the Executive Director of WASC, Kay Andersen, strongly opposed the College relationship with IPD, and in principle with nondegree courses offered by any other outside academic agency. Comments from various Commissioners were clearly negative. As a matter of fact, I was not convinced myself that the arrangement between the College and IPD was favorably comparable to the traditional on-campus undergraduate program, even

though the arguments citing academic attitudinal differences between traditional undergraduates and older-adult learners had significant merit in favoring a different approach to adult learners. I was not convinced that WASC
was substantially in error on the academic requirements of the program and
in particular on the issue of full administrative control. I did sense, though,
that the attitude and report on the College relationship with IPD was written
in stone before the official visit occurred. Perhaps had I said that the College
would divest itself of any relationship with IPD and American Field Studies as
soon as possible, the Commission would have exercised more patience. However, I was cautious in view of possible litigation at a time when there were no
financial reserves should the College aggressively pursue abridging or terminating the contract with IPD immediately. Furthermore, it would take a period of time along with a competent administrator to re-fashion the program
under the full direction of the College.

The College was placed on the newly instituted sanction of "probation" until
the next regular visit scheduled for the fall of 1980. That visit would determine whether the College had resolved its academic difficulties. This clearly
meant to me that the College had to sever its relationship with both IPD
and California Field Studies and arrange to assume major control of the
programs. The probationary status was, in fact, the major arguing point for
terminating the contract between the College and IPD. Both severance and
full College control was clearly the only judicious course of action.

Brother Dominic was indignant with the WASC sanction and suggested
that the College file suit against WASC. However, I determined that such
an action would not be fruitful in view of WASC commission objections,
particularly in terms of the written WASC standards, nor would it be helpful in future dealings with either the commission or academic colleagues in
higher education. I was persuaded that WASC had some legitimate concerns, though clearly favored existing governance models in the delivery of
academic services, expressed skepticism regarding innovation and seemed
reluctant or considered itself unable or beyond its mission to assist institutions in perfecting new approaches to higher education.

I was convinced that it would be possible for the College to incorporate a
program for older adults on its own in which significant academic standards
became the hallmark of Extended Education. Another major competitive
independent university also conducted a number of similar field studies
courses through a group different from the one the College utilized, and was
also persuaded by WASC to discontinue such programs. Unfortunately, our
contract with IPD had extended well beyond the one-year mark and thus

had over three contractual years remaining. Investigation was conducted to see what could be done to sever relationships with IPD as soon as possible and to revise the programs, so that the College could conduct them entirely with its own personnel, augmented as required. The contract was scrutinized with care which revealed that a number of actions could be taken by the College to extricate itself from the relationship. A meeting was held on Tuesday, May 29, 1979, among myself, representatives of IPD and College counsel in the College counsel's offices of Broad, Khourie and Schulz in San Francisco. Ambiguities in the contract were discussed, and it became apparent that the College could discontinue certain programs, and that if it did, IPD would find the arrangements unfavorable and would not be interested in pursuing such alternatives.

A settlement was arranged with John Sperling for the early termination of the contract. Perhaps Brother Dominic's friendship and membership on John Sperling's Faculty Advisory Board or the fact that Saint Mary's was the institution which assisted Sperling's entry into the North Central Accrediting Association and the eventual establishment of the independent, fully accredited University of Phoenix, ensured an agreeable outcome. Sperling also realized that attempting to placate the WASC commission would be a futile task, and that he would serve himself and his program much better by building a base in Phoenix under the accreditation of the North Central Accrediting Association. I also realized that settling with Sperling would be far less expensive and time-consuming than prolonged litigation, or dealing with the public or foundations in light of continued WASC sanctions.

The College personnel office designed a job description for an administrator who would be able to assume full control of the program by developing materials, hiring personnel and setting up a larger office to oversee fully the programs already in progress and, above all, to assure academic standards in vogue in the College. I was insistent that the program be examined and revised to reflect the distinctiveness and demands of a Saint Mary's baccalaureate degree for a qualified transfer student who entered Saint Mary's in his or her junior year. I believed that the awarding of a Saint Mary's diploma should announce that recipients of it had received an education which reflected the fundamental principles of the College Mission Statement.

Faculty Assembly, 1977-1978

By the Nov. 13, 1977, Faculty Assembly, discussion turned to the faculty salary scale, even though at the time the faculty carried the eight-course load to reduce the deficit and were at last aware of serious financial stringency. In

1966, the Board of Trustees had approved a salary policy that in any given year the College would, on average, adjust its salary scale to the California State University System scale of the year before plus 3 percent. The policy had not changed, even though the State System of reckoning did. During the financial downturn, the administration and the Trustees had followed the policy as consistently as they could. However, it was noted by several faculty members that the faculty workload had been altered with the assumption of the 4-1-4 calendar which rendered it to be less than that of the State University System. Comparisons with Stanislaus State University were cited, since Stanislaus State was the only State University on a modified 4-1-4 calendar. Professor Kathy Roper of the History Department opposed any comparison with Stanislaus State for she claimed from her personal experience that there was "a distinct difference between what is demanded of the faculty at the state colleges and what is expected of the Saint Mary's faculty," her implication being that the demands on Saint Mary's faculty were greater. Yet, Professor El Gelinas of the Philosophy Department observed that, in order to attain equality or parity in salary scale with the California State University system, the Saint Mary's faculty would have to demonstrate how its teaching load was equal to that of the State system. (Minutes of the Faculty Assembly, Nov. 13, 1977, Saint Mary's College Archives.) No immediate action was taken, but as the financial situation improved, faculty expressions of concern regarding the salary scale understandably increased.

Another major concern of some faculty was to seek the removal of the Academic Vice President as chairman of the Rank and Tenure Committee and to replace the AVP with the Undergraduate Dean, since the promoters of such a move contended, the Rank and Tenure Committee was concerned only with full-time undergraduate faculty. However, Brother Alfred Brousseau observed that "The role of the Academic Vice President places him over all faculty and that he should remain as chairman in light of eventual tenure considerations for faculty in graduate programs." His observation, though insightful, was ignored, and a motion by professors Pollock and Roper to place the Undergraduate Dean as chairperson of the Rank and Tenure Committee was accepted by a vote of 11 yea, 0 nay, with 2 abstentions. However, Professor Norman Springer and Brother Ronald Isetti moved that the motion be placed before the entire faculty by written ballot. The motion to poll the faculty passed by a vote of 16 yea, 1 nay. (Minutes of the Faculty Assembly, Dec. 20, 1977, Saint Mary's College Archives.) The returns from the Jan. 13, 1978, ballot proposing that the Undergraduate Dean assume the role of chair on the Rank and Tenure Committee tallied at 25 yea, 8 nay, with no abstentions.

Word of Brother Dominic's interest in quality academic standards for faculty had been circulated among the faculty prior to the distribution of the ballot. Faculty on the tenure ladder voted to make the change, along with several members of the American Federation of Teachers, who claimed that its membership supported the change as well. I refused to accept the suggested change.

A number of faculty, most of whom had been involved only tangentially in the IPD relationship, were dismayed by the temporary probationary status, and one member most likely voiced the sentiment of this particular group, namely, that had the faculty been more involved, the IPD difficulties would never have occurred. This view had credibility, since the IPD program may well have met the fate of the initially proposed MBA program a few years earlier. Several seasoned members of the faculty were more sanguine and optimistic, observing that the IPD program, as far as they could tell, and the institution of the MBA, the Paralegal Professionals Program and the expansion of the School of Education had contributed significantly to removing the College deficit and provided needed funds for the College in general. Several stated that temporary probation and a correctable upgrading were preferred to the financial straits which had developed after the turmoil of the 1972 spring semester and subsequent attrition. These same faculty voiced the opinion that with the proper leadership and the hiring of sufficient full-time faculty, older-adult programs could be developed which reflected both quality and distinctiveness, a task that the new Dean was mandated to do.

However, those who envisioned the College as a pure undergraduate liberal arts institution emulating distinctive liberal arts institutions in various locations in the nation, considered any deviation from that ideal as unworthy of Saint Mary's, even though the School of Extended Education, with shrewd and energetic leadership, could well serve a population of students in need of completion or enhancement programs, thus fulfilling one Lasallian principle of serving those in academic and financial need.

Some argued that the College should confine itself to serving younger adults, that is, those of traditional college age, because such students are more open to a liberal education and are less likely to have acquired problematical impediments to learning, due either to inept education, environmental background or their own appetites. Older students, they claimed, because of their worldly experience will be more difficult, if not impossible, to reach. This appraisal has been effectively challenged simply by the actual reaction and response of a multitude of older adults who have been inspired and intellectually enriched in significant ways by their Extended Education experience. It is observable, however, that there were a few older students who entered Extended Education programs with seemingly fixed attitudes. Such students are, on occasion, a challenge to any professor who has developed appropriate approaches to addressing older students. Even so, an overwhelming majority of Extended Education students have expressed the fact that the Extended Education experience had changed their lives, not only in securing better employment, but in enriching their personal and interpersonal attitudes and commitments.

Unrelenting Opposition - 1978-1991

During the time between the special 1977 Accreditation Visit and the regular 1980 Visit, those involved in the loyal faculty opposition remained in high gear. Their agenda was expressed clearly and persistently during this interim.

When the Feb. 27, 1978 letter from the WASC Accreditation Commission, signed by Executive Director Kay Andersen, was read to the faculty at the Faculty Assembly meeting of Sept.20, 1978, Professors Norman Springer, Virginia Snyder and several others interpreted the letter in much broader terms than the letter indicated or I clearly understood from my several interchanges with the WASC Executive Director and members of his staff regarding Commission views. I was convinced that the object of the probationary status was clear, namely, that the College take full control of any of its "graduate, off-campus, external degree and continuing education programs, and to divest itself of those programs for which the College cannot maintain controls sufficient to assure the character and quality of the institution." I knew that the joint agreements between the Institute for Professional Development or any similar arrangement for any other program were to be terminated. By 1978, the process for doing so was in high gear. Likewise clear was that Accreditation Commission pressure was being applied to any other institution in the state, and there were several, that had similar arrangements. Professor Norman Springer surprisingly saw the letter as being supportive of the criticisms of administration that appeared in the *Interpersonal Relationships* or *Love Committee Report* and claimed that the president had "misled the faculty in his comments to the faculty on March, 19, 1978." Yet, Professor Chester Aaron stated that from his vantage point as a member of the Faculty Committee on Continuing and Contract Education, "it was difficult to pin WASC down to a firm position in the interpretation of any matter." (Minutes of the Faculty Assembly, Sept. 20, 1978.)

In the face of Springer's criticism, I remained as stoical as possible and restated that the major concern of WASC was insisting that the College exercise full control over all academic programs conducted in the name of the College. I also stated that rather than assume control over the two-unit travel courses the College would simply discontinue them, which it did.

Some faculty, unsure of the facts and where the College was headed, wished to understand more fully the whole Accreditation action. Others would not be deterred from pressing their own agenda by interpreting Accreditation directives in favor of their own ends, particularly in terms of faculty membership on the Board of Trustees and in other circles of power. They called for a special meeting of the Faculty Assembly on Oct. 25, 1978, to review the March 1978 *WASC Accreditation Report* and the May 1977 *Interpersonal Relations Committee Report*.

The first to speak at the special meeting was Mary Springer, urging the faculty to discuss *A Proposed Mandate for the Faculty Committee to Study Interpersonal Relations* that had been distributed in advance. The Mandate was composed by three faculty members, Alan Pollock (English), Joseph Lanigan (Philosophy) and Mary Springer (English). The Mandate reiterated some of the issues raised in the *Interpersonal Relations Report* and included three proposals. The first took aim at the Board of Trustees; the second, the percentage of part-time faculty (a replay of the earlier AFT proposal) and the third, a review of new programs, including release-time for those involved in the review process. Professor El Gelinas rose to indicate that a Select Committee was already addressing the WASC and Interpersonal Relations reports, and that the Select Committee report would be made available to the faculty at its completion.

Norman Springer insisted that the faculty should discuss the two reports then and there, suggesting that "the faculty should move into the center of the institution," and that, "it was important to identify what is the problem that the WASC report seems to reveal." Professor Snyder, in support of Norman Springer, "quoted a WASC official's comment alleged to be made to me to the effect that there should be a democratic institution rather than an autocratic institution." I candidly stated that I had no recollection or knowledge of any WASC official or visiting team member making such a statement to me verbally or in writing, though there was reference to such a view expressed in the 1975 Accreditation Report.

Professor Norman Springer then engaged in dramatic hyperbole noting that "loss of accreditation would mean loss of credit, loss of scholarship funds, loss of prestige, loss of transferability of credit." He concluded his speculative peroration by stating that "the management of the budget should be more directly in faculty hands." A conciliatory stance was recommended by Brother Ronald Isetti, but Springer quickly indicated his disinterest in "a conciliatory stance now." Alan Pollock added to the confusion by noting that "a change in the Trustees' constituency was indicated and, in any event, greater faculty input vis-à-vis the Trustees was desirable."

A motion was made by Professors Owen Carroll and Kendall Brown that the Select Committee direct a letter to each of the Trustees individually and that a committee of three faculty present the letter to the Board of Trustees. An amendment to the motion by Professor Waddell moved that the letters to the Trustees be written by the chairman of the Faculty or someone delegated by him. The motion to amend passed by a vote of 22 yea 5 nay with 9 abstention.

Following further discussion -- with one person suggesting that a letter may be more forceful if a summary of the Select Committee's report were included, and another that no letter should be sent until the faculty receives a complete report from the Select Committee, -- motion by Gelinas/Carroll to table the motion (as amended) carried, 26-0-4, and the meeting was adjourned (Minutes of the Faculty Assembly, Oct. 29, 1978, Saint Mary's College Archives.)

I had full confidence that all significant problems would be resolved and had no anxieties that accreditation would be modified or removed. My major concern was whether the exaggerated, inaccurate and sometimes uncivil statements made during Faculty Assembly meetings and at other times and places would impede the development of the College overall, since the goodwill of the faculty majority was essential to a creative and dynamic program attractive to both students and their parents. The College had faced a difficult financial crisis, created in part by the disaffected faculty, as well as the times, and required immediate and imperative reaction. In general, the administrative reaction, pursued inexorably, though with inevitable criticism, was ultimately successful. While the concept of educating older adults who could not pursue the traditional modes of securing baccalaureate and graduate degrees was an undeniable service to a segment of society, I acknowledged that details of the Extended Education Program lacked full start-up scrutiny, whereas the MBA Executive Program, though also opposed by the same faculty members, began with a more thoughtful, imaginative and detailed foundation. While the WASC leadership had a number of legitimate concerns with the IPD program and IPD contracts with several California and out-of-state colleges and universities, it was interesting to note that the

North Central Accrediting Association, headed by what appeared be an Executive Director and Commission members who were willing to engage in reasonable experimentation, apparently found the concept of educating older adults in what was a semi-unconventional way well worth consideration. In a relatively short time, as the newly founded University of Phoenix adjusted itself to address any North Central Accrediting Association requirements, the North Central Association saw fit to grant full accreditation rights to the new enterprise. The University of Phoenix then proceeded to open numerous centers throughout California.

Frustrating as it became at the outset, the benefit of the IPD experience, once major problems were resolved, provided the College with an off-campus student body and an unusual educational system with an authentic mission to aid older adults. On the downside, the programs in Extended Education were primarily designed to appeal to those seeking career advancement in the workplace. Since the new Extended Education Program eventually included Great Books seminars called Critical Perspectives Seminars and a Religious Studies component, the liberal arts element in the program approximated what ordinary transfer students would receive in the regular undergraduate curriculum. Those who taught in the Extended Education Program were pleased to note that the more perceptive Extended Education students often remarked that the liberal arts courses were among the most influential in their lives and recommended that the program expand the number of such courses.

One Extended Education Program student commencement speaker, a Vice President at Fetzer Winery in Ukiah, stated that Critical Perspectives, which included such authors as Plato, Aristotle, Cicero, Augustine and Dante, had not only challenged his mind but changed his life, and he declared that he had become an avid advocate of reading the greatest books ever written.

The addition of strong graduate programs, the Paralegal Professionals Program and the Extended Education Degree programs, revised to reflect a Saint Mary's character and were fully supervised by the College, were not only financially helpful, but the addition of administrators and faculty as legitimate members of the College community to staff these programs emphasized the needed overhaul of academic governance, a matter to be addressed in the not-too distant future. For sure, the once small faculty faction that hoped to control the dynamics of academic life was overwhelmed by the increasing number of qualified faculty who were charged with overseeing expanded academic activities.

New School of Extended Education, 1978

In the Fall of 1978, after extensive screening, the new Academic Vice President, Brother William Beatie, recommended that Robert J. Roxby, PhD, be named Dean of Extended Education. Roxby was appointed in Jan. 1979 and presented with the mandate that he revise the Extended Education Program so that it would be fully acceptable to the Accreditation Commission and its Executive Director, Kay Andersen. Roxby held a doctorate in Higher Education from Washington State University, an MA in French and Linguistics from Georgetown and a BA in Romance Languages from Trinity College in Hartford, Conn. He had served as Dean of Carroll College in Helena, Mon., in 1969, attended graduate school in Washington for three years, and in 1973 became Director of the Evening Division at the University of Hartford in Hartford, Conn. He ably fulfilled the mandate given to him by vigorously revising the program and gaining not only WASC approval, but regular commendations on subsequent accreditation reports.

In the course of his assuming command of the School of Extended Education, Roxby extended the time required for fulfilling baccalaureate requirements and included the two major academic elements that characterized the Saint Mary's undergraduate curriculum, namely the Great Books and religious studies components. He extended the program from 33 weeks to 73 weeks and hired full-time tenure-track faculty. Furthermore, Roxby was a pioneer in guiding the library into the emerging electronic-information age, since his distance-learning students had to be able to access information differently from residential students.

The seminar method for many classes in the older adult programs became an instructional mode. Some traditional undergraduate faculty still considered Extended Education a major part of Brother Dominic's adventurism and as the cause for what they considered an embarrassing, albeit short, probationary status. Others still considered the Extended Education Program as an unneeded appendage to a quality liberal arts institution, and their unbending opposition would be untiring in its underwhelming support. Thus, Robert Roxby found that he was frequently under scrutiny and often encountered considerable opposition in his attempt to reorganize the program into what he saw as a representative and effective adult educational opportunity for the many who sought its potential benefits. However, his often obscurant, defensive mode when speaking to faculty about the program delayed not only his personal acceptance, but a trust in its viable efficacy. Later praise by accrediting visiting teams was a major factor in ameliorating most, but not all, faculty bias and resentment.

Testimony by students in the program expressed gratitude for the opportunity to complete their baccalaureate degrees and to benefit in their workplace from their continued education.

"What I appreciate most," one graduate testified: "and I think is most often overlooked are the sacrifices that the faculty and staff made to committing the time and energy to ensure that we received the top-notch education that we did…I can't thank them enough for the knowledge that they passed on, which has and will continue to allow me the opportunity to use to improve my own life and the lives of others. I feel honored as I prepare for law school to consider the professors that had such a profound impact on my life both personally and professionally, as my colleagues. I can't thank them enough." A graduate who received his baccalaureate degree at age 53 stated that: "Lifetime learning is an excellent addiction. My interest levels are higher, I feel more engaged in life and in my personal education. My interests have widened because of Saint Mary's College's curriculum. The curriculum has proved extremely valuable in the "real world." I find everyone respects a degree from Saint Mary's College — respect for the degree, respect for the school."

"On the professional side," a police lieutenant observed: "the Saint Mary's program helped me compete in a very tough captain's promotional examination where I was able to use the leadership and management lessons learned along with the fiscal and human resource development tools. The classes that I thought had the least amount of relevance to my work life: ethics, philosophy and social welfare studies, all helped me to develop a broader perspective that instilled a sense of the importance of service and compassion so critical to the field of policing. I was unprepared for just how important and special graduation was. As a mother of two young kids, an 80-hour-a-week job as a police lieutenant, I thought I would just be relieved to have completed the studying. Quite to the contrary; the sense of accomplishment and pride that I walked away with equaled the diploma in impacting my life for the better. I was so pleased with my Saint Mary's education that once I became Chief of Police, I was able to assist in bringing into existence a very special Masters Degree program in 21st Century Leadership and am very excited to be teaching in this graduate-level program. None of this would have been possible without the very special faculty and programs here at Saint Mary's. Go Gaels!"

One graduate offers a touching personal note to her experience. "I began attending Saint Mary's at a difficult time in my life. My father had passed away a year before, and my brother died in August. Classes started in September. I began to feel a sense of peace as my relationship with the instructors grew.

Critical Perspectives (Great Books Program) proved to be most helpful to me. In doing the assignments and reading from the past great philosophers, I found myself in tears as they literally touched on some of the same issues I was having at the time. I have found that my writing is much better, but the most important thing to me is my religious strength, which Saint Mary's helped me to find."

Note: After I retired from the presidency, I taught in the Critical Perspectives portion of the School of Extended Education for approximately 10 years. During those 10 years I encountered some of the brightest and most perceptive students I have ever met and was impressed by their promptness in both reading and completing assignments. A number of those older adult students claimed that the program had profoundly changed their lives.

A Respite for an Innovator

By the end of the 1978 spring semester, Brother Dominic, now 60, desired to take some time to prepare for retirement activities. He was later awarded an honorary degree during one of the Extended Education Program commencement ceremonies in recognition of his dedication and tenacity in developing programs and establishing a rationale which eventually brought the College both financial stability and appreciation by numerous graduates of the Extended Education Program. Brother William Beatie, FSC, PhD, who was serving as Undergraduate Dean, was appointed Academic Vice President commencing in the fall of 1978.

Brother William Beatie, FSC, PhD, Meticulous Progress

When Brother William Beatie, FSC, PhD, assumed the office of Academic Vice President in 1978, his incisive philosophical mind and equally sharp rejoinders were surprising to some faculty. But those of us who knew him appreciated his meticulous clarity, insight, impatience with confusion and sense of humor. His work at the University of Chicago and then his doctoral studies at the Catholic University of Louvain (Belgium) were, for his intellectual appetite, an experience of challenge, delight and fulfillment. Captivated by the relationship between philosophy and religion, he chose for his intensive study and thesis the Philosophy of Religion, a course by the same name he has taught for years. He was awarded his doctorate in 1969 and became a member of the Saint Mary's College Department of Philosophy the same year.

Students will attest that there is little doubt that Brother William is a gifted instructor whose pedagogy encourages them to develop concepts through their own intellectual effort. He normally eschews lecturing, engaging rather in the discipline of perusing a train of thought, with its normal derailments and pauses for clarification, thus evoking sufficient wonder to inspire students to engage within themselves the challenge of an intellectual discovery. The intellectual engagement of Brother William's classes may well reflect the academic excitement that occurred in the Socratic Academy. Both he and his students often enjoy enduring friendships and mutual rapport in their quest for wisdom. Students have often cited their gratitude for the experience. When students, faculty and administrators encounter him in informal situations away from the academic classroom, they often find him to be delightfully jocular and quick-witted.

As an administrator and overseer of academic programs, he displayed a meticulous attention to detail that was most beneficial in the establishment of the relationship between the College and Samuel Merritt College of Nursing, with whom the College developed an effective and beneficial cooperative nursing program leading to a joint baccalaureate degree for the registered nurse. His assiduity in selecting the right person at the right time as Dean of Extended Education, as well as his unswerving support, allowed the College to develop a baccalaureate program for older adults that became an exemplary model for adult higher education that merited praise from both members of accreditation teams and students alike.

Brother William was pleased to be relieved of the pressures of chief academic administrator in 1990, but there being no rest for such talent, he was selected as a member of the Board of Trustees in 1995, as well as a member of the New Century Committee. He became a beacon of light in a sometimes stormy sea of opinion in the formation of the College Mission Statement by the New Century Committee.

Continuing Internecine Controversy, 1978-1981

In April 1978, Professor Norman Springer submitted a five-point proposal on faculty status and remuneration for both full- and part-time members. The proposals were clearly controversial, as discussions on them within the Faculty Assembly demonstrated, and as counter proposals by other groups, i.e., the Associated Faculty, the Faculty Welfare Committee, and an ad hoc faculty committee of 10 made even clearer. The Academic Vice President ultimately formed a committee of major actors in the controversy and developed a reasonable solution. Though I remained ostensibly aloof from the give-and-take of those issues, I made my views clear to the members of the Administrative Council of which the Academic Vice President was a member. In part, the Springer - American Federation of Teachers strategy was to challenge the administration but also to seek victories in the name of the AFT, so that more members of the faculty would be inclined to become AFT members. In addition, Springer also believed that the faculty should be central in making almost all determinations on College academic policy and budget. Springer and other members of the AFT from time to time made such comments as, "faculty should move into the center of the institution, the management of the budget should be more directly in faculty hands, faculty should participate in the highest levels of administration, and membership on the Board of Trustees should be reconstituted."

One must acknowledge Norman Springer's endurance in the advocacy of both his and the AFT agenda. His election as president of the local AFT chapter gave him greater incentive and enthusiasm for promoting a new order. The discussions on the particular matter of part-time faculty status and remuneration, and the status of both full- and part-time faculty in the College as a whole began in April 1978 and ended in the spring of 1981, a span of three years. Likewise, there were other issues, such as the status of part-time faculty in College governance that Norman Springer pursued with vigor.

In the meantime, the United States Supreme Court had taken as one of its cases whether unionization efforts at Yeshiva University of New York were legally under the jurisdiction of the National Labor Relations Board. On Feb. 20, 1980, the Court rendered a decision that stated that faculty were inextricably involved in managerial and supervisory functions at the university, that is, the faculty had "extensive control" over academic and personnel decisions as well as a "crucial role ... in determining other central policies of the institution." Faculty members were, therefore, endowed with managerial status sufficient to remove them from National Labor Relations Board coverage. Since the Saint Mary's faculty participated in managerial functions in the same vein as the faculty at Yeshiva, it was not long before the unionization effort evaporated.

Dotted Line: Who's Advising Whom?
A recurring issue surfaced at a special Faculty Assembly meeting on May 24, 1978, namely a reaction to a proposed Governance Committee recommendation on a revised academic committee structure. After reviewing a chart identifying the relationship of various committees to various administrators as well as their relationship to one another, Norman Springer and Alan Pollock stated that the Academic Council, though advisory to the Academic Vice President, always submitted its resolutions to the Faculty Assembly for approval. Professor Mary Ann Mason noted that the *Faculty Handbook* stated that the Academic Council was an elected faculty body advisory to

the AVP on matters selected by him for consideration. A motion was made (Andrew DeGall/El Gelinas) to give tentative approval to the proposed academic governance model.

However, Norman Springer and Alan Pollock moved to amend the motion by having a line drawn between the Academic Council and the Faculty Assembly. Another amendment was proposed by Professor Waddell that a line also be drawn between the Academic Council and the Academic Vice President. A fourth amendment (Education Chairman Paul Burke and Sepher Zabih) required that the governance structure be subject to final faculty approval. The thrice-amended motion passed, by a vote of 24 yea, 5 nay, with 1 abstention. Norman Springer's intent in drawing a line between the Academic Council and the Faculty Assembly was to subordinate the Academic Council to the Faculty Assembly. The amendments were seen as tempering the Springer intent, but clarity did not reign after the motion with its three amendments was accepted by the faculty.

The Governance Committee proposal on the academic governance structure was again discussed, as requested, at the March 28, 1979, meeting of the Faculty Assembly. The line between the Academic Council and the Faculty Assembly had been removed by the Governance Committee. Norman Springer asked, "Why?" As chair of the Governance Committee, I responded that Brother William, Academic Vice President, had requested that the line be removed since it confused the relationship of the Faculty Assembly and the Academic Council with the Academic Vice President, since both groups are advisory to the AVP. "It should be clear," Brother William had stated, "that the Academic Council is responsible to the Dean (AVP) and is not a subcommittee of the Faculty Assembly." Professor Andrew DeGall responded to Professor Springer stating that the line was not indicative of Academic Council subservience to the Faculty Assembly. "The Academic Council," DeGall further stated," was never understood to be a committee of the Faculty Assembly, but rather, it was always understood to be an advisory body to the Academic Vice President who presents substantive matters to the Faculty Assembly for their reaction and advice." (Minutes of the Faculty Assembly, March 28, 1979.)

Norman Springer had suggested that a dotted line be drawn between the Academic Council and the Faculty Assembly, indicating that substantive matters recommended to the Academic Vice President by the Council must be considered by the Assembly for its advice to the AVP. Reference to the matter of the "dotted line" became the source for some light-hearted repartee among both administrators and some faculty when speaking of Norman Springer's interventions.

The issue as to the role of the Academic Council appeared on the Faculty Assembly docket almost a year later, on March 13, 1980. A report from the Academic Council occasioned considerable discussion. Professor Alan Pollock, who first instituted the Academic Council when he served as Academic Vice President, tapped his memory on the origins and history of its inception. Professor Albert Dragstedt (Classics/Integral) had submitted a motion proposing that the wording of the 1971-1972 and 1973-1974 *Faculty Handbooks* be re-introduced. The *Faculty Handbook* of those years stated that "the Undergraduate Dean should present major policy decisions of the Academic Council to the Faculty as a whole for discussion and approval, and the consensus of the Faculty must normally and whenever possible be accepted by the Undergraduate Dean." Dragstedt disagreed with the account in the report submitted to the Assembly by Brother William that the Academic Council is advisory to the AVP, with the comment that there had been "a recent decay of faculty influence not sanctioned by public discussion." However, at the close of the discussion by the Assembly, all three parts of the Academic Council report as submitted by Brother William were accepted (Part 1, unopposed, Part 2, by a vote of 24 aye, 12 nay, with 5 abstentions, Part 3, by vote of 20 yea, 15 nay, with 6 abstentions). (Minutes of the Faculty Assembly, March 13, 1980.)

The prolonged arguments regarding faculty role and the tasks of various committees were significant governance issues that would have long-term effects.

The Associated Faculty

A third group of faculty that brought a new voice to the mix of campus politics was a group that designated itself The Associated Faculty. Mention of The Associated Faculty appeared in the Nov. 8, 1978, minutes of the Faculty Assembly. This new association, chaired by Professor Sepehr Zabih, PhD of the Government Department, was formed by several faculty members who opposed, in principle, the formation of an American Federation of Teachers local as well as a number of interventions made by the local President. One of the purposes of the Associated Faculty was to act as an intermediary between administration and faculty, with the hope of ameliorating any differences without resorting to the draconian approach of unionization, an approach most faculty members opposed, especially some who had been involved with unionization in other institutions and did not want to repeat the experience.

One of the first actions by the Associated Faculty was to propose to the Faculty Assembly on Oct. 10, 1979, that there be a permanent Undergraduate Faculty Welfare Committee. A motion placed before the Assembly proposed that the Welfare Committee represent the faculty on the College Budget

Committee and thus would promote and protect faculty interests in matters concerning financial priorities, salaries and fringe benefits, and working conditions (office space, secretarial assistance, parking, communications). The motion also proposed that the committee would consist of three full-time on-campus undergraduate faculty members elected by the undergraduate faculty and would secure faculty endorsement before recommendations became final. The motion was divided for the vote, but all sections were approved by a large majority. The Associated Faculty next proposed a revision of faculty election procedures to the Faculty Assembly on May 7, 1980. Their proposal was accepted by the Faculty Assembly by a vote of 16 yea, 1 nay, with 3 abstentions.

Faculty Salary Policy
The faculty salary policy had been adopted by the Board of Trustees in 1966. The policy, as it appears in the Feb. 21, 1966, board minutes, states that "Saint Mary's College will, as far as possible, adopt the California State University salary scale of the prior year plus 3 percent."

The salary policy as stated was one of those motions proposed by a Board member that contained the genesis of the intention, but required subsequent interpretation to address the details. For example, the salary scales of Saint Mary's College and the California State University system were not identical: a) there were more steps in each of the categories (Instructor, Assistant Professor, Associate Professor and Professor) in the Saint Mary's scale than in the State University scale: b) the reckoning of the workload per faculty member at Saint Mary's differed from that of the California State University System. The Saint Mary's Chief Financial Officer, therefore, interpreted the Trustee policy to be that the *average* salary in the four Saint Mary's categories would be equalized with the *average* categories in the California State College scale of the prior year, with 3 percent added to the Saint Mary's scale for the current year to account for Cost of Living increases in the new year.

During the Faculty Assembly of April 15, 1978, Professors Norman Springer and Richard Wiebe moved, "that the faculty feels that the 10 percent salary increase which the President cited, as reported in the March 15 (1978) faculty minutes, and which the President will request of the Board of Trustees, is an inadequate step towards meeting the Board of Trustees' 1966 salary policy. The faculty feels that a 12 percent increase is a necessary step towards implementation of the 1966 salary policy." After discussion the motion failed, by a vote of 8 yea, 10 nay, with 10 abstentions.

Expansion for Students

Guerrieri East and West, 1980

Lewis Guerrieri was not an alumnus but became intimately associated with Saint Mary's during the Madigan Era of big-time football. However, his love of the College endured long after highly competitive football ended in 1951. As he advanced in years, he would come to the College to visit from his home in Laguna Hills, Calif. and I met him on several of his visits. I estimated his character as a hard-working, energetic and genuinely kind man who was deeply interested in Catholic education, especially at Saint Mary's, where he had seen many young men not only play the sport both he and they enjoyed, but receive an education that provided an opportunity for a productive career. Little did I realize that Lewis would provide more than one million dollars for "something related to students." Since the College needed more housing at the time, we decided to add two additional student townhouses to the four that already existed. They were named Guerrieri East and West and were dedicated in 1980.

Developing a Career Center, 1980

Brother Bede Edward, a man who did not believe in retirement would find off-campus jobs for students through taking calls from residents of the Lamorinda (Lafayette, Moraga, Orinda) area. He would collect the job offers, write the names, addresses and phone numbers of *ad hoc* job opportunities on a notepad and then walk through Oliver Dining Hall offering the jobs to students. Many eagerly sought the offers, and some even made their way through college by accepting the jobs proffered by the so-called retired Brother Bede Edward, FSC, EdD, formerly of the nominal Education Department. The administration took notice of two concerns, first, that Brother Bede was wearing down, and second, how important it was to have a placement office on campus for formalizing the part-time employment process. Negotiations were made with the State of California Department of Economic Development to set up an office on campus to serve Saint Mary's students, many young people in the area and the tax-paying citizens of Lamorinda. However, as the College grew it became evident that students required long-range career planning opportunities by professionalizing the career search process and encouraging employers to look to the College for suitable applicants for full-time positions. During the 1979-1980 academic year, Professor John Thompson developed a well-designed program that he hoped would be managed by an arm of his management firm. This plan sparked interest in Sister Clare Wagstaffe, OP, then assistant Dean of Student

Services, and Brother Brendan Madden, formerly Dean of Counseling and Guidance at Saint Mary's High School in Berkeley, who had set up a small desk in the library with catalogs for graduate study and some booklets on how to write a resume and engage in an interview. They were of the opinion that it would be more appropriate for the College to develop its own career and graduate school counseling services. They were acquainted with Bernard "Bernie" Valdez who had completed his Master's Degree at the College Department of Education in Counseling and Leadership and who had 29 years of experience in sales and human resources with AT&T and Pacific Bell. In 1980, Sister Clare named him director of the newly formed Career Development Center.

The Career Development Center became a mecca for those interested in graduate school and finding a suitable post-college career. In the early 1990s the State discontinued the State of California EDD Office on campus in a budget-cutting frenzy. The College, however, was able to do what the California EDD office had done for Saint Mary's students and much more -- in terms of training, internships, interviews, career information nights, computerized self-assessment and developing cooperation between the Center and personnel directors of various corporations. The internship program became a significant element of the College Career Development Center, and many interns were eventually hired by the institutions that adopted an internship program.

The CDC came of age with its association with the Western College Placement Association. Bernie Valdez became a member of the Association's Board and later received a Distinguished Service Award and then the Educator of the Year Award. A professional staff was hired over time and the results have been a source of student and alumni satisfaction. Valdez retired in 2001, leaving a strong program in the able hands of Brother Brendan Madden, FSC.

The Career Development Center served approximately 150 seniors and alumni and 200 undergraduate interns each year. At one time, the Center employed six full-time counselors, all with master's degrees and three administrative assistants. Part-time work opportunities for undergraduate students earn them a total of approximately $4 million per annum.

Emerging Years, 1980-1985

The Accreditation Visit of 1980—Balance and Insight

An 11-member Visiting Team, chaired by Paul E. Hadley, Academic Vice President of the University of Southern California, made an official visit on March 12-14, 1980, only two years and five months after the 1977 Visit. The opening paragraphs in the 1980 confidential report (that mistakenly found its way into a copy of the *Accreditation Report* to the College) recommended that probation be removed and accreditation be reaffirmed. "Financial deficits have been overcome; current balances are in the black, even if narrowly so; physical improvements have been made; and salaries have been raised. Key administrative changes have been made; a revised committee structure has been developed allowing for greater participation in governance; increased openness by the administration is noticeable; concurrence on the goals and objectives of the College has been achieved with some exceptions." (The last observation on *some exceptions* to "concurrence on the goals and objectives" would be a source of concern to me and the Administrative Council for years and reappears in stronger terms in the *Visiting Team Report of 1993*.)

"Both because of changes in some officers and some policies and because of what looks like a genuine and widespread effort at goodwill and trust, a much pleasanter atmosphere now pervades the campus," the Team report observed. "An atmosphere of friendly discussion and mutual respect is widely reported and seemed evident to members of the visiting team." (*Accreditation Report*, 1980, page 57.) One aspect of faculty concern, namely the voluntary eight-course teaching load had ceased, thus returning the faculty to the seven-course load.

One of the recommendations of the Visiting Team that I found most gratifying was that the College expand its liberal arts and Lasallian tradition in the Extended Education degree curriculum, thus addressing the faculty observation of 1977 that the distinctive elements of the Saint Mary's curriculum should appear in the Extended Education degree program.

Of special note is the comment in the report that, "The Team is satisfied that the College has endeavored to examine the new Standards of the Western Association of Schools and Colleges. The Self-Study reveals, however, that compliance is as yet in its initial stages." Several administrators and faculty groups charged with examining the new WASC Standards to assure compliance, experienced occasional frustration since the Association made numerous changes, some reluctantly, it seemed, to respond to rapidly advancing educational innovations associated with such new concepts as distance learning via technology, external degree programs and credit for experiential learning. Furthermore, social issues such as diversity and the need for greater financial aid, the role of women in higher education, appropriate undergraduate education, career counseling, the meaning of doctoral degrees and access to handicapped students prompted the insertion of new evaluative criteria.

The Visiting Team took note of the 1975 recommendation that the College assure itself that students truly benefit from the Collegiate Seminar (Great Books) program, considered the "heart of the liberal arts experience for all students." Evaluation or assessment was again suggested, a matter that engendered controversy, which in turn inhibited developing a report that would provide diverse anecdotal surveys or even statistical results.

In spite of whatever their intellectual and emotional maturity was when as students they encountered the Seminar Program, alumni of various stripes frequently report to faculty and administration on the value they received in both the concepts discovered in seminar texts and the experience they acquired with forming, articulating and defending their views among their peers in the seminar context. Yet, citing abundant casual or anecdotal comments from a diverse alumni population is usually insufficient for evaluators who look to professional surveys and statistical charts for evidence. They give the appearance of being more scientific! Visiting Teams were no exception. Assessment and accountability in demonstrating both immediately relevant or enduring educational results later became a major issue with the Accrediting Association, evoking complaints from a number of faculty at Saint Mary's and at other institutions as well. Inviting outside evaluators familiar with the seminar method to examine the program in order to provide a comprehensive analysis or engaging in a systematic sampling of alumni impressions through the administration of a thoughtfully designed questionnaire (written or telephonic) are two methods that could ameliorate accreditation anxieties over assessment.

One controversial recommendation was that of urging the School of Economics and Business Administration to combine the faculty of the undergraduate division with that of the newly established MBA program. The Team conjectured that both faculties would benefit if they were conjoined. As a result, over the objections of the MBA faculty, the two became one under the Dean of the School, C. J. "Mike" Walter, PhD Testimony from many faculty members later supported the notion that both undergraduate and graduate programs improved by forming a unified School of Economics and Business Administration faculty.

Though there had been significant improvement in the conduct of the January Terms since its inception in 1970, as of 1980 not all of the lacunae and ineffectiveness problems had been ironed out. The Visiting Team noted that not all students found the January Term as demanding as the regular semesters. Faculty who served as Resident Hall counselors had noted for many years that students seemed less pressured and thus more inclined to recreate or socialize during January. While there is some academic and psychological advantage in approaching a single subject during one month, reports and results had continued to be mixed. Having a particular professor for one month was difficult for some students and a vibrant intellectual experience for others. The Visiting Team noted that lower division students, particularly freshmen, felt that choice selections were less available, a concern that the January Term Director attempted to resolve. A number of students reported that the January Term contained the most fulfilling courses of their undergraduate careers and a strong core of faculty fully endorsed the challenge and effectiveness of January Term courses. Admissions officers were convinced that the January Term attracted many students to the College and that their recruitment efforts would be less effective without being able to promote the unusual merits of the "J" Term.

Academic Vice President Brother William Beatie, FSC, PhD, was intent on assuring a clear reaffirmation of accreditation through the 1980 Accreditation Visit and the removal of probation, an identity that most viewed as an academic stigma. It was clear that the traditional undergraduate program was never the cause for Accreditation disapproval. By the time of the 1980 Accreditation Visit, the College had severed its relationships with nonaccredited outside groups and had assumed full command of all its academic programs. Though some innovative programs still required maturing, the right leadership was in place to accomplish the task.

Brother William Beatie was unwilling to jettison any of the major programs that Brother Dominic had instituted, knowing that they had the potential to become effective if they had strong leadership. Since he favored the concept of older adult education, master's programs and the intercollegiate nursing program, he was determined to improve the status and reputation of Extended Education programs, both within the College and before the Accrediting Association. Under Dr. Robert Roxby's close supervision, programs were redesigned to conform more closely with the College's traditional undergraduate academic policies and requirements. In discussions among members of the

President's Administrative Council, Brother William agreed that the number of graduates from the Extended Education, older adult baccalaureate degree programs, could approximate, but not exceed, the number per annum in the traditional undergraduate program. This precaution became policy so that Extended Education programs would not overwhelm the traditional undergraduate college. The Administrative Council saw that controlling both the size of the Extended Education Program and the distance from the campus of off-campus centers would better guarantee academic oversight and quality. One of the major contributions of the Visiting Team of 1980 was to recommend with vigor that the Extended Education degree programs contain both a Collegiate Seminar and a Religious Studies component. "… Saint Mary's College may not be giving sufficient attention to what appears to be its central purpose, its fine goals, in some of its programs." (Accreditation Report of March 12-14, 1980, Paul Hadley, chair, page 23, Saint Mary's College Archives.)

The most gratifying result of the 1980 Visit was the report on Extended Education. Brother William and Robert Roxby had dedicated significant effort and insight to the reorganization and enhancement of the program. The results of their work were evident in the *Visiting Team Report* on contacts with students both in class and at the student representatives' meeting at Saint Mary's that " reassured the Team as to their maturity, sophistication, and motivation." "It appears," the report noted, "that the recruitment/admission process has selected students well-prepared to benefit from the program. The classes that were observed were generally of high quality. They began on time, lasted the prescribed time frame and reflected organized and substantive participation." (*Accreditation Report*, 1980, pages 90-91.)

Following the regular accreditation visit in 1980, Brother William Beatie and I appeared before the WASC Commission in the early summer of 1980 and recited the list of actions which the College had taken in response to earlier Accreditation Commission concerns. Probation was rescinded and accreditation reaffirmed. Probation did not at any time indicate that the College had lost its accreditation. Placing the College on probation was an action that had its desired effect, namely, the elimination of any relation between a California collegiate institution and the Institute for Professional Development or, under its new name, the University of Phoenix.

Faculty Assembly, 1981-1985

Between 1980 and 1985, the year scheduled for the next Accreditation Visit, the emphasis of faculty interest for the most part shifted from office space, welfare and political issues to more academic matters. However, a few social and disciplinary incidents were brought to the Assembly by a few members who saw them as compelling causes for action as noted below. Considerable discussion time on such causes was commandeered until exhaustion and not a little skepticism ended discussion.

The first issue that occupied the attention of the Assembly was the red swastika incident:

Two red swastikas painted on the wall of a single classroom one night in March of 1982 were cause for heightened expressions of anguish by a few faculty members who were, to use common terms in vogue, "outraged," the most egregious, followed by "offended," or the more moderate "concerned." Any faculty member would be displeased by the appearance of swastikas anywhere on campus, just as they may look askance at a student wearing a KuKluxKlan outfit to a student costume party. At the time of the swastikas incident the news media had carried a number of stories on mid-Eastern tensions, especially those between Israel and the Palestinians. In the early 1980s the College enrolled a number of graduate students from various countries where political tensions ran high. No one or group claimed responsibility for the painting of the swastikas. Some surmised that the swastikas were an expression of anti-Israel sentiment, which they may have been, but no one could identify any person or group who painted them on that lone classroom wall, nor could anyone attach a verifiable motive to the act.

Aggrieved faculty members (one who was Jewish and one whose husband was Jewish) brought the incident to the attention of the Faculty Assembly. A discussion ensued that concluded with a committee being appointed, headed by Professor Steve Woolpert of the Government Department to address what became an expanded agenda on vandalism, violence, safety and discrimination against minority groups and last, but not least, women on campus. A number of resolutions were proposed, one asking each member of the faculty to engage in introspection of his or her own attitude and another suggesting that some faculty might need human relations training. A third proposal would require all students to enroll in a course on ethnic, Third World or women's studies, and a fourth would include more works by women and minority authors in the Collegiate Seminar program. This fourth suggestion was quickly tabled, however, given that the Collegiate Seminar Governing Board reviewed all proposals affecting the Seminar and thus such a proposal should normally be sent to that Board.

One faculty member saw alcohol consumption as possibly related to the swastika incident though no evidence of such was forthcoming. The member claimed that there was probably a need for more stringent policies to reduce alcohol abuse among students living on campus. Other faculty, however, were not eager to pursue either a nonalcohol or restrictive alcohol policy, for they feared that a rigid imposition of policies to curtail alcohol usage would eliminate conviviality at dinners with older students and thus inhibit opportunities to educate students in the responsible use of alcohol, especially in the leisurely old-world tradition of European refinement.

Discussions about the swastika matter continued off and on for nearly a year, during which Professor Chester Aaron (English) was designated as a committee of one to gather possible reading lists on discrimination for use by faculty in the academic classroom. After several attempts, space on potential reading lists remained empty, at which Professor Aaron "expressed astonishment at the silence of colleagues." (Assembly Minutes, March 16, 1983.) In April of 1983, the Dean for Advising Services and Special Programs, Thomas Brown, was asked to speak to the Faculty Assembly on "underlying racism." Several unseemly incidents of discrimination were cited by Professor Chester Aaron to support Brown's claim of the presence of racism. Professor Norman Springer stressed the importance of producing a reading list. Professor Sensi-Isolani suggested that seminars and films be utilized to create awareness. Brother Timothy McCarthy noted that issues on racism, sexism and violence were often addressed in religious studies classes. The Assembly approved a motion to establish a standing committee to inform the faculty regarding reports of incidents of discrimination and violence and to advise the faculty on appropriate action. (Faculty Assembly Minutes, April 14, 1983.)

There is no evidence to suggest that volunteers could be found for the committee or that a report was ever produced. However, the *ad hoc* committee headed by Professor Steve Woolpert did deliver a report to the Faculty Assembly on Sept. 20, 1984. The following month, each recommendation was discussed and a vote recorded. The result was that a series of statements were made advising various individuals or offices to promote diversity on the basis of a Christian understanding of human dignity and to take necessary action should cases of discrimination occur. The recommendation that a study be made as to the feasibility of requiring students to enroll in a course in ethnic or women's studies passed after much discussion and a close vote of 14 yea, 11 nay, with 6 abstentions. (Minutes of Faculty Assembly, Nov. 15, 1984.) In December, the final portion of the report suggested that faculty reflect on their own attitudes, that students take courses dealing with violence and discrimination, that the Collegiate Seminar Governing Board consider adding works by women and minorities, that open discussion be encouraged both in and out of class and that a Public Affairs Society be established to encourage involvement of students in issues of ethics and public policy. A motion made to table this final portion of the report passed by a vote of 18 yea, 8 nay, with 8 abstentions. (Minutes of the Faculty Assembly, Dec. 5, 1984.)

Other issues, such as the need for renovated faculty offices, the library budget, the re-establishment of the honor society, salaries, benefits, the Collegiate Seminar, admissions, retention standards and a better writing program occupied the Faculty Assembly forum for the remainder of the year.

Problem of Part-time Faculty and Voting Rights— Progressive Platform

The Faculty Assembly approved the inclusion of full-time graduate and Extended Education faculty as electable members on a single, unified Rank and Tenure Committee for the entire College on Sept. 16, 1981. However, a policy that was seemingly understood and accepted, again became a point of controversy with the introduction of the proposal for a fully inclusive Rank and Tenure Committee, meaning both full and part-time members would be eligible for membership. Since the Rank and Tenure Committee dealt only with review, promotion and tenure for full-time members of the faculty, the current policy limited eligibility to full-time faculty members for membership. Professor Norman Springer and Alan Pollock again argued that part-time faculty were peers, that some part-time faculty had served the College with commitment for years and that their opinions were valued by the faculty. Their arguments were surprisingly persuasive and the Assembly defeated a proposition (18-32-9) that only full-time members of the faculty be allowed to vote for members on the Rank and Tenure Committee. (Faculty Assembly, Sept. 16, 1981.)

Both the Governance Committee and I found the arguments and the subsequent vote of the Assembly unacceptable. The Governance Committee was convinced that allowing part-time faculty to vote for membership on a committee that did not directly concern them was a blatant injustice to full-time faculty. The suspicion that politics, in the form of a desire to recruit members to the union effort, rather than justice, was at the heart of the argument favoring enfranchisement of part-timers, was a concern to the Governance Committee as it was to me. After hearing from the major advocates of part-time enfranchisement, I placed the issue before the Board of Trustees, since it was the Board of Trustees that had approved Rank and Tenure procedures. The Trustees were provided with copies of correspondence from both sides of the issue, as well as the Governance

Committee's unanimous recommendation against the practice. The Trustees approved the recommendation of the Governance Committee and called for a new election for members of the Rank and Tenure Committee. (Minutes of the Board of Trustees, Nov. 17, 1981, Saint Mary's College Archives.)

The Board's action was contested by Norman Springer and Alan Pollock, because the action was done "without faculty consultation." But lengthy faculty dialogue had already occurred in the Faculty Assembly on Sept. 16, 1981, and within the Governance Committee (a committee with a majority of elected faculty), which had subsequently recommended the full-time-only proposition to the Trustees. I had heard the arguments many times and consistently supported the full-time only proposition. Opponents in the Faculty Assembly grumbled that due process was ignored since the proposition came only from the Governance Committee. Since the Trustees had access to the arguments presented to the Assembly and the Assembly vote, the criticism was inaccurate. The opponents also grumbled that I did not justify myself before the Assembly before presenting the issue to the Board of Trustees. I did not recall any precedent requiring an intuition on my part that I should appear before the Assembly to rehash arguments because certain members thought I should.

More Core to the Curriculum

Another matter of academic significance was proposed by the Academic Council, namely, a revision of course requirements for all students. A number of faculty members recognized that the minimal requirements instituted in 1969 had weakened the overall liberal arts emphasis, while specific disciplines in most areas had grown stronger. Though the Academic Council was in agreement that adaptations and adjustments were required in view of demanding graduate programs in mainstream higher ducation in the United States, it also affirmed that a quality liberal arts education could not succumb to becoming a confusing educational smorgasbord for the intellectually uninitiated, a mental status that characterized most freshmen and some sophomores.

Thus, the Academic Council recommended that, in addition to the four Great Books Collegiate Seminars and two religious studies courses, additional requirements consisting of four other courses be enacted. Two would be selected by students from each of two broad categories, the first being mathematics, physical and life sciences and the second being courses in the literary, historical or philosophical disciplines. The Academic Vice President accepted the advice of his Council on this matter and presented the Council recommendation to the Faculty Assembly on Dec. 9, 1982. After several months of discussion, the recommendations, with amendments, were finally approved. (Minutes of the Faculty Assembly, Dec. 9, 1982, January 12, Feb. 17, March 16, 1983.) I applauded the Academic Council recommendation, since I believed that the changes in curriculum of 1969 had removed some critical academic requirements from the Saint Mary's curriculum that had been offered to students for at least since 1941 and that were favored by many alumni. The fact that students would be required to take courses not in their major fields as breadth requirements I, along with many faculty, viewed as a positive move. However, the proposal still lacked an integrating academic cohesiveness beyond that garnered through the chronological reading of literary, historical and philosophical texts in Collegiate Seminar. Emphasis in the Collegiate Seminar focused on students developing and articulating critical thought through conversation with supporting textual evidence. The chronological sequencing of texts allowed students to witness the development of thought in what was termed "ways of knowing" in the Western intellectual tradition. But an integrating element, such as a few selected courses in philosophy or a combination of several integrated courses from several disciplines, was still absent from the curriculum as a whole.

Music, Dance and Theater: A Major

Faculty members dedicated to the performing arts had developed a proposal for a coordinated program in the performing arts. A representative met with the Curriculum Committee to discuss the educational, financial and staffing aspects of such a new program. The concept was introduced to the Faculty Assembly on Dec. 10, 1981 by Professor Dan Cawthon (Religious Studies/ Performing Arts) who, in addition to his doctorate in theology and literature (Union Theological Seminary and Columbia University), also held active membership in Actors' Equity Association. No action was taken at this time, but the initial furrowing of the soil for a *bona fide* performing arts department was engraved in faculty minds.

Writing for All — Waivers an Exception

In the spring of 1982 a Faculty Committee on English Composition submitted a 31-page report on student writing. A student writing analysis by faculty reported that only one quarter of entering freshmen were considered good or superior writers, but that approximately 55 percent of upperclassmen were considered good or superior. Comparable data for institutions in the area, for example, the University of California, Berkeley, noted that only 33.3 percent of freshmen passed the Entrance A English Examination. At Stanford University only 300 out of 1,500 entering freshmen were exempted from the freshman writing requirement. (Ad Hoc Committee on English Composition, Report of spring 1982) The Report recommended that the required two -semester English Composition courses, titled *Better Writing*, be maintained, and furthermore, that remedial English courses be required of transfer students who did not measure up to the standards of the two required courses for freshmen. Also recommended were the offering of optional workshops for all faculty conducted by the Better Writing faculty, so that all faculty in all courses would be aware of the writing standards expected of students. The Faculty Assembly accepted and endorsed the recommendations contained in the Committee Report, by vote of 27 aye, 0 nay, with 2 abstentions. (Minutes of the Faculty Assembly, April 20, 1982.)

The Assembly also considered a recommendation by the Curriculum Committee that there "should be no retreat from the current College practice of requiring two semesters of composition for most students." Student writing was a critical concern for faculty, since the writing skills of entering students was so inconsistent. In too many cases, faculty claimed, the development of writing expertise as students moved toward graduation did not reflect collegiate-level standards. Motions with amendments were heard, with the Assembly overwhelmingly approving the need to continue with the writing program for most all students. A student could be exempted from the second course with an A or A- grade in the first course or was able to provide clear evidence of writing competency to a faculty jury. (Faculty Assembly Minutes, May 14, 1981.)

The Seminar Requirement

Controversial discussions on whether there should be two semesters centering on texts from the Greek World, followed by two or three seminars of other Great Books, chronologically arranged, selected from the remainder of Western literature, transpired over several months, namely from October 1982 to March 1983. In December, the Assembly maintained the two seminars for freshmen but declined to specify content. By March 1983, fixed on two seminars for freshmen and one in each of the two following years. (Faculty Assembly Minutes, March 16, 1983.) An argument against requiring five seminars focused on two difficulties, first, the need for as many as twenty additional sections, as well as additional faculty to teach the added seminars, and second, that additional requirements would reduce the opportunity for students to enroll in elective courses in their majors, a stance found unacceptable by those who supported a greater acquaintance with liberal arts for all students.

Suggestions were made to add an optional seminar. In May 1986 the Curriculum Committee recommended that an optional honors course in Collegiate Seminar for seniors only be added to the Collegiate Seminar program, to which the Governing Board acquiesced. Those who understood the extraordinary influence of Greek thought and literature on the Western world, argued for two semesters of Greek World. A secret ballot to faculty affirmed that the first two seminars be in Greek Thought by a vote of 46 yea, 37 nay, with 1 abstention. However, considerable dissatisfaction was expressed by some faculty who believed that one semester of Greek Thought was sufficient, and that other eras in the history of great thought were being shortchanged. After considerable discussion with various faculty members, Brother William, Academic Vice President, in a letter to the faculty dated March 23, 1983, noted that his discussions disclosed that "The importance of a two-semester requirement for Freshmen to lay the groundwork of both a unique educational experience and the development of the Seminar method of inquiry, was carefully examined, but the importance of a return to the content of the original program of a four-semester requirement which covered the spectrum from ancient to modern thought outweighed requiring Freshmen to take two semesters of Greek Thought." (Letter of Brother William Beatie, FSC, PhD, Academic Vice President, March 23, 1983.) The seminar program, therefore covered the four eras, a) Greek Thought, b) Roman/Early Christian/Medieval, c) Renaissance, 17th and 18th Century Thought, d) 19th and 20th Century Thought. Optional seminars included: Multicultural Thought in the United States and World Traditions: Asia, Africa and Middle-East. However, most students did not seem interested in the optional seminars, and the option was soon discontinued.

Additional Requirements

In February 1983, the faculty approved a Curriculum Committee recommendation that in addition to the four required seminars and two religious studies courses, that there be six required courses, two from each of three areas, an increase from the previously required four courses. It passed by a vote of 22 ayes, 7 nays, with 8 abstentions. (Minutes of Faculty Assembly, February 17, 1983) The three areas were divided according to disciplines: a) mathematics and the empirical sciences, b) the social sciences, and c) the humanities, including the fine and performing arts. In April 1984, in a 30-0-8 vote, the Faculty Assembly recommended to the Curriculum Committee the reinstitution of a one-year language requirement if a student could not demonstrate the collegiate equivalent of a one-year foreign-language study in secondary school or at another collegiate institution. One argument in favor of a one-year collegiate language requirement was the increasingly global nature of scientific, academic, economic and political interchange. The major argument for language study is proficiency in understanding the logic and nature of language, especially one's own. The faculty requested the Curriculum Committee to consider the institution of a foreign-language requirement and a plan for its implementation. The vote was 34 ayes, 9 nays, with 4 abstentions. (Faculty Assembly Minutes, March 26, 1987.)

An Honor Society—At Last

English Professor Phyllis Stowell, chair of an *ad hoc* faculty group on rees-tablishing an Honor Society, introduced the idea to the Academic Council. Rather than reactivate the former *Alpha Pi Gamma Upsilon* College honor society that had disappeared during the 1960s, a group preferred joining an existing national honor society to take advantage of possible benefits available to student members. The *Phi Kappa Phi* national honor society was recommended as the society of preference. The Academic Council's discussion on initiating an honor society was reported to the Faculty Assembly in December, 1981. Serious consideration of re-establishing some kind of honor society was a clear sign that attitudes from the turbulent 60s and 70s had changed, and that the then pervading socially egalitarian influences among faculty had waned. After discussing a possible application for membership with *Phi Kappa Phi* administrators, the Academic Council recommended to the Assembly in January 1982 that the College officially apply. The Academic Vice President announced to the Faculty Assembly in December 1982 that an application had been made to *Phi Kappa Phi.* However, acceptance required that the society directors be unanimous in granting approval but one director withheld approval because he noted that the College fell short of the 125,000 hardbound volumes required for the library. The nonapproval prompted lengthy Faculty Assembly discussion on library allocations. In November 1984 the Academic Council recommended the formation of an Honor Society based on the constitution of *Phi Kappa Phi,* while efforts to obtain affiliation with society continued. On Dec. 5, 1984, the Faculty Assembly unanimously endorsed the Academic Council recommendation that an Honor Society based on *Phi Kappa Phi* principles and organization be formed. The inaugural installation of officers and induction of honor society members was held on April 12, 1985, with Wayne Booth, Pullman Professor of English at the University of Chicago as the guest speaker. Sister Clare Wagstaffe and Dean C. J. Mike Walter were the first faculty members to take a lead role in the formation of the Society, and it has continued as it was formed, but was not officially a chapter of *Phi Kappa Phi* as of 1997.

Student Life in the Early '80s

Tantalizing the Palate, 1983

Rich Crisman, '84, was a man of discriminating taste who desired to cultivate both a gourmet attitude and savory palate among his student body associates. Thus was born the Gourmet Club. The overall plan was to print reviews of local restaurants in *The Collegian* and to provide students with opportunities to experience delectable culinary taste as well as delight in the nectars of the gods with such offerings as exquisite desserts, champagne, wine and other scrumptious foods. Rich was assisted by Kristine Kozlowski, Carrie Jackson, Francesca Farolan and Christopher Davis in organizing monthly meetings. Though early attendance at meetings was impressive, like many elegant ideas, the concept was attractive but short-lived in the face of the cost of jet-set living and the awarding of a diploma to Rich Crisman.

Stuffing Pac-Tel, 1984

Dwight D. Eisenhower was President and the Cold War and Conservatism were the prevailing attitudes that characterized the nation. A student prank in Durban, South Africa reported in the news was noticed by students in several American institutions from MIT to Saint Mary's. American collegians joined in what was called the Telephone Booth Squash. Just how many students can fit into a telephone booth? Saint Mary's students tried to beat the numbers achieved by students from other institutions one evening in the phone booth in Aquinas Hall, but its size precluded a record. An inventive student by the name of Leo LaBelle, '61, who later became Rev. Patrick L. LaBelle, OP, motivated interested students to stuff a Pacific Telephone and Telegraph booth that was borrowed and set up on the Chapel lawn. Local and national news media were invited to witness the event when 23 students stuffed the booth. Time and Newsweek Magazines reported the feat and Life displayed a full-page photo, placing Saint Mary's in the national and international news. The photo reappeared in the *Best of Life* 50 year edition. Fifteen years after the event I was walking on a side street not far from the Louvre Museum in Paris when to my surprise I noticed a small, colored plaster replica of the 1959 stuffing in a novelty shop window. Unfortunately, the shop was closed (it was probably August, vacation time for many French shops), and no purchase was possible.

In 1984, Father LaBelle remarked to students that it had been 25 years since the 1959 Telephone Booth Squash and suggested an anniversary re-creation. On Homecoming Day, Oct. 6, 1984, a Pac-Bell booth was again set up on the

Chapel lawn and, with paramedics and an ambulance on hand, 24 students carefully engineered the stuffing of the 3' x 3' x 7' booth, beating the record of 23 in 1959. Bay Area newspapers and television stations covered the story, and headlines appeared worldwide. One of the "stuffed" students, Peter Dowley of Menlo Park, was flown to New York to appear on ABC's *Good Morning America* to present his firsthand experience of the caper. Letters and telegrams were received from all over the world, some expressing amazement and a few others admonishing the administration for allowing such a dangerous demonstration. Twenty-two of the students who participated were: Robert Solari, Peter Contini, Tim McCaffrey, Rich Bruni, Bill McKenna, Jeff Disdati, Brian Foss, Joe Viera, Scott Edgar, Peter Dowley, Ivan Padilla, Robert Holloway, Tim Soldati, Bill Clark, Alberto Canizares, Mike Wilson, Steve Seriani, Chris Agular, Joe Fitzsimmons, Eric Cesenare, Irwam Kamadini and Mark Desrochers. I could not find records including No. 23 or No. 24.

Diving From De La Salle Residence

I was returning to campus on a Friday evening at the close of the 1986 spring semester following a delightful evening at the San Francisco Symphony when the guard at the gate flagged me down. "There's been an accident," he said, "a student has fallen off the roof of De La Salle Hall." De La Salle Hall is four stories, with the ceiling of the first floor higher than the others. As I traveled over to De La Salle Hall, my imagination led me to believe that I would encounter a catastrophe and a possible funeral to be scheduled in the middle of examination week. When I arrived, the Moraga Paramedics were already on the scene. The young man who had fallen off the roof was lying on the ground protesting a trip to the hospital, claiming that he was uninjured. He had attended a small party in the room of one of his friends, became sleepy and decided to go down to his room to secure a good night's rest. He found he had locked his room and forgotten his key. He went back to his friend's room, climbed out the dormer window, crawled across the roof and when he arrived at the window to his room, he stood up on the small platform outside of his window. He lost his balance, fell over backward and slid off the roof. A balcony on floor two broke his fall and turned him over so that he fell on his back. A few days before his fall, the maintenance crew had removed the asphalt paving next to the building to make way for landscaping. Thus the young man fell on fairly soft earth. His forced trip to the hospital, amid some injudicious complaining, revealed a broken shoulder blade. With his arm in a sling he was able to sit for his final examinations and graduated with his class. I was grateful for a happy ending to what could have been a major personal disaster.

269

New Facilities and New Ideas

Claeys North, 1984, South, 1987

Alumnus Linus F. Claeys, '32, an astute farmer and the owner of 1,600 acres of grazing and farmland in the Rodeo area of the Contra Costa County, was a devoted Gael. A member of the first class that spent four years on the new Moraga campus, he played football until an injury ended his athletic career. When suburban development made its way to Rodeo, Linus seized the opportunity to capitalize on his extensive landholdings, selling a portion to an oil company and most of the rest to residential developers. Linus was not a man of many words, but when he spoke he said much. His first wife and business partner, Edna, pre-deceased him, and he later married Ruth Giammona, a devoted friend. An interest in both students and education prompted him to establish the Linus F. Claeys Scholarship for needy students. A member of the Board of Regents, he attended the dedication of the new Guerrieri townhouses in 1980 and realized that student housing was a pressing need if the College were to expand and become self-sufficient. He later pledged to support the construction of the first Claeys Hall, dedicated in 1984, and then a second, Claeys South, dedicated in 1987. He was also inspired to support both the construction of the football stadium in 1972 and the Soda Center in 1989 by contributing funds to build Claeys Lounge. His donations were in the millions. Modest in his acknowledgement of the gratitude he received he would say, "All I did was make the downpayment." Linus Claeys, a hard-working, unassuming, practical, shrewd and generous man, was named Alumnus of the Year in 1982 and Rodeo Citizen of the Year in 1986. A portion of the freeway near Rodeo was named in his honor in 1990, with State Senator Dan Boatright citing him as a "distinguished rancher and supporter of education."

The Disney Forums

In 1985, Roy and Patricia Disney provided the Communications Department under Professor Rev. Michael Russo, PhD, an endowment fund to enhance the academic and professional goals of the department. Initially, the funds purchased a *state-of-the-art* mobile video truck. A crew of Saint Mary's undergraduate men and women produced the very first cablecasts of Gael football, basketball and cultural events. Several alumni, including Kent Camera, who became a senior producer for Fox Sports Television, entered the ranks of the broadcast and cable industry, inspired by the experience gained from these campus productions. For some time, the video truck and its equipment helped support the student effort of Gael TV, an on-campus cable television channel.

A part of the academic enhancement made possible by the generous Disney endowment was the development of a lecture series. In 1992, the Communications Department established the *Roy E. and Patricia Disney Forum* for the purpose of inviting to campus nationally recognized academic and media professionals. Over the years a scintillating array of guests have come to speak to collegewide forums and participate with students and faculty in classroom conversations. Among the speakers have been Neil Postman (NYU), Marvin Kalb (Harvard University), George Gerbner (University of Pennsylvania), Joan Acocella (writer, *The New Yorker*), Alice Walker (author), Sister Joan Chittister (social activist), Daniel Ellsberg (social activist), Father Ellwood "Bud" Kieser (Paulist Productions), C. W. Nevius (writer, *San Francisco Chronicle)*, Robert Wussler (Vice President, Turner Broadcasting), Danny Glover (actor), Deborah Amos (correspondent, National Public Radio), Sanford Ungar (Director Voice of America) and Walter Murch (film editor, Academy Award winner). Father Michael Russo, PhD, Chair of the Communications Department and occasional CBS religious and political commentator and advisor guided the Disney Forums.

Appointment of Deans, 1985

Beginning in the fall of 1984, discussion among members of the Administrative Council was directed to alleviating the increasingly functional complexity encountered by the Academic Vice President in fulfilling his role as academic leader. The three traditional Schools of the College, formed under Brother Albert Rahill's presidency in the mid-1930s, were the School of Liberal Arts, School of Science and School of Economics and Business Administration. A chairman had been named for each of the Schools, but they were more coordinators than creators, with little authority or impact. With the addition of the growing Departments of Education and Extended Education, the administration concluded that the Department of Education should be renamed The School of Education and that Extended Education be identified as the School of Extended Education with a dean overseeing each entity. As the College grew, so did faculty and various administrative officers who reported to the Academic Vice President. Brother William Beatie decided to research the policies and structures of other Catholic universities in California and, following his investigation, recommended that the chairmen of the Schools of the College likewise be elevated to the rank of deans with specific duties that would alleviate his diverse responsibilities. After a year of discussion, mainly between the Governance Committee and the Faculty Assembly, the concept of appointing Deans for each School was approved.

The appointment of the Deans and the institution of the Council of Deans was finally achieved in the fall of 1985, just as the 1985 Accreditation Visiting Team was about to commence its official Comprehensive Visit.

The first Deans were: Brother Brendan Kneale, FSC, Acting Dean for the School of Liberal Arts; Professor Phil Leitner, PhD, for the School of Science and Professor C. J. "Mike" Walter, PhD for the School of Economics and Business Administration. Those previously appointed as directors or chairs for Schools outside of the traditional undergraduate college continued in their respective roles under the new deanships: Professor Paul Burke became Dean of the School of Education and Professor Robert Roxby was retained as Dean of the School of Extended Education.

Dean of the School of Liberal Arts:

Brother Brendan Kneale agreed to serve as Acting Dean for an additional year, 1986-1987, at the request of the search committee, which asked for more time. Having an extra year to search proved fruitful. Paul Zingg, PhD (history, University of Georgia), who had been Assistant to the President at the University of Pennsylvania, was named Dean of the School of Liberal Arts in 1987. Zingg was an author, historian and academician who had distinguished himself through having published a number of articles on higher education, including, *Quality in the Curriculum: Renewed Search for Coherence and Unity.* (Journal of General Education, v.39, n.3, 1987.) One of his historical interests was the history of baseball, and he found Saint Mary's a resource for baseball information. He authored a book on alumnus Harry Hooper, a member of the National Baseball Hall of Fame, *Harry Hooper, an American Baseball Life* (University of Illinois Press, 1993), was a consultant to Ken Burns for his TV series on baseball, and was both editor and contributor to *The Sporting Image, Readings in American Sports History* (University of America Press, May, 1988.) Dr. Zingg served as Dean of Liberal Arts until 1993, when he accepted an appointment as Dean of the College of Liberal Arts at Cal Poly, San Luis Obispo. A productive, energetic, articulate, principled and congenial personality, he was appointed President of California State University, at Chico in 2005.

Faculty member Steve Sloan, PhD (UC Berkeley, Political Science, Captain, USN, Ret.), served as an effective and personable interim Dean from 1993 to 1995 for the School of Liberal Arts. Joseph Subbiando, a linguistic scholar and former Dean of the School of Arts and Sciences at Santa Clara University and former Dean, College of Humanities, University of the Pacific, was appointed Dean of Liberal Arts in 1995. When he accepted an appointment as President of the California Institute of Integral Studies in San Francisco in 1999, he was replaced by alumna, Frances Sweeney, PhD, '86, (Modern Language, University of Texas) as Interim Dean in 1999.

Dean of the School of Science:

Phil Leitner, PhD (UCLA), who had been chair of the School of Science, was named Dean in 1986. He retired in 1992. Faculty member Allan Hansell, PhD, served as interim Dean for one year (1992-1993) and was succeeded by, Keith Devlin, PhD, (UC Berkeley, Mathematics), who came to Saint Mary's from Colby College, in Maine. A mathematician, author and national PBS-TV celebrity, Devlin served until 2001, when he was appointed Executive Director of the *Center for the Study of Language and Information* at Stanford University. Faculty member, Judd Case, PhD (UC Riverside), a vertebrate paleontologist, was named Dean in 2001.

Dean of the School of Economics and Business Administration:

Professor William Tauchar, PhD, who retired in 1983, was replaced by faculty member and accountant Stanford White, who served as Acting Chairman of the School of Economics and Business Administration while the search committee sought a permanent replacement. Following a national search, C. J. "Mike" Walter, PhD (University of Iowa), a Senior Vice President of Levi-Strauss, Inc., San Francisco, was named Dean of the School in 1984. Walter served for 10 years when he was appointed Dean of the much larger School of Business at California State University, Long Beach in 1994. Faculty member Professor Kris Chase, PhD (University of Maryland) was then named Acting Dean for a short time. Named Dean, July 1, 1994, was Edwin Epstein, JD (Yale University.), former Associate Dean of the Haas School of Business, UC Berkeley, who served until June 2001, when he returned to UC Berkeley to serve as Director of the Rotary Peace Center for International Studies in Peace and Conflict and Professor in the International and Area Studies Teaching Program. Epstein retired from academia in 2007. Faculty member Roy Allen, PhD, (UC Berkeley) was appointed Dean in 2001.

Dean of the Inter-institutional Nursing Program:

The Intercollegiate nursing program began in 1977 with an Associate of Arts Degree plus the normal Registered Nurse (RN) certification. Shirlee Snyder from Samuel Merritt Hospital School of Nursing served as Dean of Instruction for the program between 1981 and 1984. When the program entered into the baccalaureate-RN program, Samuel Merritt dropped the word Hospital from its appellation, and a permanent dean was sought for the academic oversight position. The Academic Vice President began the search process and received a recommendation that Abby Heydman, RN, would be an ideal Dean for the Intercollegiate Nursing Program. After interviewing her, it was evident to the Academic Vice President and the President of Samuel Merritt School of Nursing, Sharon Diaz, that Heydman had the personal qualities and academic acumen to serve as Dean for the new venture. Heydman's performance as Dean was exactly what the program required, to the delight of both Samuel Merritt College of Nursing and Saint Mary's College. Intelligent, experienced, outspoken and blessed with a sense of humor, Abby assumed the Dean's role in 1985 and at the same time was completing her doctoral studies at UC Berkeley. In 1993, she was named Dean at Samuel Merritt and was succeeded at Saint Mary's by Phyllis Easterling as Acting Dean for 1993-1994 and Alice Conway for the fall of 1994. A family problem required that Alice Conway reluctantly resign, and Marilyn Chow assumed the role for the remainder of the 1994-1995 academic year. Sarah Keating was named Dean in 1995 and served until 2000.

Dean of the School of Education

Imaginative and organized, Joseph Beard assumed direction of the Education Department following the departure in 1970 of H.O. Brown. An innovator and energetic administrator, Beard quickly expanded the Education Department's student body and faculty. He served from 1970 to 1974 and was followed by Brother John J. O'Neill, FSC, EdD (Columbia University Teachers' College), who assumed the role of Acting Chairman for the 1974-1975 academic year. During that year, Brother John conducted a national search for a full-time Chair. The major innovation in the search process was for Brother John to visit candidates in various parts of the country and tape-record responses to uniform questions which were later played for search committee members. He discovered Paul J. Burke, EdD (Columbia University Teachers College), who was Associate Dean, School of Education at the City College of New York. Dr Burke guided the department for 12 years, doubling the programs and the student body. He was responsible for its becoming a School under the guidance of a Dean in 1985. He retired from the School of Education in 1987 and was replaced by Peter Garcia, PhD, (Oregon State University), who served from 1987 to 1988. A faculty member, Tory Courtney, EdD, (University of San Francisco) served as Interim Dean, from 1988 to 1991, when Fannie Preston (EdD, UC Berkeley), Associate Dean of Education for Academic Affairs at San Francisco State University, was selected. An articulate and academically astute leader, she guided the School through accreditation and organizational changes. An expert in organizational process, she began studies on whether the College should offer a doctoral program in education but retired in 1998 before her vision of a doctoral program leading to the EdD, could be completed. The concept was implemented after her retirement.

Dean of the School of Extended Education

Robert Roxby, PhD, (Higher Education Administration, University of Washington) was appointed the first Dean of the School of Extended Education in 1979 and served until 1995, when he became a Professor in the Extended Education Program. Roxby came to Saint Mary's from the University of Hartford in Connecticut, where he served as Director of Administrative Services. He was able to remake the Extended Education Program so that it was acknowledged as a quality educational program by the Accreditation Commission. He was succeeded by Penelope Washbourn, PhD (Union Theological Seminary, New York) in 1995. Washbourn had been Director of the Procurement and Contract Management Master's program and the Continuing Education Program. She served during the transition from my presidency to Brother Craig Franz, FSC, PhD, who desired that Washbourn begin an expansion program in the School of Extended Education. Several sites were acquired and staffed in such locations as Fairfield, Sacramento, Oakland and San Jose.

Leaping Forward

Preserving the Past, Securing the Future
The Capital Campaign, 1984-1991

A comprehensive capital campaign proposal, the first of its kind for the College, was initiated by Brother Jerome West, Vice President for Development, and his staff in the fall of 1983. After considerable discussion, in January 1984, the Board of Trustees approved the selection of a professional fundraising organization to investigate the feasibility of a major fundraising or capital campaign. The proposal clearly stimulated my imagination, and that of the members of the Boards of Trustees and Regents, the administration and the faculty. It anticipated raising funds for endowment for student financial aid, faculty chairs, needed facilities, faculty development, technology and other wishlist items that would enhance the academic quality, competitiveness and stability of the College. The fundraising consulting firm of Barnes and Roach, Inc., of Rosemont, Penn., was selected to evaluate the effectiveness of development and public relations functions and the fundraising potential of the College. If the internal organization was deemed capable and the fundraising potential seemed positive, the consultants would then suggest the appropriate timing for a capital campaign. Positive results from the analysis encouraged the Board to approve the appointment of Michael Ferrigno, Development Director, as Campaign Director. Barnes and Roach, Inc. then appointed its Vice President, Mr. Kelsey Murdoch, as the Saint Mary's consultant. (Minutes of the Board of Trustees, Sept. 27, and Nov. 25, 1984)

Following successful research and analysis, the second phase of the campaign consisted of a silent, but comprehensive, fundraising effort conducted by Development personnel over a year and a half to gather sufficient pledges and gifts that would provide evidence of support for approval by the Board of Trustees to engage in a full-scale, public Capital Campaign. Concurrently with the silent phase, the administration of the College formed a strategic planning committee entitled the Institutional Planning Group. The IPG consisted of members from the administration, faculty, Trustees, Regents, and alumni. The successful results of the silent phase and the initial publication of the 63 page draft of the Institutional Planning Group Report moved the Board to approve engaging in a public Capital Campaign at its Nov. 8, 1986, Board meeting. (Minutes of the Board of Trustees, Nov. 8, 1986.)

After several months of research and writing, I was able to produce what was named *The Institutional Planning Group Report*, which presented an expansive and expensive list of future needs. It was up to the Board, however, to establish priorities among them. The setting of priorities was more difficult than at first anticipated. For example, Brother Jerome favored a higher percentage of funding for endowment, particularly scholarship endowment, while I thought that endowment and funding for the construction or renovation of needed facilities should be equal. In conversations with Brother Jerome, I understood that he believed the College should grow but at a slower pace, while providing financial aid through endowment to more students in need. What I saw was a long-range program that provided needed facilities that would allow the College to grow by providing attractive housing and student recreational facilities and would modernize and expand facilities for science, faculty offices, and the fine and performing arts. Likewise, addressing the advances in technology so as to reach all faculty offices, student rooms, the library and computer laboratories seemed imperative. I agreed that endowment was essential for the future and was clearly in keeping with the Lasallian interest in students with financial need, but I also cited the need for adequate facilities for a College that had to be competitive in faculty accommodations, academic offerings, recreational facilities and a modern technological environment. A stable financial base through a student body of reasonable size would allow the College to increase its support of students in need in due time, after essential facilities were funded. The Trustees agreed that funds for facilities and endowment should be divided equally, though everyone understood that a balance between raising funds for endowment and facilities depended largely on the interest of donors.

The final *Institutional Planning Group Report* was published on March 14, 1986, and accepted by the Board of Trustees at its June 1986 meeting. Planning Group members from the Boards of Regents and Trustees were Hon. Donald D. Doyle, James R. Harvey, Arthur Latno, Jr., Elaine McKeon, Alexander R. Mehran, Raymond O'Brien (Chairman), Thomas W. O'Neil, Raymond Syufy and John Thompson. From the administration and faculty, the participants were, Brother Mel Anderson, FSC, Rev. Michael Carey, OP, Brother William Carriere, FSC, Wilber Chaffee, PhD, Michael Ferrigno, MA, Philip Leitner, PhD, Katherine Roper, PhD, Brother Jerome West, FSC, and Raymond White, PhD Consultant Kelsey Murdoch of Barnes and Roach, Inc., worked closely with me and the Vice President for Development.

Following its extensive research and interviews, Kelsey Murdoch and Associates suggested that a goal of $32.1 million seemed reasonable and achievable. There were provisions in the study that would allow for a reduction in the estimates should the campaign prove to be more difficult than expected or should some adverse or unexpected circumstances reduce necessary momentum and enthusiasm. The report assured the Trustees and the Administration that no one would be embarrassed or disheartened should the goal not be reached.

The next step was to appoint a Fundraising Steering Committee approved by the Board of Trustees. The tasks of the Steering Committee were to, "identify possible prospects, develop a cultivation and solicitation strategy …." The success of the Capital Campaign was viewed as being, "a necessary and important threshold" to the future progress of the College, as it proved to be. With the agreement of the Steering Committee on priorities set by the Trustees, the strategy for cultivation and solicitation could then commence. The Steering Committee would develop the Case Statement, derived from the *Institutional Planning Group Report*, for presentation to possible donors.

Through Brother Jerome's excellent leadership, enthusiastic membership on the Steering/Planning Committee and the active participation of the administration and Development Office personnel, Michael Ferrigno, Dennis Koller, John McClenahan and staff, the Public Relations, Alumni Relations and Publications offices, the five-year estimate for achieving the Capital Campaign goal of $32.1 million was exceeded by $2 million by the end of the fourth year. The President's Council, the Steering Committee and the Board of Trustees agreed to continue with the campaign as projected. A gratified Steering Committee as well as the Boards of Trustees and Regents joyously celebrated the end of the campaign in June 1991. It had reached a $51.2 million mark.

Accreditation, 1985
Overarching Fresh Air and Attitude

The mandate given to the Accreditation Team of 1985 by the WASC Accreditating Commission of Schools and its Executive Director was to focus on, "administration, governance and academic organization."

The 11 member 1985 Visiting Team was welcomed, perhaps with some trepidation, to the College from Oct. 14 to 17, 1985. The team was chaired by Donald R. Gerth, PhD, President of California State University, Sacramento, a man who understood *Great Books* programs through his association with the University of Chicago and who had been a member of the 1969 Visiting Team to Saint Mary's.

The opening paragraph of the final Accreditation report stated the overarching view of the Visiting Team, namely that, "Saint Mary's College of California is a fine institution with a past filled with real accomplishment, a present of considerable substance and a future of great promise."

I had for many years expressed my discontent in one way or another with the basic academic governance of the College and believed that a comprehensive Academic Senate would be the one body to tie the separate academic entities together in the academic tapestry that constituted Saint Mary's College. A senate would be comprised of representative elected faculty members who would be responsible to their constituency, would attend almost every meeting and would be accountable for their presence, views and votes.

One benefit of the Faculty Assembly was that it provided a forum for the airing of faculty concerns by giving every faculty member equal footing to express views without recrimination under the protocol of Academic Freedom and the concept of a community of scholars. Though the Assembly gave equal voting rights to all faculty members, tenured and untenured, full- and part-time, attendance by faculty was spotty. Some members vigorously opposed the concept of a senate, saying that such a body would move the College closer to becoming more like a corporation. While it was generally accepted that an institution of higher education is not operated as a business corporation, there are business concerns that must be taken into account. Some other objections to the elimination of the Faculty Assembly were with good reason, since those who made use of the Assembly forum for delivering perorations of one kind or another would lose a convenient platform, even though Senate meetings would be open to all faculty and staff, who would be free to speak their minds. One of the most compelling arguments in opposition to the Senate was that it would be a representative body, and though its membership would be elected by the faculty, individual faculty members not elected to the Senate who had become accustomed to introduce motions and vote on anything that surfaced in the Assembly would be partially disenfranchised. Philosopher and political observer Steve Cortright maintained that the absence of the Assembly diminished faculty interest in comprehensive concerns of the institution. He may have been right, but any group of faculty could call for a town-hall meeting at any time.

The recommendation by the Visiting Team that, "The President should propose to the Board of Trustees and to the Faculty a process and a set of principles for the creation of a comprehensive academic senate" was a recommendation that in my estimation would move the College to a new level of faculty responsibility and thoughtful involvement as well as faculty-administration rapport. Fortunately, the Chairman of the Visiting Team perceived the need for more comprehensive and effective academic governance, a need that could not be fully addressed by the addition of Deans for the five Schools.

The Governance Committee, chaired by myself, almost immediately set about implementing the Academic Senate recommendation. Major academic committees were reorganized so that they included representatives of all Schools and would report their findings or recommendations to the Senate. Subordinate committees would report or consult with major committees, the Deans of their respective Schools or Chairs of departments.

One of the major issues of concern to the Visiting Team was a restatement of the Mission of the College to include the new activities then in its academic portfolio, such as graduate, Extended Education degree, Education credential and paralegal certificate programs. The recommendation of the Visiting Team was an appropriate one, namely, update the Mission Statement, and all else will logically flow from the Mission. The Visiting Team was critical of what seemed to be a topsy-turvy approach of preparing a case statement for a capital campaign before revising the Mission Statement that would include all academic activities of the College. A new Mission Statement would be forthcoming, but no one expected a drastic change in mission. The Board of Trustees and the College administration believed that the time was right for inaugurating a capital campaign, in view of the needs of the College and the receptivity of potential donors. The Board also believed that the major organizational elements, such as the appointment of Deans and the formation of a Senate, would foster clarity in updating and expanding a revised Mission Statement at a later date. It was also determined that the current Mission statement contained the basic principles required to operate the College.

Concurrently, the Development Office would make use of the *Institutional Planning Group Report* for writing a succinct case statement that Murdoch strongly recommended for the commencement of the Capital Campaign. A clearer, crucial and more extensive revision of the Mission Statement occurred a few years later in response to what was perceived not only as a growing secularization within the institution, but a greater mimicking of mainstream, departmentalized scientific research institutions in American higher education and a diminution of an overarching liberal arts philosophy and pedagogy that had historically characterized a Saint Mary's undergraduate education. The technological revolution likewise accelerated the imitation of secular research-based higher education to the detriment of comprehensive liberal education, two aspects of which were the *Great Books, Collegiate Seminar* program for all students and area requirements and requirements in theology or its more popular title, Religious Studies. John Henry Cardinal

Newman claimed in his major work that if theology were not part of the core curriculum, "… its province will not simply be neglected but will actually be usurped by other sciences, which will teach without warrant, conclusions of their own in a subject matter which needs its own proper principles for its due formation and disposition." (John Henry Cardinal Newman, *The Idea of a University*, Discourse IV, Ch. 15) The *Great Books, Collegiate Seminar* program has likewise been subject to attempts of invasion by those who saw it as an academic potpourri that could accommodate books on the politically correct agenda, such as: Liberation Theology, Ethnic Studies, Far-Eastern history, philosophy and religions and gender studies.

There were a number of legitimate inquiries and opinions about the criteria that governed the formation of the canon of the Great Books, a controversy unfortunately subject to the ebb and tide of sometimes fleeting, sometimes objective and principled interests. What I and the other administrators of the College attempted to avoid was the tidal wave of ephemeral political interests, uncompromising secularization and scientific narrowness that tended to intrude upon American Catholic higher education in general.

While the College had not endorsed a publish-or-perish policy, the Accreditation Team was impressed that, "the revitalization of the undergraduate faculty has been manifested also in a remarkable number of professional accomplishments in the years 1980-1985. Books of literary criticism, poetry and children's fiction, as well as books on historical and theological subjects, have brought recognition to Saint Mary's faculty. Many published articles in their professional fields with regularity. Others received major grants from the National Endowment for the Humanities. An Irish National Fellowship was awarded to one faculty member in the spring of 1985; another received a grant from the Canadian Embassy to study Canadian literature. The College community was pleased in 1984 when the MacArthur Foundation selected Saint Mary's English professor and poet, Robert Hass, PhD, to receive an award of a quarter of a million dollars. A growing number of faculty participated actively in conferences by presenting papers in their fields of expertise." (1985 Accreditation Report, page 4.) Once the financial crisis was resolved, the College was able to grant faculty more sabbaticals and other kinds of support, and organizations such as the Alumni Association were able to fund various faculty research projects. Though funds had to be guarded expeditiously, the direction was indicative of the future.

The College also funded a modest faculty publication edited by Brother Brendan Kneale followed by Professor Steven Cortright, that in due time could possibly become both a rival and/or a revival of the old *Moraga*

Quarterly, published in the '30s and early '40s. The publication was named *Educational Perspectives.*

As stated earlier, the 1975 Accreditation Visiting Team had expressed its skepticism regarding the conduct of Extended Education programs in conjunction with the Institute for Professional Development. Definitive effort had been invested in disassociating the College from the IPD and in an intense oversight and improving the School of Extended Education under Dean Robert Roxby, PhD It was gratifying to note that the 1985 Visiting Team reported that: "The Team found the Extended Education programs, now fully conducted by Saint Mary's, to be well conceived and conducted in an academically sound manner. The programs fill a need for lifelong learning. Satisfying the specific concerns of the adult learner is arguably within the tradition of Christian Brothers education." (*1985 Accreditation Report,* page 28.)

There is little doubt that Dean Robert Roxby had accomplished what he had set out to do. He had vigorously reorganized the Extended Education Program so that it would be not only acceptable, but positively endorsed by the Accreditation Association.

Accreditation was reaffirmed early in February 1986, but with the disappointing proviso that an Interim Visit would be conducted in the fall of 1988 "to address progress made by the College in addressing governance issues identified throughout the report." Having another Accreditation Visit, interim though it might be, so close to the regular visit seemed to be unusual and untimely. It would take several years to smooth out the initial functions of the Academic Senate and develop a comprehensive understanding among the diverse elements of the faculty. Furthermore, the College was embarking on a major capital campaign that would provide the necessary funding to improve the institution in numerous ways. To distract the administration and others from addressing both governance and enhancement initiatives became a confusing intervention.

Establishing the Academic Senate: the Governance Committee

I was gratified that the Visiting Team recommended the establishment of an Academic Senate, inclusive of all persons and Schools of the College academic community. There were misgivings from several factions, including those few who claimed the Faculty Assembly as their own. There were also those who enjoyed the give-and-take of the Assembly, even though the process was often time-consuming and sometimes inconsequential. A third group thought the free exchange of ideas created academic tension that in turn generated thoughtful articles and ideas on liberal and not-so-liberal education. And there were those who saw the inclusion of members of the College community not from the traditional three schools of the College (Liberal Arts, Science and Economics/Business Administration) as a selling out of authentic liberal arts undergraduate education to graduate education and dubious kinds of careerism, better left, they believed, to other institutions. And there were some Christian Brothers who saw the Extended Education Program as one of the genuinely Lasallian programs in the College, not unlike surprisingly similar programs for thousands of older adults conducted by the Christian Brothers of France in the 19th century. Replacing the Faculty Assembly with an Academic Senate would not preclude either the administration or groups of faculty from calling for Collegewide colloquia on both scholarly and pragmatic academic issues as needed or at intervals of opportunity or necessity. As it turned out, several colloquia were conducted by faculty that paralleled the work of the Senate.

The task for the Governance Committee was to determine how to structure a fully representative, acceptable and functional Academic Senate as soon as possible after the final report from the Accreditation Visiting Team was received. "The governance structure," the Visiting Team remarked, "should flow from the Mission Statement." Though the College had an existing Mission Statement, it had to be augmented to represent the expansion in the Schools of the College and their personnel. The Governance Committee began consideration of a revised Mission Statement in March 1986. Several attempts at revising the Mission Statement occurred in the 1986 spring semester. Faculty member Clinton Bond (English) and Assistant to the President Rev. Michael Carey, OP, delivered two notable attempts. By April 16th, 1986, the Governance Committee believed it had developed a suitable Mission Statement that was forwarded to the faculty as a whole for comment. In the meantime, a detailed copy of a College governance structure was submitted by Committee Member Valerie Gomez, PhD.

Valerie Gomez who held her BA, MA. and PhD in Romance Languages from the University of California, Berkeley was a meticulously thoughtful Dean of Academic Services committed to orderly processes and sensitive to faculty concerns. She saw communication and appropriate organization as the means for ameliorating complaints and focusing all entities on their respective responsibilities, including the primary teaching function of faculty members. She was the editor in chief of the Faculty Handbook, a document that was an extension of the contract between the College and faculty members that grew larger and more legalistic with each passing year, and the College Bulletin or Catalog, that provided students with available courses and academic regulations. In addition to serving students, the Bulletin was sent to high school counselors and to all other colleges and universities. She also managed the academic calendar, tracked students on academic probation and compiled the Dean's Honor Roll. As a member of the Governance Committee, she worked assiduously in developing the structure of the Academic Senate. In other words, she was one of the unsung heroines whose diligence held many of the diverse academic issues together and who embodied a wealth of accurate information. Prior to her first teaching assignment at the College, Gomez was employed by the U. S. Government, first in the Department of Agriculture in Mexico (1950-1954) and then in the American Embassy in Mexico (1954-1956). In addition to the Governance Committee membership, Valerie Gomez also served on the Undergraduate Council, and the Curriculum, January Term and Student Orientation Committees. Always cheerful and positive in attitude she was the ideal provider of services to the faculty through her accuracy, and common sense. She retired in 2001 and is presently engaged in research for writing a history of her colorful family.

The Governance Committee did not anticipate its role coming to an end with the installation of the Senate. In fact, it saw its role as a "committee on committees," or "a committee on structure," as being essential to the good functioning of College governance. It functioned much like one of the entities in a bicameral system, as is characteristic of both state and federal government in the United States. This function provided, in my view, what was a much needed balance, as I did not think it wise to allow the Senate to have sole power in formulating its own rules of conduct. Having another body concentrating on protocol and structure, yet composed primarily of faculty, would provide balance in faculty politics. Furthermore, having the President as chair of the Governance Committee and a minority of other key administrators on the Committee created an authentic community of scholars, with administration and faculty working closely together, as should be the case.

A Surprise Visit From Mrs. Ageno

In the spring of 1988, I received a call from Mrs. Edward (Marjorie) Ageno who requested an appointment to see me. I knew who Marjorie Ageno was, since she usually purchased a full table of 12 for the annual Saint Mary's College Guild Fashion Shows, and I customarily greeted her on those occasions. I knew Ed Ageno a little better, since Ed was the owner of the Galileo-Capri Salami plant and offered slices of his finest salami and pepperoni, along with fresh French bread, at the annual Contra Costa College Committee Wine Festival. I set up the appointment for the afternoon of the next day. Mrs. Ageno arrived on time along with Barbara Ageno, her daughter-in-law, whose husband, Michael Ageno, '63, died from a heart attack at age 40.

After the introductory pleasantries, Mrs. Ageno came right to the point of her visit. "We came here to discuss the possibility of building a residence hall in honor of my son, Michael. How much would a residence hall cost?" she enquired. We had just completed the construction of Claeys Halls North and South and we knew the cost to be $2 million each. I explained that we sought a donor for one-half the cost of a residence hall and assumed a California Educational Facilities Act bond for the other half which the students would pay off over a 30-year period through the rental fees for their rooms. "If we asked the students to pay a rental fee to cover the full cost of a residence hall, the room charge would be much too high," I said. "Then," she responded, "a residence hall would cost a donor $1 million?" "That is correct," I said. "We can do that," she responded. I was both shocked and elated, since we needed residence hall space for many applicants who had to find housing either off-campus or who enrolled elsewhere. Ageno then announced triumphantly, "We will have a residence hall in honor of Michael! Well, Barbara, we can go now," she said, and stood up. I thanked her and opened the door. They both smiled and made their exit. The next day a stone-faced Ed Ageno came to see me and asked, "What did my wife do yesterday?" I repeated the conversation. He smiled and said, "Yes, we can do that, and we will!" I was delighted. We needed a residence hall and did not yet have potential donors for one. It was a gift that flowed like honey from the heavens: "*Hodie, meliflui facti sunt coeli!*" I recalled from my pre-Vatican II days of reciting the Divine Office in choir and in Latin.

The celebratory dedication for Michael Ageno Hall was held on Sept. 11, 1988. As the dedication ceremonies were drawing to a close, Ed Ageno came to me and asked whether it would be possible to build another residence hall in honor of his wife, Marjorie. "Of course," I said, "we need residence hall space." "Then could you design one for Marjorie? he asked." "We'll start tomorrow," I responded.

About two weeks later, I received a call from Ed who asked whether it would be less expensive per unit if an additional hall to the one being designed in honor of Marjorie were built at the same time. I responded that I thought so, given the efficiency of building two at one time. I noted, however, that as the construction of new residence halls would extend the distance of student housing from the center of the campus, the cost of extending utility lines would increase the total cost of each building. "Even so," he said, "I would like to build a third residence hall in honor of my parents, Ferdinand and Camille Ageno." We commenced designing the third Ageno hall immediately. The dedication of both the Marjorie David Ageno and the Ferdinand and Camille Residence Halls was conducted on Sept. 12, 1992.

Every so often after the dedication of Michael Ageno Hall, Ed and Marjorie would drive on campus after dinner and park near Michael Ageno Hall to watch students enter and exit. Occasionally Marjorie would ask a student how he or she liked the hall, and was pleased with the responses. Unfortunately, Marjorie suffered a stroke and succumbed shortly thereafter, never to see the completion of Marjorie David Ageno and Ferdinand and Camille Halls.

But that is not all. By 1995-1996 we were still in need of additional residence space, designed differently for upper-division students. We turned to Ed, suggesting that a fourth Ageno hall be named after him. Though Ed was not feeling as physically well as he had been, he was interested in funding a fourth residence hall. I noted to him that our loans through CEFA bonds were at capacity and that an additional CEFA bond at that time was not feasible. I told him that because of grading and extended utilities, the cost for a new residence hall would be about $5 million. He thought about it and agreed to the whole cost. Realizing that his physical condition was failing, he agreed to sign a document to that effect, though in the past his word and a handshake were considered as binding as a written document.

As we proceeded with the design, Ed's condition, due to cancer, worsened and the Lord called him in August 1997. The concept of a different kind of residence hall for older students led us to dividing the one dorm with a capacity for 85 students into two smaller ones, each holding 41 students, but with more agreeable accommodations. Thus came into being Edward Ageno Hall West and Edward Ageno Hall East, forming what has been dubbed the "high-rent district." Ed Ageno East and West were dedicated on Sept. 10, 2000.

Inspiration: Convocations, Colloquia and Institutes

Convocations

With the intention of clarifying the College mission, several convocations, colloquia and an Institute were convened to discuss the major characteristics of the College goals statement. Events centering on the liberal arts and liberal arts education, the Catholic character of the College and its Lasallian spirit were conducted over several years.

At the suggestion of Dean C. J. "Mike" Walter, PhD, formal convocations inaugurating the second semester were held for several years in the College Chapel. Faculty were invited to process into the Chapel in academic regalia and students invited to attend. Classes were suspended to allow for attendance.

The first convocation, held on Feb. 11, 1987, featured Theodore Roszak, PhD, professor at California State University, Hayward and the author of a current and choice, but controversial book entitled *The Cult of Information: the Folklore of Computers and the True Art of Thinking.* His address was entitled *The True Art of Thinking.*

The second convocation celebrated the 125th anniversary of the founding of the College in 1863 by Archbishop Joseph Alemany, DD, of San Francisco. The theme of the convocation , *Values: Catholic Education in the 21st* Century, was highlighted in an address by Brother Luke Salm, PhD, chairman of the Religious Studies Department at Manhattan College in New York. Honorary doctoral degrees were awarded to the Most Reverend Joseph Cardinal Bernardin, DD, Archbishop of Chicago, who spoke at the evening banquet; Brother Luke Salm, FSC, PhD and Lisa Sowell Cahill, PhD, Professor of Theology at Boston College.

The convocation for 1989 convened on Feb. 7, featuring I. Michael Heyman, JD, former law professor and then Chancellor of the University of California, Berkeley. His address described societal challenges, including the plight of the homeless and the nuclear threat, suggesting that upon graduation students would discover serious challenges facing them. The Chancellor saluted the College for its outstanding academic reputation and attentiveness to human issues.

Donald Kennedy, President of Stanford University addressed the convocation on Feb. 16, 1990. Kennedy issued a call to students to make a difference, especially with regard to America's children, 23 percent of whom live in poverty. He urged students to consider engaging in tutoring programs and teaching as a career. Other activities for graduates, he noted, might include serving the poor, the homeless and the sick. In terms of the environment he urged seeking regional solutions, and in terms of society in general he stressed the importance of a continued fight against bigotry and intolerance.

The newly appointed Academic Vice President, William J. Hynes, was the featured speaker for the Feb. 21, 1991 convocation. He challenged the Class of 1991 by asking, *How Courageous is the Class of 1991?* Adapting a quotation from Martin Luther King, "It is always the right time to do right," Hynes encouraged students to "pursue the important things in life," noting that the courageous person is he or she who is passionate about both the pursuit of truth and the pursuit of right. Faculty members, who have continued higher studies in spite of their moments of poverty, frustrations and often near despair associated with writing a thesis, are examples of courageous souls. Those who pursue the good of others by giving back generously to family, school, nation and the world were cited as other examples of courageous individuals.

Even though noted personalities were featured, it was difficult to lure students (even with time off) to attend. Interest in perspectives from higher education on the issues of the moment was thin, unlike the political turmoil of '60s and early '70s that would attract larger numbers. Thus, the second semester convocations came to a close. The permeation of young adult culture by electronic media and various forms of entertainment often trumped interest in the intellectual perspectives of academic personalities. Academic convocations, such as the Thomas Aquinas debates in the '50s, would attract numerous students, engaging them in discussions and controversial argumentation. At that time, almost all students were exposed to philosophical issues and problems and many found such convocations of interest. A seminar led by famous American philosopher Mortimer J. Adler on *Oedipus Rex* drew a capacity audience in Dryden Hall in the early '50s. But the '50s were without the benefits and distraction of emerging high technology.

Colloquia on Mission

Other colloquia, usually held in the afternoon among faculty, staff and students, dealth with the three issues of the College Mission Statement, namely, its liberal arts, Catholic and Lasallian character. A number of such colloquia featured faculty members from the College who provided their personal interpretations of and insights into the nature of liberal arts education or the meaning of the College as Catholic.

The Catholic Character of the College was the focus of the faculty symposium on April 14, 1988. Several faculty members wrote essays on the topic that were distributed to the faculty to be read a week in advance. At the commencement of the symposium, each of the authors provided a short precis of his essay prior to opening the floor to discussion. The authors were Brother Brendan Kneale, MA (mathematics), Professor Ed Biglin, PhD (English), Professor Steven Cortright, MA (philosophy), Professor Lawrence Cory, PhD (biology), Professor John C. Dwyer, STD (theology), and Professor Joseph Lanigan, PhD (philosophy).

The Lasallian Tradition was discussed on Oct. 3, 1988 when Brothers Raphael Patton, FSC, PhD, (mathematics), Brother Brendan Kneale, FSC, MA (mathematics) and alumnus Thomas O'Donnell, JD, a practicing attorney from the South Bay, delivered papers and engaged in discussion on the meaning and effect of being a Lasallian institution.

A major convocation on liberal arts was convened on Nov. 8 1990, featuring Eva T. H. Brann, PhD, Dean of Instruction at Saint John's College, Annapolis, Md., whose address, *Take No Thought For The Morrow,* created an academic stir. Her address has been published twice in *Educational Perspectives* because of its discussion on such issues as relevance, globalization and diversity in higher education in light of an authentic liberal arts education. Also on the program were Professor Hazard S. Adams, PhD (English), from Washington University, Seattle; and Paul Zingg, PhD, Dean of Liberal Arts at Saint Mary's.

A one-day Winter Colloquium on Values was convened on Jan. 24, 1996. The first morning speaker was Professor Robert Bellah, PhD, from UC Berkeley, (sociology), co-author and editor of *Habits of the Heart* and *The Good Society.* He delivered the opening address entitled *Values in Community and Society: American Values.* Other speakers included Sanford Ungar from the American University in Washington, D.C., who spoke on California's role-model status and Ed Epstein, Dean of the School of Economics and Business Administration, who considered values in economics. Michelle Dillon from the Sociology Department of Yale University provided reflections on *Why Catholics Want to be Catholics.*

The afternoon session discussions considered the College Mission Statement. Professors Ed Biglin, Rebecca Carroll and Wayne Harter provided views such as *Translating What Really Matters into Our Lives* and *Teaching Decency and Courage.* Ben Wang from the Chinese Institute of New York spoke on *Eastern Values: Chinese Language and Culture.* Professor Woody Weaver addressed *Community Values in an Electronic Age.* Rev. David Gieb, OP, closed the *Winter Colloquium* by leading an interfaith prayer service, and I delivered a reflection on *Values in the Undergraduate Years.*

A March 1, 1996 colloquium on Ethics in the Catholic Academy was sponsored by the School of Economics and Business Administration featuring speaker Kenneth Goodpaster, a graduate of Notre Dame University and the Harvard Business School who served as a faculty member at the University of St. Thomas in St. Paul, Minn.

A January Term or Winter Colloquium on Catholic Social Thought in 1997 brought several intellectual luminaries to campus for a discussion on Liberal Arts education. Michael Naughton, PhD, Director of the John A. Lyon Institute for Catholic Social Thought at St. Thomas University in St. Paul, Minn., addressed *The Integration of Liberal and Professional Education.* Four faculty panelists, Scott Myers-Lipton, Kathleen Taylor, John Thompson and Ed Tywoniak discussed *Liberal Arts in the Workplace.* Richard Tarnas, Professor of Philosophy and Psychology at the California Institute of Integral Studies spoke on the *Passion of the Western Mind,* the title of his recent book. The former president of the American Association of University Professors, Linda Ray Pratt of the University of Nebraska, addressed *Liberal Arts and the Post-Modern University.* The perennial topic of *Liberal Arts and the Core Curriculum* was discussed by Brother Kenneth Cardwell, FSC, PhD, (Integral, rhetoric), Greg Eisler, Professor Gretchen Lempke-Santangelo, PhD, (history), and Professor Jacob Lester, PhD (biology).

More on Mission

Professor Dan Cawthon, PhD, graciously accepted the task of organizing a program on the essentials of the College liberal arts mission by enlisting noted scholars to deliver papers on liberal education. This session was to be followed by two others, one on the Catholic nature of the College and the third on its Lasallian character. Entitled a Festschrifft on the Liberal Arts, it was dedicated to me because I was retiring at the end of the 1997 spring semester. Held in the LeFevre Theater on Friday, April 18, 1997, the well-attended audience of faculty, students and administration heard lectures and engaged in discussion with four scholars: Ralph McInerny, PhD, Professor of Philosophy at the Jaques Maritain Center, University of Notre Dame, who delivered a paper entitled, *Survival of the Liberal Arts;* Rev. David Tracey, PhD, Professor at the Divinity School of the University of Chicago, prepared a paper with an eye-catching title *The Surprising Return of God.* Illness prevented the appearance of Father Tracey, but Dan Cawthon delivered his paper. M. Katherine Tillman, PhD from the Program of Liberal Studies at the University of Notre Dame, whose scholarship has concentrated on John Henry Cardinal Newman, presented insights on *Newman and the Art of Learning,* and Douglas Sloan, PhD, Professor of History and Education at Teachers College, Columbia University, delivered a paper on *Opening the Gates of Knowledge: The Primacy of Meaning.*

The Henning Institute

The Honorable John F. (Jack) Henning, '38, JD, was appointed Director of

Industrial Relations for the State of California under Governor Edmund. G. "Pat" Brown, Undersecretary of Labor in the Kennedy Administration and U. S. Ambassador to New Zealand during the Johnson Administration. He then served as Executive Director of the AFL-CIO for the State of California. Shortly before his pending retirement in 1996 was imminent, alumnus and attorney Ernest Pierucci, '72, JD, Catholic University of America, and faculty member Professor Steven A. Cortright, '75, philosophy, Saint Mary's College, inaugurated a plan to honor the former Ambassador, Executive Director and alumnus for his work in Catholic Social Justice. Thus was born the John F. Henning Institute, founded to promote both Catholic social thought and the dignity of the worker and work. Three major conferences on Catholic Social Thought were presented in 1997, 1998 and 1999. For several days following the annual Commencement ceremonies, prominent speakers were featured under the J. F. Henning Institute. Faculty, their colleagues in other institutions, students, alumni and friends of the College were invited to attend.

Speakers for the first conference in 1997, which had as its theme *Solidarity and the Common Good* were Professor James P. Murphy, PhD, Government, Dartmouth College, *The Quest for a Balanced appraisal of Work in Catholic Social Thought;* Professor James Gordley, JD, Law, University of California, Berkeley, *Labor and Communicative Justice;* Professor Thomas A. Cavanaugh, PhD, Social Ethics, University of San Francisco, *Aquinas's Account of the Ineradicable Social Character of Private Property;* Professor Michael A. Naughton, PhD, Management, University of Saint Thomas, *Managers as Distributors of Justice: An Analysis of Just Wages within the Tradition of Catholic Social Thought* and Professor Michael Stebbins, PhD Moral Theology, Woodstock Theological Center, *The Meaning of Solidarity.* The speeches were compiled and printed under the title, *Labor, Solidarity and the Common Good,* edited by Professor S. A. Cortright of Saint Mary's College and published by Carolina Academic Press in 2001.

Speakers featured for the 1998 John F. Henning Instgitute were Professor Michael Naughton, *Work, Leisure and Worship: The Person in Catholic Social Thought;* Al Gini, Associate Editor of Business Ethics Quarterly; Daniel Kolb, Tutor, St. John's College, Annapolis, Md.; Professor Maria T. Carl, '76, Seattle University; Professor Daniel McInerny, University of St. Thomas, Houston; and S. A. Cortright, Director, J. F. Henning Institute.

Coming of Age

Transition From Faculty Assembly to Academic Senate: 1985-1989

After the Accreditation Visit of 1985, the Governance Committee addressed in earnest the transition from the Faculty Assembly to the Academic Senate. I employed the word *Academic* in conjunction with the word *Senate* when speaking of the new legislative body with the hope that academic issues would be the focus of Senate activity rather than tangential contemporary political or relevant concerns. Modest reorganization of existing academic committees that now would report to the Senate, was seen to be in order. Committee reorganization would officially include representatives of all academic activities the College had undertaken since 1975. The formation of the Senate would end the ad hoc committee oversight of nontraditional programs and call upon all faculty elected to the Senate to exercise academic responsibility for the whole institution. Both the graduate and undergraduate business programs had already been placed under the direction of the Dean of the School of Economics and Business Administration, and the Inter-institutional Nursing Program had been incorporated within an Inter-institutional Council, but with all the normal undergraduate councils and committees assuming their respective oversight duties.

General discussions could be and were conducted, and discussions on core curriculum or similar matters could be instituted if administrative leadership, e.g., the President, Academic Vice President, the Dean of a School, the Academic Senate or a group of faculty could persuade colleagues to attend such a meeting. In fact, such persuasion was not difficult. The Governance Committee, for example, held hearings on the formation of the Senate, and General Senate meetings were open to all faculty members, any one of whom could intervene in the discussions. The major benefit of the Senate was that issues were more carefully refined and defined when proposals were forwarded from standing academic committees. If not, proposals could be returned to committees for clarification. Members of the Senate, who were beholden to various segments of the faculty, carried out their responsibilities in the sight of all, who could thus judge the effectiveness of each member.

The issues that came before the Assembly during the interim, that is, since the Accreditation Visit of 1985, and the inauguration of the Senate in the fall of 1988, were of several types: a) concerns regarding social, moral and political attitudes and conduct, b) academic requirements, regulations, additional majors and the core curriculum, and c) faculty concerns regarding salary, sabbaticals, research opportunities and the appropriate number of courses a professor should teach per year (otherwise known as the "teaching load.").

Since the faculty was primarily charged with recommending the hiring of new members of the faculty, one recommendation urged that Affirmative Action principles be employed more vigorously in hiring. Some of the more exaggerated or controlling proposals, or those that impinged upon certain academic terrains, were tabled and eventually forgotten.

The other ethical issue that occupied the attention of the Assembly was presented by Professor Mary Springer of the English Department, who was particularly concerned with student plagiarism. As access to the Internet increased among both students and faculty, the temptation for students to make use of quotations or ideas from essays by noted writers without acknowledging sources became more widespread. It was often difficult for faculty to locate the source of suspiciously well-conceived or written themes or sections thereof unless faculty members were familiar with ever-increasing Internet sources or could spend the time, often extensive, on the Internet tracking down sources. The resolution of the plagiarism issue was to institute a number of academic penalties, as well as state the ethical impropriety of plagiarism. In due time, Internet providers made it easier to trace essay or book sections among an expanding store of essays, articles, précis, book condensations and whole books on various topics.

The Institution of the Academic Senate

I presented a Governance Committee Report, dated May 6, 1988, to the Assembly on May 11, 1988, on the institution of the Academic Senate. After considerable discussion, the Assembly Chair, Professor Jane Sanguine-Yager, stated that the report constituted a motion and a second. The Assembly approved the motion that replaced the Faculty Assembly with the Academic Senate, by a vote of 25 yea, 7 nay, with 11 abstentions. (Minutes of the Faculty Assembly, May 11, 1988, Saint Mary's College Archives.)

Professor Kris Chase of the School of Economics and Business Administration was named Acting Chair of the Faculty Assembly to conduct the transition. Her first task was to identify faculty who were willing to serve as chair, vice chair and as members. Her second was to conduct elections for the Chairman, Vice Chairman and the 14 members of the Academic Senate, representing all academic entities of the College. Her third task was to conduct elections for the various academic committees that report to the Senate. Her final assignment was the set a date for the first executive meeting of the Senate. That date was Oct. 12, 1988.

The Academic Senate, 1989-1990

Members of the first session of the Academic Senate: Chair: Professor Gerald Brunetti (Education); Vice Chair: Professor Chester Aaron (English); Members: Professors Leonard Auerbach (Graduate Business), Fred Anderson (Economics and Business Administration), Lillian Barden (Extended Education), Edward Biglin (English), Phyllis Easterling (Nursing), Paul Giurlanda (Religious Studies), Robert Gorsch (English), Allan Hansell (Biology), Sandra Hellman (Extended Education), Ron Olowin (Physics), Kathy Perez (Education), Tony Roffers (Education), Kusum Singh (Communications) and Diana Wu (Economics and Business Administration). Secretary to the Senate: Deirdre Harper.

The Senate met twice a month. The first meeting, named an *Executive Meeting*, was convened to review items for the agenda and to assign agenda priorities. If two-thirds of the senators voted that an item should be sent immediately to the Academic Vice President with or without comment, the item was placed on a *Consent Agenda*. The second meeting was called a *General Meeting*. General meetings were open to all faculty and staff.

A review of both the Executive and General Senate Meeting minutes of the first academic year of the Academic Senate, 1988-1989, would lead one to come to the conclusion that members of the Senate, the Chair and the Vice Chair understood and conducted meetings with professional efficiency and worked effectively with both the Governance Committee, the Academic Vice President and the faculty in general. Or so it seemed.

Senators for the second year (1989-1990) were Chester Aaron, Chair (English), Fred Anderson (Economics and Business Administration), Paul Giurlanda (Religious Studies), Robert Gorsch (English), Allan Hansell (Biology), Brent LaMon (Psychology), Kathy Perez (Education), Alden Reimonenq (English), Gordon Rieger (Extended Education), Rev. Michael Russo, Vice Chair (Communications), Kusum Singh (Communications), Christine Vourakis (Nursing), Leonard Auerbach (Graduate Business), Sandra Hellman (Extended Education), Barbara Smith (Economics and Business Administration). Elected the second semester were Allan Pollock (English), Carole Swain (Education) and Candy Boyd (Education).

Within the first few months of the 1989 fall semester, the Chair of the Senate, Professor Chester Aaron (English) threatened to resign on the grounds that there was lack of cooperation and interest in the Senate from both administration and faculty. In spite of urgings by his colleagues that he complete his term, Professor Aaron clearly affirmed his intention to resign at the end of the semester, which he did. For reasons not entirely clear, the fall of 1989 was a test for the viability of the Academic Senate. Possible reasons for what appeared to be dysfunction were suggested, but the difficulties may have been legitimate growing pains. There did not appear to be any subterfuge in the resignation of the Chair. Senator Kusum Singh also resigned at the end of the first semester.

With the resignation of Chair Aaron, the position of Chair was bestowed upon the Vice Chair, Rev. Michael Russo (Communications). As Father Russo assumed leadership of the Senate, the WASC Interim Visiting Team had completed its short Visit and submitted its report. The Visiting Team only exacerbated the growing pains of a Senate that had been in existence for less than a year and a half when the Team arrived. The Visiting Team could not help but criticize the problems of the new Senate that appeared in the WASC Interim Report. Fortunately, Father Russo was able to bring an orderly process to the Senate proceedings, while managing at the same time problems created by Visiting Team criticisms and the fact that one Senator, who had been a member of the President's Task Force on Minority Presence, was determined to push the Task Force Report recommendations as far as he could.

A lengthy controversy between the Senate and myself began in the Senate in September 1989, when Senator Alden Reimonenq expressed his concern regarding the report from the *President's Task Force on Minority Presence*. Professor Reimonenq, an African-American (English), had been a member of the *Task Force*. He stated that the report had been presented to me in February 1989, but neither the report nor the President's response to it had been made public. Professor Hansell moved that the Chair of the Senate contact me to request that I present the report to the Senate for discussion, since he thought that it would be an appropriate forum for a discussion on minority presence. The motion passed. I would subsequently find that my enthusiasm for the Senate, at least on this issue was miscalculated, a hoisting of myself on my own petard.

By the Academic Senate meeting of March 29, 1990, Senator Reimonenq insisted that the Senate discuss the Task Force Report. Some Senators quickly proposed that the Senate adopt all of the report's recommendations. However, the final resolution called for a committee review of the Task Force Report and a list of the Task Force recommendations by priority, as determined by the Senate committee, be made and then presented for action by the whole Senate.

Professor Allan Hansell was elected chair of the Senate for the 1990-1991 academic year and Professor Gerald Brunetti Vice Chair. An impressively balanced and objective 39-page Annual Report to the Faculty was issued by Chairman Rev. Michael Russo in June 1990.

The President's Task Force on Minority Presence

The Task Force on Minority Presence was formed by myself in consultation with the Administrative Council, as requested by the Board of Trustees on a motion by Trustee and alumnus, the late LaRoy Doss, that "steps should be taken to ascertain the image of Saint Mary's College within the Black (African-American) and Hispanic communities, both to discover ways by which that image can be improved and to increase enrollment by Black and Hispanic students." (Minutes of the Board of Trustees, June 1987.)

In April, 1988 I appointed a diverse task force of approximately 16 members, co-chaired by the Dean of the School of Liberal Arts, Paul Zingg, PhD, and Thomas Brown, Dean of Special Services. By May 1988, the Chair reported that the work of the Task Force was moving forward. (Administrative Council Notes, May 6, 1988.) I had hoped that the Task Force would reveal an imaginative yet realistic plan for increasing the number of African-American, Hispanic and other ethnic groups on campus, as well as suggest ways to make the College attractive to such students. Several on the Administrative Council expressed concern regarding the growing Hispanic population in California, a majority of whom were raised as Catholics. The completed Task Force Report was presented to me early in the 1989 spring semester. When I read the Report of nearly 50 pages, I realized that I was holding a controversial conundrum in my hands. What I had envisioned was a helpful straightforward report on the attitude of underrepresented ethnic and racial groups toward the College in the traditional undergraduate programs along with recommendations that would increase and enhance their presence. What I received was a major injunction for a radical remake of the College admissions and financial aid policy, as well as changes in curriculum, including the Collegiate Seminar program, and in campus life and governance. It was in my estimation an over-the-top plan that went well beyond the mandate given the Task Force via myself from the Board of Trustees. Complying with its recommendations, I conjectured, would disrupt the financial, academic and governance stability of the institution and would create controversial positions within the faculty. I brought the report to the Administrative Council for analysis and discussion.

A letter from the Chair of the Faculty Senate arrived after the Sept. 22, 1989,

Executive Meeting of the Senate, requesting the President's presence to engage in discussion on the Task Force Report with the Senate. I responded to the Chair that "neither I nor the members of the Administrative Council consider the Task Force Report, as helpful as it stands, as either the initial or final document upon which we would base our ultimate policies." I further stated that, "I am not ready to discuss whatever proposed policies we may develop on minority presence, and neither I nor the Administrative Council consider the Report of the Minority Task Force an appropriately developed vehicle for discussion." I urged the Senate to wait for the joint initial text that I and the Administrative Council would develop and, "which will provide material for addressing the minority presence issue." (Letter to Chester Aaron, Chair, Sept. 29, 1989.)

My letter was read to the Senate at its Oct. 12, 1989 Executive meeting, but some members were dissatisfied with my response, and, as expected, moved to invite me to the November Senate meeting to discuss the Task Force Report, which they thought should be made public. The discussion with the Senate would be, some thought, an important element in the decision-making process. More diplomatic members suggested that it would be more productive to wait for my response, which some speculated, perhaps facetiously, would be "ready after Christmas." The motion was withdrawn. (Minutes of the Academic Senate Executive Meeting, Oct. 12, 1989.)

An historical rendering of the discussion among the members of the Administrative Council as it considered the Task Force Report is as follows: the Administrative Council had addressed the Task Force Report in the course of several meetings, the first being in March 1989. (Administrative Council Notes, March 30, 1989.) The minutes note the reception of the Report and a method for analyzing each section. The second discussion was held by the Administrative Council on April 10, 1989. Discussion was limited to the first part of the Task Force Report in which the Council ascertained that numerous assumptions were made without support. The Council stated that the policy of the College had been that it was clearly interested in offering a quality education to underfunded, underprivileged and ethnic minority students, and that such was in keeping with its Catholic and Lasallian mission. The Catholic mission of the College must be considered, the Council noted, since more than 50 percent of the entering class identified its religious preference as Catholic.

Council members stated that they needed time to consider each of the recommendations thoughtfully and were also concerned about possible campus disruptions, especially by some on the Task Force, who may call for demonstrations or otherwise stir the embers of discontent, thus creating adverse public relations that would negatively affect overall recruitment efforts. The Task Force Report, some on the Council observed, was reminiscent of efforts characteristic of the late 1960s to forge radical change. Little was said about the liberal arts or the philosophy and theology that lay at the heart of the mission of the College, a mission that is applicable to all students. The Report, for example, criticized the traditional Collegiate Seminar program for not having readings and discussions consistent with the vision the Task Force would impose, such as various ethnic readings. The issue seemed to be whether the College curriculum should change the students or should the students change the College curriculum for some vague and indeterminate multicultural end that may dilute the strong academic goals of the Collegiate Seminar (the use of recognized Great Books) for everyone. (Administrative Council Notes, April 10, 1989.) During the end-of-the-academic-year workshop, June 12, 13 and 14, 1989, the Task Force Report was assigned first place on the agenda and was discussed at length. The Report had recommended specific quotas for various ethnic groups: 60 percent Caucasian, 13 percent Hispanic, 10 percent Asian, 8 percent African-American, 1 percent Native American and 8 percent International. The Council would not accept the concept of either recruitment or admission by quotas. Such a concept did not seem either possible or even just and reasonable under the circumstances. Though international students were welcomed, a quota of 8 percent was deemed clearly arbitrary. The Task Force Report claimed that the benefits of having international students were "clear and persuasive," yet the Council was not convinced that such was the case, especially if a number of international students were deficient in English, as our experience demonstrated.

When questioned, the Dean of Admissions noted that he was consulted on some issues by members of the Task Force, but on the matter of quotas and other critical issues he was not. The Council expressed interest in stronger efforts to recruit underrepresented minorities but would not accept a specific quota system as being academically or economically wise. While the quota numbers closely reflected the general percentages for each of the selected ethnic populations in the state, those numbers did not represent the percentage of students from those respective ethnic groups who were college eligible. Demographic studies indicated that among high school graduates in 1987, 32 percent of Asians, 4.5 percent of African-Americans, 19.4 percent of Filipinos, 5 percent of Hispanics and 15.8 percent of Caucasians were University of California eligible. Fifty percent of Asians; 10.8 percent of African Americans, 29.5 percent of Filipinos, 13.3 percent of Hispanics and 31.6 percent of Caucasians were California State University eligible. (Data from

Toward Educational Equity, 1989, published by the California Postsecondary Education Commission.) Competition for recruiting those eligible among certain groups, particularly African Americans and Hispanics, was becoming more intense statewide.

The Council strongly opposed radical changes in the Collegiate Seminar program. While it did not object to offering a limited number of courses that addressed the culture, history, psychology and other aspects of certain ethnic groups, the council opposed making ethnic studies a requirement. It also strongly opposed changes proposed in governance, including requiring additional personnel empowered with intrusive oversight to monitor hiring and student recruitment in other departments, such as the Personnel (Human Resources) and Admissions offices, academic Schools and individual departments. As for additional recruiters, the Council stated that the recruiting, hiring and supervising of admissions personnel was solely within the jurisdiction of the Dean of Admissions, yet, if financially possible, it would be helpful to hire one or two minority recruiters. Serious doubt was expressed with the recommendation that implied that only Hispanics or African-Americans should, or could, recruit students from their respective ethnic groups. The Council also noted that financial aid policies were within the oversight of the Board of Trustees, and that if there are to be changes in policy then it was the Board that would make them, usually on careful analysis and recommendation from the administration, and in particular the Financial Aid Director and the College Chief Financial Officer. The Council was opposed to the recommendation on either blanket or selected loan forgiveness. Appropriately educated minority graduates were sought for employment by various employers and thus, such graduates would be in a position to repay their college loans, as were all other graduates. The overall cost to fulfill the recommendations of the Task Force on minority presence would place an untenable burden on the budget and would curtail legitimate requests from other sectors of the community.

The Council was also made aware of an oral minority report from several members on the Task Force who claimed that the Task Force Report was "steam rollered," to use their terminology, that members were intimidated into following the lead of the Chair and the Dean of Special Services, that certain researched information was ignored, and that meetings were haphazard and without minutes. The final Report, the representatives claimed, was never given to all the members of the Task Force for comment or approval and was, they observed, basically the work of the Chair and the Dean. Its overall negativity was not supported by the data gathered from students, and its radical stance was the creation of the most outspoken and apparently activist Task Force members. The difficulty for me and the Council was that the Report was in print and touted before the Senate by a member of the Task Force.

I began the compilation and composition of an initial text on diversity from the administration of the College to be reviewed by the council, which was clearly concerned over possible reactions -- or even protests and demonstrations -- that certain statements could possibly evoke from different segments of the College community.

With thanks to the Task Force on minority presence for its input, I distributed a document entitled *Educating Leaders for the Next Millennium, Diversity, Quality and Tradition,* dated Jan. 6, 1990. The carefully written, "next-step" document presented both the philosophy of the College mission as well as its serious interest in increasing ethnic and racial representation within the student body. It was moderate. It also outlined the numerous and continuing efforts to recruit and support minority high school students, but at the same time indicated the restraints on the College in terms of financial aid and the highly competitive recruitment both within California and from outside the state of high school minority student graduates in view of the limited eligibility pool. The statement provided a philosophy for encouraging minority presence on campus and noted that budgets had been increased to augment both admissions and counseling efforts. It also noted that for nearly 20 years the High Potential Program and the appointment of an Assistant Dean for Special Programs had been in place. For eight years a program for the recruitment of international students from Asia and from Christian Brothers institutions in Hong Kong and Mexico had been sponsored. The admissions recruitment film had been edited to express both a welcoming attitude toward minority students as well as promoting the advantages to them in attending Saint Mary's. A special Spanish-language version had also been developed. The appointment of a special admissions officer for recruiting both Hispanic and African-American students was scheduled for the 1990 fall semester. The publication of *Educating Leaders, et al,* prompted a less than objective commentary by some in the Senate and ultimately by leading members of the Task Force, who were not satisfied with either my or the Council's response to the Task Force Report.

By May, 1990, a Senate committee claimed that it had carefully reviewed the Task Force Report and arranged issues according to what it considered important. At the end of a lengthy discussion on the recommendations the committee deemed important, Senator Alan Pollock moved that: "We, the members of the Academic Senate, after careful review and consideration of the *Report of the President's Task Force on Minority Presence* dated 15 March '89, endorse the report and urge implementation of the recommendations as stated in the *Executive Summary* of the report." The Senate also empowered a *Progress Committee* to "monitor and implement the recommendations of the Task Force" and report regularly to the Senate. The motion passed 12-0. (Minutes of the Academic Senate, May 17, 1990.)

The bravado of the Senate vote to "implement the recommendations" seemed to be a test of its muscularity, especially given its weak second-year first-semester showing.

William J. Hynes, PhD, appointed the Academic Vice President as of July 1, 1990, appeared before the Academic Senate at its first meeting of the academic year, Sept. 6, 1990. He reported that the he, I, and members of the Task Force would schedule a meeting to discuss both the Task Force Report and the subsequent Administrative Council document, "to focus on improving minority presence at Saint Mary's, and specifically, the recommendations contained in the Task Force Report as endorsed by the Senate last year." (Minutes of the Academic Senate, Sept. 6, 1990.)

Hynes had previously spoken to me to suggest a meeting between myself and members of the Task Force, so that potential adverse reactions could be ameliorated before some Task Force members and Senators became overly reactive. I agreed, though with some reluctance. Since Hynes was new, he believed that he would be considered an objective mediator.

After four meetings between myself and the Task Force, Vice President Hynes, who chaired the meetings, informed the Senate on Feb. 28, 1991, that progress had been made in effecting agreement on a number of items. The sharpness that characterized the first meetings with the Task Force had diminished, most likely because some concessions were made. One of the creative initiatives by the Academic Vice President was to enlist the assistance of the Development Office in contacting the James Irvine Foundation for financial assistance in implementing some of the recommendations, since financial constraints were a factor that inhibited their implementation. The Foundation found his proposal worthy of consideration and indicated that it would be considered by its Board at its May meeting. In May 1991, Hynes reported to the Senate that a report would be forthcoming on the meetings. The compromise report entitled *Celebrating Diversity* was presented on May 22, 1991, and stemmed the controversy. The issue of establishing specific quotas based on the general percentages of ethnic populations in the state was ameliorated, and those modified numbers were considered ranges and goals rather than quotas.

Referred to the Curriculum Committee and the Collegiate Seminar Governing Board were recommendations on curriculum and the Collegiate Seminar. Though Deans and department chairs were willing to examine curriculum so that "multicultural awareness, understanding and respect" could be achieved through offering certain ethnic-based courses, there was no requirement that all students enroll in them. A watchdog person or committee with authority to investigate and require action of various Deans and departments was considered obnoxious and unnecessary in an institution that cherished its academic freedom and the free exercise of its responsibility. I was uneasy with several of the compromises. Uppermost in my mind was my personal concern for the liberal arts background of the College, including the canon of Great Books, the philosophy and pedagogy that supported the Great Books program and the dialogue between theology and reason, none of which was considered in the Task Force Report. While I honestly welcomed the increase in minority candidates for the baccalaureate degree, I had to ask myself the questions: "What is a quality education for under-represented minorities, and is not such a quality education fundamentally the same for all students?" In my experience I believed that the cultivation of the mind through liberal arts education was in the best interests of every student. Such an education would, I was convinced, play well in the marketplace; in creating family life, where education begins; and or in the pursuit of graduate work after commencement. Given the circumstances of the moment, accepting and modifying a number of the recommendations avoided an unnecessary confrontation and continued agitation. Furthermore, I surmised that some of the suggestions or recommendations would be reconfigured when they entered the machinery of academic processes.

As is the case with many projects, in due time memory and enthusiasm are soon distracted and diverted to other interests. However, a plan for follow-up was put in place, and subsequent reports were issued. The High Potential Program was later enlarged (with the aid of a grant) and in time, under-represented minority enrollment increased. The pressure was continuous by those who saw their cause as the major issue both within College confines and nationwide. While the complaints and pressure for more funding were persistent, often annoying and pointed, it must be said that unless the minority advocates pursued their concerns, minority issues may have been given less attention. My only wish was that civility, balance and respect for hard facts had been considered. Unfortunately, I do not believe that those agitating for unusual changes in several areas understood the value of an objective, nonpolitical liberal arts education, an education and intellectual environment that would move the disadvantaged in many ways away from whatever disadvantages they faced and would focus their minds on more universal principles that would provide them with greater intellectual and self-improvement opportunities.

The Interim Accreditation Visit of 1989 - Ambiguity

When the appointed chairperson for the *Interim* Accreditation Visit of 1989 (postponed from 1988) arrived for a pre-Visit dialogue, the purpose of the Interim Visit was discussed as outlined by the WASC Accreditating Commission for Schools, namely, that the Interim Visiting Team would see what progress had been made with regard to mission, governance, graduate programs, extended education and the library. The conversation with Team Chair Carolyn Ellner, Dean of the School of Education at California State University, Northridge, was cordial and followed the format and agenda the Commission outlined. The College administration noted that it was prepared to address each of the issues and Dean Ellner was satisfied that the College had responded to the concerns of the Accrediting Commission.

However, when the full interim Team of four visitors arrived in November 1989, both I and the Administration were chagrined to discover that new issues had been added to the agenda without prior notification. The written Team Report noted that although the College response to the Commission had addressed "all issues raised by the previous team, the (self-study) document was literal and specific, narrowly focusing on each issue. It might have been more useful," the report continued, "as an assessment tool if the focus of the report had gone beyond these specifics and had been future-oriented. The document might have been used for planning. In addition it appears in conversations with faculty and staff that only individuals who were expected to respond to the recommendations of the 1985 visit were involved in its preparation."

The latter observation was, in the minds of those involved in preparing the interim self-study report, an unjustifiable extension of what the College was told by WASC officials and that the interim Visiting Team or the College was expected to do. The College administration had responded as professionally required, involving those who were responsible for the stated issues, and clearly understood, from both the Executive Director's letter and the pre-visit consultation, that the interim Visit was not a Comprehensive Visit. The College had just completed an extensive planning document for securing the future and was midstream in what became a gratifying over-achievement of a vigorous Capital Campaign.

As for the new governance organization, the interim Team arrived just as the new organization was experiencing its second-year introduction to the faculty, as well as its normal growing pains. Even though the Governance Committee had crafted the Academic Senate bylaws thoughtfully, there were, as expected, those who thought the organization should be different, as well as those who longed for the freewheeling former Faculty Assembly. Some faculty who supported the Academic Senate concept were suspicious that some individuals had tried to undermine the new governance model by acting less than responsibly within the Senate, but such suspicions could not be substantiated.

The interim Visiting Team also took sides in the disagreement between some in the faculty who wanted the Senate to determine its own bylaws, thus eliminating the Governance Committee as a separate entity. The intention behind an independent Governance Committee was to establish a separate branch of faculty governance, much like an upper and lower house in state or federal government or a committee on committees system. Furthermore, a separate Governance Committee would allow for the forging of a coalition among administrators and faculty so that the concept of a "community of scholars" might be a substantial working reality. The alternative model, acquired from corporate business, would be mimicking the division between capital and labor, a concept not in keeping with academic notions of shared governance.

What was also troublesome with the interim Visit were additions to the agenda that were disclosed to the interim Visiting Team prior to the Visit, but not to College administration. Additional standards would normally be promulgated and any institution would be expected to respond at its next regular Comprehensive Visit. Thus, when the interim Team added *assessment, student services, cultural diversity, and residential life* to the agenda, both administrators and some faculty members viewed the additions as impositions of philosophy and praxes emanating from the appetites of a new WASC administration. A generous estimate of the confusion in the Interim Visit most likely reflected an overworked and/or understaffed accrediting office. The College had responded as requested, only to be criticized for doing what it was asked to do and for not doing what some team members or WASC administration thought the College should anticipate or conjecture.

Enduring what seemed an unnecessary, ill-timed and ill-organized interim Visiting Team was not only a disruption, but frustrating. The next regular Accreditation Visit was scheduled for 1993. Unfortunately, the 1993 agenda also contained a surprise section on diversity formulated under the direction of the new Executive Director.

Faster Forward

Timothy Korth Tennis Courts, 1990 and the Korth Tower, 1996

Howard and Gerri Korth had a history of generous support for Catholic causes, particularly for Catholic education. Howard Korth was an engineer who graduated from the University of Notre Dame. He served in the United States Navy during World War II and was honorably discharged as a Lieutenant Commander. He was employed by the Chrysler Corporation's Aviation Division. Exercising his entrepreneurial spirit, Howard and two associates established Aaxico Airlines, which became Saturn Airways in 1965 with Howard as Chairman of the Board and C.E.O. In 1976, Saturn was purchased by Transamerica, Inc., and renamed Transamerica International Airlines, with Howard as Vice Chairman of the Board of Transamerica, Inc.

James Harvey, CEO of Transamerica, Inc., not only sat on the College Board of Trustees, but the summer home he shared with his wife Charlene was on the land adjoining the southeast side of the campus. Jim suggested inviting Howard to join the Board of Regents, which the College did. Howard responded positively.

Among the Korth children was a son named Timothy, also a Notre Dame graduate, who unfortunately died at age 42. Since Howard was a tennis enthusiast, Development Office personnel asked if he would be interested in helping to relocate and enlarge the tennis courts, thus allowing conference tournaments to be held on campus, as well as providing tennis offices and storage facilities near the courts. Howard and Gerri agreed to do so in honor of their deceased son, Timothy. The Timothy Korth Tennis Courts and Offices were dedicated in 1990.

A few years later Howard and Gerri agreed to fund the remodeling of the facilities on both sides of the College Chapel. The offices of the Academic Vice President and a classroom on the east side of the Chapel and the tower containing the brass bell from the first Saint Mary's campus in San Francisco (1863-1889), campus ministry offices and seminar offices and classroom on the West side of the Chapel were named *Korth Academic Offices* and *Korth Tower* (respectively) in honor of Howard and Gerri Korth.

The Gala Opening of the Soda Center, 1989

A much needed facility for various College functions, such as student and faculty dinners and dances, receptions, civic functions, meetings, lectures, luncheons, special dinners for auspicious occasions, fashion shows, music performances and the like, finally came into being through the generosity of former Trustee and Regent Y. Charles "Chet" Soda, the Y. Charles and Helen Soda Foundation and Regent and alumnus Linus Claeys. It contained a state-of-the-art kitchen capable of serving over 500 guests at a formal dinner and could seat 2,000 for an opening day parents' meeting or a Moraga Town Hall event. The main indoor area, like Caesar's Gaul, was divisible by folding sound walls into thee parts named the Orinda, Moraga and Lafayette Rooms which could be used simultaneously for different meetings or dinners. An attractive reception area which could be used as a fourth dining area was named Claeys Lounge, honoring both Linus and Ruth Claeys. A patio suitable for outdoor barbecues adjoined the main dining/meeting area.

Y. Charles "Chet" Soda, of Italian descent, was well-known in the East Bay and had long been associated with Saint Mary's College, having been named a Regent in 1952. He served as the Board of Regents' President for two years, 1975-1977, and as a member of the Board of Trustees from 1977 to 1988. Chet became a life member of the President's Club in 1971 and was named an honorary alumnus in 1972. He was one of the early partners in the Oakland Raiders, served on the Oakland Port Commission, was a director of the California Racing Commission Board and helped form an Oakland Salesian Boys Club. He began construction on a dream home for retirement for himself and his wife Helen, in Southern California when she became terminally ill. When she gained her eternal reward in 1983 Chet turned his attention to forming a charitable foundation and became interested in the construction of the student activity center by pledging funds toward it. The College architect, Kazuo Goto, AIA, began its design in earnest, and groundbreaking was held on Nov. 2, 1986. At that time neither Chet, a robust and stately man, nor anyone at the College suspected that he would soon become seriously ill. He was feted as the Easter Seal Humanitarian of the Year in 1987 and honored as a Gaelsports Director Emeritus also in 1987. Chet visited the construction site of the Soda Center several times before he realized that he was suffering from a fatal illness. He died in March 1989, just five months before the dedication of the Soda Center on Aug. 27, 1989.

Town and Gown Reprise

A revised Master Plan was submitted to the Town of Moraga in March 1990. However, while the Master Plan was under consideration, the College requested permission to begin construction on two residence halls, shown on the Plan, so that they would be completed prior to academic year 1991-1992.

If the deadline were not met, the College would not be able to offer some out-of-town students on-campus housing at the beginning of the academic year, which would most likely mean a loss of enrollment. The response of the Town was unexpected, since the construction of residence halls was in accord with the Town's Master Plan which recommended that the College construct residence halls for students on campus in order to reduce traffic in and around Moraga. There were several members of the Moraga Town Council who believed that whatever regulations were devised should be observed regardless of the hardship, be it financial, for student life, or to relieve traffic in the Town. The argument was the normal one that fear inspires, namely, that if an exception was made for the College, the same argument could be made by a developer or some other petitioner. Thus, the College had to wait for the Council to discuss the Master Plan at length. The residence hall construction was delayed, precluding an opening for the 1991 fall semester. In order to address issues the College Administration enlisted the services of an attorney versed in presenting master plans to municipalities. Furthermore, the Advancement Staff and I enlisted the assistance of citizens from the Town who would support the Master Plan concepts and who understood the mind of the Town Council. Among the citizens who attended the Council meeting were several who first supported the incorporation of the Town and some who had served on the Council in the past. The Master Plan was finally approved on Oct. 23, 1990 but placed some restrictions on College enrollment.

The request for approval of the construction of the two residence halls (Majorie David Ageno Hall and Ferdinand and Camille Hall) triggered a disturbing discussion within the Town Council, namely whether to impose what are called user fees on the construction of the two residence halls.

The Moraga Park and Recreation Commission had developed plans for the construction of a community recreation center and the Town Manager, Ross Hubbard, discovered that other communities had imposed fees on independent collegiate institutions for certain services provided by the cities in which they were located. Hubbard, working with the Town counsel, applied this concept to the College, suggesting that the College pay safety and recreation user fees. When the College applied for permits for the construction of two new residence halls, he saw an opportunity to secure parkland dedication fees for use in building a Town recreation center. The College administration and Board of Trustees were disturbed by the proposal, given the openness of the College to community activities and the cooperative relationship that had seemingly been developed. The imposition of park dedication fees on the College and her students to construct a recreation facility for Moraga citizens, whose financial resources were clearly above average, was considered particularly odious in view of the College nonprofit public benefit status that saves taxpayers millions of dollars annually. Government grants, numerous donors, interest from endowment and, most importantly, tuition and fees support the significant cost for each student at the College. If the same students enrolled at the University of California or one of the California State Universities, each student would be subsidized by the state at taxpayers' expense.

Of significant benefit to taxpayers is the fact that the College, through its arduous and time-consuming fundraising efforts, acquires funding for the construction of its needed facilities for academic, housing and recreational needs. The construction of facilities at state-supported institutions is paid for mainly by taxpayers. The College is not a developer involved in constructing homes, apartments or other residential facilities for profit. It's property of approximately 420 acres -- 100 of which had been donated by the Moraga Land Company and the rest purchased in 1927 specifically for the construction of collegiate facilities, namely for the education, housing and recreational needs of students, as well as the housing of supervisory faculty in residence halls and the faculty of the religious or monastic community. Independent colleges and universities are viewed by state and federal legislatures as benefits to the public at–large, and thus low-income students are eligible for grants and loans from both state and federal sources, though usually at a subsidy lower than costs to taxpayers if such students were to attend public institutions. User fees are charged to developers (who pass on the costs to buyers) in order to construct parks, public schools and common recreation facilities, as well as roads and facilities for fire, police and other emergency services. The clients of the developers benefit from their own user fees as an investment in their community.

Legal counsel to the College demonstrated that the campus had never been divided into parcels for development and therefore a parcel-use fee would not apply. Furthermore, Counsel noted, the College had been cooperative in opening its facilities to the citizens of Moraga, provided it did not compromise normal student use. In order to satisfy all parties, a compromise agreement was fashioned that did not impose user fees and at the same time formalized the existing College policy of public use of College facilities as was the practice in vogue at the time.

There were two other difficulties that occurred with the Town that centered on commencement ceremonies and the celebrations following. The first difficulty was the College failure to notify surrounding civic entities of the date and time of the commencement ceremonies. As the ceremonies grew in size, and as many as 5,000-6,000 parents, relatives and friends arrived on campus to attend them; traffic on roads leading to the campus became congested on the Saturday morning of the commencement ceremony. On a particular Commencement Day in the mid-1980s traffic on the roads from both Orinda and Lafayette was reduced to one lane because of tree trimming. The trimmers and the civic entities that hired them had viewed the Saturday morning hours as having light traffic and did not anticipate the commencement date and the corresponding overwhelming traffic. The resultant traffic congestion was uncompromising, and many attendees, including some of the graduates, did not arrive on time for the ceremonies. One female graduate, caught in traffic, drove on to the campus and when advised by a campus security guard that she could not enter a certain road drove forward in spite of the guard's warning. The guard fell and was slightly injured. After the commencement ceremonies, the woman was arrested, much to her and her guests' consternation. The problem was addressed the following year by the College sending letters indicating commencement date and time to all local entities well in advance. Furthermore, final examinations were scheduled so that almost all nongraduates would leave the campus no later than the Thursday prior to commencement, thus vacating approximately 70 percent of the parking spaces on campus for use by commencement attendees.

An unusual difficulty occurred on Commencement Day in May 1991, when an aggressive police officer decided, with the Chief's approval, to address what the Moraga police department considered difficulties related to alcohol consumption during post-commencement family celebrations that took place on campus. Families brought their own food and drink, including beer, wine and champagne, to celebrate the graduation of sons and daughters. Graduates are normally 22 years of age or older. However, there are usually underage family members or friends of the graduates who attend the ceremonies. Junior year students who work during commencement are normally over 21 by the end of their junior year. The police officer brought with him a mature appearing young man under 21 who circulated among the various family groups and helped himself to beer (in other words, he purloined it). This was taken as a sign of ill-controlled alcoholic beverage use by the College. The College Dean for Student Life, Ron Travenik, who was present to assure good order among the guests, was given a citation for failing to observe liquor laws, even though neither he nor the College sponsored any of the family celebrations. As word leaked out around town of such police action, a number of citizens wrote letters to the police chief and to local newspapers decrying such activity and expressing fear that police would be looking over back fences at subsequent family gatherings in their own backyards. For reasons undisclosed, neither the chief nor the officer remained much longer with the Moraga Police Department. The following year, notices were sent by the College to parents stating that if they brought alcoholic beverages to the post-commencement gatherings it was illegal to serve such beverages to underage persons, including family members.

I was named Moraga Citizen of the Year, on May 11, 1994. The Proclamation was signed by Mayor Al G. Dessayer, Vice Mayor James J. Sweeny, and Council members Cherie T. Grant, Susan L. Noe, and Michael G. Harris and Town Manager, Ross Hubbard.

A mutual benefit for both Town and Gown occurred in 1997 when Ross Hubbard, the Town Manager, approached me with a plan to bury the utility lines that were strung across the front of the campus along Saint Mary's Road. The Town regularly received an allocation from Pacific Gas and Electric Co. to bury utility lines along roads designated by the Town as scenic corridors. If the College were willing to pay half the cost, the Town would devote PG&E allocations to fund the other half of burying the lines that had for years been an eyesore. I secured approval from the Board to fund the College portion, namely $250,000, and the project proceeded. It was completed in 1997 to the delight of all, especially since the tally for the project was under budget There is no doubt that this project contributed to the beautification of both the Town and the view of the College from Saint Mary's Road.

Thinking of the Millennium

Planning Ahead

As a follow-up to the initial *Institutional Planning Group Report* (March 14, 1986), written as a framework for the first major Capital Campaign (1984-1992), I completed a second document on May 30, 1990. It reviewed the same elements as the original IPG Report noting where progress had been made, where aspirations had been fulfilled and where next steps were to be made. It projected ambitious goals for the forthcoming five years, including an extensive and, in some cases, expensive list of needed facilities. Overall, it provided a blueprint for future planning and action in every facet of the College as a comprehensive liberal arts, coeducational institution with graduate and older adult programs.

In light of a Papal document entitled *Ex Corde Ecclesiae* (From the Heart of the Church) on the mission of Catholic higher education worldwide and the mandates from Christian Brothers General Chapters, discussions on the inherent nature and outward expression of the Catholicism of the College seemed imperative, while keeping in mind the necessity for academic freedom as applied to both faculty and students. Likewise, the efforts and funding required to enhance the quality of its academic endeavors became an increasing concern. These two issues soon became the focus of what was titled *The New Century Committee* that was to be formed in anticipation of the excitement generated by looking forward to the new century and the next millennium.

Changing of the Academy Guard, 1990

A scholarly study could be made of the *Weathering of Academic Vice Presidents,* given the emotional and intellectual pressure that any Academic Vice President must endure. He or she occupies a pivotal place in the administration of an academic institution, since the AVP stands between the President and his advisors on the one hand and his own official advisors, namely, the Academic Senate and the Council of Deans on the other. Administration and members of the faculty both have agendas that are occasionally at odds with one another. One role of the Academic Vice President is to mediate between both agendas. After 12 years of listening, negotiating, winning and losing some strategic issues as Academic Vice President, Brother William Beatie expressed his intense desire to retire from that post at the end of the 1990 spring semester. I appreciated his gallant efforts and hoped that he would remain but understood his fatigue and accepted his resignation. A

311

search committee was formed to conduct a national search under the leadership of Rev. Michael Russo, PhD, who had been elected chairman of the Academic Senate. At the completion of reviewing applications and conducting interviews, a bright, scholarly, inventive and energetic man who had been serving as Academic Dean at Regis University in Denver, Co., was selected.

William J. Hynes, PhD, Academic Vice President, 1990-2000

William J. Hynes received his doctorate in the History of American Religious Thought from the University of Chicago in 1976. As Academic Dean at Regis University, a Jesuit institution, he was intimately aware not only of traditional academic programs, but of programs for older adults, since Regis University had conducted programs for older adult students in conjunction with IPD similar to those Saint Mary's had instituted some 15 years previously. (and like Saint Mary's, Regis had assumed full command of the IPD joint program.) As scholar himself with numerous published essays and three books, it was evident that Hynes held a strong interest in encouraging faculty scholarship. His academic background was indicative of a commitment to philosophy, Christian thought, and religious and ecumenical studies. His studies in English provided him with an eloquence fitting an Academic Vice President. Having served at Regis University and Saint Xavier University, which is located in Chicago, and sponsored by the Sisters of Mercy, and having studied at Marquette University (MA, 1969), also a Jesuit university, as well as Immaculate Conception College (BA, 1962), Hynes was acknowledged by the Screening Committee for his extensive experience with Catholic higher education the committee and recommended that he be appointed.

Having been exposed to Jesuit higher education as a student, teacher and administrator, it took some time for Hynes to adjust to the academic spirit and pedagogy characteristic of Saint Mary's. He was academically imaginative and held strong views on such matters as an Affirmative Action program for Catholic faculty and on faculty scholarship. Hynes also saw the need for hiring academic models as chief administrators or, as some faculty regarded them, at times facetiously, as "stars," to serve as Deans of Schools when vacancies occurred. It was not long however, before he made significant contributions to liberal arts education, religious insight, the College mission, Christian Brothers' pedagogy, California academic lifestyle and the encouragement of quality teaching. His inauguration of three major summer institutes by noted scholars for the benefit of faculty and administrators on issues related to the mission of the College were presented successively over a dozen summers and were an imaginative and enlightening opportunity for developing insight. His appreciation for faculty accomplishment through honoring and rewarding exceptional teaching left its productive mark on the academic life of the College. Hynes was also successful in securing grants to sponsor *Visiting Woodrow Wilson* and *Marshall Scholars.*

For the first of the summer institutes, Hynes invited Professor Bruce Kimball of the Warner Graduate School of Education, University of Rochester, an international authority on the history of Liberal Arts to hold at least six summer workshops for faculty. Hynes grew to appreciate the value of the Collegiate Seminar approach for developing students' minds and eventually hearts through the reading and discussion of Great Books and saw a summer institute in Liberal Arts Education as a resource for all faculty and especially for those leading students in Collegiate Seminars. He also observed that having as many faculty members as possible teaching in the Great Books program would deepen their understanding of liberal education and their ability to converse with one another beyond the confines of their own disciplines.

The second invitee was Professor Scott Appleby, PhD, Director of the Cushwa Center for Catholic Studies at the University of Notre Dame. He conducted workshops on the development of Catholic Higher Education, primarily in America. Appleby was a well-known academician who had been called upon as an expert by various national television news organizations and had addressed the National Conference of Catholic Bishops at its annual Conference. Professor Appleby conducted three summer workshops.

The third set of summer instructional institutes addressed the Lasallian Heritage of the College by investigating the writings of and about St. John Baptist De La Salle, Founder of the Christian Brothers. The first Lasallian Heritage workshop was conducted by Brother Luke Salm, FSC, PhD, of Manhattan College in New York and three subsequent summer workshops were conducted by Assistant Vice President Brother Michael Meister, FSC, PhD.

To encourage faculty teaching, Hynes established a *Professor of the Year* event awarding a selected faculty member with a stipend and the opportunity to deliver an address to the faculty followed by a celebratory dinner. The list of *Professor of the Year* awardees from its inception in 1992 to 1997 is recorded in the Appendix.

As a member of the President's Council, Hynes developed a strategic five-year plan for the enhancement of academic life. Though his timelines were sometimes considered overly ambitious by me, his vision for improving the academic life of the College was worthy of attention. One of his more ambitious goals was to achieve a better balance between faculty members' instructional and scholarly duties. He believed that a faculty member's teaching would maintain currency and develop depth if the member could devote appropriate time to scholarship, as evidenced by scholarly articles, books, appearances before peers both on and off campus, the development of creative approaches to his or her teaching and participation in developing insights for fulfilling the threefold mission of the College. The difficulty in achieving such a lofty goal was the proposition of reducing teaching obligations with the questionable hope that the majority of the faculty would devote themselves to scholarship. It would also be an expensive aspiration.

Hynes indicated his deep commitment to welcoming diversity among both students and faculty and unifying those diverse elements through a dedication to liberal arts education, the Catholic nature of the College and its Lasallian heritage. The Lasallian heritage, taken from the spirit of St. John Baptist de La Salle, would advocate attentiveness and encouragement to those students who found themselves in both financial and personal need. Hynes solicited over $3 million from the James Irvine Foundation to increase College efforts to recruit diverse students, faculty and staff. In formal addresses to the faculty, he relied on his ability to articulate goals and observations with cogency and extensive literary allusions peppered with a congenial sense of humor.

In November 1995, in an address to the faculty, Hynes encouraged the faculty to be a community of scholars saying, "If we are a community in which we expect our students to be able to look twice and cultivate liberating habits of mind, as well as value both faith and reason as mutually enriching each other, we are no less a community in which faculty must feel actively animated and similarly engaged." (Address to Faculty, Nov. 21, 1995, Saint Mary's College Archives.)

In his quest for excellence, he enunciated the following comments in an address to the faculty in 1994: "To the extent that an institution and its faculty are truly excellent, to this same degree they will have carefully distilled a cohesive core curriculum. Is a core simply a loose amalgam of courses gathered from departmental offerings? Is a core little more than the autobiographies of faculty? Is a core, in the words of Phil Leitner (Former Dean of the School of Science), simply a fossilized record of past battles and détentes? The core curriculum that emanates from an institution tells us to what degree the faculty of that institution have achieved as a distinctive and coherent sense of the whole." (Address to Faculty, Sept. 9, 1994, Archives, Saint Mary's College.)

His aspirations for excellence as demonstrated in many ways and in such trenchant remarks as those noted could not be denied. However, certain faculty members grew uneasy with what they perceived an elitism and an impishness in what appeared to be vacillating academic postures. Hynes insisted on national searches for faculty and administrative positions, thus bringing a diversity of personalities to the campus, including some "stars." However, some who voiced complaints believed that outstanding members of the faculty were passed over in favor of outsiders who may have acquired a reputation elsewhere but were not known in the Bay Area. Some critics thought that too many faculty and administrators were appointed who had minimal understanding of, or even sympathy for, the Catholic guiding principles of the College, as well as its special liberal arts character. His insistence on being better led to interpretations that he had in mind the model of some other institution, rather than simply focusing on fulfilling the worthy mission of the College. "Did he really embrace the fundamental spirit of Saint Mary's?" some asked.

One problem Hynes attempted to address was to overcome a slowly waning but persistent historical attitude that insisting on excellence was detrimental to minority or low-income students. He adopted the contrary view that with proper support, insisting on excellence would enhance the potential and personal satisfaction of all students. He had put in place a plan entitled *Proactive Guidelines for Hiring Faculty*, suggesting that personal and intellectual qualities of viable candidates should be able to contribute to the three traditions of the College, especially the education of disadvantaged students who could be inspired by an insightful and compassionate faculty.

A few grumbled, because they believed that he had raised the bar for full professorship by requiring greater scholarship. Even though Saint Mary's was considered primarily a teaching institution, Hynes' view was that without scholarship, teaching excellence would falter. For the most part, faculty knew that he was an advocate for the good of the institution and thus its reputation in the wider academic community. They recognized his insight, professionalism and scholarly approach, as well as his congeniality. However, his demeanor made it clear that he was the Academic Vice President, and some found that daunting.

When he entertained faculty groups, his familiarity with the connoisseur's wine list and his ability to evaluate the nectar of the gods was indicative of a well-cultivated palate.

Bill Hynes was named President of Saint Norbert College in De Pere, Wisc., a suburb of Green Bay, in February 2000 and assumed office in July of that year.

Academic Senate in the Throes of Progress, 1991-1993

The Academic Senate continued to mature into a lively and intensely serious academic think tank, and during academic year 1990-1991 under the guidance of Chair Allan Hansell (biology), it became engaged in extensive debate. The debate, at times both complex and passionate, was over such interconnected issues as salary; reduction in and equalization of teaching duties (often called teaching load, a terminology some considered plebeian); and rank and tenure standards, including faculty scholarship expectations. The semester calendar was also on the table, that is, with a proposal to return to the standard 15-week semester without the January Term or continuing with an optional January-like term following the traditional academic year. The calendar became an emotional issue involving both faculty and students, with the latter intensely advocating the continuation of the January term with its opportunity for travel courses. Included in the calendar discussion was a return to the standard unit evaluation of courses, i.e., two-, three-, four- or five-unit courses with a standard 50-minute class session While a little over half the faculty supported the continuation of the January Term (33 percent strongly supporting, 20 percent supporting), another poll showed that almost two-thirds (61 percent) of the faculty favored dropping the January Term *if that would guarantee a maximum six-course teaching load.* However, the six-course teaching load proposal on the faculty wish list neglected to demonstrate its financial implications, or what that would mean under unit system of reckoning. The teaching load issue would surface again in the late '90s coupled with expectations for greater faculty scholarship. As President, I was intent on receiving a package of proposals on calendar, workload, January Term, and salary scale, since they were all intertwined. The financial and curricular issues (including the January Term), research funding, teaching load and greater availability of faculty to students were issues that I saw as being weighed equally, even though availability to students topped my personal list.

Other items on the Senate agenda were extensive, including a proposal for an anthropology - sociology major, standards for promotion, faculty course load, library development policy, librarians on major academic committees, standards for selecting students as valedictorians, School and departmental awards, and participation in commencement ceremonies. Recommendations on diversity were previously discussed.

Recommendations for curriculum changes highlighted the pressure many institutions and faculty faced in reviewing time-honored curricula in the face of demands for social awareness, international understanding and mutual respect. Social goals enunciated at various times and places were often critical of the canon (reading lists for the Collegiate Seminar), and requests were made to include books by various ethnic authors or women, which had the taint of promoting social and political positions rather than generating objective formation of mental habits through reading the most influential authors in world history. Pressure was applied on the members of the Seminar Governing Board to make the reading list more relevant. It should be noted that a few faculty were only too eager to augment or substitute texts in the Seminar canon in order to address and embrace multicultural or gender awareness. Substituting social engineering in place of the intellectual arts was not something that I believed was within the fundamental mission of the College, and I was deeply concerned that the intellectual goals of the Collegiate Seminar would be compromised. Dean Thomas Slakey, (1971-1974), who had a wealth of experience with Great Books education having been both a tutor and Dean of Instruction at Saint John's College in Annapolis, Md. and Santa Fe, N.M., was able to hold the great texts line in 1972, when political issues prompted by the Draft, the Vietnam conflict, the Free Speech, Civil Rights, and other movements of the time attempted to replace authentic and objective liberal arts education with the social and political issues of the moment. "All Saint Mary's students," I noted, "should be exposed for the most part to the traditionally recognized canon of Great Books, thus fostering the development of habits of mind so essential to analyzing the current mercurial political, moral, social and technological movements. A quality liberal arts education for all students will allow them to speak to one another across ethnic, gender and cultural lines, raise the intellectual colloquy and achieve a lasting diminution of prejudice as well as cultural and gender awareness firsthand without indoctrination."

What was impressive about the Academic Senate was that both members of the Senate and the faculty in general were methodically well-informed, though some were still influenced by current issues, as was evident from the end-of-the year *Reports to the Faculty* for both 1991 and 1992. It became apparent that the Senate was clearly more professional and effective in addressing academic and faculty affairs. With the Academic Senate and Governance Committee in quasi-bicameral balance and with the Governance Committee limited to process and committee structural matters, the overall academic management had clearly matured.

Years of Administrative Consolidation

Frank and Olivia Filippi Hall, 1992
Brother Jerome West Hall, 1992

Frank and Olivia Filippi's first major gift to Saint Mary's College was discussed one evening in my suite in Augustine Hall, where I was at the time the Resident Director (as well as President) for 60 students, mostly sophomores. With the assistance of student Chuck Carter, I was Chef de jour for dinner. Frank, Olivia and Brother Jerome West, Vice President for Development, all arrived on time. I assigned Brother Jerome the task of libation bearer and pourer. During the course of a congenial repast Frank announced that he and Olivia had decided that they wanted to see a building on the St. Mary's campus bearing the Filippi name during their lifetimes. That joyfully welcome announcement was the genesis of embarking on plans for the Filippi Hall Administration Building, now proudly standing at the entry to the campus. Groundbreaking for both the Frank J. and Olivia C. Filippi, and Brother Jerome West Halls was a modest event, accomplished with decorum on June 8, 1990. I have served Steak Diane to potential benefactors ever since, hoping for a similar result.

After being suggested for membership on the Board by Fred Ferroggiaro, Frank served on the Board of Regents from 1980 to 1995. The law offices of Filippi and Mullen dealt mainly with Workers' Compensation Claims and Insurance matters. William. T. Mullen died in 1967 leaving Frank as CEO of a firm of 90 attorneys with several offices in Northern California. Being of Italian descent, Frank lived modestly with his wife Olivia, investing his dividends from the firm in securities and real estate from San Francisco to San Jose. They had no children.

On April 29, 1985, Frank asked to meet with me, College Counsel, John W. Broad, Brother Jerome, Brother Norman Cook, the then Provincial and Brother Gary York. We gathered for a congenial and tasty lunch in the President's Dining Room. Following the luncheon, Frank told us that he and Olivia had agreed that the bulk of the Filippi Estate would be bequeathed to the College, since Frank believed that he could have a greater impact at Saint Mary's than anywhere else. His fist pounded the table like a judge's gavel as he declared, "And that will not change!" As it turned out, to the surprise of all of us, the bequest of Frank and Olivia was the *single largest gift in College history* up to that time. Frank was made an Affiliated Member of the Christian Brothers in 1994 in a special ceremony in the Saint Mary's Chapel. I was named the Executor and Fred Weil, JD, who became College counsel when John Broad retired, the attorney.

Olivia died in March 1993 after a long illness. Frank lived until August 2001, though his last years became increasingly difficult for him.

The Board of Trustees, 1989-1993

At the outset of the first meeting of the 1989-1990 academic year (Oct. 10, 1989), Board Finance Committee Chair Elaine McKeon announced to the Board of Trustees that $850,000 had been transferred from the operating budget of 1988-1989 to the Reserve Fund. A spirit of optimism permeated the Board meeting, as it was announced that the Y. Charles and Helen Soda Center was completed and in full use and, the Silvio Garaventa Soccer Field and the Patrick Vincent Rugby Field were nearing completion along with the Timothy Korth Tennis Courts. I stated that plans were nearing completion for a high-tech classroom building (Garaventa Hall) and the two adminis-tration facilities (Frank J. and Olivia L. Filippi Hall and Brother Jerome West Hall). The Executive Director for Development, Michael Ferrigno, then an-nounced to the Board that the Capital Campaign, Chaired by Trustee Ray-mond O'Brien, was clearly on the road to achieving its projected five-year goal of $33.5 million by June 30, 1991, a year ahead of initial projections. Board members euphorically expressed their astonishment and immediately discussed whether the goal should be increased as the Campaign entered its fifth year, with the option of extending the Campaign to achieve a revised goal. As the first meeting of the year evolved, the Trustees authorized me to engage the architects in developing drawings for the renovation of the two arcade wings on either side of the Chapel and for a student health and recreation center as well as the design of additional campus parking and a right-turn lane at the entry to the campus.

I somewhat dampened the euphoria by presenting the Trustees with a list of 20 items from landscaping, renovation and computers to faculty salaries and library acquisitions that required attention, some sooner than later. Faculty representative Brother Raphael Patton added the need for an astronomical observatory to the list. Eight days after the Board Meeting, on Oct. 18, 1989, the Loma Prieta Earthquake struck the Bay Area at 5:04 p.m., damaging the library, the McKeon Pavilion and the Chapel, including the statue of St. John the Baptist, which was beheaded (again!) as the statue fell to the sanctuary floor. All of the full-length first-floor windows in the library were shattered, lighting fixtures had fallen, some furniture and computers were ruined, and hardly a book remained on the shelves. One student, an international stu-dent from Jerusalem, was injured when shattered plate glass from the library entrance door fell on his arm as he hurriedly exited the building. Many students were attending the World Series in Candlestick Park, but most were in the dining hall where there was considerable rocking and rolling, without the music, but little damage. The Board surveyed the damage at its January meeting. With the exception of the Chapel, for reasons of separation of church and state, FEMA covered most of the necessary repairs, totaling some $400,000, including the installation of several sheer walls on the library arcades and reinforcements to the foundations under the Chapel floor.

In May 1990, the Board recommended that the College return to the standard academic system of two 17-week semesters, each with 15 weeks of instruction, one week of examinations and one week of holidays for each semester. The Board also recommended that faculty teach 21-22 Carnegie units per academic year with a target of a student to faculty ratio of 16-to-1. These recommendations were subsequently debated among faculty, students and administration for approximately a year, after which the Trustees were presented with several difficulties encountered during the energetic debates.

By October 1990, the Board was pleased to learn that Moody's Investor Service had assigned an "A" rating to the $18 million California Educational Facilities Act Bond granted to the College, thus assuring lower interest rates for the construction of the Frank J. and Olivia C. Filippi and Brother Jerome West Halls.

Considerable discussion in October 1990 and January 1991, revisited the recommendation by the Board to eliminate the January Term, reduce the faculty teaching load and return to the two semester calendar. Student officers representing all four class levels presented statistics on student attitudes toward the January Term that were overwhelmingly positive. Remarks noted that the return to the two-semester calendar with a reduced faculty load would create financial burdens on students, and thus any change should be made over several years. The Board quickly realized that such a change should be considered more carefully with all implications clearly in mind.

Vice President for Business and Finance Alan Holloway resigned as of June 30, 1993, and Raymond J. White, PhD, Vice President for Research and Planning was named in his place with a new title: Vice President for Administration and Chief Financial Officer.

In June 1993, the Board approved the completion of working drawings for the renovation of the facilities on one side of the Chapel arcade and approved the upgrading of electrical service for the Campus as a whole in light of the need for service as the Campus Master Plan was fulfilled.

The Administrative Council, 1991-1993

In the fall and spring semesters of academic year 1991-1992, the Administrative Council was composed of Vice-Presidents William J. Hynes, Academic; Alan Holloway, Financial; Brother Jerome West, Advancement; William McLeod, Student Services; and Raymond White, Research and Planning.

The Council discussed a number of items that paralleled the Academic Senate, but often did so from a perspective that recalled the experience of the College in debt, both after 1929 and in the late '60s and early '70s. The Council clearly understood the intrinsic need for a reasoned, balanced approach to certain critical issues based primarily on principles relating to the liberal arts, Catholic and Lasallian mission of the College. The Papal document, *Ex Corde Ecclesiae* (From the Heart of the Church), had been issued to Catholic institutions worldwide. The first part of the document was well-crafted and even inspiring in celebrating a university as a community of scholars in light of the Catholic dedication to developing the relationship between reason and faith. The second part of the document, the implementation, created considerable controversy within Catholic higher education, not only in the United States, but in other parts of the world as well.

Diversity discussions within the Administrative Council consumed considerable time. The issue carried some degree of state and national urgency. A few of the more outspoken college and university presidents in California expressed their concern with vigor that more must be done for including California minority students in the higher educational community. Their major arguments were not without foundation, and the need for minority students to secure higher education was supported by considerable data. The presidents, and most notably the President of the Claremont Graduate School (later renamed Claremont University), John D. Maguire, PhD, did not have difficulty in urging the placement of the diversity issue on the agendas of annual meetings of such organizations as the Western Association of Schools and Colleges, which encompasses both public and independent institutions, and the Association of Independent Colleges and Universities. For several years WASC exerted considerable pressure on institutions during official accreditation visits in view of the need for including a greater number of minority students among the student bodies of both public and independent California schools. At times the pressure was applied unexpectedly, as was the case with the Accreditation Visits of November 1989 and spring 1993. While both the College Administrative Council and I were committed to increasing diversity among the student body in view of the Catholic and Lasallian principles enunciated in the College Mission Statement, there were financial limits in doing so.

The College had commissioned Thomas Brown, Dean for Special Programs, to recruit foreign students by traveling to Asia and other areas of the world. He did so with significant success. Council discussion on requests for increased recruiting efforts for international students turned up with divided opinion. One member opined that given the great need domestically, the College should concentrate on domestic students, and while not discouraging international students from applying, it should focus on national societal needs. Financial aid was not normally granted to foreign students. Another comment was made that the supposed desirability of international students enriching the institution may be over-emphasized in that international students come to American institutions because they offer both American intellectual and cultural values and opportunities that international students find attractive. Thus, international students are just as much learners as their American counterparts, and their academic acuity on average is not much different from that of contemporary American students. Daunting difficulties do arise, however, when certain students are not sufficiently in command of English. What international students can offer best is good example, if they are serious students themselves. Such example will earn them respect and contribute to the intellectual quality of the College. If there are enough from one country, such as Mexico or the Philippines, such a group could present aspects of their cultural traditions for the appreciation, understanding, and entertainment of all students.

The discussion also included the consideration of transfer students from other four-year colleges and from two-year community colleges. A transfer from another four-year institution is usually accomplished without much difficulty, if most courses taken fit the normal requirements of the College and the Grade Point Average (GPA) is equivalent to a student in good standing at Saint Mary's. Difficulties occasionally arose from transfer students from certain community colleges. In many cases a minimum Grade Point Average of "C" was not sufficient to predict success at Saint Mary's, based on past experience with grading at certain institutions, and thus a higher GPA was required in transferable courses, especially if the potential transfer student was not eligible at the end of his high school career.

Successful efforts had been made to recruit honor students from high schools, especially those conducted by the Christian Brothers. Both the Administrative Council and I deemed such activity as critical to the academic enthusiasm and ultimate quality of the College. The Council recommended a continuance of such a recruiting program, especially since both myself and the Academic Vice President were intimately involved.

Brother Jerome West, who had been the Vice President of Advancement since 1968, had reached his 71st year in 1989 and expressed his desire to step down from that demanding post. Plans were laid to begin searching for a replacement, with the hope of having a new Vice President for Advancement in place by the second semester of academic year 1991-1992. Brother Jerome would then be appointed Vice President for College Relations, with Trustee approval, and continue as a member of the Administrative Council. He would continue to foster relations with Alumni, donors and members of the Boards of Trustees and Regents, but he would serve at the pleasure of the new Vice President and be relieved of his former administrative responsibilities.

Brother Jerome stepped down as Vice President of Advancement in February 1992, having been replaced by Marianne Briscoe, a seasoned development officer with considerable background. In less than two years, however, it became evident that his replacement was not able to continue at Saint Mary's, and Brother Jerome was asked to resume his former post as Vice President for Advancement until another appointment could be made. Michael Ferrigno, who had been Director of Development and was in the process of completing the Capital Campaign, was selected as Vice President for Advancement in 1994. After the appointment of Mike Ferrigno, Brother Jerome reverted to his recent appointment as Vice President for College Relations. By 1996, Brother Jerome became cognizant of his increasing difficulty in recalling names and facts and in following dialogue during Council meetings. Yet he remained a positive asset in his relationships with Trustees, Regents and Alumni until such time as he could no longer contribute with his usual incisiveness, charm and vivacity. He retired to the Christian Brothers Retirement Community in Napa in 2000 and died of a brain tumor on Dec. 1, 2002, at age 84.

The Administrative Council in 1995 included Academic Vice President William Hynes; Vice President for Advancement (the au courant name for Development) Michael Ferrigno; Vice President, Student Affairs William McLeod; Vice President for Administration and Chief Financial Officer Raymond White; Vice President for College Relations Brother Jerome West; and Assistant Vice President for Research, Planning and Technology Michael Beseda.

Achitectural drawings were in various stages of completion for a new, high-tech classroom facility, the renovation of buildings on either side of the Chapel, facilities for the Communications Department and an addition to the library. Serious thought was being devoted to finding donors, perhaps through another capital campaign, for the construction of such facilities,

In light of Council discussions on diversity during the previous year, Vice President William Hynes sought funds from the James Irvine Foundation to support diversity initiatives, such as special recruiters and a program for developing minority teachers and scholars. Likewise, to increase the number in the *High Potential Program,* that enrolls students with potential and provides them with special study and guidance; and to review the curriculum to assure that minority history, literature and other elements of the curriculum are not excluded from a comprehensive academic view in a shrinking world. "The more we appreciate diversity, the more we glimpse God's creative plan," one Council member noted.

Since the Town of Moraga had attempted to attach a costly developer's or User Fee to the construction of new residence facilities for students, a lengthy discussion addressed the value of establishing more congenial ties with the local community. A more friendly relationship, the Council opined, may obviate the attitudes of some to look upon the College as a source of Town revenue, or the students as out-of-towners. A number of public-relations efforts were suggested, as well as proposals to offer events that would encourage community participation, such as a *Moraga Day on Campus.* Both faculty and students could be enlisted in various community-relations projects. Local churches, such as the Lutheran, Presbyterian and the Orthodox, could be invited to utilize the Soda Center for annual events. Many in the Moraga community were unaware of either College offerings or the welcoming spirit of the campus, and even though it is in their midst do not feel that they are indeed welcome.

The insistence by the Accreditation Association for assessment was also discussed, since the Association would appear on campus for its official Visit in February 1993 and would undoubtedly exert pressure for initiating research on student assessment. The Council expressed concern regarding preparation for the Accreditation Visit in addressing the assessment issue when the Accreditation Visiting Team arrived. The Council also found the National Collegiate Athletic Association proposals on division classification troublesome. A number of larger institutions with major football interests were attempting to pressure the NCAA membership to reclassify institutions with major basketball programs, but without major football programs, out of competition with institutions with major football programs, especially in view of national television exposure and revenues in Division 1 basketball. Presidents of many Division 1 basketball institutions, that didn't have Division 1 football programs were appalled by the attempt of some institutions with major football programs to exclude institutions or conferences with quality basketball programs from competition at the highest levels. The major argument offered by the football powers was that the competition would be unfair if smaller Division 1 institutions without major football expenses were thus able to divert greater funding toward basketball.

The Accreditation Visit of 1993 — A Mixed and Mixed Up Review

From the outset, the preparation for the Accreditation Visit of Feb. 16-19, 1993, followed the normal procedures. A steering committee was formed, and the preparatory work was divided among the committee membership. Numerous meetings were conducted for the sole purpose of analyzing the state of the College and compiling both strengths and weaknesses of the institution under various headings or standards as determined by the WASC Accreditating Commission. Reactions to criticism of earlier accreditation procedures -- that were directed to an analysis of structural, procedural and academic statistical data rather than to the nature and effectiveness of the educational program -- prompted the Commission to adopt what in fact was a more scientific approach to scrutinizing the academic mission, curriculum integrity, academic standards, and the effectiveness of methodology through a measurement of educational outcomes by means of assessment.

The more scientific approach by the Commission and Visiting Teams is reflected in the Visiting Team Report of 1993, with some thoughtful reservations. Questions were raised, for example, as to the meaning and measure of assessment and the methods employed to achieve them. This is not to say that statistical data is unimportant, as noted in the criticism of the Visiting Team that "in spite of the College's dedication to liberal arts and its pride in its Collegiate Seminar Program as a unique aspect of its liberal arts tradition, the team was surprised to find that 57 percent of the courses taught in the Collegiate Seminar program during fall 1992 were taught by part-time faculty." (*Visiting Team Report*, page 41) While this criticism did prompt changes in some faculty appointments, it neglected to note that in the San Francisco Bay Area, with its preponderance of institutions of higher education and a high-tech and corporate workforce, there are a significant number of highly qualified individuals who are available and willing to serve as part-time instructors. The criticism that "60 percent of the graduate business courses are taught by part-time faculty, a situation that could be remedied by an increase in full-time appointments," (*Visiting Team Report*, 1993, page 42), also neglected to note that some of the College part-time business instructors are members, some full-time, of nearby prestigious business faculties. Furthermore, it should be noted that highly experienced leaders in quality business enterprises were also academically qualified to be faculty members, a benefit to higher education in the intellectually vibrant San Francisco Bay Area. Academically qualified and highly experienced business leaders are considered by many critics of higher education to be essential to an insightful MBA program, if even on a part-time basis.

A commendation of the School of Extended Education noted that a "carefully designed sequence of courses is scheduled to fit the full-time professional and personal commitments of students. Sixteen months of weekly four-hour seminars combining instruction intensity and cohort collaboration result in theoretical and practical learning that will long endure after graduation ... Assessment in the School of Extended Education is thoughtful and well integrated, and could well serve as a model for the institution." (Op., Cit., page 44)

While the 1993 evaluations by the Visiting Team were both numerous and in the aggregate costly, the Team did draw heavily upon the institutional self-study, as well as its own interviews, to develop its recommendations. Many recommendations were thoughtful and desirable, and most were not surprising. The College was still growing and attempting to address its essential needs, as it matured into a more distinctive academic enterprise. The imperative for financial operating stability -- while at the same time addressing the need for competitive salaries for administration, faculty and staff, the improvement of academic services, financial aid, technological advances, maintenance, student residence and recreational needs as well as the improvement of opportunities for faculty research, -- was a juggling act that required stringent control and decisions that undoubtedly did not satisfy everyone.

There were two areas that the Visiting Team Report cited that were a cause for chagrin. One of those criticisms focused on the Board of Trustees and the role of the Christian Brothers in the oversight of the College. As noted earlier, the Governing Board is divided into two sections, a *Corporation* and the *Board of Trustees*. The *Corporation* has certain limited, but significant duties and the *Board of Trustees* is entrusted with the general overall management of the College. The *Corporation* is composed of 15 Christian Brothers, 10 from the College administration or faculty and five from institutions outside of the College. The *Corporation* may dissolve the bylaws and create new ones, and must agree to amendments to the bylaws and to a dissolution or merger of the corporation that is Saint Mary's College. The Accreditation Report claimed that the membership of the *Corporation* "places them in conflict with the intent of WASC Standard 3, since that Standard requires that the *Board of Trustees* not include predominant representation by the employees of the institution, and that Standard 3.A.12, requires that the board have a policy precluding participation by any of its members in actions involving possible conflict of interest …" (*Visiting Team Report*, Pages 31-39)

The Christian Brothers are the sponsoring religious body and are not considered employees of the institution. As the sponsoring religious body, it is their preeminent role to safeguard the apostolic, that is, both the evangelization and intellectual aspects of the mission of the College as expected by the Church. As for the Board of Trustees, the regular managers of the College, there have been Christian Brothers from the Province, from the faculty and from other Christian Brothers institutions and provinces as members. There are strong reasons why Christian Brothers on the faculty may be members of the Board of Trustees, for the same reasons as cited for the Corporation. The presence of Christian Brothers faculty from the College on the Board of Trustees clearly keeps the Trustees in close contact with the culture and mission of the College, a point that is often overlooked but is critical to keeping Trustees in touch with the realities of the enterprise.

A few Brothers on the Board of Trustees are in a pivotal position to safeguard the religious mission of the College, to communicate to the other Christian Brothers on the faculty and to support the President when necessity so requires. What could be the so-called conflict of interest? Since the Brothers do not receive a salary and are there to assure that the mission of the institution is fulfilled, what possible benefit would a Christian Brother receive that would constitute a conflict of interest? *The Christian Brothers Community is the sponsor of the institution not its beneficiary.*

The Accreditation Report was also critical of the role of the Provincial in appointing the president. (*Visiting Team Report*, pages 32-34) Though the Board now screens possible candidates for the presidency and submits its recommendation to the Provincial, it is possible for religious and perhaps other grave reasons for the Provincial to act otherwise than the Board recommends, though such is most probably unlikely. In these times, it would be appropriate for the Provincial to discuss his reasons for his refusal to appoint the recommended candidate with the Board. If in the future a recommended candidate for President were not a Christian Brother, a change in the role of the Provincial in the appointment of the President may change, yet for apostolic reasons, it may not.

A lengthy section of the *Report on Diversity* (Pages 84-99) was particularly disconcerting, since it extended beyond the role of the Accreditation

Commission by delving into social engineering. The Accreditation Team had been provided with an extensive checklist of items by the Accreditation Commission and its Executive Director to measure so-called appropriate diversity in an institution. The College administration did not receive the checklist in advance, rather, a copy was given to me toward the end of the Visit by a member of the faculty who received one from a Visiting Team member. The Diversity section of the *Visiting Team Report* is a list of admonitions, recommended correctives and anecdotal evidence, made without regard for financial stability, the worthy efforts that had been made to increase diversity and establish programs, or a sensitivity toward the preponderance of faculty and staff who conducted their classes and normal functions with respect for all. In reading the report it becomes clear that the Visiting Team and its Chair, Kent M. Keith, then President of Chaminade University in Honolulu, Hawaii, appeared as social crusaders, seemingly with the encouragement of the WASC Executive Director and the Commission. The Report cast the Team as a regulatory governing body intent on imposing its social agenda on the governance, mission and academic purposes of the College as soon as possible, regardless of the cost, time or difficulties, for example, of finding minority faculty and personnel whose profile fit the Liberal Arts, Catholic and Lasallian Mission of the College, especially a candidate's familiarity with the Catholic intellectual tradition. Likewise, it ignored the difficulties of recruiting certain minority students from a limited pool of college-eligible candidates. The Report emphasizes social goals, celebrating cultural differences and the mistaken notion that academic quality and diversity are inextricably and necessarily linked. It ignores the principle that cultivating minority student interest in the intellectual life is a process that proposes to liberate all students from ignorance and prejudice and provide each, regardless of culture, ethnic or gender differences, with intellectual skills and insights based on the commonality and unity of humankind. This universal process, the Administrative Council observed, should assume first place in a liberal arts institution.

In spite of the disturbing elements of the Accreditation *Visiting Team Report*, the Accreditation of the College was reaffirmed with an interim visit, scheduled for the spring of 1997, to review diversity, assessment and governance. I was invited to participate on a WASC panel as a basis for discussion on diversity among WASC institutions that was to take place in November 1993 in San Francisco. The 1997 interim visit was later postponed.

The WASC Panel on Diversity

Following the spring 1993 Accreditation Visit, a regular meeting of representatives of WASC institutions was scheduled for Nov. 5, 1993 at the San Francisco Holiday Inn near Chinatown. I was invited to be one of four panelists to address the members of the Association. The topic was the *Draft Policy on Diversity* as proposed by Executive Director Steve Weiner and the WASC Accreditation Associating Commission for Schools.

Seated among the regular academicians who attend such meetings was an unusual group of attendees (estimated to be approximately half of the attendance) that eventually proved to be mostly gay. The unusual attendees and the opening statement initiated a contentious discussion on the principle of egalitarianism with ethnic, racial and gender diversity. However, it soon became clear that the presence of the gay group was an attempt to link the concept of egalitarianism in diversity to the assumption that academic quality would be diminished or compromised unless there existed widespread diversity in any academic institution. The link was an unwarranted assumption.

The four panelists, one of whom declared himself to be a gay man at the outset, as if that mattered, spoke first. The four speakers were then followed by numerous interventions from the audience, who spoke, some vigorously, in support of the inclusiveness of gays and lesbians in the definition of diversity in higher education in the WASC region. Many member institutional representatives in the audience and especially several from Biblically-based Protestant-sponsored institutions were affronted by the monologues, interchange and some insulting remarks that transpired.

In my 11-minute address as a panelist, I stated, among other items, that "linking diversity with quality provides the Accrediting Commission with the justification it could use for judging an institution's educational quality in light of racial, ethnic and gender diversity." To make such a dubious linkage between intellectual or academic quality and diversity with such dogmatic emphasis was, in my view, truly reaching. There are many famous institutions that produced quality graduates with little diversity in enrollment. I cited Oxford and Cambridge, and La Salle (Christian Brothers) Universities in Mexico and the Philippines as examples. If quality is linked with anything, it is linked with the way an institution seeks the truth, be it scientific-mathematical, philosophical, theological, moral, political, and so forth." Most representatives from higher education left the meeting somewhat uneasy and wondering what principles the Executive Director anticipated inserting into a WASC policy document on diversity and its link to academic quality. Other institutions (a number of them public) also objected strongly to the proposed linkage between academic quality and diversity, and within a short time the WASC Executive Director found himself the focus of a growing controversy. A new Executive Director, Ralph Wolff, was appointed shortly thereafter.

Hope in the Future

The New Century Committee, 1993-1995

In considering the success of the Capital Campaign of 1984-1991, the various needs the College faced and its aspirations for the future, the Administrative Council began discussions on the development of an overview document similar to the *Institutional Planning Group Report* that guided the capital campaign. (Administrative Council Notes, Dec. 11, 1992.) As Brother Jerome observed, the new committee would be different from the Institutional Planning Group, since the IPG had a somewhat different focus. A new planning committee would first concentrate on rewriting the Mission Statement, the intention of which would impact every facet of the College. With the year 2000 not far off, I considered the advent of the new century and millennium an advantageous time to reexamine the College Mission Statement, since it would sharpen the focus of the entire College on its commitment to its liberal arts, Catholic and Lasallian characteristics. A new edition of the Mission Statement would also include all programs instituted since 1975, and the next broad step would be to investigate how it would effectively inform each of the Schools, departments and activities of the College. The name of the committee, the *New Century Committee,* and its potential participants evolved during the 1993 spring semester.

The Administrative Council participated in suggesting membership for the Committee drawn from the Boards of Trustees and Regents, administration, faculty, staff, alumni, Christian Brothers communities and students. A total of 31 members responded to the invitation to participate. Arthur Latno, former Vice President of Pacific Telesis, former U. S. Ambassador-at-large during the Reagan Administration, and former Chairman of the Board of Trustees, agreed to chair the *New Century Committee.*

In my 1993 address to the faculty at the beginning of the 1993-1994 academic year, I stated that "The major project on the administrative agenda ... will be the work of the *New Century Committee*. It seems that the time has come to specify our mission with more clarity. While we state that the fundamental characteristics of the College are liberal arts, Catholic and Lasallian, and we have conducted a number of colloquia over the years on these topics, we still find that the meaning and implementation of these characteristics are not fully clear or that sufficient agreement is not fully in evidence." At the same time, I also cited a number of quotations from the papal document, *Ex*

Corde Ecclesiae, that His Holiness John Paul II considered appropriate for a Catholic institution of higher learning, such as, "A Catholic university pursues its objective through its formation of an authentic human community animated by the spirit of Christ ... As a result of this inspiration the community is animated by a spirit of freedom and charity; it is characterized by mutual respect, sincere dialogue and protection of the rights of individuals." (Address of Brother Mel Anderson to the faculty, Sept. 10, 1993.)

Preliminary reading material that was sent to the members of the Committee consisted of the letter reaffirming Accreditation (1993), statements from various institutions such as the University of Notre Dame, (*Notre Dame Magazine,* Fall 1993); Boston College, *The Challenge,* an article by Michael Buckley, SJ (Boston College Magazine, August 1993); and articles such as *Catholic Higher Education: Worth Supporting?* by Edwin Fussell, (New Oxford Review, September 1993); *Authority and the Academy, Reflections on Ex Corde Ecclesiae* by Robert F. Sasseen, President of the University of Dallas (FCS Newsletter, June 1993); *Catholic Higher Education: What Happened?* by Kenneth Woodward (Commonweal, April 9, 1993); *Can Higher Education Foster Moral Development?* by James Heft, SM, of Marist University, Dayton, Ohio (Origins, Jan. 28, 1993) and many others. A translated copy of the Papal Encyclical, *Ex Corde Ecclesiae,* and a compendium of articles reacting to *Ex Corde Ecclesiae,* entitled *Challenge and Promise* edited by Rev. Theodore M. Hesburgh, Notre Dame Press, were also provided to each member.

The following accepted Committee membership, with my gratitude and that of the Council: From the Board of Trustees: Arthur Latno, Chairman; and Bernie Orsi; the Board of Regents: LaRoy Doss; Thomas O'Donnell, JD; Elaine McKeon; the Alumni Association: Sherie Dodsworth; Ernest Pierucci, JD; the Administration: Raymond White, PhD; William Hynes, PhD, Academic Vice President; Dean Fannie Preston, PhD; Michael Beseda; Ron Olowin, PhD; the Faculty: John Thompson, MBA; Sandra Hellman, PhD; Clark Moscrip, JD; James Temple, PhD; Kathy Roper, PhD; Carole Swain, PhD; Steve Cortright, MA; Daniel Cawthon, PhD; the Christian Brothers: Brother Willilam Beatie, FSC, PhD; Brother Kenneth Cardwell, FSC, PhD; Brother Stanislaus Sobczyk, FSC, PhD; Brother Gary York, FSC, MA; the Staff: Personnel Director Barbara Nicholson; and Students: Carl Reed, K.C. Estenson, Mark D.Berger and Megan Wilson. Ex Officio: Brother Mel Anderson, FSC, President, and Brother Mark Murphy, FSC, Provincial.

Though some thought that *Catholic* should be listed first in the sequence of Liberal Arts, Catholic and Lasallian, since the truth of Revelation should be paramount, others thought that the institution should be an excellent academic enterprise leading toward truth on the premise that grace builds on nature. Furthermore, Catholicism should not be embarrassed by linking it with a second- or third-rate academic institution, no more than Catholic should be linked to a hospital that is inept at assisting patients. That the College be Catholic in its encompassing of all truth there was no quarrel within the Committee. Catholicism enhances the rational exploration of reality by pointing to realities that extend beyond natural wisdom. In her quest for the understanding of faith through theology, the Church has developed extraordinary intellectual traditions as reflected in her study of scripture, her extensive systematic theology, her discerning of moral distinctions, her spirituality and her evocative liturgical rites, all of which enrich, direct and enlighten the journey of life. Being Lasallian incorporates a Christian approach to the intellectual life and reinforces commitment to the dignity of the person, especially those in disadvantaged positions, since all students seek fulfillment as beings made in the image and likeness of God.

From the heart of the Church (*Ex Corde Ecclesiae*) arose the great centers of learning that spread throughout the world, because the Church has understood that the gift of intelligence should be cultivated in freedom, with the blessings of grace, to achieve both ultimate wisdom and self-direction of the heart. The Lasallian spirit of the Christian Brothers untiringly encourages each student to enhance the dignity that is his or hers in both mind and heart.

In my remarks to the faculty at the beginning of the 1994-1995 academic year, I expanded the notion that a major work, among others, of the *New Century Committee* was to address the College commitment to its Catholicism. "Some faculty may hold that secularization is the only course to follow if the College is to gain national recognition among reputable collegiate institutions. Such members may be embarrassed by the College relationship with a religious tradition, no matter how venerable and influential it might be, viewing a faith commitment as inappropriate for or even an impediment to evolving as a quality modern American college or university ... I hear reports that some faculty members will say things like, 'If only Saint Mary's could be like Reed, Claremont-McKenna, Wittenberg or Grinnell, wouldn't that be wonderful.' It is statements such as these that cause many, myself included, to wonder about how our traditions are understood, whether our reason for existence, our mission, has been clearly enunciated ..."

The recasting of the Mission Statement occupied over one year, more time than was anticipated, but it evolved into a well-turned basic document from which the future academic quality of the College, the guidance of revelation and theology, and the spirit of the Christian Brothers would flow. Professor

Dan Cawthon, a member of the Committee, added a touch of cohesive literary polish to a document written by a committee, and was designated the Committee spokesman to present the new Mission Statement to the Board of Trustees. He did so on June 7, 1995, indicating an 82 percent approval rate from the faculty. The Board accepted the document as written with gratitude. (Minutes, Board of Trustees, June 7, 1995.)

Sixteen subcommittees were identified and members named to examine the relationship between the Mission Statement and each of the diverse facets of the College. Subcommittee reports were in the process of development prior to the finalization of the Mission Statement, since its essence had sufficiently emerged in the minds of the membership. Each subcommittee developed a rationale based on the Mission Statement that guided the subcommittee in developing recommendations for the future. (Subcommittee Minutes, Dec. 15, 1995, Feb. 16, 1995, April 27, 1995 and May 11, 1995.)

The Papal document on higher education wisely supports the need for Catholic intellectuals and those appreciative of the Catholic intellectual tradition who will create the living environment of the Catholic higher educational institution. Thus, *Ex Corde Ecclesiae* states without equivocation that the majority of the faculty be representative of the Catholic intellectual tradition.

The *Highlights* section of the *New Century Report*, was composed by committee member Michael Beseda, at that time, Director of Enrollment Management, and scrutinized and approved by the Administrative Council. It provided a summary of the extensive efforts of the Report to "engage all members of the institution in comment and review of drafts." What follows is a summary of the highlights.
- The power and influence of the new Mission Statement is evident in the remarkable impact that the process of its creation has already had on the College community.
- The subcommittee reports reveal the profound effect of the preceding Mission Statement discussions.
- Each report makes a special effort to measure the unit or activity examined in terms of the College's Liberal Arts, Catholic and Lasallian character.
- Instead of using the familiar Liberal Arts College terminology, the new Mission Statement refers to Saint Mary's as an "institution where the liberal arts inform and enrich all areas of learning." This significant alternation reflects the evolution of the College over the past several years.

- The reports of the Schools of Economics and Business Administration, Extended Education, Science, Education and Liberal Arts all express their commitment to the Liberal Arts tradition and in varying ways raise the question of their role in it.
- The School of Science report suggests a designated core course in Science for all undergraduates.
- Historically the School of Liberal Arts has had a primary, but not exclusive responsibility to foster the liberal arts identity of the College. It is time for the School to reexamine its role given the broader conception of the scope of Liberal Arts as articulated in the Mission Statement.
- Several committee reports call for improvements in the core curriculum to insure that the College provides the level of Liberal Arts education to which it aspires.
- As noted in the report on Faculty, Saint Mary's must recruit and hire faculty members who are deeply committed to its view of the Liberal Arts (as well as the other characteristics of the College.)
- The visual and performing arts take rise from wonder at the nature of existence and the human person. They give wonder its form, make it intelligible and affirm its essential beauty,
- Economies of scale suggest that in order to remain competitive with similar independent institutions of higher education, the College must plan for moderate growth over the next decade.
- The Mission Statement presents an eloquent, challenging and provocative description of the relations between the academic and religious faces of Saint Mary's as it strives to live up to its Catholic nature: the College understands the intellectual and spiritual journeys of the human person to be inextricably linked.
- The subcommittee on faculty states that the College should continue to improve the way it actively recruits excellent academically qualified faculty who are dedicated to the Catholic, Lasallian, and Liberal Arts character of the College.
- The report on the School of Economics and Business Administration examined ways in which the School could make the Catholic tradition manifest in its activities and noted the necessity of recognizing the ethical, social, spiritual and temporal implications of this tradition in its curriculum and courses.
- The passionate discussion concerning the Catholic nature of the College within the *New Century Committee* and with members of the Saint Mary's community concerning drafts of the Mission Statement showed that spirited dialogue between faith and reason has characterized and continues to characterize the College's intellectual community.

- The report on Student Affairs noted that residence hall regulations be reviewed for their propriety and effectiveness in view of promoting both the Catholic and Lasallian spirit on campus.
- The importance of recruiting and hiring staff and faculty members who are either committed to or open to the student-centered Lasallian philosophy is emphasized in several subcommittee reports.
- The appointment of one individual or group responsible for the coordination and support of efforts to enhance the Lasallian character of the College is recommended.
- The work of the *New Century Committee* clearly shows that Saint Mary's is blessed in having three remarkably rich intellectual and spiritual traditions from which to draw, the Liberal Arts, Catholic and Lasallian traditions. While restatements of fundamental animating traditions often fall into nostalgic fixations on the past, the *New Century Committee* looks ahead and describes the College's fundamental traditions as dynamic forces capable of ensuring a promising future ... It is to this future, in which the College more fully realizes its commitment to the Liberal Arts, Catholic and Lasallian traditions, that the work of the *New Century Committee* is directed.

As many involved themselves in developing the aspirations of the *New Century Committee*, a sense of optimism seemed to permeate the spirit of the College. There was much to satisfy administrators, faculty, alumni, Regents and Trustees, but there was also much to reach for in terms of progress, especially in the area of core curriculum development, a widespread understanding of both our Catholic and Lasallian commitment within the entire College community, and the unswerving march into the technological age. The more difficult issues, such as cultivating the necessary elements for developing a *diverse but unified* intellectual community as envisioned by *Ex Corde Ecclesiae*, required thoughtful consideration in exercising sometimes subtle and at other times compelling initiatives to assure the full implementation of the Mission Statement.

Being a Catholic Institution of Higher Education

By the beginning of academic year 1996-1997, I was in my last year in office. In light of the final report of the *New Century Committee* presented to the Board of Trustees on Nov. 1, 1995, I reflected on the work of the Committee and challenged the faculty to consider seriously the implications of the Mission Statement, especially its Catholic commitment. "There are," I said, "a number of concerns which surface as a result of our stating that we are a Catholic institution of higher education, an institution which is striving to become an outstanding collegiate institution by honoring theology, by seeking a metaphysics which brings cohesiveness to the curriculum in its search for truth, by the understanding and exercise of academic freedom, by being an institution that is fully alive to contemporary world progress as well as its difficulties, and which understands that its commitment as a Catholic institution by fostering the promotion of dialogue between faith and reason, 'so that it can be seen more profoundly how faith and reason bear harmonious witness to the unity of all truth' (*Ex Corde Ecclesiae*) (Brother Mel Anderson, Address to Faculty, Sept. 6, 1996.)

The Academic Senate, 1992-1997

Historian Brother Ronald Isetti was elected to Chair the Senate for the 1992-1993 academic year. Subsequent Chairs were Education Professor Gerald Brunetti, 1993-1994; History Professor Katherine Roper 1994-1995; History Professor Ronald Isetti 1995-1996; and Economics Professor Ted Tsukahara, 1996-1997.

The many issues brought to the Senate soon required full attention, and senators responded as faculty are wont to do with well-crafted studies and reports. The WASC Visiting Team of 1993 noted that: "The Academic Senate has been established, and is becoming an effective body. A number of policy issues have been passed and approved by the Academic Vice President." (*WASC Visiting Team Report*, Feb. 1993.) Concerns over frequent requests by both faculty and students for full access to technological advances required not only the efforts of faculty committees, but also administrative appointments and a Board of Trustees professional assessment and consequent funding. Misunderstandings prompted a few seemingly intemperate comments regarding the relationship between the Academic Senate and the Governance Committee.

While tension between the Senate and the Governance Committee was partly due to misunderstanding and some headiness, it was also due to a deep-seated desire on the part of other senators, to conduct its business entirely under its own rules. I saw my fundamental role as participating in overall College governance, and in the case of the faculty, I saw academic governance as a working relationship between myself and a qualified, elected faculty committee charged with governance structure. I believed that, once the structure was established, various committees, councils and the Senate would determine policy within their respective responsibilities. The Senate would address academic policy in conjunction with the Academic Council, the Curriculum Committee and the Academic Vice President, though it was understood that the President ultimately held veto power. Veto power was used sparingly by me and only after thoughtful interchange with the Senate and the Vice President and his Council. I did not think that it was wise for the Senate to determine all of its own rules, given the hubris of a few senators who saw the Senate, and their role in it, as the dominant force in the College, even in some matters beyond the academic. The time required by the Governance Committee to conduct its work convinced me that the Senate would have more than enough to do without assuming governance as well. However, several senators found difficulty with what they termed "parallel committees." Discussions between both Senate and Governance Committee representatives were conducted so that distinctions in the tasks of each could be clarified, and efficiencies without haggling would result. The discussions seemed to resolve difficulties, at least for the time being.

Another issue, perhaps more symbolic than crucial, was whether the Academic Vice President or a faculty member should chair the Rank and Tenure Committee. The Academic Vice President normally chaired that committee and made use of his overview and secretarial resources to organize and often compose extensive paperwork in a timely manner. Debate on the issue was heard from time to time for over a year and ended in January, 1994, with the motion that a faculty member chair the Rank and Tenure Committee being soundly defeated 13-0.

Time was allotted in several Academic Senate meetings in 1992 for developing a proposed academic calendar that included a reduction of faculty teaching load, a return to the standard two-semester system and shifting the remnants of the January Term to an optional end-of-the-academic-year three-week program, renamed a May Term or Maymester. The proposed change was to occur in the 1993-1994 academic year. At the end of several discussions with the Calendar Implementation Committee (at first named Blue-Ribbon Committee), I met with the Board of Trustees, which had mandated the change in the first place, to suggest that the Board mandate be deferred until the work of the *New Century Committee* could be completed, including the writing of a new Mission Statement and then recommending curricular changes. The curricular changes, I stated, "should drive the new calendar." (Minutes, Board of Trustees, Jan. 19, 1994.) Thus, for the time being the retention of the January Term, and the status quo of the calendar prevailed. It also became clear to me that some faculty were willing to reverse their previous vote in favor of retaining the 4-1-4 calendar with its January term because its elimination would reduce the seven-course teaching load to six. The six-course teaching load carried with it weighty economic considerations that needed thoughtful analysis. Thus, the six-course teaching load would become a matter for serious discussion in the near future. To change to the standard two-semester system would also require a major public relations effort, since the January Term had been proffered in advertising as an exciting rarity in higher education and a significant Saint Mary's offering. The desire to retain the 60-minute hour for a class would also confuse the return to the standard two-semester calendar and the reckoning of courses by the widely understood Carnegie units in higher education.

Other issues that came before the Senate were varied and legion, from the need for parking spaces to an improved campus bookstore, from the ineptitude of duplicating services to a law school proposal, from a Performing Arts Major and women's study minor to a Master's degree in Creative Writing, and from the inadequacies in the library to internationalizing the curriculum, whatever that meant! The Master's Degrees in Creative Writing, the Performing Arts Major and the Women's Studies minor (with serious reservations) were all approved. The Master of Arts in Creative Writing became a greater success than was first anticipated. The Performing Arts Major provided cohesion and stature to a program that deserved full recognition and peer approbation. The Women's Studies minor eventually grew, though not without controversy. There was anxiety among some that a minor would evolve into a major. While there are recognized differences between men and women, several faculty observed that the intellectual life, from anthropology to philosophy and theology, was the same for all human beings. The political or psychological concerns of the moment such as the often negative position of women in paternalistic societies or inequities in our own, even in the Church, should not prompt a morph into a major study, a kind of study that seemed more appropriate for graduate research, and especially not for a liberal arts undergraduate program. Some also thought that the assumptions that prompted the minor in Women's Studies should be examined with greater care, especially in view of the three-fold mission of the College. Some who opposed the Women's Studies minor advocated a more generic study of the human person that would include serious consideration of the human person in terms of the Judaic-Christian vision of human destiny and dignity as well as social justice.

The Senate also hammered out some impressive policy reports on promotion and tenure, faculty development and scholarship, and sabbatical and leave policies; a statement on academic freedom in a Catholic academic institution; policy on endowed chairs; a study on faculty rank and compensation and a proposal for requirements in language, lab science and mathematics for all students. It also produced reports on such matters as the College bookstore, an analysis on a proposal for undergraduate summer offerings, an evaluation process for academic administrators and expanded high school course requirements for admission.

The Academic Senate became a positive and essential element in the conduct of the academic life of an expanding and more complex collegiate enterprise. Its success depended on its working relationship with the Academic Vice President and the attitude of the President, who viewed the Senate as a crucial element in developing an authentic community of scholars.

Mary Candida Garaventa Hall, 1996

In the foyer of the elegantly designed Garaventa home in Concord, the inlaid marble inscription, *La Famiglia Garaventa*, announces the cohesiveness, spirit and taste that characterized the home of Silvio and Mary Garaventa. Silvio Garaventa, Sr., arrived in the United States as an Italian immigrant at age 15 and found work in San Francisco, as did a number of his compatriots, collecting trash. Not only was Silvio a man of energy and astute shrewdness, he was also a man of exceptional good taste. Embodied in his Italian genes and in the great European tradition of culture and refinement there was a profound love of opera, sculpture, painting and quality architecture. He and his beloved Mary Candida Garaventa, raised a family with an understanding that loyalty, high standards of conduct and an appreciation for beauty were intrinsic to leading good lives. He knew that Catholic education, from grammar school through college, something he was unable to enjoy fully himself, was essential for each of his children and grandchildren. In developing his own business, Concord Disposal, he insisted on creating a class act, based on integrity, quality and decorum. Sil was invited to join the Saint Mary's Board of Regents and graciously accepted. He was a soccer enthusiast and when asked to help with the installation of a soccer field, he funded the entire project. The Sil Garaventa, Sr., soccer field is to the left of the College entrance. While I was visiting the Garaventa family summer home in Palm Desset in 1994, Sil wore his chauffeur's hat as we toured celebrity homes in the area. In the course of our conversation, he stated that he would be willing to provide funding for the proposed classroom building. As we prepared plans for the new facility, I visited with Sil in his Concord offices and suggested that he consider naming the building in honor of his gracious wife, Mary. After speaking to his family, that is what he did. With appropriate solemnity, blessings, speeches, expressions of gratitude and a reception, the Mary Candida Garaventa Hall (a high-tech classroom facility) was dedicated on Oct. 10, 1996. After a short illness, Silvio was called to his eternal reward in February 1998 to the great sorrow of his family and friends. Saint Mary's and her students lost a man truly devoted to the importance of Catholic education.

Other donors to Garaventa Hall were the Wayne and Gladys Valley Foundation of Oakland, Calif. and John and Georgiana Warta of Portland, Ore.

The Board of Trustees, 1993-1997

The Board of Trustees had examined the existing 4-1-4 academic calendar and moved to return to the traditional two-semester calendar, a controversial move, but politically possible, since a number of faculty anticipated reducing the teaching load from seven courses per year to six. Upon considering the complications in such a move, it seemed that the timing proposed by the Trustees was perhaps too hastily considered. I was therefore caught in a dilemma between the urging of some Trustees and the difficulties that needed addressing before a movement to the two-semester system could be made. I requested a postponement that some Trustees found disconcerting. Though some Trustees did not favor postponement, the Board agreed to review the calendar issue at a later date.

Howard and Geri Korth had pledged $1 million for the remodeling of the office areas on either side of the Chapel. The Trustees' audit committee reported that the outside auditors, KPMG Peat Marwick, determined the College to be in a healthy financial condition, in view of its systematic maintenance program, particularly in the residence halls and a growing reserve fund. The Board authorized the development of plans for several academic and student services facilities.

Financial Vice President Alan Holloway announced his retirement, effective Dec. 31, 1992. Vice President Raymond White, PhD was appointed Vice President for Administration and Chief Financial Officer as of Jan. 1, 1993.

Giles Miller, MD., '54, President of the Board of Regents, proposed a plan to bring members of the Board of Regents into closer collaboration with the Board of Trustees by including members of the Regents on Trustee subcommittees. The Trustees approved the addition of members of the Regents on the Academic Affairs Committee and the Architectural Planning and Administration Committee. The plan was an attempt to provide the Board of Regents with an opportunity for greater involvement in substantive recommendations for consideration by the Trustees. It would also reveal Regents for potential membership on the Board of Trustees in the future.

By June 1993, gifts for 1992-1993 exceeded the previous year, and transfers to both the reserve emergency fund and the plant fund were made. With plans for new facilities already on the drawing boards, architect Kazuo Goto advised the Board that a costly electric supply upgrade would be required before any future buildings could be completed.

Brother Mark Murphy completed his unprecedented second term as chair, a total of four years, and Mary Ellen Cattani, JD, Senior Vice President and General Counsel for American President Companies, was named chair of the Board for the next two years (1993-1995.) Chair Cattani continued the semicorporate practice initiated by Brother Mark Murphy that an Executive Meeting be held following the regular meeting of the Board to allow only members of the Board to discuss and vote on all motions made during the regular meeting. Some members preferred these executive sessions, while others stated that they saw no reason for them and preferred the open discussions followed by a vote during the regular sessions, with the exception of personnel issues or financial matters specific donors deemed confidential.

In January 1994, I was again asked to discuss my reasons for requesting a postponement of the Board action on implementing the academic calendar change. My main objection to a change at the moment was that the curriculum should determine the calendar, and given that the New Century Committee had begun its work on a revised Mission Statement, I hoped to see what could be done with the calendar following a curriculum change inspired by the revised Mission Statement. In investigating the report from the Calendar Implementation Committee, it was clear that the faculty still thought in terms of courses rather than units and hoped to reduce its standard workload by one course, a serious financial consideration. The faculty mind-set was still working with the existing 4-1-4 course concept, that is, all courses would remain the same unit value instead of the standard practice of other institutions that offered various meeting times per week for different courses, thus allowing for more flexibility in instituting requirements and offering more variety in course offerings.

The Dean of Liberal Arts, Paul Zingg, was busy campaigning with the Implementation Committee for the existing 60-minute class hour that had become the Saint Mary's norm under the 4-1-4, as opposed to the standard 50-minute "hour" found in most other institutions using the Carnegie unit, a complication in implementing the two-semester calendar not anticipated by the Board. The sixty-minute class hour did not seem necessary in terms of the standard two-semester system. There was also a public relations problem in addressing the elimination of the January Term and substituting an optional, three-week May Term for an extra tuition cost that the Board also did not seem to have fully considered. Students had already started a movement to save the January Term and I was concerned with the effect dropping it might have upon prospective students and current student retention. I was not satisfied with the report of the Implementation Committee, since I saw no significant change in the curriculum and a continuation of the inflexibility that was inherent in the existing 4-1-4 calendar, without the attractiveness of the January Term, that so many students seemed to find appealing. I hoped that the New Century Committee would be able to inspire a change in curriculum, which would require the creation of a more flexible calendar without greatly increasing the academic budget by approximately 14.28 percent through a reduction of the normal faculty teaching load, a teaching load that had been slightly reduced when the 4-1-4 came into effect in 1969. Several discussions on the 1990 mandate by the Board followed, with a final discussion being held on Jan. 17, 1996. The result was to allow the New Century Committee to continue developing a curriculum with an appropriate calendar to follow. Thus, no specific action was taken, although some grumbling from a few Trustees was reported.

With my four-year appointment expiring in 1995, the Board was asked to evaluate my performance and submit its recommendation for reappointment or noreappointment to the Provincial. After conducting its research that included multiple interviews, the Board unanimously recommended that I be appointed to another four-year term, ending in June 1999. (Minutes, Board of Trustees, June 7, 1995.) I had earlier stated that, if approved, a 1995-1999 term would be my last.

Though the Trustees had recommended a regular four-year term, a short time after the Board meeting, the outgoing Provincial granted a two-year term for reasons neither clear nor discussed. Thus with only two years allowed before my retirement, changes in calendar or curriculum, the positioning of the January Term program or the enhancing of the Catholic intellectual tradition could not occur. A new administration, as is usually the case, developed its own agenda. However, following my retirement, the faculty, seizing the opportunity of the interregnum and supported by the Academic Vice President, was able to achieve a six-course teaching load (a reduction of 3.5 Carnegie units) on the premise that the faculty would have more time for research, writing and advising students. The reduction of the teaching load would obviously incur a significant increase in cost, since additional faculty would be required to fill the needs of the unchanged curriculum.

During the two years Mary Ellen Cattani, JD, served as chair, the Board moved forward with its usual optimism and progress. Concerns regarding residence hall fire safety and adequate parking were addressed, as were major capital expenditures for remodeling the wings on either side of the Chapel arcade and the construction of the new high-tech classroom facility, later to be named Mary Candida Garaventa Hall. The budget remained healthy, and controls were effective. Technology claimed considerable attention, and a special committee of the Board of Regents headed by Regents Russ Harrison (CEO of Three Net Systems) and Bill Jasper (CEO of Dolby Laboratories) outlined the requirements for providing the College with high-tech electronic capability. Their conclusion was that the College had to upgrade its technology in every academic facility and residence hall to remain competitive with other institutions as well as to provide all students with opportunities for full computer literacy and research capability. The plan included not only equipment but personnel to maintain equipment, install new software and to instruct students and staff on its use.

Brendan J.,"B.J.," Cassin was elected Chair of the Board to serve from 1995 to 1997. Brother Mark Murphy completed his term as Provincial and was replaced by Brother David Brennan, FSC, who then became an ex-officio member of the Board. Almost at the outset of his term as Provincial, he brought to the attention of the Board that plans had to be made in the near future to search for a new President who would be taking office on July 1, 1997.

During a budget discussion in November 1995, a question was posed by one member of the Trustees regarding whether the Vice President for Advancement could hire a consultant without Board approval, even though the consultant's fees appeared in the annual budget that is approved by the Board. Another questioned whether the President could approve a multiyear contract or project without approval. The only multiyear contracts were personnel contracts for coaches, vice presidents and selected administrators, and for faculty who received lifetime contracts with the awarding of tenure. Such contracts never required Board approval, though each was listed in the annual budget submitted to the Board for approval. Though little came of the discussion, it was curious that interest in approving multiyear contracts became a concern, unless someone had complained to a member of the Board that someone (a coach, vice president or dean) with such a contract was inept and was not being appropriately scrutinized by the President. Tenure decisions which only affected faculty were by policy the responsibility of the President, after receiving recommendations from both the Rank and Tenure Committee and the Academic Vice-President.

The Mission Statement developed by the New Century Committee was presented to the Trustees in November 1995.

Chairman B. J. Cassin proposed increasing the members on the Board of Trustees by three, making the total membership 18. Cassin was surprised to discover that such a proposal would be presented to the Board at one meeting and approved at the next, and that a substantive change in the bylaws would require the approval of the majority of the members of the Corporation. Approval of the Corporation members could be secured through phone contact, email or regular mail. Cassin's interest in expanding the Trustees was to secure the membership as soon as possible of an alumnus he believed would be a valuable asset to the Board of Trustees. The bylaws were revised after both Corporation and Trustee Members approved to expand the Board to 18 members. The revision was approved in October 1996.

During my last year as President (1996-1997), I was gratified to hear George Vukasin, Chairman of the Finance Committee, offer a commendation to me and my staff for the excellent financial results of the previous year. He noted that the $1 million assigned to the reserve fund brought the fund to two-thirds of its goal or $9.5 million. The goal was to maintain a reserve fund that could support the College for three operational months in case of an emergency, e.g., earthquake, fire or some other unforeseen catastrophe.

I requested that $250,000 be allocated from the Plant Fund to begin the restoration of the Chapel organ, and that $500,000 be allocated from the Chapel fund to renovate the Chapel. I also requested that an additional $297,000 received from foundations and donors for the renovation and landscaping of the courtyard in the front of the Chapel, including a statue of the founder of the Christian Brothers, Saint John Baptist De La Salle (a gift of the Soda Foundation), be approved. Since funding was available, the requests were granted.

In January 1997, I requested that two townhouse buildings in Ageno Park be designed, given the commitment of Ed Ageno to fund them. The cost would be approximately $5.6 million. Approval was granted based on the quality of the pledge.

The Board also accepted the gift of $4.5 million from Mr. and Mrs. B.J. Cassin to renovate Dryden Hall and the former bookstore and to construct a new courtyard, bookstore and post office facility attached to the College Union. The project would be named after the B. J. Cassin family.

A resolution honoring the late Raymond White, PhD., was unanimously accepted, noting his extraordinary contribution to the College as an admissions officer, financial aid director, vice president for research and planning and lastly as vice president for administration and chief financial officer.

Ray White succumbed to cancer following an illness of several months. I and other members of the Administrative Council were deeply saddened, not only because of his loyalty, devotion and critical insight, but also because of his management expertise, personal style and sense-of-humor. William (Bill) McLeod, Vice President of Student Affairs, was appointed in November 1996, to Ray White's position.

McLeod was a former superintendent of Catholic schools for the Diocese of Fresno-Monterey, had been a conservative financial manager at the College for 25 years. He had carefully scrutinized and managed the student affairs budget, then amounting to over $6 million annually and had developed a long-range replacement plan for residence hall furniture and facility refurbishing. Members of the Administrative Council recognized his consistently prudential voice as the annual budget was formulated and was intimately involved in controlling the annual athletic budget. Controlling the athletic budget was not an easy task considering the demands made by the Athletic Director, coaches, students, parents of athletes and athletic fans. He also was confronted with gender equity requirements mandated by the Federal law, and additional requirements from the NCAA and the West Coast Conference. McLeod's awareness of overall College goals and endowment policies would be an asset in the CFO Office and he would have four certified public accountants assisting him. His personal traits would also work well with the Regents investment committee.

The interregnum that occurs between the final months of one administration and the anticipation of the next, has its moments of amusement, curious planning and some chagrin. Such was the case in the aftermath of McLeod's appointment and title which secured regular Board approval at its regular meeting of January 28, 1997. I was surprised that the incoming president questioned the appropriateness of the contract between the College and McLeod for his new assignment and I wondered whether someone had made a negative intervention with the new president. I also received a phone call from the chairman of the Board sometime in April or May expressing doubts about the appointment and suggested that I rescind it. I objected. However, the matter was brought before the final Board meeting in June 1997, an issue that turned into an interminable brouhaha that Board member Frank Brown described as "making a mountain out of a mole hill."

Brown was right. The contract was prepared by competent legal counsel, was signed by both McLeod and myself and was in keeping with normal policy. The contract recognized the right of the new president to assign McLeod to another position as he saw fit, provided California labor laws were observed. The issues, or more likely, misunderstandings could have been resolved in a separate discussion among College legal counsel, a select Board committee, and both the outgoing and incoming presidents. College counsel was told by the chairman not to attend the Board meeting, an unheard of intervention by the chairman. Such a move left the Board without the legal rationale of the contract and the absence of understanding current California labor law mandates. The Provincial had brought his own counsel to the meeting who falsely claimed he represented the College and who failed to do his homework. He embarrassed his firm by misrepresenting the action of the Board in the previous January meeting. In a divided but close vote the Board, obviously under pressure from both the chairman and the provincial rescinded McLeod's contract. I left the meeting chagrined and disgusted as did several other Board members.

Shortly after assuming office, the new president informed McLeod that his contract had been rescinded and that he should seek employment elsewhere. Given the care with which the rescinded contract was drawn and current California labor law, the threat of lawsuit hurriedly produced a favorable alternative contract. After serving as chief financial officer until January 1998, a total of 14 months, McLeod was assigned to the Advancement Office where his gracious familiarity with alumni, donors and friends of the College led to a gratifying success for both the College and McLeod. He happily retired in 2011, following his 70th birthday.

My Final Year

The Gala Send-Off, April 25, 1997

As my 28 years as President came to a close, the Advancement Office contacted Trustees, Regents, alumni, faculty and friends of the College to propose a grand celebration and the establishment of an endowed scholarship in my name. The celebration was held at the San Francisco Hilton on April 25, 1997. Alumnus Brian Stevens, '77, then Vice President of Hilton Hotels arranged for a special private reception for the family and selected guests of the President prior to the major event in the grand ballroom. Hors d'oeuvres and libations were plentiful to the delight of the guests. One could sense the excitement in the air as guests moved from the special reception to the grand ballroom. Vivacious banquet guests filled hallways and reception rooms near the ballroom, as the joyous and friendly Saint Mary's spirit enveloped the atmosphere. On display in the lobby was a small model of the statue of Saint John Baptist De La Salle that would soon grace the Chapel plaza. The grand ballroom was at capacity of nearly 1,000 guests. A special table was arranged for my family and the Most Reverend John Cummins, Bishop of Oakland and a long-time family acquaintance. Brian Stevens favored the table with elegant champagne and other tokens of appreciation. Senator Dan Boatwright of Concord; Michael Marjchrzak, Mayor of Moraga; Brother David Brennan, Provincial; Members of the Boards of Trustees and Regents, Presidential colleagues from neighboring universities; administrators; faculty; alumni; students; their parents; and many friends of the College were among the attendees. A testimonial film was prepared by faculty member Ed Tywoniac recalling highlights of my tenure. My remarks were cast in the spirit of the revelry of the evening relating the mishaps and unexpected events that occurred in abundance on the occasion of the Commencement Ceremonies of 1988, one of the hottest Moraga days in years. I also made a few remarks regarding the College history and my vision for the future: In my thanks to so many who supported the College in so many ways, I also reminisced by citing experiences with students. "What a cause for delight," I said, "as we observe the maturing of souls before our eyes, as we discern students reflecting upon their lives as they encounter profoundly serious and perplexing questions, when we glimpse significant moral resolutions taking shape as a consequence of intellectual insights. Learning well and living authentically is a conversion of soul. Nothing is more gratifying than to witness a genuine conversion: to see a student dedicate his or herself with passionate commitment to the quest for understanding, human and divine, and the pursuit of unselfish love."

The endowed Brother Mel Anderson scholarship was revealed that evening and has grown to well over $1 million dollars. I was also presented with a generous check that would allow me to travel the Baltic Sea by ship for 10 summer days, something I enjoyed a few years later.

Yearning

This memoir was written about an institution with a colorful, but phoenix-like, history that was financially struggling in 1969 and had concurrently adopted a new calendar, core-curriculum and philosophy that in important ways was different from that of its previous 28 years. This major change created a restlessness that prompted the title *Years of Yearning*. It seemed to me that the postmodern, deconstructionist secular philosophy of the time had influenced the designers of the new format to some extent and, unfortunately, several faculty who tenaciously held to the pre-1969 concepts did not demonstrate a creative spirit of adaptation to the evolving changes in both the Church and the times. However, it is doubtful that creative adaptation would have stemmed the tide of the change that occurred. When I came on the scene, neither my philosophy nor views of governance nor my changes in personnel set well with the 4-1-4 reformers, but, it soon became evident to the faculty that certain academic requirements that were omitted from the post-1969 curriculum were absolutely necessary, and changes were made. I was convinced that the reduction of philosophy requirements to zero deprived a number of students of the intellectual structures that would have enhanced the learning process in almost all courses and majors, as well as provide a necessary understanding of Christian anthropology of the human person, so critical to such issues as the emerging civil rights movements and for coping with the mindless excesses of an emotive sexual revolution. While philosophical texts were included in the Collegiate Seminar requirement of four courses for all students and thus provided some encounter with philosophical principles, they did not provide a major in-depth philosophical experience that would be found in a full course or courses, though many students voluntary enrolled in courses in philosophy, and students in the Integral Program had the benefit of an unusual educational experience based on the Great Books. In the ensuing years there were times of trial and error and moments of success and even triumph, but as with most human endeavors the work seems never to be complete.

After successfully muddling through the financial crises of the 1970s and engaging in a planned building program to accommodate both student housing and academic improvement for both students and faculty, we were able to pull together the many thoughts about the purposes of the College that had developed over many years by several individuals and committees. Through the formation of a cooperative cross-section of faculty and administration we were able to develop a Mission Statement that defined and clarified the philosophy of the College. The next step in the plan was to intentionalize the meaning of the Mission Statement in each School and department. This part of the plan embodied the hope of fulfilling the "yearning" expressed in the title. But like many yearnings, it is the destiny of some to sow and for others to do the reaping, and we were only able to suggest the next step. Perhaps some day it may be taken.

Appendices

FINANCIAL SUMMARY, 1969-1976 (SPRING)					
Year	Income	Expenses	Operation (+) or (-)	Accrued Deficit	Endowment Market Value
Prior to 1969				-122,000	1,717,667
1969-1970	3,273,000	3,436,000	-163,000	-285,000	1,447,920
1970-1971	3,780,600	4,091,712	-309,412	-557,581	1,727,914
1971-1972	4,111,646	4,112,834	-1,188[1]	-558,769	1,915,000
1972-1973	3,860,570	4,187,091	-326,521	-885,290	1,951,000
1973-1974	4,110,992	4,403,346	-292,354	-1,058,736	1,827,000
1974-1975	4,124,272	4,257,438	-133,166	-1,191,902	2,034,000
1975-1976	4,723,318	4,851,606	-128,288	-1,320,190	2,269,000

[1]an unrestricted gift provided almost break-even support

FINANCES, OPERATIONAL AND ENDOWMENT, 1976-1985 (SPRING)						
Year	Income	Expenses	+ or	Deficit (Accrued)	Plant Fund	Endowment Mkt. Value
1976-1977	5,637,328	5,416,028	+221,300 (2)	- 799,000		2,249,000
1977-1978	7,447,000	7,067,000	+380,000 (2)	- 119,000		2,450,000
1978-1979	8,396,000	8,370,000	+26,000 (2)	0		2,557,000
				Reserve		
1979-1980	9,430,000	9,392,000	+38,000	64,000	10,373	2,877,000
1980-1981	12,020,874	11,523,865	497,009	141,846	13,272	3,338,087
1981-1982	14,538,000	13,848,000	690,000	438,422	0	3,041,790
1982-1983	16,089,000	15,375,000	714,000	739,795	3,177	5,133,480
1983-1984	17,838,000	16,970,000	868,000	994,701	86	4,974,545
1984-1985	19,964,000	19,796,000	168,000	728,623	363	7,224,740

[2]De La Salle Institute loaned the College $300,000 in 1977 and again in 1978; and $119,000 for 1979, a total of $719,000.

FINANCES, OPERATIONAL, RESERVE AND ENDOWMENT, 1985-1990 (SPRING)					
	Income	Expenses	Accrued Reserve	Plant Fund	Endowment
1985-1986	21,987,000	21,799,000	565,794	408	9,031,320
1986-1987	24,323,000	23,316,000	1,139,741	710	15,326,686
1987-1988	27,711,000	26,601,000	1,971,717	1,075	14,824,299
1988-1989	31,636,000	30,249,000	3,379,741	-65,059	15,130,972
1989-1990	36,392,000	33,892,000	3,657,674	52,730	16,847,622*

*Fluctuations in value of endowment were contingent on the market value of investments.

FINANCES, OPERATIONAL, RESERVE & ENDOWMENT, 1990-1997 (SPRING)					
	Income	Expenses	Accrued Reserve	Plant Fund	Endowment
1990-1991	40,312,000	38,953,000	4,288,554	82,496	17,463,403
1991-1992	42,397,000	42,274,000	3,859,166	104,896	21,499,996
1992-1993	46,780,000	46,151,000	4,638,299	643,790	23,121,776
1993-1994	49,792,000	48,720,000	5,193,394	521,033	23,479,268
1994-1995	53,256,000	51,888,000	7,071,179	373,394	28,599,790
1995-1996	55,711,000	54,573,000	8,487,760	791,966	31,598,023
1996-1997	57,899,000	57,276,000	9,423,865	444,012	41,710,812

Members of the Board of Trustees, 1969-1997

A review of the members of the Board of Trustees from fall of 1969 to the end of the 1997 spring semester, discloses an impressive roster of wise and dedicated advisors and policy-makers. The direction from the Board and the Board partnership with the administration allowed the College to resolve both difficult financial and some academic issues in the '70s and beyond and to develop optimistic and enthusiastic plans for the '80s and '90s, a time some have called golden years of financial, faculty, facility and enrollment progress. The complete list of Board members who served from 1969 to 1997 is noted below.

Barbara Jean Ageno, FSC, 1996-2004
Brother Mel Anderson, FSC, '51, 1968-1997, (Ex officio, 1969-1997)
Edmond J. Barrett, DDS, 1969-1970, Dentist, Barrett Transportation and Barrett Hotel, San Francisco
Brother William Beatie, FSC, PhD, '52, 1978-1988, 1994-2003, Academic Vice President
Peter B. Bedford, 1984-1994, President, Bedford Properties
Brother Dominic Berardelli, FSC, 1981-1986
Brother David Brennan, FSC, 1983-1993, (Provincial, ex officio) 1995-2003
Frank Brown, 1997-1998, Connell Co.
Harry R. Buttimer, PhD, 1978-1984, Chancellor, Contra Costa County Community Colleges
Brendan J. "B.J." Cassin, 1994-2000, B.J. Cassin Inc, Menlo Park, Calif.
Maryellen Cattani, JD, 1990-1999, Attorney, American President Lines
Ruth Claeys, 1992-1995
Brother Bertram Coleman, FSC, 1966-1974, (Provincial, ex officio)
Sister Samuel Conlon, OP, PhD,1980-1986, President, Dominican College, San Rafael, Calif.
Brother James Norman Cook, FSC '52, 1976-1980, Provincial, ex officio, 1980-1987
Brother Lawrence Cory, FSC, PhD, 1961-1971 , biologist
Daniel J. Cullen, 1967-1972, CEO, Walston Co. Brokers, San Francisco
Rt. Rev. Msgr., and in 1974, Bishop John S. Cummins, 1969-1979, Auxiliary Bishop, Diocese of
    Sacramento, Calif., 1974; Bishop of Oakland, Calif., 1977-2003
Brother Louis DeThomasis, FSC, PhD, 1990-2000, President, St. Mary's College, Winona, Minn.
Sister Ambrose Devereux, SNJM, PhD, 1970-1980, President, Holy Names College, Oakland, Calif.
Mrs. Roy E. (Patricia) Disney, 1987-1992, Shamrock Enterprises, Burbank, Calif.
Laroy Doss, '59, 1980-1990, Ford Motor Co., Pittsburg, Calif.
Donald Doyle, 1989-1998, President, San Francisco Chamber of Commerce
Brother Timothy Edwards, FSC, '60, 1969-1973, Principal, St. Mary's College High School, Berkeley,
    Calif.
Brother Patrick Ellis, FSC, PhD, 1986-1997, President, La Salle University, Philadelphia, President,
    Catholic University of America, Washington, D. C.
Hon. Carlos R. Freitas, '22, JD, 1967-1972, Judge, Marin County
Brother Cassian Frye, FSC, '22, MBA, 1969-1970, 1971-1980, Dean of Studies,
William C. Garcia, '32, 1973-1980, Garcia and Sons, Inc.
George R. Gordon, JD, '28, 1969-1978, Attorney, Chairman, Contra Costa County Community College
    Board
James R. Harvey, 1983-1991, President, CEO, Transamerica, Inc., San Francisco
Hon. John F. Henning, '38, 1970-1972, Executive Secretary--Treasurer, AFL-CIO State of California,
    Former U. S. Ambassador to New Zealand, Undersecretary of Labor
Kenneth H. Hofmann, 1980-1990, President, The Hofmann Company, Owner Seattle Seahawks,
    Oakland A's
William Jasper, 1997-2006, President, Dolby Laboratories, San Francisco
Thomas G. Kenney, 1973-1983, President, Transamerica Title Insurance, Inc.
Hon. Arthur Latno, 1986-1996, Vice President, Pacific Telesis, Former U. S. Ambassador-at-Large
Edward L. Lammerding, '51, 1993-1999, Lammerding and Associates, Sacramento, Calif.
Richard H. Matzke, MBA, '77, 1996-1997, President, Chevron Overseas
James McCloud, 1972-1983, President Raymond Engineers, Oakland, Calif.
Elaine McKeon, 1980-1990, Chairman of the Board, San Francisco Museum of Modern Art
George R. McKeon, 1970-1976, McKeon Development, Inc .
Brother Michael Meister, FSC, PhD, 1988-1997, Professor, Religious Studies
Giles Miller '54, MD, 1993-2002, Cardiologist, Saint Mary's Hospital, San Francisco
Nicholas Moore, '63, 1997-2006, President, CEO Coopers and Lybrand, Inc.,(retired)
Brother Gabriel Murphy, FSC, STD, '48, 1969-1976
Brother Mark Murphy, FSC, '65, 1987-1995, (Provincial, ex-officio)
William P. Niland, '42, PhD, 1968-1978, President, Diablo Valley College, Pleasant Hill, Calif.
Raymond F. O'Brien, 1983-1992, President, CEO Consolidated Freightways, Inc.

Edward C. Massa, 1970-1980
Richard H. Matzke, 1993-1999
G. Joseph Bertain, 1980-2001
Edward B. McCaffery, Jr., 1993-2001
James W. McClenahan, 1968-1974
James F. McCloud, 1972-1988
Daniel J. McGanney, 1954-1979
　President, 1956-1958
George V. McKeever, Jr., 1986
George V. McKeever, Sr. 1952-1976
William E. McKenna, 1995-2009
Elaine McKeon, 1977-1994
　President, 1986-1988
George R. McKeon, 1968-1976
Alexander R. Mehran, 1984-1988
Masud R. Mehran, 1991-1996
Giles Miller, MD, 1976-2002
　President, 1992-1994
James P Miscoll, 1983-1986
Ernest L. Molloy, 1956-1971
Nicholas G. Moore, 1993-2006
Judith Murphy, 1995
Weller Noble, 1952-1971
Donald L. O'Brien, 1973-1979
Raymond F. O"Brien, 1979-1996
Thomas P. O'Donnell, 1989-2005
　President, 2003-2005
Thomas W. O'Neil, Jr., 1976-1998
Bernard A. Orsi, 1987-2001
George W. Pasha, III, 1983-1985
Louis Petri, 1958-1972
Irene Pope, 1975-1980
John A. Powers, 1975-1978
Lee B. Price, 1968-1975
James Quandt, 1993-
James Radnich, 1989-1993
Kenneth Ranin, 1991-1993
Carl E. Reichardt, 1983

Donald C. Rego, 1993-2001
John J. Reilly, Jr., 1963-1983
　President, 1972-974
James B. Rettig, 1992-2001
Quinten Reynolds, 1970-1978
James E. Roberts, 1952-1977
　President, 1960-1963
Jack Martin Roth, 1964-1983
Gary M. Sabatte, 1996
Remond C. Sabatte, 1972-1985
Albert E. Schlesinger, 1956-1976
J. Gary Shansby, 1981-1984
Henry G. Sheehy, 1958-1982
Charles H. Shreve, 1984-1996
　President, 1994-1996
Hugh Sill, 1952-1984
William G. Simon, 1989-1992
Earl W. Smith, 1984-1989
Rosemary Soda-Maricic, 1989-1993
Y. Charles Soda, 1952-1953, & 1963-1989
　President, 1975-1977
Michael C. Stead, 1996-2000
Albert E. Stevens, 1975-1999
　President, 1978-1980
James N. Sullivan, 1988-1991
Raymond J. Syufy, 1970-1993
John J. Taylor, 1990-1999
John E. Thompson, 1975-2004
William J. Timmings, 1958-1973
Henry Trione, 1986-1989
George Vukasin, 1988-1999
Robert. E. L. Walker, 1972-1982
John Warta, 1995-2003
Kathryn Westfall, 1975-1984
William G. White, 1964-1972
Arthur P. Williams, 1962-1985
Ross B. Yerby, 1964-1985
Carlo Zocchi, 1987-2001

Alumni Directors, 1969-1997: John Cunningham '57, 1966-1974; Michael Ferrigno, '66, 1974-1976; Tim Gilmore, '71, 1976-1978; Mary Patricia Fink Butler, '75, 1978–1982; Susan Rickenbacker Stabler, '81; 1982-1992; Ron Turner, '79; 1992-1996; Mark Trinidad, '93, 1996-1998; Giles G. Miller, '84, 1998-2004.

Alumni Presidents, 1969-1997: Bernard Cummins, '57, 1969-1970; Elwood, "China" Lang, 1970-1971; Giles E. Miller, MD, '54, 1971-1972; Daniel Scannell, '57, 1972-1973; Thomas O'Donnell, JD, '60, 1973-1974; Al Heeg, '59, 1974-1976; John Powers, '60, 1976-1978; Don DeLong, '51, 1978-1979; David Kelly, '62, 1979-1980; James Forkin, '59, 1980-1982; Joseph Crane, '53, 1982-1984; Ernest Pierucci, JD, '72, 1984-1985; Donald Dickerson, '70, 1985-1986; Louis A. Meyer, '59; 1986-1987; Sherie S. Dodsworth, '78; 1987-1988; Martin Haley, JD, '56; 1988-1989; Ric Rosario, '80, 1989-1991; Frank Brady, '56, 1991-1993; Rita K. Walljasper, '84, 1993-1994; Janet Holbrook, '85, 1994-1996; Betsy Madruga Weber, '86, 1996-1997.

National Alumni Association Statistics
Total traditional baccalaureate degrees from the three undergraduate schools, including the inter-institutional degrees jointly granted by St. Mary's College and Samuel Merritt College, 1970 to 1997: 10,197 (the number of traditional undergraduate graduates in 1970 was 192. There were 544 in 1996 (highest) and 516 in 1997.

Inter-institutional baccalaureate degrees, Saint Mary's College and Samuel Merritt College, 1989 to 1997: 812 (included in the total traditional undergraduate degrees listed above.)

Extended Education baccalaureate degrees in public management, law studies, social science, humanities: 1976-1997, 7,654
Extended Education baccalaureate degrees in Procurement and Contract Management: 39
Extended Education baccalaureate degrees in Health Services Administration: 1,325

Total Extended Education baccalaureate degrees: 9,018

Graduate MBA Program, 1977 to 1997: 2,438
Graduate (MA) International Business Program, 1977 – 1991: 246 (merged into MBA after 1991)
Graduate (MA) Psychology Program: 350
Graduate (MA) H., P.E. and R. Program: 263
Graduate (MA) Theology Program, summers 1970 to 1988: 184
Graduate Education (MA) Programs: 1,253
Extended Education Graduate (MA) program in Health Services Administration: 741
Extended Education Graduate (MA) program in Procurement and Contract Management: 180
Total graduate (MA) degrees to 1997: 5,379

Paralegal Certificate Program (ABA approved in 1981): 1,903
Doctoral Program in Education commenced after 1997

Since the State of California issues the teaching credential, no records are currently available as to how many credential students were certified by Saint Mary's College.
Total of living alumni, all programs, was reckoned at approximately 35,000 as of 1997.
Note: Estimates on the number of graduates from various programs are as close as possible, given that statistics were gathered within various programs and Schools. Some entities were more proficient at record-keeping than others.

Professors of the Year 1992-1997

1992   Professor Marguerite (Candy) Boyd, School of Education
1993   Brother Ronald Isetti, School of Liberal Arts, History
        Address: *The Catholic Character of Saint Mary's College: Intellectual Tradition*
1994   Professor Mary Springer, School of Liberal Arts, English
        Address: *The Question of Modesty in College Affairs.*
1995   Professor Dan Cawthon, School of Liberal Arts, Theology/Performing Arts
        Address: *Wondering at the Edge: Reflection on the Role of Teacher at Saint Mary's College*
1996   Professor Carole Swain, School of Education
        Address: *Saint Mary's College in Communion with Itself. The Sign of a Healthy Community.*
1997   Professor Joseph Lanigan, School of Liberal Arts, Philosophy
        Address: *Recollection and Presence.*

Major Donors 1969-1997

The reception of gifts, large and small, in terms of legal tender, securities, real estate or in-kind gifts through advice, influence, referrals, materials, labor or volunteer service, are deeply appreciated by the officers of the College, the faculty, staff and legions of students who may not even be aware of the generous benefaction that has been bestowed upon them. All of us involved with the College are deeply appreciative of the generosity of De La Salle Institute (Christian Brothers), the donated services of the Christian Brothers on the faculty and staff, former and current Trustees and Regents, many friends and parents and thousands of Alumni, who faithfully supported the College, its students and faculty in various ways. The College has been blessed through the Alumni Annual Fund, the Capital Campaign, the College County Committee, Genesian Awards, the Saint Mary's Guild, the Saint Mary's College East Bay Scholarship Fund, Inc., local Alumni Chapters, Gaelsports, Gael Auto Raffles and the many who became members of the President's Club. Furthermore, a significant number of the same donors generously included Saint Mary's in their planned giving program, the benefits of which are yet to be realized and will be received with gratitude in the future.

Undergraduate Valedictorians and Commencement Speakers, 1969-1997

Traditional undergraduate commencement ceremonies were scheduled at the end of each academic year, normally in May, and included addresses by a valedictorian selected by the senior class from among those graduating with highest academic honors, and normally a guest Commencement speaker. Honorary Degrees and special awards, when bestowed, are normally awarded at commencement ceremonies. Since commencement ceremonies occurred within one day of the completion of final examinations, it was not possible to ascertain completion of all requirements for all graduates, thus the diploma case was presented at the ceremonies, and official diplomas were mailed to each graduate within a week or two of the commencement ceremonies.

Undergraduate Valedictorians, 1970-1997

1970   Dennis Hedgecock, School of Science
1971   James R. Davis, School of Liberal Arts
1972   William Francis Gray, Integral Liberal Arts

1973 John Randall Andrada, School of Liberal Arts
1974 Daniel Anthony Doherty, School of Liberal Arts
1975 Jeffrey N. Dennis, School of Liberal Arts
1976 Louis F. Pierotti, School of Liberal Arts
1977 Brian J. Mahaney, School of Liberal Arts
1978 David Fregeau, School of Science
1979 Robert Wiley, School of Liberal Arts
1980 Calvin Edward "Ted" Wood, School of Science
1981 Philip Frederick Nash, School of Liberal Arts
1982 Bobby Lee Hagle, School of Economics and Business Administration
1983 Elizabeth A. Della-Santina, School of Liberal Arts
1984 Richard Donald Bechtel, School of Liberal Arts
1985 John Kevin Kitchen, School of Liberal Arts
1986 Frances Mary Margaret Sweeney, School of Liberal Arts
1987 Barton Lee Jacka, Integral Liberal Arts
1988 Mary Elizabeth Hutcheson, School of Liberal Arts
1989 Karen Lynn Cline, School of Liberal Arts
1990 Paul William Rickey, School of Liberal Arts
1991 Jenny T. Olin, School of Liberal Arts
1992 Craig Milton Elliott II, School of Liberal Arts
1993 Joanne N. Clemitson, School of Science
1994 James C. Oleson, School of Liberal Arts
1995 Colin P. Daly, School of Liberal Arts
1996 Cindy Neander and Jason Eisele, School of Liberal Arts
1997 Mollie Flint, School of Liberal Arts

Undergraduate Commencement Speakers

1970 Hon. Jerome Waldie, Member of Congress (D)
1971 Hon. Wilson C. Riles, State Superintendent of Public Instruction
1972 Hon. John C. Akar, MBE, Former Ambassador of Sierra Leone to the United States, Canada and Jamaica.
1973 Hon. John Vasconcellos, LLB, Member of the California Assembly
1974 Rev. James T. Burtchael, CSC, PhD, Provost, University of Notre Dame, Indiana
1975 Earl F. Cheit, PhD, Associate Director, Carnegie Council on Policy Studies in Higher Education, formerly of the University of California, Berkeley.
1976 Hon. John F. Henning, '38, LLD, Executive Secretary-Treasurer, California AFL- CIO.
1977 Mr. Al Collins, '27 and Leo J. Roney, '27, representing the Class of 1927, celebrating 50 years of the College in Moraga.
1978 Hon. Daniel Keenan Whitehurst, '69, Mayor of Fresno.
1979 Sister Samuel Conlon, OP, President of Dominican College San Rafael, Calif.
1980 Steve V. Allen, Author, TV Personality, Composer, Musician, Entertainer.
1981 James Ferdinand McCloud, Member, Board of Trustees, President, Kaiser Engineers.
1982 Hon. John Gavin, Entertainer, United States Ambassador to Mexico
1983 Hon. Peter H. Dailey, Advertising Executive, United States Ambassador to Ireland
1984 Robert Hass, '62, PhD, Professor and Chairman, Department of English
1985 James De Preist, Conductor, Music Director, Oregon Symphony
1986 Kevin Starr, PhD, Author, Historian, Lecturer, Journalist, Professor, Chief State Librarian
1987 Brother Patrick Ellis, FSC, PhD, President, La Salle University, Philadelphia
1988 Brother Mark Murphy, FSC, Provincial, Brothers of the Christian Schools, District of San Franciso
1989 Hon. Manuel Lujan, Jr., United States Secretary of the Interior
1990 Lynn Cheney, Chairperson, National Endowment for the Humanities
1991 Richard K. Donahue, LLB, President and CEO, Nike, Inc.
1992 Herman D. Lujan, '58, PhD, President, Northern Colorado University
1993 Most Rev. John S. Cummins, Bishop of Oakland
1994 Professor Norman Springer, PhD, Professor of English
1995 James Roosevelt, Jr., JD, Choate, Hall and Stewart, Boston, (50th Anniversary of the death of Franklin D. Roosevelt, President of the United States)
1996 Robert Hass, '62, PhD, Poet Laureate, United States of America, and Brenda Hillman (Hass), Poet in Residence, St. Mary's College
1997 Brother Mel Anderson, FSC, Retiring President of the College

Honorary Degrees, 1970-1996

Though most Honorary Degrees were awarded at the end of the undergraduate academic year, several were awarded on special occasions, one in 1975, one in 1984, and three in 1988 apart from traditional undergraduate commencement ceremonies.

1970 (Doctor of Laws) Hon. Jerome R. Waldie (D), Member of Congress.

1971 (Doctor of Humane Letters) Wilson C. Riles, State Superintendent of Public Instruction.

1972 (Doctor of Humane Letters) John J. Akar, MBE, Former Ambassador of Sierra Leone to the United States, Canada and Jamaica.

1973 (Doctor of Humane Letters) John Vasconcellos, Member of the California State Assembly. (Doctor of Humane Letters) Karl O. Drexel, First Chancellor, Contra Costa County Community College District.

1974 (Doctor of Humane Letters) Rev. James T. Burtchael, CSC, PhD Provost, University of Notre Dame, Indiana.
(Doctor of Humane Letters) Brother Bertram Coleman, Former Provincial of the District of San Francisco of the Christian Brothers.
(Doctor of Humane Letters) Mr. Alfred Fromm, President of Fromm and Sichel, Inc. Distributors of Christian Brothers wines and brandy. Founder with Mrs. Hanna Fromm of the Fromm Institute of Lifelong Learning at the University of San Francisco.

1975 (Doctor of Divinity) Rev. Patrick LaBelle, OP, '61, President Dominican School of Philosophy and Theology. Awarded Jan. 9, 1975 in a special Convocation at Saint Mary's College Chapel.
(Doctor of Humane Letters) Earl F. Cheit, PhD Associate Director, Carnegie Council on Policy Studies in Higher Education and formerly Vice Chancellor, University of California, Berkeley.
(Doctor of Humane Letters) Henry Schaefer Simmern, MA, Professor of Art Education.

1976 (Doctor of Law) John F. Henning, '38, Executive Secretary-Treasurer, California AFL-CIO.
(Doctor of Law) Hon. Lloyd Burke, '37, JD, United States District Judge, District of Northern California.

1978 (Doctor of Humane Letters) Rev. Alfred Boeddeker, OFM, Director, Saint Anthony Dining Room and Farms.
(Doctor of Science) Brother Timothy Diener, FSC, '33 , Chemist, Cellarmaster, Christian Brothers Winery, Napa, Calif.

1980 (Doctor of Arts and Letters) Steve V. Allen, musician, composer, author, entertainer, originator of *The Tonight Show* and *Meeting of the Minds*, a series on the great intellectual and personalities who influence the world.
(Doctor of Arts and Letters) (in absentia) Jayne Meadows Allen, entertainer and collaborator with husband, Steve Allen, on *The Meeting of the Minds*.

1984 (Doctor of Humane Letters) Brother Dominic Ruegg, FSC, PhD Former Academic Vice President (Awarded at Extended Education Commencement, June 14, 1984).

1985 (Doctor of Arts and Letters), James De Preist, Conductor and Music Director, Oregon Symphony.

1986 (Doctor of Arts and Letters) Kevin Starr, PhD, author of California: A History, lecturer, journalist, professor of history, Librarian for the State of California.

1988 (Doctor of Humane Letters) Most Rev. Joseph Cardinal Bernardin, DD, Archbishop of Chicago; Lisa Sowle Cahill, PhD Associate Professor of Theology, Boston College; Brother Luke Salm, FSC, PhD, Professor of Theology, Manhattan College New York. (Brother Luke delivered the address: *Values, Catholic Education in the 21st Century*. Degrees awarded on the Occasion of a special convocation celebrating the 125th Anniversary of the College founding in 1863. Convocation held in the College Chapel, April 7, 1988.

1989 (Doctor of Humane Letters) Manuel Lujan, Jr., United States Secretary of the Interior.

1990 (Doctor of Literature) Hon. Lynn Cheney, Chair, National Endowment for the Humanities.

1991 (Doctor of Humane Letters) Richard K. Donahue, LLB, President and CEO, Nike , Inc.
(Doctor of Laws) Raymond J. Syufy, '40, President and CEO, Syufy Enterprises, Century Theaters.

1992 (Doctor of Humane Letters), Herman D. Lujan, '59, PhD, President Northern Colorado University.

1993 (Doctor of Humane Letters) , Most Rev. John J. Cummins, DD, Bishop of Oakland.

1994 (Doctor of Humane Letters), Benjamin A. Frankel, PhD Professor of History, Saint Mary's College. (At Saint Mary's since 1949.)

1996 (Doctor of Humane Letters) Robert Hass, '62, PhD United States Poet Laureate.

Student Body Chaplains, Directors of Campus Ministry & Associates, 1969-1997

1968-1970	Rev. Paul Feyen	1984-1985	Rev. Basil De Pinto
1970-1971	Rev. Ed Martin, OMI		Sister Judith Renik, SNJM
1971-1972	Rev. Ed Martin, OMI		Bro. Ronald Roggenback, FSC, PhD
1972-1973	Rev. Ed Martin, OMI	1985-1986	Rev. Basil De Pinto
	Rev. John Fearon, OP		Sister Judith Renik, SNJM
	(in res. Brothers' Chaplain)		Rev. Emerich Vogt, OP (in res.)
1973-1974	Rev. Patrick LaBelle, OP	1986-1987	Rev. Basil DePinto
	Brother Martin Verducci, OP		Sister Bernice Bittick, OP
1974-1975	Rev. Bernard Cranor, OP	1987-1988	Rev. Michael Sweeney, OP
	Rev. Martin Igoa, OP		Sister Bernice Bittick, OP
	Sister Noelle O'Shea, CSJ	1988-1989	Rev. Michael Sweeney, OP
	Rev. Denis Reilly, OP		Rev. Emerich Vogt, OP
1975-1976	Rev. Cassian Lewinski, OP		Sister Bernice Bittick, OP
	Rev. Kent Burtner, OP	1989-1990	Rev. Michael Sweeney, OP
	Rev. Neil Wise, OP (in res.)		Sister Bernice Bittick, OP
	Sister Doloes Fencil	1990-1991	Rev. Michael Sweeney, OP
	(Greymore Franciscan-student)		Sister Bernice Bittick, OP
1976-1977	Rev. Cassian Lewinski, OP	1991-1992	Rev. Michael Sweeney, OP
	Rev. Raymond Rindau, OP		Rev. Jude Eli, OP
	Rev. Neil Wise, OP (in res.)		Sister Bernice Bittick, OP
1977-1978	Rev. Jerry Milizia, OP	1992-1993	Rev. Jude Eli, OP
	Rev. Mark Ziefle, OP		Rev. Salvatore Ragusa, SDS
1978-1979	Rev. Jerry Milizia, OP		Rev. John McDonough, OP
	Rev. Martin Diaz, OP		Brother Norbert Finn, OP
1979-1980	Rev. Bruno Gibson, OP		Sister Bernice Bittick, OP
	Rev. Martin Diaz, OP	1993-1994	Rev. Jude Eli, OP
	(transferred to Seattle, Oct. 1979)		Rev. Salvatore Ragusa, SDS
	Katie Regal		Rev. John McDonough, OP
	Rev. Michael Dodds (in res.)		Brother Norbert Finn, OP
	Rev. Emerich Vogt (in res.)		Sister Bernice Bittick, OP
1980-1981	Rev. Bruno Gibson, OP	1994-1995	Rev. John McDonough, OP
	Rev. Michael Sweeney, OP		Rev. Salvatore Ragusa, SDS
	Katie Regal	1995-1996	Rev. John McDonough, OP
	Kevin Ewen		Rev. Salvatore Ragusa, SDS
	Rev. Michael Dodds, (in res.)		Rev. David Diebel, JD, JCD
	Rev. Emerich Vogt (in res.)		Rev. Michael Morris, OP
	Sister Clare Wagstaffe, OP		Rev. Michael Carey, OP, JD
1981-1982	Rev. Michael Sweeney, OP	1996-1997	Rev. John McDonough, OP
1982-1983	Rev. Michael Sweeney, OP		Rev. Salvatore Ragusa, SDS
1983-1984	Rev. Basil DePinto		Rev. David Diebel, JD, JCD
	Sister Judith Renik, SNJM		Rev. David Gieb, OP
	Brother Ronald Roggenback, FSC, PhD		Brother Michael Murphy, FSC
	Brother Martin DeMartini, FSC (pt.time)		Brother Gary Hough, FSC
	Mark Sullivan (music)		Rev. Michael Morris, OP
			Rev. Michael Carey, OP, JD

Undergraduate Dramatic Performances, 1969-1997

Drama directors: Brother Matthew Benny, FSC, MA, Theodora Carlile, PhD, Brother Charles Marin, FSC, MA, Sally Wilson, Dan Cawthon, PhD, Jane Armitage, Katherine Mazur, Rebecca Engle, M.A., Larry Russell, Ken Ross, Frank Murray, PhD, Michael Cook, M.F.A.

Fall 1969, *Tartuffe* by Moliere, Directed by Brother Matthew Benny, FSC
Spring 1970, *Blood Wedding,* by Federico Garcia Lorca, Director: Phil Larson
Fall 1970, *"J.B."* by Archibald McLeish, Directed by Brother Matthew Benny, FSC
Spring 1971, *Man for All Seasons* by Robert Bolt Director: Brother Matthew Benny, FSC
Spring 1971, *The Birds,* by Aristophanes, Director: Theodora Carlile (Integral Program students)
Fall 1971, *Scapin* by Moliere, Director: Brother Matthew Benny, FSC,
Spring 1972, *Lion in Winter,* by James Goldman, Director: Brother Matthew Benny, FSC
Spring 1972, *As You Like It,* by Wm. Shakespeare, Director: Theodora Carlile (Integral Program students)
Spring 1972, Scenes from Shakespeare, Director: James Townsend, PhD English
Spring 1973, *The Tempest,* Wm. Shakespeare, Director: Theodora Carlile (Integral)

Spring 1974, *Bacchae,* by Euripides, Director: Theodora Carlile (Integral)
Spring 1974, *Hadrian VII,* by Peter Luke, Director: Brother Matthew Benny;
Fall 1975, *The Importance of Being Earnest,* Oscar Wilde, Director: Brother Matthew Benny
Spring 1976, *The Romancers* by Edmond Rostand Director Brother Matthew Benny, FSC
Fall 1976, *Happy Birthday Wanda June,* by Kurt Vonnegut, Jr., Director: Brother Charles, Marin, FSC
Fall 1976, *The Woody Guthrie Story,* Director: Sally Wilson;
Fall 1976, *The Maids* by Jean Genet, Director: Steven Sowash (student)
Fall 1976, *Waiting for Godot* by Samuel Beckett, Director: Brother Charles, Marin, FSC
Fall 1977, *Grease,* by Jim Jacobs and Warren Casey, Director: Brother Charles, Marin, FSC
Spring 1978, *Taming of the Shrew,* Wm. Shakespeare, Director: Brother Charles, Marin, FSC
Fall 1978, One *Flew Over the Cuckoo's Nest,* by Dale Wasserman, Director: Brother Charles Marin; FSC
Spring 1979, *You Can't Take It With You,* by Kaufman and Hart, Director: Jane Armitage
Spring 1979, *That Championship Season,* by Jason Miller, Director: Terry O'Brien (student)
Fall 1979, *A Flea in Her Ear,* Georges Feydeau, Director: Brother Charles Marin, FSC
Spring 1980, *The Fantasticks,* by Tom Jones and Harvey Schmidt, Director: Brother Charles Marin, FSC
Fall 1980, *Equus,* by Peter Shaffer, Director: Brother Charles Marin, FSC
Spring 1981, *Dracula,* by Hamilton Deane and John L. Balderston, Director: Dan Cawthon,
Fall 1981, *America Hurrah* by Jean Claude Itallie, Director: Katherine Mazur
Spring 1982, *Our Town,* Thornton Wilder Director: Dan Cawthon
Fall 1982, *Carnival,* Music and Lyrics by Bob Merrill, Book by Michael Stewart, Director: Dan Cawthon
Spring 1983, *Imaginary Invalid,* by Moliere, Director: Rebecca Engle
Fall 1983, *Miracle Worker,* by Wm. Gibson, Director: Rebecca Engle
Spring 1984, *Sweet Charity* based on play by Neil Simon, Adaptation: Cy Coleman, Lyrics: Dorothy
      Fields, Director: Dan Cawthon
Fall 1984, *Antigone,* by Sophocles, Director: Dan Cawthon
Spring 1985, *Hello Out There* by Wm. Saroyan, Director: Rebecca Engle
Spring 1985, *Winners,* by Brian Freil, Director: Rebecca Engle
Fall 1985, *Dark of the Moon* by Howard Richardson & William Berney; Director:: Dan Cawthon
Spring 1986, *The Secret Life of Walter Mitty* based on the short story by James Thurber, Book by Joe
      Manchester, Lyrics by Earl Shuman, Music by Leon Carr, Director: Dan Cawthon
Fall 1986, *The Dybbuk* by S. Anski, Tr. Mira Rafalowicz, Director: Larry Russell. .
Spring 1987, *The Importance of Being Earnest* by Oscar Wilde. Director: Dan Cawthon.
Fall 1987, *The Absurd World of Eugene Ionesco,* two, one-act plays by Ionesco, The Lesson and Jack or
      The Submission, Director: Dan Cawthon
Spring 1988, *Working,* based on the book by Studs Terkel, Adapted by Stephen Schwartz, Nino Faso,
      Director: Ken Ross
Fall 1988, *The Crucible,* Arthur Miller Director: Dan Cawthon
Spring 1989, *You Can't Take It With You,* by Kaufman and Hart. Director: Frank Murray
Fall 1989, *The Bacchae* by Euripides. Director: Frank Murray
Spring 1990, *Joseph and the Amazing Technicolor Dreamcoat* by Andrew Lloyd Webber and Tim Rice.
      Director: Dan Cawthon, Music Direction by Chris Kula, Choreograpy by Claire Sheridan
Fall 1990, *Rashomon* by Fay and Michael Kanin. Director: Dan Cawthon
Spring 1991, *She Stoops to Conquer* by Oliver Goldsmith. Director: Frank Murray
Fall 1991, *Our Town* by Thornton Wilder. Director: Rebecca Engle
Spring 1992, *The Fantasticks* by Tom Jones and Harvey Schmidt. Director: Dan Cawthon.
Fall 1992, *The Life of Galileo* by Bertolt Brecht. Director: Frank Murray
Spring 1993, *True Beauties* by Julie Hebert, Director: Rebecca Engle
Fall 1993, *Hippolytus* by Euripides, Director: Dan Cawthon
Spring 1994, *House of Blue Leaves* by John Guare, Director: Rebecca Engle
Fall 1994, *The Little Shop of Horrors* by Howard Ashman and Alan Menken, Director: Frank Murray
Spring 1995, *The Little Prince* by Rick Cummins and John Scoullar, Director: Dan Cawthon
Fall 1995, *Little Women* by Marion DeForrest, Director: Michael Cook
Spring 1996, *Spunk* Adapted by George C. Wolfe, Music, Chic Street Man Director: Rebecca Engle
Fall 1996, *The Trojan Women* by Euripiedes, Director: Frank Murray
Spring 1997, *Man From La Mancha* by Dale Wasserman, Music by Mitch Leigh, Lyrics by Joe Darion,
      Director: Dan Cawthon; Music Director: Colleen Lenord; Choreography: Claire Sheridan.

Alumnus of the Year Award, 1969-1997

Hon. Edwin Regan, '28, 1969; Brother Cassian Frye, FSC '42, 1970; Dr. Louis "Dutch" Conlon, '26;
1971; William Fischer, '32, 1972; Brother U. Albert Rahill, FSC, '26, 1973, 1974; George W. McKeever,
Sr. '17, 1975; Elwood B. Lang, '35, 1976; Joe Shally, '32, 1977; Brother Timothy Diener, FSC, '33, 1978;
Joseph McTigue, '30, 1979; George Gordon, '31, 1980; Louis Guisto, '16, 1981; Linus Claeys, '32, 1982;

Ken Hofmann, '45; 1983; Brother Jerome West, FSC, '40, '1984; Raymond J. Syufy, '40, 1985; Brother Mel Anderson, '51, 1987; George V. "Val" McKeever, Jr., '49, 1988; Thomas O'Neil, Jr. '52, 1989; George R. Canrinus, '34, 1990; Donald F. DeLong, '51, 1991; Jerry Fitzpatrick, '42, 1993; Giles Miller, M.D., '54, 1994; Tom Walsh, '49, 1995; Bob Haas, '63, 1996; and Louis Geissberger, DDS, '53, 1997.

St. John Baptist De La Salle Award for Excellence in Teaching, 1969-1997
Elmer Gelinas, 1981; Benjamin Frankel, 1982; John Correia, '59, 1983; Stanford White, 1984; Lawrence R. Cory, '39, 1985; O. De Sales Perez, '53, 1986; Katherine Roper, 1988; Jerry Bodily, 1989; Roy Schmaltz, 1990; Sally Stampp, 1991; Steve Cortright, '75, 1992; Norman Springer, 1993; Mary Doyle Springer, 1994; Carl Guarneri, 1995; Kristine Chase, 1996; and Jane Sanguine Yager, 1997.

Signum Fidei Award for Participation in the Spirit of St. J. B. De La Salle
Brother Haig Charshaf, FSC, '69; Brother W. Thomas Levi, FSC '69; William McLeod, '69; Paul Ascenzi, '69; Thomas O'Neil, '69; Bernard Cummins, '70; Brother Matthew McDevitt, FSC, PhD '70; Robert McAndrews, '71; Brother Virgil Eastham, FSC, '71; Rev. George Kutches, '71; Rev. Benjamin Bowling, '71; James "Jimmy" Phelan, '71; George Canrinus, '73; William S. Whitehurst, '73; Richard Didion, '73; Joseph Shally, '73; John A. Whalen, '73; Bernard Clougherty, '75; Joseph McTigue, '75; Francis Coakley, '75; Thomas Coakley, '75; Albert H. Heeg, Jr. '76; G. Joesph Bertain, Jr. JD '76; Donald J. Cariani, MD, '76; Don DeLong, '77; George Pagnelli, '77; John Powers, '78; Rod Arriaga, '78; LaRoy Doss, '79; Lou Pometta, '79; Brother Ferederick U. Portillo, FSC, '79; Charles Heinbockel, '81; John G. Bannister, '81; Brother Bertram Coleman, FSC, '83; Mary Doyle Springer, PhD '83; C. Joseph Crane, '84; Brother Alfred Brousseau, FSC, PhD '84; Ronald MaArthur, PhD'85; Robert Hass, PhD '85; Brother V. Dominic Barry, FSC, '85; Lawrence Bliquez, PhD'86; Rev. Patrick LaBelle, OP, '86; Thomas Lyons, '88; Brother Brendan Kneale, FSC, '88; Benjamin Frankel, Ph.D '89; Brother William J. Beatie, FSC PhD, '90; Leo O. Oakes, '90; George Silvestri, '91; John W. Broad, JD, '91; Christian Brothers of SMC, '91; the Alemany Community, '91; Brother Robert Lee, FSC, PhD '92; Bother Arnold Stewart, FSC, '93; Herman Lujan, PhD '93; Frank Brady, '94; Ernest Pierucci, JD, '95; Brother Manuel Vega, FSC, PhD '96; and Brother Jerome West, FSC, '97.

Requiescat in Pace
The list that follows is a compilation of the Brothers who served at Saint Mary's College either as members of the faculty or in the administration between 1969-1997 and who were called to their eternal reward during the time between 1969 and 2011. The date of decease is listed in front of the name.

9/8/72 — Brother Austin Crowley, FSC, PhD, Faculty, President 1941-1950
6/28/79 — Brother Virgil Eastham, FSC, MA , English
Faculty 1928-1941, 1947-1969. (During WWII he taught at Cathedral H.S. in Los Angeles)
3/01/81 — Brother Ives Patrick Tracey, FSC, MA (Oxon) History and Seminar, from District of England, Faculty 1978-1980
7/21/81 — Brother V. Julian Royer, FSC, Faculty, Education
8/06/82 — Brother Matthew McDevitt, FSC, PhD Faculty, Professor of History
4/23/83 — Brother Albert Rahill, FSC, Past President, Assistant to the President
Faculty 1935-1941. President, 1941-1943, Dean of Men, 1935-1941
VP, Relations with Schools, Asst. to President, 1962-1983.
6/27/83 — Brother Cassian Frye, FSC, MA, Dean of Studies, Faculty 1950-1951,
Dean of Studies, 1953-1972, Chair, Board of Trustees 1982-1983.
4/26/84 — Brother Alvan Maluvius, FSC, MA, Chemistry Faculty 1941-1949, 1953-1973
5/31/88 — Brother Alfred Brousseau, FSC, PhD Physics, Mathematics Faculty, 1930-1941, 1962-1978.
Former Provincial, Fibonnaci Society Co-founder.
7/5/91 — Brother Edward Behan, FSC, MA, Counselor, 1972-1975, Director of Brothers Community, 1975-1978
9/7/91 — Brother Anthony Pisano, FSC, PhD History, Served at Saint Mary's College, 1990-1991
10/21/91 — Brother Matthew Benney, FSC, MA, English, Dramatics Faculty 1955-1991
5/23/94 — Brother Benedict Reams, Faculty, Mathematics and Physics, 1946-1968
7/28/94 — Brother Gary York, FSC, MA, '69 Assistant to President, Seminar
Faculty, Asst. to President, 1993-1994 Served on the Board of Trustees, 1993-1994. Died unexpectedly, brain aneurysm.
11/22/95 — Brother Dominic Barry, FSC, MA, Mathematics Faculty, 1939-1945, 1946-1980
11/28/95 — Brother Manuel Vega, FSC, PhD Spanish, Seminar
Faculty, 1985-1988, Chair Mod. Lang. 1990-1992,

2/15/98   Brother Robert G. Lee, FSC, PhD Religious Studies Faculty 1977-1979, Director of Student Brothers 1979-1982, Faculty 1982-1989, 1997-1998. 1989-1995, study and Director, Christian Brothers Alemany Community

6/19/2000   Brother Carl (James Joseph) Lyons, FSC, Religious Studies, Performing Arts. Faculty 1964-1965, Faculty 1967-1997. Chair Perf. Arts.

6/24/2000   Brother Eric Vogel, FSC, PhD Physics Faculty, 1974-1976, 1984-1994. U. of Bethlehem, Faculty, 1976-1982

12/1/2002   Brother Jerome West, FSC, MA, Vice President for Development, 1969-1992 and 1994; Vice President for College Relations 1994-2000. Faculty, School of Economics and Business Administration

8/1/03   Brother Dennis Goodman, FSC, MS, Head Librarian, 1953-1983; Archivist 1983-1992.

8/24/03   Brother Edmond Dolan, FSC, PhD, Philosophy, Seminar Faculty, 1948-1957, 1958-1992

10/1/03   Brother DeSales Perez, FSC, PhD Modern Language, Seminar Faculty 1967-1977, 1995-2003 (Died during heart operation)

11/2/03   Brother Theophane Ke: Faculty, part-time, French, Latin, 1976-2003

10/14/04   Brother Walston Thomas Levi, President, 1950-1956

11/20/04   Brother Raymond C. Berta, PhD Communications, 1978-1981, 1985-2004

9/12/06   Brother Robert Smith, FSC, PhD Philosophy, Integral Director, Faculty, 1941-1952, 1953-1964, 1966-1972 (Taught at St. John's Annapolis, 1972-2005)

3/15/09   Brother Michael Quinn, FSC, PhD, President, 1962-1969; Psychology Department, Chairman, Faculty Chairman.

7/8/2010   Brother Martin Fallin, FSC, MA, English and Collegiate Seminar

Faculty who served at the College, 1969-1997, now deceased

Professor Byron Bryant, PhD, English, Collegiate Seminar, Appointed, 1955; Retired 1976

Dean, Professor Paul Burke, EdD, Appointed, 1975; Retired 1987; d. 2009.

Professor Gerard M. Capriolo, PhD, Biology, Appointed, 1977; d. 2009

Professor William L. Civitello, MBA, Economics and B.A. Appt. 1956, Retired 1975, d.

Professor Andrew L. De Gall, MA, JD, Appointed, 1965; Retired 1995; d. 2001

Professor John Dennis, PhD, Appointed, 1979; d. 2008

Professor Donald DePaoli, PhD, Appointed, 1977; d. 2002

Professor Joseph Dongarra, MA, MLS, Appointed 1961; Retired 2000; d. 2001

Professor Frank Ellis, Ph.D, Appointed, 1964; d. 1993

Professor Benjamin Frankel, PhD, D. Litt, AFSC, Appointed, 1949; d. 2001

Professor Alan Garrett, Economics and Business Administration Appointed, 1949; Retired 1975; d.

Professor Elmer T. Gelinas, PhD, Philosophy and Religious Studies, Appointed 1960; Retired 1987; d. 1988

Professor (Brother) Timothy McCarthy, PhD, Appointed, 1982; d. 1998

Professor Monsignor Edgar McCarren, PhD Appointed, 1974; Retired, 2002; d. 1/13/2003

Athletic Director, Professor Donald McKillip, EdD, Appointed A.D. 1970; Retired 1998; d. 2007

Professor Arthur Ortin, MA, JD, Psychology and Ethnic Studies, Appointed 1972; d. July 2011

Professor Rosemary Peterson, PhD, Education, Appointed, 1973; Retired 2009; d. 2009

Professor LeRoy Smith, MA, Philosophy, Classical Language, Appointed, 1949; Retired 1970; d. 1972

Professor Mary Doyle Springer, PhD Appointed, 1965; Retired, 1999; d. 2008

Professor John E. Thompson, MBA, Appointed, 1980; d. 2004

Professor James Townsend, Jr. PhD Appointed 1953; Retired, 1982-3; d.

Sister Claire Wagstaffe, PhD Appointed, 1980; Retired, 2004; d. 2007

Professor John Wellmuth, PhD, Philosophy, Appointed, 1958; Retired, 1970; d. 1979

Professor Stanford White, MA, CPA, Accounting, Appointed, 1963; Retired, 1995; d. 2009

Professor Sepehr Zabih, PhD Government, Appointed 1963, Retired, 2004; d. 2009